BOUND TO BE FREE

BOUND TO BE FREE

*Evangelical Catholic Engagements
in Ecclesiology, Ethics, and Ecumenism*

Reinhard Hütter

WILLIAM B. EERDMANS PUBLISHING COMPANY
GRAND RAPIDS, MICHIGAN / CAMBRIDGE, U.K.

© 2004 Wm. B. Eerdmans Publishing Co.
All rights reserved

Wm. B. Eerdmans Publishing Co.
255 Jefferson Ave. S.E., Grand Rapids, Michigan 49503 /
P.O. Box 163, Cambridge CB3 9PU U.K.

Printed in the United States of America

09 08 07 06 05 04   7 6 5 4 3 2 1

Library of Congress Cataloging-in-Publication Data

Hütter, Reinhard, 1958-
    Bound to be free: evangelical Catholic engagements in
  ecclesiology, ethics, and ecumenism / Richard Hütter.
       p.   cm.
    Includes bibliographical references and indexes.
    ISBN 0-8028-2750-0 (pbk.: alk. paper)
    1. Church. 2. Liberty — Religious aspects — Christianity.
  3. Christian union. 4. Theology, Doctrinal.   I. Title.

BV600.3.H88   2004
262'.001'1 — dc22
                                      2004047169

www.eerdmans.com

For my children

Hanna

Sara

Joshua

Jonathan

Contents

Acknowledgments	ix
1. Bound to Be Free: *Ekklēsia — Eleutheria — Parrhēsia*	1

I. *Ekklēsia* — or, Free to Be Church

2. The Church as Public	19
3. The Knowledge of the Triune God	43
4. Hospitality and Truth	56
5. Karl Barth's "Dialectical Catholicity"	78
6. Beyond Dialectics: *Est* and *Esse*	95

II. *Eleutheria* — or, Free to Live with God

7. (Re-)Forming Freedom	111
8. Freedom and Commandment	145
9. The Fallen Tongue and the Freedom of Praise	168

III. *Parrhēsia* — or, Free to Speak Ecumenically

10. Christian Unity and the Papal Office On the Encyclical *Ut Unum Sint/That They May Be One*	185

Contents

11. Freedom, Truth, and the Will   194
    On the Encyclical *Fides et Ratio*/On the
    Relationship between Faith and Reason

12. "In"   208
    On the Declaration *The Jewish People and Their
    Sacred Scriptures in the Christian Bible*
    (Pontifical Biblical Commission)

Notes   218

Credits   297

Index of Persons   299

Index of Subjects   305

Acknowledgments

Thanks are due to my wife, Nancy Heitzenrater Hütter, who suggested the title *Bound to Be Free* on a memorable walk in which we discussed the contours and content of this volume. I thank my colleagues at Duke University Divinity School. It has been a privilege to teach systematic and philosophical theology in such a hospitable, ecclesially committed, and intellectually stimulating context. I am indebted to the Center of Theological Inquiry, Princeton, and its directors Wallace Alston and Robert Jenson, as well as the Center for Catholic and Evangelical Theology and its directors Carl Braaten and Robert Jenson, two institutions that are together the epitome of intellectually robust and ecumenically committed theological dialogue in the United States. I am grateful to the Center for Catholic and Evangelical Theology, the Deutsche Forschungsgemeinschaft (DFG), the Lilly Foundation, and the Luce Foundation for their crucial support during the years in which I worked on several of these chapters.

A book like this, which has grown over many years, would be inconceivable without the innumerable conversations that have influenced its shape and substance. For these essential exchanges, thanks are due to Robert Benne, Markus Bockmuehl, James J. Buckley, J. Kameron Carter, Michael Cartwright, Amy Laura Hall, David B. Hart, Stanley Hauerwas, Timothy Hinton, Nancy Heitzenrater Hütter, Willie Jennings, Robert Jenson, L. Gregory Jones, William H. Lazareth, George Lindbeck, Lois Malcolm, Joseph L. Mangina, Bruce Marshall, Philip Rolnick, Kendall Soulen, Hans G. Ulrich, Geoffrey Wainwright, Bernd Wannenwetsch, Vítor Westhelle, Susan Wood, David Yeago, Matthias Zeindler, and my graduate students Daniel Barber, Jason Byassee, Holly Taylor Coolman, Edgardo Colón-Emeric, Beth Felker Jones, Jeff McCurry, and Brian Madison. Special thanks go to Paul J. Griffiths and Stan-

Acknowledgments

ley Hauerwas for crucial advice in putting this volume together, to Daniel Barber and Daniel Rhodes for the onerous work of indexing, and to Carol Shoun for her wonderful way of turning my Germanic prose into something proximate to good English.

Some of the chapters in this book have appeared, in earlier forms, in *Kerygma und Dogma, Modern Theology, Neue Zeitschrift für Systematische Theologie und Religionsphilosophie,* and *Pro Ecclesia.* I thank these journals, as well as the Biblioteca dell' 'Archivio di Filosofia,' William B. Eerdmans Publishing Company, and Fortress Press, for granting me permission to reprint material that is included here. For further publication details the reader is directed to the credits at the end of the volume.

I dedicate this book to my children, Hanna, Sara, Joshua, and Jonathan, who have taught me much about *eleutheria* and *parrhēsia* — in short, about what it means to speak the truth in freedom.

All Saints' Day, 2003 REINHARD HÜTTER

1. Bound to Be Free:
Ekklēsia — Eleutheria — Parrhēsia

In this book you will find an exploration of church, freedom, and truthful speech: *ekklēsia, eleutheria,* and *parrhēsia*. In the course of this investigation I am going to show how *ekklēsia, eleutheria,* and *parrhēsia* interrelate and, indeed, interpenetrate. This mutual interpenetration, or *perichoresis,* has long been obscured by ongoing Christian division. Separated from each other, many Christians assume that freedom can be maintained and truthful speech preserved only at the cost of Christian unity. Others assume that Christian unity can be attained only if freedom and truthful speech are narrowly circumscribed in their proper exercise. Christian division issues in the all too familiar individualistic accounts of church, freedom, and speech that have haunted modernity and clouded the proclamation of the gospel. At the beginning of the twenty-first century there is indeed nothing that Christians can less afford than to remain blind to this crucial interrelationship and its source in the God of the gospel. Each of the three parts of this book will illuminate in a different way the *perichoresis* between church, freedom, and truthful speech.

I. *Ekklēsia* — or, Free to Be Church

What is so great about being Christian? The freedom to be church. This answer drives the first part of the book. What makes the answer so odd is the apparent grammatical tension between the intuited singular in the question and the equally intuited plural in the answer. For the question suggests an individualistic answer that the actual response undercuts: there is no way to be church on one's own, despite the many rather resourceful attempts of modern liberal Protestantism to achieve something of the kind. In contrast to these attempts, I will make the case in part I of the book that unless the church reclaims its genuinely public character as *ekklēsia*, that is, as the eschatological gathering of God's people from Israel and the nations, Christians indeed forfeit the freedom to which they are called. Likewise, I will argue that any Christian theology that fails to think through the answer to the above question gives involuntary witness as a remainder of a bygone Constantinian establishment or a participant in the late modern designation of the church as simply one private association of religious belief among many.

One obvious rejoinder to these admittedly controversial claims is how I can even talk about "the church" in the singular. Are there not numerous churches and church communities, some in fellowship, but most separated from each other? This question, which haunts everyone who takes up the subject of the church under the condition of Christian division, is addressed most explicitly at the end of chapter 2. There I contend that the only way to think about the church theologically that is neither sectarian, claiming the fragment as the whole, nor "Platonic," forgoing the church's concrete existence and settling for its bare idea, is specifically and forthrightly ecumenical. In short, ecclesiology — thinking theologically about the *ekklēsia* — must be done *ecumenically* or it amounts to a self-deceptive sham that is bound to fail before it even begins.

There is no one who has addressed more squarely the theological implications of living under the condition of Christian division as if it did not exist than Ephraim Radner. In *The End of the Church: A Pneumatology of Christian Division in the West*,[1] Radner forcefully suggests that a facile Protestant ecumenism of "reconciled difference" — a euphemism for denominational pluralism — is nothing short of ecclesial self-deception. At the same time, Radner challenges the more "conservative," institutional ecumenism that is bent on the unification of divided church bodies. In recent decades, for a range of complex reasons — and despite mainline Protestantism's best efforts and great labors — the élan of institutional ecumenism has largely faded. Meanwhile, the Roman Catholic Church, at least since the encyclical *Ut Unum Sint/That They May Be One*, has taken up the ecumenical initiative in what has been proclaimed as an irreversible way. As Cardinal Walter Kasper stated recently in a remarkable public lecture, as clearly and — in light of the ever recurring Protestant worries about a "return-to-Rome" ecumenism — as helpfully as possible:

> The ecumenical aim is . . . not a simple return of the others into the fold of the Catholic Church, nor the conversion of individuals to the Catholic

Church (even if this must obviously be mutually acknowledged when it is based on reasons of conscience). In the ecumenical movement the question is the conversion of all to Jesus Christ. As we move nearer to Jesus Christ, in him we move nearer to one another. Such unity is ultimately a gift of God's Spirit and of his guidance. Therefore, the *oikoumenē* is neither a mere academic nor only a diplomatic matter; its soul is spiritual ecumenism. Only by a renewal of the spiritual ecumenism, by common prayer, and common listening to the Word of God in the Bible can we hope to overcome the present ecumenical impasses and difficulties.[2]

Such spiritual ecumenism is currently the best and possibly the only available response to Ephraim Radner's prophetic indictment of the church's end under the condition of persistent Christian division. For next to that indictment is the prophetic promise that "a bruised reed he will not break, and a dimly burning wick he will not quench" (Isa 42:3).[3]

However, the freedom to be church on which this ecumenical theology is based cannot consist in the negative freedom to "do our own thing." On the contrary, the freedom to be church must consist in the positive freedom of being committed and accountable to the common faith and its teaching. As I argued in *Suffering Divine Things,* the very point of the freedom to be church is to become obedient to the "form of teaching" (Rom 6:17) to which Christians are entrusted precisely when they become Christians.[4] In the church, therefore, freedom and obedience do not contradict each other. Rather, the former becomes complete in the perfection of the latter. I am aware that this sounds most counterintuitive to late modern sensitivities. Yet in part II of the book I will elaborate why and how this claim reflects the proper theological understanding of human freedom. Like human freedom, the church's freedom is received in a specific *form,* or *gestalt,* that consists of constitutive, core practices and distinct, normative teachings expressed in doctrine and dogma.

Part I of *Bound to Be Free* takes up my arguments from *Suffering Divine Things.*[5] Chapters 2 and 3 spell out the central argument of *Suffering Divine Things* in a more direct and accessible way; chapters 4, 5, and 6 push the argument further than did the earlier volume. Chapter 4 is my attempt to display the interaction between worship and doctrine as a necessary correlate for understanding the practices of *hospitality* and *honoring the truth.* Both practices supply the one well from which genuine spiritual ecumenism springs and continually renews itself — lest it turn into a deadly, quasi-bureaucratic interaction between various franchises of a troubled global organization. In this sense, chapter 4 establishes the horizon in which all of part III, "*Parrhēsia* — or, Free to Speak Ecumenically," is to be read.

Chapters 5 and 6 develop two additional aspects of *Suffering Divine Things*. In chapter 5 I continue my conversation with Karl Barth, by far the most productive — and most paradigmatic — Protestant theologian of the last century. Barth developed a fascinating and complex ecclesiology that sublates the concrete divisions among Christians into the dialectic of a quite seductive but ultimately abstract catholicity. The distinct abstractness of his "dialectical catholicity" culminates in Barth's treatment of Israel in relation to the church — far ahead of his time. It is only in chapter 12, in which I unfold the word "in" as it constitutes the silent fulcrum of the Roman Catholic Declaration *The Jewish People and Their Sacred Scriptures in the Christian Bible*, that an alternative way of relating Israel and the church emerges, one that cannot afford Barth's abstract ecclesiology.

Chapter 6 returns to the question of dialectics, this time as a mode of theological discourse. Somewhat to the dismay of many a Barthian, in *Suffering Divine Things* I pressed an implication of the Lutheran and, I think, genuinely catholic *finitum capax infiniti* by identifying the churchly utterance of God's word with God's Word — and this, contrary to any curtailment of God's sovereignty, as the most genuine expression of divine freedom. It is not surprising that Barthians worry about such an assertion, because it might suggest a latent idolatry, against which the virtues of Barth's distinct theological dialectics are invoked. This Barthian concern is not completely without warrant. For if we want to move beyond dialectics, for reasons offered in chapters 2, 3, and 5, we have to find a viable alternative to account for the categorical difference between Creator and creature. The alternative to dialectics proposed in chapter 6 is *negative theology*. There I claim that negative theology — far from being a neoplatonic intrusion into Christian theological discourse and thereby foreign to the nature of the Christian gospel and its Hebrew roots — must rather be understood as a necessary moment of proper theological discourse. More importantly, however, I understand the negative moment to be a *corrective* moment. The primary aspect of theological discourse is the affirmative — and this, for trinitarian and christological reasons, all the way down. In the third section of chapter 6 I undertake the move beyond dialectics by drawing upon the theology of the icon. For in iconic theology the negative moment expressed in the schematism of the icon is christologically assumed and transfigured. Likewise, and contrary to dialectical theology, iconic theology rests upon an analogical participation in the gift of being *(esse)*, a gift in which the affirmative and the negative are antecedently one and the same.[6]

This might be a problematic path for many a modern Protestant theologian to travel. It allows, however, the constructive reception of a vast tradition of profound patristic and medieval theology that has been prematurely banished by modern Protestantism with a consequent loss of rich theological possibilities. The move beyond dialectics is therefore a move toward "resourcement," a return to theology's roots, to fecund and promising sources for an ecumenical theological discourse.

I have written this book with the intention of engaging both Protestants and Roman Catholics, but with the equal intention of avoiding the abstract ecclesial nowhere that so often is assumed to be necessary for such an endeavor. Indeed, the particular perspective and ecclesial location that makes the simultaneous engagement of Protestants and Roman Catholics possible and in fact crucial is probably only all too visible throughout the book. In short, I have written this book for those living in the midst of the "Christian division in the West" (Radner), or, in starker and perhaps more accurate terms, for those living in "the church in ruins" (R. R. Reno).[7] We find ourselves in a distressingly fragmented ecclesial space. However, as long as the gospel is publicly proclaimed, the Lord's Supper or Eucharist publicly celebrated, and the triune God publicly praised and confessed, the Holy Spirit dwells within the broken parts of Christ's body in a way that holds before us the freedom to be church — indeed, to be church as *one public*. It is the false modesty of much of modern theology (Milbank) not to live by and act according to this hope.

II. *Eleutheria* — or, Free to Live with God

What is so great about freedom? This is the question that drives the second part of the book. The answer is, Nothing and everything. Nothing at all is great about a freedom that we claim as our possession. Yet nothing is greater than a freedom that is received as the gift of *eleutheria*, the freedom of living with God; such freedom is everything. Much is at stake between that nothing and that everything — nothing less than our very lives.

At the end of the popular movie *Braveheart*, just before being beheaded, the protagonist, a Scottish hero who has fought for freedom from English domination, utters his last word: Freedom. In light of this cruel ending, many might want to respond with a sigh of relief and a sense of pride: "I'm proud to be an American, where at least I know I'm free" — a statement that can be variously applied to any other modern democracy. For in modern democracies we usually need not fear that we might be beheaded when we fight for our own freedom or for that of others. And this surely is one great thing about freedom.

Yet the purpose of the book's second part is to convince you that we profoundly deceive ourselves when we stop where many might want to stop when they answer the question, What is so great about freedom? Why? Because, strangely enough, there are worse things that can happen to us than being beheaded. So when we ask what is so great about freedom, we should recognize that this is a dangerous topic. If we get freedom wrong, our mistake will ultimately kill us. Yet if we get freedom right, we will live, often painfully and sometimes even dangerously, but always truthfully in an ever expanding horizon that will lead us deeper and deeper into the Giver of true freedom.

In order to answer our question, What is so great about freedom? we must first ask about the nature of freedom. What do we mean when we talk about freedom? And who has this freedom? In our day-to-day thinking and conversation we tend to confuse three levels of freedom.

First, when the topic of freedom comes up, we tend to think of political freedom: the freedom of *Braveheart,* the freedom that was at stake in the American Revolution — that is, Jefferson's, Franklin's, and Washington's freedom, and by extension, the freedom sought by Rosa Parks and Martin Luther King Jr. Yet when we reflect longer and push further, we arrive, *second,* at that freedom that is the very presupposition of political freedom. It is moral freedom: the freedom on the grounds of which we are morally responsible. This aspect of freedom was most famously and lastingly developed by Immanuel Kant in his concept of autonomy.[8] Moreover, according to the principles of Enlightenment political thinking, only truly autonomous — that is to say, free — persons can be entrusted with the complex project of political self-governance.[9]

Classical modern thinking about freedom stops at the point of autonomy, and postmodern thinking despairs long before. Yet in order to grasp what is so great about freedom, we have to push beyond Kantian autonomy. Moving to the *third* level, we suddenly find ourselves in strange but exhilarating company. There are Gregory of Nyssa and Augustine, Thomas Aquinas and Martin Luther, John of the Cross and Teresa of Avila, Jonathan Edwards and Søren Kierkegaard, Karl Barth and Hans Urs von Balthasar, Edith Stein and Sergius Bulgakov. While they undoubtedly differ in numerous important respects, they all agree that this third level of freedom is the most fundamental and decisive. Here push comes to shove, because only here do we find the answer to our question. If we think we can rightly claim the greatness of freedom by attending solely to moral and political freedom, we simply commit the modern fallacy, which repeats the bad habit of the Enlightenment. If we think we can altogether escape the call to freedom by denying that there are basic imperatives of moral and political responsibility, we simply commit the postmodern fallacy, a more recent bad habit.[10] When we examine these two bad habits, we come to see that they make a hidden decision about the third, fundamental level — *eleutheria*, the freedom of living with God.

But what am I talking about when I suggest that here and here alone freedom stands or falls? At stake on this third, most fundamental level is the question, *What constitutes the human as human? What makes us who we essentially are?* The epoch of modernity defined itself by rejecting Christianity's answer to the question, What is so great about freedom? Modernity offered instead a new and different answer. Freedom itself was the very core of what constituted the human as human. Goethe's famous poem "Prometheus" captures best the modern answer to this question: moral sovereignty and self-sufficiency. By heroically defying the gods, Prometheus claims freedom for himself and the whole human race. Moreover, he shows that freedom makes him Prometheus in the first place: "Here I sit, forming men / In my own image, / A race, that is like me, / Made to suffer, to weep, / To take pleasure and to enjoy itself, / And to pay no attention to your kind, / Like me."[11] I call this perspective, in which the Promethean "I" imagines itself as sovereign, the *modern daydream*.

Having been foreshadowed in various ways for about 150 years, the modern daydream of the sovereign self came to full bloom at the end of the eighteenth century. What had happened? A disastrous and deeply pretentious "exchange of attributes" between God and human had occurred: freedom for contingency. Humanity had usurped *libertas*, the full and ungrounded freedom of sovereignty. For Luther and previous orthodox Christian theology, sovereignty had been solely a divine attribute. In exchange for sovereignty, humanity had handed over to God *contingency*, the essential attribute of what it means to be a creature. The world was now thinkable without God. Like Prometheus, humanity was now completely its own sovereign.

It did not take long for the nihilistic implications of this usurpation of the divine sovereignty to be felt. God not only became contingent but was even pronounced dead, this death of God being shockingly envisioned in Jean Paul's gripping "Speech of the dead Christ, looking down from the empty sky, that 'there is no god'"[12] and famously announced by Friedrich Nietzsche's "madman."[13]

This move is the presumptuous last consequence of modernity's answer to what is so great about freedom: God is dead and the human is divine. Yet in humanity's utmost presumption lies the seed of the fall from the modern daydream into the postmodern nightmare. It is important to remember that part of the modern daydream was a fundamental exchange of juridical positions between God and humanity, that is, between bench and dock. In C. S.

Lewis's apt description: "The ancient man approaches God (or even the gods) as the accused person approaches his judge. For the modern man the roles are reversed. He is the judge: God is in the dock. He is quite a kindly judge: if God should have a reasonable defence for being the god who permits war, poverty and disease, he is ready to listen to it. The trial may even end in God's acquittal. But the important thing is that Man is on the Bench and God in the Dock."[14] Yet during reason's trial of God, the god of the deists died in the dock. And with this god dead, there is only humankind left to blame for the miseries that we inflict upon each other. Theodicy turns into anthropodicy. That is, in view of evil and suffering, now humanity, instead of God, needs to be acquitted. Moreover, the nature of salvation has changed. If we don't save the world, no one else will. Progress has turned from an optimistic possibility into a sheer necessity. If we don't decide and thus choose who we are or what we want to be and do, some other human will. In Jean-Paul Sartre's famous dictum: "We are condemned to be free."[15] Faced with the infinite responsibility that accompanies the claim of infinite freedom, the Promethean self loses its nerve, capitulates, and flees from the posture of heroic sovereignty into the self-deceptive camouflage of petty license. License promises ultimate relief, because it allows the exhausted and overextended modern self to let its desires rule without accountability. "Freedom" now means living out whatever drives us. Such freedom, however, is eventually exposed as a life that consists in nothing other than the search for the next sensual pleasure, the empty, restless existence of the condomized and narcoticized Hades of instant gratification.

The modern daydream of sovereignty has turned into the postmodern nightmare of bondage. Friedrich Nietzsche, the first and already the last genuine postmodern, attempted to fuse radical freedom and absolute determination as he celebrated the endless will to power and the eternal return of things.[16] Nietzsche's profound postmodernity was not the faddish contemporary postmodernism; he took a lonely, radical, and ultimately deadly path. Today's postmodernists, by contrast, tend to occupy chichi coffeehouses and the "humanities" departments of countless colleges and universities — a lifestyle option secured by a TIAA-CREF pension plan. And so in late modernity, both "modernity" and "postmodernity" have become lifestyle options in a consumer society that mistakes license for freedom. It is no surprise that this kind of society finds itself caught on a manic-depressive roller-coaster ride between the dizzying heights of the modern daydream suggesting that our freedom is endlessly expanding and the despairing depths of the postmodern nightmare intimating that our freedom has been totally eclipsed.

What does all this mean? Whenever "freedom" becomes simply an issue and a catchword, limited to the political and moral levels, and especially when it is reduced simply to license, we become dangerously oblivious to the fundamental crisis of freedom that threatens humanity. Our concern for political and moral freedom in the face of the real *crisis of freedom* resembles a homeowner's preoccupation with a fire in the backyard trash can as her house burns down behind her. In the midst of the presumptuous "public sphere" daydream of cloning humans and tinkering with the human genetic code — not to mention the unchallenged "private sphere" supremacy of license — we may simply lose the ability to ask, What is so great about freedom? and still expect an answer that truly liberates and transforms our lives.[17] We should have a serious look again at Aldous Huxley's prophetic novel *Brave New World*.[18] We find there hauntingly displayed how license and genetic programming go together: the late modern subject understands itself to become at once completely "free" and completely "determined." And we should read right afterwards the equally prophetic encyclical *The Gospel of Life*[19] by Pope John Paul II. Living for a while between these two texts, we will start to understand: *With the present turn of things we have come to the very brink of denying human freedom and dignity on its most fundamental level, a denial that ultimately encompasses moral and political freedom as well.*

Yet how can we open ourselves to a truthful answer to the question about freedom? How can we gain access to an answer that truly liberates and transforms? We must start by allowing ourselves to be awakened from both the daydream and the nightmare. And waking happens first by hearing.[20]

It was common consensus for centuries of Christian thinking that creation's whispering sound has always already been around us and in us, addressing us constantly in the sheer fact of creation. Our being God's creatures, that is, our being constantly dependent on the Creator and called to acknowledge the Creator in gratitude, is thus an evident truth — yet one from which we have fled into daydreams and nightmares. Even though creation ceaselessly addresses us, our dull ears need a stronger signal, God's own waking call, God's own Word become incarnate.[21]

In short, the deep insight of the Christian faith into the question, What is so great about freedom? is that genuine freedom is an original gift that we find already spoiled and wasted. The modern daydream and the postmodern nightmare are only two more instances of this spoiling and wasting of what was originally given — and lost. Chapters 7 and 8 focus on one exemplar from the long history of profound Christian thought on this matter: Martin Luther's reading of the Genesis narrative, as he renders it in his long-neglected *Lectures on Genesis*. Luther reads the Genesis account, the human being in original communion with God, as a realist novel that tells us about our fundamental predicament in the form in which our creaturely life is structured, that is, as narrative.[22] In his interpretation of Genesis 2, Luther offers us a reading of the freedom we received in original communion with God. As we will see, this freedom is characterized in two ways. First, genuine freedom is a *gift* that connects the human in profound delight with God and all the other creatures. Second, genuine freedom has a concrete *form:*

> And so when Adam had been created in such a way that he was, as it were, intoxicated with rejoicing toward God and was delighted also with all the other creatures, there is now created a new tree for the distinguishing of good and evil, so that Adam might have a definite way to express his worship and reverence toward God. After everything had been entrusted to him to make use of it according to his will, whether he wished to do so for necessity or for pleasure, God finally demands from Adam that at this tree of the knowledge of good and evil he demonstrate his reverence and obedience toward God and that he maintain this practice, as it were, of worshipping God by not eating anything from it.[23]

Luther assumes that humanity was originally created for a freedom that is grounded in an intense and joyful communion with God, a communion that receives its proper creaturely form by following God's commandment. Thus genuine freedom and God's commandment stand in no contradiction to each other whatsoever. Rather, as I argue at length in chapters 7 and 8, God's commandment gives concrete creaturely shape to genuine freedom. In breaking God's original commandment, humanity abandoned the very form of genuine, received freedom and thus lost the original communion with God. Only then did God's commandment, originally supplying freedom's proper form, turn into the law that both constrains and unmasks the human pretension to self-grounding. Only then did God's law turn into the yoke that only Christ can lift.

In Christ the triune God restores the original communion as a gift received by faith alone through Christ's self-donation on the cross, thereby fulfilling the law in an exemplary way and granting life in God's spirit of love. The law is abrogated through Christ insofar as it constrains, unmasks, and convicts the sinner. Since sin, however, is still present in the life of the Christian, the law continues to unmask sin, keeping the believer focused on the need to continuously receive the gift of Christ's self-giving that constitutes genuine freedom. In short, there continues to exist in every Christian an ongoing struggle between flesh and Spirit (Rom 8:13-14). Yet this struggle must not be conceived as a static dialectic, an unending back-and-forth between sin and forgiveness, but must be seen as a dynamic — whose subject and agent is Christ through the Spirit — that results in an ongoing growth in faith, as Luther would put it in his treatise *On the Councils and the Church*.[24] It is on the basis of the latter that God's commandment, God's law, can become a source of genuine delight — which *is* the enactment of genuine freedom. Thus the law's content is restored to its original intent as the genuine expression of God's will: *the law of love*.[25] It provides the creaturely form of genuine freedom, the freedom of communion with God as received by faith. Now it is God's own law of love received in Christ, a "law" therefore welcomed with delight: *"Whenever there is this delight, it does what God commands. Then the law does not cause a guilty conscience, but causes joy, because one has become another person already."*[26]

Genuine freedom comes only when it is received by faith. There is no other source. Genuine freedom grows out of the restored and redeemed relationship with the One who, as Luther put it so memorably in his *Small Catechism*, "has created me together with all that exists."[27] The very heartbeat and life of this relationship and thus of true freedom is love, the *caritas* created by the Holy Spirit in the human heart. St. Augustine remains the unsurpassed ecumenical teacher of the West, ceaselessly instructing us about the intrinsic relationship between true freedom *(vera libertas)* and love *(caritas)*.[28] Charity restores our will's undivided desire for God. Now our will delights and trusts in God's goodness and is set free from its bondage to fear and lust; propelled by the heartbeat of *caritas*, true freedom unfolds.[29]

The central point of chapter 8 is to argue that this freedom receives God's commandments as its own proper form, longs to embody those commandments, and regards living joyfully according to them as its rightful enactment. Moreover, chapter 8 displays both what is at stake for Christian ethics in taking this claim seriously and how Christian ethics should operate in light of this claim. Although certainly a matter of contention among quite a number of Lutheran theologians, it seems to me beyond dispute that there is no strand of theology in greater danger of misconstruing *eleutheria*, the freedom of living with God, as a purely negative freedom — a freedom "from" — than Lutheranism. Hence, for reasons developed at length in chapter 8, chapter 9 contends on almost exclusively Lutheran grounds that this assumption is fundamentally wrong. However, the argument put forth in chapter 9 applies mutatis mutandis to any other form of Protestant ethics that succumbs to antinomian temptations.

At the end of chapter 8 I make the case that the signs of true freedom are, first, true worship and, second, delight in God's commandments through unceasing meditation on them and joyful obedience. Psalm 119:129-131 puts it this way:

Your decrees are wonderful;
  therefore my soul keeps them.
The unfolding of your words gives light;
  it imparts understanding to the simple.
With open mouth I pant,
  because I long for your commandments.

In the precise sense of God's commandments giving the proper form to genuine freedom, Psalm 119 longs for and celebrates freedom. However, a close reading shows that the Giver of the commandments and hence the Giver of freedom is first of all celebrated and praised. This is possible only through the gift of truthful speech, which has its true end in praise. And precisely for this reason, chapter 9, a consideration of the Decalogue's eighth commandment, transitions from *eleutheria*, the freedom of living with God, to its necessary consequence, *parrhēsia*, speech that is as free as it is truthful, speech that ends in the freedom of praise.

III. *Parrhēsia* — or, Free to Speak Ecumenically

Eleutheria, the freedom of living with God, must give rise to free and truthful speech, to *parrhēsia*, or it is not genuine freedom. Indeed, I submit that the practice of speaking the truth freely is the test case for genuine freedom, for *eleutheria*, in the church. Here we need to attend for a moment to the word *parrhēsia* itself, for it by no means signifies simply "free speech" in the contemporary, ordinary sense of having the right to express whatever is on our minds. It is that, but in a way that is simultaneously more radical and more profound. For, as Michel Foucault has pointed out with admirable clarity in his lectures on "fearless speech":

> The one who uses *parrhēsia*, the *parrhēsiastēs*, is someone who says everything he has in mind: he does not hide anything, but opens his heart and mind completely to other people through his discourse. In *parrhēsia*, the speaker is supposed to give a complete and exact account of what he has in mind so that the audience is able to comprehend exactly what the speaker thinks.[30]

But there is another crucial element: "The *parrhēsiastēs* is not only sincere and says what is his opinion, but his opinion is also the truth. He says what he knows to be true. The second characteristic of *parrhēsia*, then, is that there is always an exact coincidence between belief and truth."[31] Any individual practitioner of Christian theology must be a *parrhēsiastēs*. And if indeed ecumenical theology must be understood as nothing other than freely speaking the truth in the church under the condition of schism, ecumenical theology is the test case for how much genuine freedom is left in the church's speech when, for centuries upon centuries, persistent separation has haunted its existence and weakened its witness.

Finally, *parrhēsia* always involves some risk of personal or relational loss. Foucault would even say that such risk is a requirement: "Someone is said to use *parrhēsia* and merits consideration as a *parrhēsiastēs* only if there is a risk or danger for him in telling the truth."[32] To be clear, we do not need to return to the times of the persecution of Christians or to the Great Inquisition in order to secure the possibility of genuine Christian *parrhēsia*. Foucault expresses in a way that is immediately applicable, mutatis mutandis, what the nature and risk of ecumenical *parrhēsia* entails:

> Of course, this risk is not always a risk of life. When, for example, you see a friend doing something wrong and you risk incurring his anger by telling him he is wrong, you are acting as a *parrhēsiastēs*. In such a case, you do not risk your life, but you may hurt him by your remarks, and your friendship may consequently suffer for it. If, in a political debate, an orator risks losing his popularity because his opinions are contrary to the majority's opinion, or his opinions may usher in a political scandal, he uses *parrhēsia*.[33]

Similarly, speaking for our own situation, when we risk drawing criticism or even repudiation as "crypto-other" by offering a prophetic critique of our own communions, we are practicing *parrhēsia*. "*Parrhēsia*," says Foucault, "demands the courage to speak the truth in spite of some danger."[34]

Yet while Foucault helpfully spells out the nature of *parrhēsia*, we would go seriously amiss if we did not acknowledge first and foremost the source from which Christian *parrhēsia* arises, a source that makes it distinct as both a Christian and an ecumenical imperative. The source from which Christian *parrhēsia* arises is nothing other than *parrhēsia* itself — that is, in its sense of "confidence." The Letter to the Hebrews uses *parrhēsia* in this sense with great emphasis. In Christ we have confidence (*parrhēsia*) to enter the sanctuary of God's presence (Heb 10:19); "we are [Christ's] house if we hold firm the confidence [*parrhēsia*] and the pride that belong to hope" (Heb 3:6); "do not, therefore, abandon that confidence [*parrhēsia*] of yours" (Heb 10:35). This *parrhēsia* is the true sign of the Christian existence, which must be preserved to the end.[35] Without this antecedent confidence, any ecumenical *parrhēsia* will sound hollow and shrill.

Having clarified the nature and source of ecumenical *parrhēsia*, we can attend to its centrality for contemporary Christian theology. At the end of chapter 2, the constitutive chapter on *ekklēsia*, I claim that the only way to regain the church's public character in the world of modernity is by overcoming the church's internal schisms and thereby (re-)creating a truly catholic and evangelical church and theology — or, better put, by praying ceaselessly for the Holy Spirit to do the overcoming and creating. And the other side of that prayer is for nothing less than the practice of ecumenical theology. At the end of chapter 7, the central chapter on *eleutheria*, I claim that to enact genuine freedom is to presuppose and require the existence of communities that embody the practices in and through which freedom is received. Essential among these practices is ecumenical *parrhēsia*.

One aspect of this *parrhēsia* is to speak the truth freely to the churches or church communities that are separated from our own. From the Roman Catholic side, the single and most consistent speaker for — and perhaps the most uncomfortable practitioner of — this form of *parrhēsia* has been Pope John Paul II in his numerous encyclicals, especially the most recent, *Ecclesia de Eucharistia/On the Eucharist in Its Relationship to the Church* (2003). From the Protestant side, this ecumenical *parrhēsia* has been practiced by numerous individual theologians, among whom I should mention representatively Gottfried Maron,[36] Eberhard Jüngel,[37] and Miroslav Volf.[38]

Of equal if not greater importance — and surely of greater difficulty — is the form of *parrhēsia* practiced inside and toward our own communions, a *parrhēsia* that gives free and truthful witness to the truth seen in other, separated communions in a way that comes to bear critically upon our own. Paradigmatic for this aspect of *parrhēsia* are the efforts that produced the *Joint Declaration on the Doctrine of Justification* between the Roman Catholic Church and the churches assembled in the Lutheran World Federation.[39]

Finally, there are those voices that unite both aspects of ecumenical *parrhēsia* into one, as most recently in the United States the prophetic call by an ecumenical group of noted theologians from a broad spectrum of churches: *In One Body through the Cross: The Princeton Proposal for Christian Unity*.[40] These collective efforts, incubated in many cases for years by ecumenical working groups of theologians, are undoubtedly crucial forms of such *parrhēsia*. But important as well are the individual efforts undertaken on a regular basis across the abyss of the various schisms.[41]

No one has expressed more clearly the nature of this *parrhēsia* than did Cardinal Walter Kasper in the lecture with which we began. Because of its significance, I quote here at length:

> Ecumenism is quite different from an easy irenism, relativism or indifferentism, which forgets and disregards the question of truth. True ecumenism takes serious the claim of truth of its proper Church as it respects the claim of truth other churches or church communities raise. Only Christians or church communities which have and preserve their own identity can enter in dialogue. But the personal identity as the identity of a people of the Church as well is not an isolated monad and is [not] in itself a closed, arrogant, self-satisfied and self-sufficient reality. As every person so every culture, every nation and every church has its own identity only in relation and communication with its neighbor persons and with other cultures, nations and church communities. Identity is a dialogical reality, and ecumenical dialogue is therefore dialogue in truth and in love. Therefore, ecumenism is no one-way street, but a reciprocal learning process, or — as stated in the ecumenical Encyclical *"Ut Unum sint"* — an exchange of gifts.[42]

The final chapters of this volume take the form of an evangelical catholic engagement of Roman Catholic teaching documents. As such, part III can be read as a kind of coda, an attempt to inhabit the space of ecumenical *parrhēsia*. Free and truthful speech within and among communions can be difficult and costly. Undertaken in a way that gives due account of the Spirit's embodiment in the concrete traditions, doctrines, and practices of the church, it calls us to nothing less than radical ecumenical conversion. But enabled by the God who grants true speech through the Word and sets it free in the Spirit, genuine ecumenical *parrhēsia* — always pressing for the truth in love — will find its end in communal praise.

I. *Ekklēsia* — or, Free to Be Church

2. The Church as Public:
Doctrine, Practice, and the Holy Spirit

I. The Eclipse of the Church in Modernity

The dynamics of advanced modernity[1] seem to be forcing the church in America (especially Protestantism)[2] in two directions: either toward an ever intensified understanding of faith as an essentially private gnosis or experience made "relevant" through various subject-related activities or toward more and more objectified forms of faith — as especially in fundamentalist biblicism or traditionalist ecclesiasticism. Common to both of these Christian reactions to modernity's forces of dissolution[3] is that the church as a genuine "public" is eclipsed.

Yet we might very well ask why this should be deemed an important issue at all. What is lost if the church is just an association of religiously interested individuals? Under the conditions of modernity, can the church be anything other than a private association — and even if so, can it be a "public" in any full sense?

But then the counterquestion could be raised: If the church is in fact nothing other than a private interest group, does this realization not undercut its own self-understanding, its covenantal promise, and its mission? Does the church not dissolve into an ever increasing number of private circles that mirror the religious interests, likings, longings, and tastes of its members? Does it not, in other words, become the bearer of the "American religion," a "faith" that sanctions and undergirds democracy and that — while "free" to be exercised within the confines of democracy as an idiosyncratic private enterprise — is finally determined by the project of America?

II. The Protestant Church — an Oxymoron?

Questions similar to these were raised in a sharp and paradigmatic way about seventy-five years ago by the German New Testament scholar Erik Peterson[4] in a letter exchange with the then internationally famous historian of Christian doctrine and *spiritus rector* of liberal Protestantism Adolf von Harnack.[5] Many events and world historical changes obviously separate the present American situation from post–World War I Germany. Yet we can read the correspondence almost as if it were written yesterday. With the revolution of 1918/19 the Protestant churches in Germany experienced a shock of disestablishment from which they only, and only partially, recovered in the restoration period after World War II. This correspondence is particularly interesting and challenging seventy-five years later in an American context — a context characterized by the legal disestablishment of (Protestant) Christianity simultaneous with a cultural and social establishment unparalleled in the Western world. Our situation has radically changed since the 1960s. The place of a culturally established mainline Protestantism is subtly but increasingly being usurped by a post-Christian American religion with some lingering Christian overtones — in Harnack's words, "the aroma of an empty bottle."[6] In this very context the questions raised by Erik Peterson to Adolf von Harnack take on a pressing relevance. Ironically reframing the question, we might ask, Who needs the church after all?

The thesis I am going to argue in this chapter is that it is essential for the church to be a "public."[7] When the church is not characterized by those aspects that constitute it as a public in its own right, the church is a church in crisis. It is not God's crisis; rather, it is a crisis self-inflicted by the church's accommodation to modernity's norm for the organization of a public that is shaped by the liberal nation-state and the free market.[8]

While I would claim that the church's essential marks of apostolicity, catholicity, oneness, and holiness designate it as a public in its own right at all times and in all places, my thesis is nevertheless a highly contextual claim. While the church's designation as a public in its own right might be implied in its essential marks, the question of the church as public emerges with special urgency under the conditions of our ever advancing modernity.[9]

As a political project, modernity is constituted by a particular way of organizing the "private" and the "public" that entails the dichotomizing — and thereby the effective taming — of religion. On the one hand is a "civil religion" destined to justify and stabilize the project of a liberal society. On the other hand are those idiosyncratic opinions that particular individuals and traditions might hold on their own. The latter are strictly relegated to the realm of privacy. The freedom of religion becomes, for individuals, the right of privacy in religious opinions and, for the church, the "right" to exist in denominations — which is synonymous with the crisis of the church as public. This politico-religious context, in which the church as public has to a high degree been eroded or even lost, makes it imperative that the church explicitly claim its public character as a *nota ecclesiae,* an essential mark of the church.

The central contention of my argument here will be that the church has to break out of the iron cage of privatism set up by modernity's specific way of defining "private" and "public" in order fully to be the church. The church is either fully church and thereby a public in its own right or a bundle of denominations. So the key question concerns what a public is and how a public is constituted. I will argue that any public is constituted by binding teachings and practices. At this point a short lexical clarification is in order: In the following, I will use "doctrine" or "church doctrine" as a designation for those normative and binding principles that define and thereby make possible a public in the first place. This designation acknowledges the schismatic predicament under which the church currently exists. The pre-schismatic ecumenically acknowledged form of church doctrine is "dogma." Hence, only the teachings declared binding by the early ecumenical councils will in the following be called "dogma" in the strict sense. Moreover, I understand "doctrine" to be an unfolding and specification of its constitutive source, the *doctrina evangelii,* that is, the preaching and teaching of the gospel as the church confesses it in the Apostles' and Nicene Creeds.

First, I will show how Erik Peterson forcefully argues that the church has to be a public in order to be the church. He does this in light of Harnack's liberalism, which has capitulated in regard to modernity's private/public dichotomy.

Second, I will argue with Karl Barth against Peterson that the church as public involves God's own agency in the Spirit. Barth's pneumatological advance is crucial for avoiding the ecclesiastical objectivism that dangerously looms in some of Peterson's construals. Yet Barth's own suggestions remain unsatisfying. His newly recovered understanding of theology as a public enterprise normative for the church remains inherently unstable if the church to which it belongs fails to recover itself as a public. This insight was cogently voiced by the New Testament scholar and *Kirchenkampf* pastor Heinrich Schlier. He raised Peterson's question "after Barth" in a renewed and sharp form: Can there be a church in the New Testament sense if it is not a public that is defined and circumscribed in an *unambiguously binding* way? He saw the Confessing Church already hedge on this question, and post–World War II Protestantism in Germany, even more. Western Protestantism has inherited this question, and the unresolved problems related to it have only intensified.

Third, I will engage Schlier's concern by developing a politico-religious analogy that shows how *church doctrine* as binding teaching and norm makes sense if we draw upon the understanding of *polis* in its ancient sense and relate it, via Israel, to the church. This will allow me to sketch out some of the key practices that mark and characterize the church as public.

Finally, I will make some suggestions toward a pneumatological ecclesiology, in which the binding nature of the church's doctrine and practices is understood not as "against" the Spirit but rather precisely as the Holy Spirit's *(Spiritus Creator)* creation of that which makes the church possible as a public in its own right. Nothing less will suffice if the church is to be recovered as such a public — under the conditions of modernity. This, of course, means a return neither to Constantine nor to an established church in the Reformation or post-Reformation sense. Rather, it points forward to a recovery of the full political import of the church's being the church under the subtle and not so subtle pressures of modernity's "freedom of religion."

III. Objectivism versus Subjectivism: The Peterson-Harnack Impasse

The correspondence between Peterson and Harnack reflects in a paradigmatic way two reactions to Christianity's existence under the conditions of an increasingly secularized modernity. On the one hand, Harnack gives in to secularity and espouses an essentially individualistic and relativistic perspective:

> What will become of the Evangelical Church, I do not know; but, as you correctly state, I can only welcome the development which leads more and more to independence and purely intentional community [*Gesinnungsgemeinschaft*] in the sense — I do not shrink from this — of Quakerism and Congregationalism. . . . We will indeed find a way and forms free of *ecclesiastical* absolutism (absolutism only has a place in a lively spirit) — of course in the meantime we are still severely dependent on the remains of Catholic tradition among us, as it were, on the aroma of an empty bottle, and I am also not of the opinion that we should intentionally hasten the process, which will proceed slowly but surely, of its own accord.[10]

All that remains is nonbinding moral exhortation and voluntary association with those who hold similar convictions — of whatever sort. The church as distinct, identifiable public disappears.

On the other hand, there is Peterson's option, the return to Roman Catholicism, a step he took, after long hesitation and inner struggle, on December 25, 1930. Peterson raises the question of the church under the conditions of modernity. If the Protestant church has lost its public character by being disestablished (whether culturally or politically) and by increasingly being pressed into modes of privacy, can it still be church?

It is worthwhile to listen to Peterson's analysis of modern Protestantism in Germany:

> It seems at first sight one of the most astonishing features of modern Protestantism that it stands in alienated, uncomprehending opposition, not only to Catholicism — which at least makes psychological sense — but to its own past in traditional Protestantism, and, let it be noted, not just in "liberal" circles, but today quite generally, even among those of the so-called "positive" theology. The only way to grasp this incomprehension is to realize that the ontological basis of Protestantism has changed. The civil and public character of the Protestant church and theology, which was essentially definitive for traditional Protestantism, has vanished with the extinction of the Christian state, that is, of a confessionally defined territory. Along with it, the dialectical relationship to the Catholic church and to Catholic theology with its authentically *ecclesiastical* public character has been dislodged. As I see it, a good part of the development of the Protestant church makes sense in light of this slippage in the foundations.[11]

Peterson's analysis is, I think, of considerable importance for understanding some aspects of the dynamics internal to mainline Protestantism in the Western world. Having lost itself as a distinct public, mainline Protestantism is constantly in search of its own relevance in that public that is the currently determining and normative one, namely, that of secular society. Peterson anticipated already in 1928 the three dominant ways in which current mainline Protestantism makes itself "relevant" in this public: rationalism, mysticism, and activism — until quite recently the three most popular strands of American mainline Protestant theology. Yet Peterson's insight is suggestive beyond anticipating the major trends of contemporary Protestant theology: his insight suggests a crucial link between Protestantism's lack of a public nature and its ongoing crisis of relevance. The very collapse of its public character might be the reason that American mainline Protestantism took the national project of America as its subject matter, overcoming its crisis of relevance by becoming culturally established as civil religion. And accordingly, it is the loss of precisely this status as civil religion that has thrown mainline Protestantism into a renewed crisis of relevance in the last decades. Only by becoming *itself* a distinct public can mainline Protestantism overcome this systemic crisis of relevance. But then again, mainline Protestantism is not a church but a conglomerate of loosely affiliated denominations.

In the present context, the strong and obvious attraction of Peterson's suggestions clearly rests in their objectivism, which seems, at a time of rampant ecclesial and secular subjectivism and individualism, to promise a wholesome medicine. Yet on second look, we realize that his suggestions are born of a mere reaction, albeit a necessary reaction. And this is hardly sufficient. While it might be tempting to drive out the devil with Beelzebub, to get rid of Harnack via Peterson, it is not sufficient. This becomes obvious if we attend to a hidden "text" between the lines of their correspondence, namely, their tacit agreement in rejecting Karl Barth's option, which differs from each of theirs. It is exactly this undercurrent that shows why the one almost needs to invent the other in order to justify and hold his own ecclesiological position.[12]

I would argue that Harnack and Peterson are caught in an impasse exactly because they dismiss Barth's option out of hand. Yet only after having gone through Barth's alternative to both Harnack's subjectivism and Peterson's objectivism can we take up Peterson's pressing questions again — after Barmen, after Vatican II, and in light of the ecumenical movement.

IV. Beyond Objectivism and Subjectivism: Karl Barth

With the exchange between Peterson and Barth we turn to a question that, on the surface, appears to sidestep the present issue. The focus seems to shift from the church's public nature to questions of what theology is, how theology obtains its subject matter, and to what theology as a discourse practice is normatively bound. Yet these questions, as I will argue more closely in the next chapter, are far from sidestepping the central issue at stake. Rather, they display the problem at issue as it is paradigmatically embodied in one particular practice of the church, namely, theology.

In an essay as short as it is sharp with the simple title "What Is Theology?" Peterson critically engages Karl Barth's early dialectical theology. He applauds Barth's attempt to recover Protestant theology as a serious (i.e., public) enterprise, yet he criticizes dialectical theology for ultimately failing because it lacks a concrete and tangible object from which to draw. In other words, it has no binding dogmatic foundation on which the enterprise can stand. Rather, it remains an endless dialectical play with possibilities. Its seriousness, according to Peterson, is a false seriousness that only conceals its self-preoccupation.[13]

For Peterson, theology gains its unique function by submitting to the authority of dogma. If dogma falls away, we do not enter the realm of absolute freedom — as some contemporary theologians might assume and hope. According to Peterson, we rather again fall under the law. In other words, it is the sheer arbitrariness of "free" theological opinions in a market of endless possibilities that keeps theology captive and forever secluded from its objective — the God of Jesus of Nazareth. Is theology not in need of an objective grounding, which it finds in a dogma that is in continuity with Christ's speaking about God? Does theology not receive its substance, authority, and distinctive character as a unique inquiry solely from dogma?

Karl Barth and the whole group of dialectical theologians (to which, at that time, Bultmann and Gogarten also belonged) clearly felt the force of this attack.[14] Moreover, for Barth, Peterson's attack was crucial for his own development from dialectics to analogy.[15]

Barth's rejoinder, "Church and Theology," is a fascinating and skillful *sic et non*, a "yes and no," far from an all-out rejection of Peterson from that supposedly simplistic biblicist position that Peterson and Harnack see looming behind Barth's theology. Instead, Barth raises crucial questions regarding Peterson's way of relating theology to dogma and thereby to the very way he understands dogma.[16]

Barth agrees with Peterson that there are, as a matter of fact, significant and crucial forms through which theology receives its object. Yet, at the same time, he presses the relevance of pneumatology and God's present activity and work for theology in a twofold way. First, God's present activity is a constitutive element of the mediating forms in which theology receives its object; and second, that activity is a constitutive element of any ongoing Christian practice here and now — and that means also of theology as one of these practices. While Peterson seems to look for a clearly identifiable "object" of theology, Barth insists that this "object" is inexhaustibly present as subject, agent — as God the Holy Spirit. Theology takes place in the presence of God and is shaped by and in God's presence.

The question of the extent of concrete authority that Peterson presses leads Barth to point to a more complex reality in contemporary Roman Catholic dogmatics than Peterson might be willing to acknowledge: biblical references, theologians of the church, dogma, and recent papal decisions are, according to Barth, constitutive of the concrete authority under which Roman Catholic dogmatics operates. Barth actually can go along with some aspects of this practice by claiming that the concrete authority to which theology has to be concretely obedient is constituted by the ecclesial decisions on canon and canonical text and by more or less broadly acknowledged principles on which church proclamation rests as unfolded by the Fathers. By this line of acknowledging concrete mediating forms to which theology is concretely obedient, Barth succeeds in undercutting Peterson's tight connection between "logos," "dogma," and "theology" and in placing "dogma" into the realm of the church's teaching activity together with other significant teaching activities to which theology is equally concretely obedient, as to the canon or the teachings of the Fathers.

Barth concludes that in this sense, theology lives from dogma, but only insofar as the church has "authority." But what kind of authority? Here he rightly challenges Peterson's understanding of *jus divinum* (divine right), on the grounds of which Peterson can claim: "The gospel is not good news directed 'to everyone' — else how could it be distinguished from the Communist Manifesto? — but rather is God's positive legal claim [*Rechtsanspruch*] that from the body of Christ affects every one of us concretely, and does so *iure divino*" (p. 146; my translation).[17] Barth rightly maintains: "The authority with which the church sets the canon, proclaims dogma, etc., is clearly Christ's authority in a secondary sense; it is temporal, relative, formal authority" (p. 161/294). Its authority is an authority on earth (and not in heaven!), the authority of forgiven thieves; it is representative authority in relation to Christ's genuine authority; and it is authority that does not supersede revelation. In this precise sense, dogma and other aspects of church authority encounter us *jure divino* (by divine right). It is not the kind of authority on the grounds of which the church could cease praying for the Holy Spirit before and after its decisions, that the Spirit may lead the church into all truth. Thus Barth rightly claims the term *jus divinum* but interprets it again in a strictly pneumatological sense.

Yet, Barth asks, where is the exact point at which the church's mediate authority visibly and concretely submits to Christ's authority? "Word" and "Spirit" in their togetherness constitute the critical point at which Christ's immediate authority grounds the church's mediate authority and at the same time limits it. Only in relation to Christ's immediate authority does the church exercise mediate authority. By submitting to Word and Spirit in their concrete occurrences, the church explicitly acknowledges and practices concrete obedience and authority. Barth locates this concrete authority in a "third" place between God's Logos and Spirit on the one hand and human religious opinions on the other: "It is in this intermedium that the church knows God and confesses him through God's full grace, but does both with human limitations according to the measure of faith given to it, to the church of sinners. There the church receives and proclaims God's Word, but does both in weak, human words. There it makes its decisions by the divine law, but then sets up a human law. There the infallibility of the God-given and the fallibility of the human acceptance of God's gift make an exclusive antithesis as little as the covenant of grace into which the individual is taken is an absolute antithesis to the daily penitence of which, precisely as begraced, he is in need. In this intermedium 'there is' concrete authority, 'there is,' along with whatever else comes under the concept of such authority, also dogma" (pp. 165/297-98). Theology's obedience is the concrete obedience of a concrete practice in service of the proclamation of the gospel: "Theology becomes possible as position and science only if it carries that special burden, that special eager fidelity of the church to its Lord, that anxious guardianship of a zeal for the purity of the church's preaching" (p. 305).

Barth's rejoinder to Peterson is, I think, of paradigmatic significance for our own present theological context, since it fends off two problematic options: on the one hand, liberal subjectivism and relativism in theology and Christian life, and, on the other hand, traditionalist objectivism. Both, Barth would claim, operate *etsi Deus non daretur*, as if God were not presently active as Holy Spirit. This very pneumatological emphasis allows him precisely to go beyond both Harnack and Peterson.

I think at least two conclusions can be drawn from Barth's rejoinder to Peterson: *First*, there are concrete mediating forms — with a concrete authority — through which theology receives its subject matter and which are normative — as mediate — for Christian existence today as well as yesterday. In other words, there is no Christian theology and Christian existence without and outside of the scriptural canon, without and outside of the dogmatic consensus of the ecumenical councils, and without and outside of the theological discernment of the normative traditions.

Yet, *second*, it is not we who actualize God's presence here and now through our theologizing or any other activity.[18] Rather, both take place in the very presence of God's own activity. Barth moves pneumatologically beyond Harnack *and* Peterson. We are not canceled as human agents (pro liberal subjectivism), but the mediating forms are instantiated and authorized (pro traditionalist objectivism). Yet Barth makes two significant shifts. First, the focus of agency is taken away from us. We become recipients — we suffer God's salvific presence and activity — in and through our acknowledging and witnessing activity. Second, the reification of tradition is undercut. Creeds, dogmatic formulations, councils, and normative theologians themselves witness to God's salvific presence and activity and thereby obtain their mediate authority.[19]

Yet despite Barth's constructive pneumatological response to Peterson's challenge, I think all the questions Peterson places on the doorstep of Protestantism are still to be answered.[20] The reason for this is that Barth failed — despite his pneumatological advance — to make his theology ecclesiology, in other words, to interpret the concrete mediating forms in a way that shows their ecclesiological relevance.

Barth's understanding of theology is pneumatologically sophisticated yet ecclesiologically deficient precisely because the relationship between Spirit and church is far from clear.[21] While Barth was able to recover Protestant theology as a serious practice inherent in the life of the church, he did not render one necessary implication of this enterprise ecclesiologically explicit — namely, that the church itself has to be a public in order to make sense of and to sustain in the long run the very practice of theology that he envisioned. Thus the debate between Peterson and Barth about "What Is Theology?" was and still is today also a debate about the church as a public in its own right — or else an acknowledgment of its privatization!

V. Pneuma and Dogma: Heinrich Schlier's Renewal of Erik Peterson's Question

There is an almost forgotten witness — very uncomfortable for Protestantism[22] — to the fact that Barth's solutions were only partially successful, that is, successful in reviving theology as a serious, ecclesially public and accountable enterprise. Where Barth's project failed was in reviving that church in which this theology would have an ongoing viable existence. The witness to this failure is the New Testament scholar Heinrich Schlier, who succeeded Erik Peterson in his chair at the University of Bonn in 1945.[23] The crucial experience to which he points is his own deep involvement and activity in the Confessing Church's struggle in Nazi Germany. For Schlier, this struggle was, among other things, an effort to regain the church in Protestantism.[24]

Yet he saw the Confessing Church fail exactly in this effort because it did not achieve a common acknowledgment of concrete and binding teachings. To regard the confessions of the Reformation, for example, as concrete doctrinal foundations of the church was, according to Schlier, decried as "confessionalism" by the majority in the Confessing Church. Instead of the dogmatic principle, the majority espoused a charismatic principle. While Schlier fully acknowledges the charismatic principle — that is, the ongoing activity of a confessing faith — he sees that it replaces the dogmatic principle as foundation only at the price of losing the church and falling back behind Barth's efforts into Harnackian subjectivism.

Schlier's critique fully resonates with a comment Dietrich Bonhoeffer made in 1940 in a letter to Eberhard Bethge in regard to the *Kirchenkampf*: "The question is whether, after the separation from papal and from secular authority in the church, an ecclesial authority can be established which is grounded solely in Scripture and confession. If no such authority is possible, then the last possibility of an Evangelical Church is dead; then there is only return to Rome or under the state church, or the path of individualization, [e.g.,] of the 'protest' of authentic Protestantism against false authorities."[25]

This question, shared by Bonhoeffer and Schlier, is so uncomfortable for Protestantism because it is raised — "after Barth," so to speak — from the very core of Protestant resistance in the *Kirchenkampf* and from that core of Protestantism from which came most impulses for the church's renewal after World War II in Germany. Thus in the wake of Barth, Peterson's trenchant questions are, via Heinrich Schlier, still on the doorstep of Protestantism today. In continuation of our inquiry, I would like to formulate them in the following way:

1. Does the church need church doctrine — that is, binding teaching — to be the church as a recognizable public in its own right, transcending the privacy of all individually held convictions? Does the church have to maintain its public character even more so after having lost the support of the state, that is, after the creation of a separate secular public from the Enlightenment on?
2. How is God's present activity in the Holy Spirit related to those binding teachings that make the church a public? Does God's present activity as Holy Spirit relativize or undercut the mediate forms? Or are they, as mediate forms, still bindingly and concretely authoritative? In other words: Do the scriptural canon, the creeds, the dogmatic decisions of the ecumenical councils, and the confessions have an authority that makes a concrete difference here and now *in* God's presence? Are they a form (albeit mediated) of God's presence and therefore authoritative and binding? Or are they just actualizations of human witness in their concrete time, historically interesting to study and consult but ultimately nonbinding and unauthoritative? Are some of these mediate

forms a binding teaching for the church, or are they "sources" we might want to consult from time to time and whenever we are in need of orientation?

Half a century later, these questions have become ecumenically relevant insofar as all churches in the West are increasingly being "Protestantized" — in the sense of the last of Bonhoeffer's above-mentioned alternatives — under the pressures of an advanced modernity where "all that is solid melts into air." Is there an ecumenical alternative for the church beyond a reifying objectivism on the one hand — the very modern drive of reaction, to keep things solid — and an individualizing subjectivism on the other — the likewise very modern drive of accelerating the process of liquefying everything for the sake of "freedom"?

In order to advance our inquiry beyond these two alternatives we must address the following questions: (1) How are church doctrine and the church as public interrelated? and (2) How are God's own activity and presence and the binding nature of those doctrines and norms that make the church a public interrelated? In regard to the first question, I want to argue — with the help of classical political theory — that the church as public necessarily requires doctrine, binding teaching, and that doctrine has a public church as its necessary consequence.

VI. The Church as "Public" — a Political Analogy

Here it will be helpful to draw on the insights of political theory. By way of interpreting Plato and Aristotle, Hannah Arendt[26] develops a structural notion of "public," of which the polis is only one unique instantiation. Any public is defined by a particular set of normative convictions, embodied in constitutive practices, and directed toward a distinctive telos.

We can easily see how the ancient polis would be one particular instantiation of this notion of "public." First of all, the polis was a specific *space* circumscribed by the city walls. A totally open and unstructured space (a seemingly endless plain, for example) would contradict one of the central purposes of the polis, namely, to be a space for the free citizens to come together to speak, act, and cooperate. Second, and much more important, the laws of the polis prescribed its constitutive practices and underwrote its normative convictions. Thus just as much as the walls of an ancient polis surrounded and defined it as a unique physical space, its laws framed and defined it as a unique public space. The laws preceded the public; they were the result of a *poiesis,* an intentional production, in order to provide the distinct practices through which *praxis,* the political activity of free citizens, was made possible. And third, it was a very particular telos that characterized the whole enterprise of the polis in its distinction from the *oikos:* the escape from the endless cycle of production and reproduction, from the fragility and finality of mortal life into a space where heroic praxis (both in speech and act) would be praised by equals and where a specific kind of immortality in the memory of the polis could be achieved.[27] This telos, in addition, was precisely what informed the kind of freedom *(eleutheria)* for which the polis stood.[28]

This structural notion of a public as suggested by Hannah Arendt helps us understand also a "democratic society" or a "university" as a distinctive public, each defined by a particular telos, circumscribed by constitutive practices, and underwritten by normative convictions. Similarly, we have to understand the Torah and especially the Decalogue as defining the public in which the praxis — "following the way" — of God's covenant people, Israel, takes place.[29] The Torah is thus not an idiosyncratic limitation of an otherwise "free" existence but rather the very condition of the possibility of Israel's praxis of following the way of God — the latter being the defining telos of Israel as a distinct public. The Torah's binding nature creates precisely the "space," the public, that makes this praxis possible in the first place.[30]

In a similar way we have to understand the church's doctrine and core practices as constituting and defining the church as a distinct public, the telos of which is nothing less than the triune God's economy of salvation. Pentecost initiated an eschatological, albeit very concrete, *novus ordo seclorum.*[31] A new public was created; the *ekklēsia* of the eschatological polis (Heb 13:14) was gathered. After initial struggles, it became increasingly clear that this public was no longer constituted and informed most fundamentally by life according to the mitzvoth.[32] Rather, the *ekklēsia* was constituted and informed most fundamentally — christologically and pneumatologically — by the *kerygma*[33] and peculiar *practices* (especially the breaking of the bread and baptism).[34] The earliest creeds, the scriptural canon, the *regula fidei,* and the office of ministry that provided the continuation of the kerygma and the kerygma's practices were the elements that constituted the church as an identifiable public both in distinction from the theologico-political public of the Pax Romana[35] and from Judaism.[36]

In summary, there is no public without clear visibility, without a defining and constituting set of binding convictions, rules, and core practices. It is essential to this understanding that "public" and "political" are synonyms, that the activities in and of this public are political by its very nature.[37] It is only in the Western world from early modernity on that the *saeculum*[38] has monopolized the political for itself as normative and dominant public. The ironic result is that a "political theology" that attempts to "politicize" the church can only and unavoidably deepen the church's irrelevance and undermine the church's public (political) nature by submitting and reconditioning the church according to the *saeculum*'s understanding of itself as the ultimate and normative public. Peterson was arguing — together with Bonhoeffer, Barth, and others — against this politicization of the church already in the 1930s in Germany.[39]

As mentioned above, it is not crucial whether this public coincides with a state, as it did in the Byzantine Empire or in the Protestant states in sixteenth- and seventeenth-century Germany, or as it does in present-day Israel in regard to Judaism — or whether the public in question is categorized as a "sect," as the Amish, the Hutterites, or the Eastern Orthodox might be in the United States, or as Roman Catholics were in the former Soviet Union or former East Germany. Rather, the crucial dividing line runs between, on the one hand, a public that is constituted by church doctrine (as conciliar and papal decisions, or Scripture and confessions, or the Amish Ordnung) and, on the other hand, a religion that is thought of as something essentially private, that "motivates," "guides," or "directs" our ways of "going public" — "public" being the normative political public. The latter is "religion within the limits of the *saeculum* alone," and I wonder whether in at least some cases where modern liberalism identifies "fundamentalisms" around the globe, those are precisely Judaism, Islam, and Christianity reclaiming their own inherently public nature and thereby unavoidably exploding modernity's foundational dichotomy between public and private.

In this precise sense Peterson is right: because of its unwillingness to understand itself as a public constituted by concretely binding teachings and practices, modern Protestantism has collapsed into private piety that can at best "make" itself "public" by incessantly striving after "relevance" in the dominant, secular public, be it on the path of Gordon Kaufman et al. (religion within the limits of reason alone), Matthew Fox et al. (unitary mystical experience), or Dorothee Sölle et al. (political and social activism). The strength of Peterson's insight is that as soon as the church abandons its self-understanding as public, it falls into a ceaseless crisis of legitimation. All three Protestant "ways out" ironically only intensify this crisis in that they seek to legitimize the relevance of faith according to the criteria of the *saeculum*'s public nature, thereby acknowledging the latter's inherent primacy and further undermining the understanding of "public" appropriate to the church.[40]

Doctrine, as it delineates the church as public, lies beyond the alternatives of persuasion and coercion, the categories by which modernity tends to interpret dogmatic authority. In fact, I would argue that if one or the other needs to take place in relation to that which constitutes the church as a public in its own right, this public has already broken down and we are in a situation defined by Rorty or Lyotard or Habermas. And this is exactly where Protestants currently are: some (still) in "conversation," most involved in "paralogy," and all searching for that discourse that they hope might finally lead to a "consensus."

Yet as long and insofar as the church exists as a public in its own right, the teaching and the theological exploration of those convictions, rules, and practices that constitute it will continue. Ongoing persuasion[41] is an inherent element of the practice of theology, and forms of discipline (the office of the keys) might be a necessary element alongside it. Yet this discourse practice of theology is a practice of the church as public only insofar as it is bound to those convictions and rules that constitute it as public. Such persuasion or discipline cannot be foundational in the sense of justifying or critiquing the convictions and rules that constitute this public on grounds other than those very convictions and practices themselves![42] This is precisely why theology makes sense only as a church practice bound to those norms (doctrines) that constitute the public that is the church. A theological discourse that attempts to justify or critique the very constitutive convictions and practices on alien grounds is unavoidably part of another public constituted by other normative convictions and practices. Insofar as specific modern theologies have attempted to do just that, they were and are precisely part of that public that John Milbank rightly calls *saeculum*. This is why Peterson resolutely related theology to that church doctrine that constitutes the church as public and why Barth understood theology as a "church science" *(kirchliche Wissenschaft)*. Thus there is an irreducible conflict of contesting publics, and as public enterprise, theological discourse is necessarily and unavoidably accountable to the *binding doctrines* of one of these publics.[43]

This is one way to defend both the persuasive and the normative aspects of doctrine. In another, closely related perspective, I fully agree with current concerns about coercion in relation to doctrine. Peterson himself exemplifies, sadly, why these concerns are not and, historically, were not at all unjustified. The reason is that Peterson — in his strong reaction to the way the *saeculum* submits the church to privacy — got trapped by the very logic with which the *saeculum* understands "public." The dogma becomes, in Peterson's construal, as coercive as constraints by force in the *saeculum*: "The objective and concrete expression for the fact that in the incarnation God has come up against humanity, is dogma. It is the adequate expression of this fact that each turning against dogma, as, for example, done by the heretic, logically results in a corporal punishment of the heretic."[44] Here Barth responded rightly and sharply: "The custom of 'physically' punishing heretics which Peterson mentioned, not without a certain Spanish warmth, is to be judged discreetly as abuse *(abusus)* and not as use *(usus)* of the church's authority, since it obviously rests upon a disastrous deviation at precisely this point" (p. 161/294).

The key issue here, it seems to me, is how we understand this eschatological *novus ordo seclorum*, this assembling of an *ekklēsia* of the eschatological polis that took place at Pentecost. Does not this *civitas* explode the understanding of "politics" of any *civitas terrena* by constituting another distinct public? And if church doctrine is the prolongation of the body of Christ in any significant pneumatological and eschatological sense, does that not have precise consequences for how we understand church doctrine — *jure divino* — that is, precisely christologically and pneumatologically? In other words, we have to understand doctrine as a form of the gospel *(doctrina evangelii)* in the "upside-down kingdom" (Kraybill), with the consequence that doctrine is not "defended" at the body of the heretic through burning, drowning, or other, more subtle forms of discipline but that it is precisely the life and death of the martyrs and the confessors that defend church doctrine![45] In other words, doctrine has to be understood strictly along christological and pneumatological lines — lest it become distorted as a means for the exercise of force.

VII. The Church as a Public in Its Own Right

Clearly, it is important to remember that what we have elaborated in relation to Greek politics is an analogical argument. The church is not just another instantiation of the overarching genus "public." It is, rather, a public in its own right; its nature as public is defined by its own very particular and concrete designation. The ancient concept and reality of the polis has been used solely — and in immediate correlation to Israel — in order to elucidate the crucial role of doctrine for the church.

One way to show that the church is a public in its own right in distinction from the polis is to draw upon the "other" of the ancient polis, namely, the *oikos*, or household. Ephesians 2:19 shows wonderfully how the church can be understood as something similar to a polis and to an *oikos*, though not identical with either one: "So then you are no longer strangers [*xenoi*] and aliens [*paroikoi*], but you are citizens [*sympolitai*] with the saints and also members of the household [*oikeioi*] of God."[46] If we take this sentence in all its radicality, we have to conclude that the *ekklēsia* explodes the framework of antique politics, which is precisely built on the strict dichotomy between polis and *oikos,* or, in John Milbank's felicitous formulation: "[T]he polis itself . . . was partly constituted as a machine for minimizing the *oikos,* or as a kind of cultural bypass operation to disassociate continuity and succession from wombs and domestic nurture. Hence a virtue (like Christian virtue) that can also be possessed by women, and be exercised as much in the home as in the forum (and perhaps also as much by the immature as the mature) cannot be 'virtue' in the same 'political' sense at all: it must be an entirely transvaluated virtue."[47] Thus the church was nothing less than a revolution of the ancient political superstructure of polis and *oikos.* God's own *oikonomia,* God's own salvific activity — encompassing all of creation and culminating in the eschaton of a new heaven and a new earth — becomes tangible in a unique "space," a public in its own right. Here those who are by definition excluded from the ancient polis and relegated to the *oikos*[48] (namely, women, children, and slaves) become through baptism *sympolitai,* citizens, of that unique public that is governed by God's *oikonomia,* God's household rule. This is what Paul refers to in Galatians 3:27-29: "As many of you as were baptized into Christ have clothed yourselves with Christ. There is no longer Jew or Greek, there is no longer slave or free, there is no longer male and female; for all of you are one in Christ Jesus. And if you belong to Christ, then you are Abraham's offspring, heirs according to the promise." It is exactly this *oikonomia* of God that is specified and enacted by doctrine and the core practices.[49]

God's household rule, God's *oikonomia,* becomes specifically embodied through doctrine and particular core practices, and these two are inherently interrelated. Doctrine preserves bindingly and normatively in its formulations the very essence and the characteristics of God's salvific agency. The core practices embody and enact bindingly and normatively various specific aspects of God's *oikonomia.* The doctrine and practices are interrelated insofar as doctrine also bindingly teaches about these core practices, while the core practices enact church doctrine. Thus there is an "inner circle" of constitutive practices through which God's *oikonomia* instantiates itself. These practices are themselves dogmatic in the sense that they are constitutive of the church. They identify, or mark, the church as the space of God's *oikonomia.*

Martin Luther called them the marks of the church, and it was his way of approaching ecclesiology via these public marks that gave me the idea of thinking about these practices as the other side of doctrine, as equally instantiating the church as a public in its own right.[50] For this very reason, and also because it might be wholesome for us to be challenged by Luther's often forthright formulations, I will give (in the notes) some longer quotations of his in regard to each of the marks. Luther lists the following constitutive marks of the church:

- proclamation of God's word and its reception in faith, confession, and deed[51]
- baptism[52]
- Eucharist[53]
- office of the keys[54]
- ordination/offices[55]
- prayer/doxology/catechesis[56]
- way of the cross/discipleship[57]

I would suggest, surrounding this inner circle, an outer circle of practices that extend and support the inner circle in crucial ways. The outer circle is an open, extensive list, being mainly an expansion of the first and the last practices of the inner circle. They are not suggested as the church's only practices, but as those necessary to maintain the church as the public of God's own *oikonomia*.[58]

- the remembrance of the saints and martyrs and an ongoing procedure of identifying exemplary lives and witnesses[59]
- theology as a distinct practice of the church (as I will argue in the next chapter)
- an ecclesial procedure (at the least, if no public pacifist stance) of discerning between just and unjust wars[60]
- an increasing understanding that our primary vocation is Christian and that not all secular vocations are compatible with that[61]
- the regular practice of church visitations, as mutual support and admonition *(öffentliche Seelsorge)*[62]
- the encouragement of concrete communities that practice "life together" in such a way that they become challenges for all Christians (base communities, *integrierte Gemeinde,* Taizé, et al.)
- mutual public recognition and fellowship among historically divided churches, toward a Christian witness that is not paralyzed by internal divisions[63]

These suggestions for the outer circle of practices are, of course, inherently vulnerable to various misunderstandings. There is, first, the obvious critique that the church I am talking about does not exist. This is a truism if we choose

The Church as Public: Doctrine, Practice, and the Holy Spirit

to cast the church's "existence" into sociological categories. There the church never "exists" as church but exists merely as a sociological reality predetermined by the conceptual limitations of its own vocabulary. If we shift the description into the theological conceptuality proper to the object as given, the issue changes from existence to faithfulness and unfaithfulness in regard to both doctrine and church practices. The other critique (and misunderstanding) — that this represents a proposal for realizing the ideal "superchurch" beyond all existing churches — is only the flip side of the first critique. The church practices as listed do not suggest any *poiesis*, any production of a new and better ecclesial "system" in analogy to all the bureaucratic and managerial systems that characterize modernity. Both the descriptive truism that this church does not exist and the poietic desire to produce or (re-)create the church according to our own best (recent) insights are misunderstandings born of the conditions of a modernity that presupposes a conception of the church *etsi Deus non daretur*. It is nothing less than we ourselves and our commitments to and investments or entrenchment in key convictions of modernity that make the church a "problem." Especially for those who claim the battle cry *ecclesia semper reformanda* as constitutive of their ecclesial — or should I say "denominational"? — identity, it should not come as a surprise that they might be called to a *metanoia* for the gospel's and — thereby necessarily and implicitly — the church's sake, a *metanoia* that only the Holy Spirit will be able to accomplish.

VIII. The Holy Spirit and the Church

While the relationship between the Holy Spirit and the church is broadly acknowledged in the theological tradition, how this relationship is to be precisely understood has been and still is a matter of intense debate in various corners of the *oikoumenē*.[64] Nothing will be resolved with the following few comments — although they are necessary to an understanding of one crucial point of our concern thus far: the church as a public in its own right. Consequently, I will only gesture toward a pneumatological ecclesiology in which the binding nature of the church's doctrine and core practices is understood to be not "against" the Spirit.[65] Rather, it is precisely the Holy Spirit who creates — as *Spiritus Creator* — that which makes the church possible as a public in its own right: doctrine and the core practices. Yet, on the other hand, it is the church — constituted by doctrine and the core practices as a public in its own right — in and through which the Holy Spirit's work becomes public, is announced and interpreted.

I will situate my argument in the horizon of the following canonical text, the promise of the presence and work of the Holy Spirit among Jesus' disciples — the Spirit as the one who, in a unique sense, represents Jesus in the time of his absence: "But the Advocate, the Holy Spirit, whom the Father will send in my name, will teach you everything, and remind you of all that I have said to you" (John 14:26). This text gives us, I think, a clue to how the relationship between the Holy Spirit and the church is to be understood. While the initiative clearly lies with the Holy Spirit, the activities of teaching and reminding presuppose, on the church's side, structures and practices of learning and remembering as well as ways of communally embodying that learning and remembering so that it can be passed on as that which the Holy Spirit has given and in light of which new learning and remembering can take place.

Exactly this is the role and place of the church's doctrine and core practices. Yet in order to account for the continuing initiative of the Holy Spirit, these mediate forms have to be understood as creatures of the Spirit through which the Spirit does the work of teaching and reminding. In other words, the Spirit's teaching and reminding do not remain disembodied. It is to be expected that the Holy Spirit creates procedures — doctrine and the core practices — through which the teaching and reminding occur. These procedures are the Spirit's gift in service of God's *oikonomia*.[66]

To put the matter in a variation of a famous formulation of Kant: Pneumatology without ecclesiology is empty; ecclesiology without pneumatology is blind. Without the Holy Spirit, the church would be blind: it is God the Holy Spirit at work bringing about God's *oikonomia* who is both origin and objective of the church. Without seeing itself in the horizon of God's *oikonomia* — being created, shaped, and informed by the Holy Spirit, and serving God's *oikonomia* — the church becomes blind, that is, loses the sense of its own unique vocation. It is exactly in and through doctrine and the core practices that the church is taught and reminded of its origin and telos. The church learns and sees through them what it is to which it is bindingly committed. Doctrine and the core practices — as they enable the church to be that public in which the announcement of God's *oikonomia*, discipleship, and the formation of other practices and habits take place — are the Spirit's work, although they do not exhaust, by far, the Spirit's work.

When there is no insistence on the inherent relatedness of the Spirit's work to the church and no understanding that the church is nothing less than the Spirit's creature in time, the Spirit's "announcer" and interpreter, then the Spirit's activity can easily be seen and claimed everywhere — and, therefore, nowhere in particular. Claiming the Holy Spirit becomes an empty claim. In other words, without the concrete mediation of the church's doctrine and core practices, the character of the Holy Spirit's work becomes questionable: How does the Spirit teach and guide if not in and through what Barth calls the "mediated forms," namely, the church's doctrine and core practices? If the Spirit's activity is completely severed from that mediation, the lordship of the Spirit turns into a void to be filled by all sorts of human projections. How, then, are the Spirit's work and the church related?

Pentecost provides one clue. If we understand the event at Pentecost as the beginning of the eschatological pouring out of God's Spirit over all the nations (Acts 2), we have to ask how this pouring out of the Spirit is characterized. It clearly is the effective "making public" of God's *oikonomia*, God's salvific activity, through Jesus Christ's death and resurrection. At Pentecost, the Holy Spirit's activity stands for this overwhelming and transforming "publicity" of God's mighty deeds, the effective communication of the gospel. This event, the Spirit's effective communication of the gospel of Jesus Christ, the Spirit's "publicity," creates and characterizes the church as a public in its own right. Yet while the public nature of the church and the Holy Spirit's publicity are intricately interrelated, they are not identical. The church as public is constituted by the Holy Spirit in and through the mediating forms, doctrine and the core practices. It is through these that the church participates in the Holy Spirit's publicity.

Yet the Holy Spirit's publicity goes beyond the church's limits, in that the Spirit creates new things and can act as a critic of the church from both within and without.[67] At the same time, the Holy Spirit's activity clearly becomes public in and through the church's practices of proclamation and witness. So while the Holy Spirit is active in all of creation, this activity is announced and interpreted in that particular public that is the church. And without doctrine and the core practices constituting the church as public, there is nothing to be publicly announced and interpreted! In other words, while the church clearly cannot lay claim to the Holy Spirit as if the church's doctrine and practices could "manage" the Spirit (in this sense the Spirit always remains Lord over against the church), the church's doctrine and practices are far from being irrelevant for the Spirit's own publicity and activity. To put it another way: The Spirit can do a "new thing," guide the church into all the truth (John 16:13), only if there is a binding set of doctrines and practices in the church. Only in such a context can something new be discovered, minds and practices be changed, and a new aspect of God's *oikonomia* emerge as a newly binding practice or doctrinal formulation. Where there is no public constituted by the binding nature of doctrine and the core practices, everything becomes a matter of "personal choice" — that is, of private arbitration — and that is precisely the situation in which the church ceases to discover or encounter anything new! Where everything is arbitrary, everything and nothing is new. It might sound like an ironic paradox, but if the Holy Spirit is to lead the church into all the truth and teach the church new things by constantly reminding the church of Jesus Christ, the binding nature of doctrine and certain core practices is essential. This is precisely why Acts 15:28 mentions the Holy Spirit in the very formulation of a new doctrinal decision: "The Holy Spirit and we have decided...."[68] In this instance of doctrine a new practice was defined that helped constitute that very public in which Jews and Gentiles could be together without offending those living according to the Torah. It was something new the church had to decide — in the power of the Holy Spirit — as a way of learning and remembering what the gospel of Jesus Christ and the way of discipleship concretely imply.

One of the key questions in light of this claim is, of course, whether and how the church can legitimately use this formulation after 1054, the split between the Western and the Eastern Church, or after the Reformation events and the ensuing Council of Trent. Which church can legitimately claim the Holy Spirit for its doctrinal decisions — especially if they are explicitly directed against doctrinal decisions of another body that claims to be church? I think this is a valid and very urgent question — yet one that should precisely *not* be solved either by claiming the exclusive identity between the Spirit's work and one church-body or by assuming a pneumatological agnosticism on this point. It seems to me that the right way to pursue this question would be to exclude both alternatives and address the question as ecumenical: Which doctrinal formulations and which practices point to, promote, and even embody the church's unity — and thereby become again, in the mode of an ongoing ecumenical *metanoia*, vessels of the Holy Spirit's teaching and remembering?[69] No one has expressed the nature of such a *metanoia* more clearly and courageously and thereby already also enacted it than Cardinal Walter Kasper in the public lecture from which I quoted in chapter 1. Because of its long-range significance I shall again quote at length:

> [E]cumenism is no one-way street, but a reciprocal learning process, or — as stated in the ecumenical Encyclical *"Ut unum sint"* — an exchange of gifts.
>
> The Catholic Church too is wounded by the divisions of Christianity. Her wounds include the impossibility of concretely realizing fully her own Catholicity in the situation of division. Several aspects of being Church are better realized in the other Churches. So we can learn from each other in order to grow in the one truth of Jesus Christ, to comprehend and to realize more and more the richness he revealed to us. Thus,

since the Councils we Catholics learned a lot from our Protestant brothers and sisters about the importance of the word of God and its proclamation, and who knows only a little on orthodox icons gets aware what spiritual richness we can draw from them. The *oikoumenē* is a spiritual process, in which the question is not about a way backwards but about a way forwards by mutual exchange....

Besides, The Council [Vatican II] is aware of the sinfulness of the members of its own Church, and of sinful structures existing in the Church itself; and it knows about the need of reforming the shape of the Church. The Constitution on the Church and the Decree on Ecumenism state expressly that the Church is a pilgrim Church, and ecclesia *"semper purificanda,"* which must constantly take the way of penance and renewal. Thus, the ecumenical dialogue fulfils the task of an examination of conscience. Ecumenism is not possible without conversion and renewal.[70]

In his statement Cardinal Kasper exemplifies the ecumenical truth that "[t]he disciplines of unity are penitential," as aptly put by the recent *Princeton Proposal for Christian Unity.*[71] My candid engagement of Roman Catholic teaching documents in part III should be understood as modest and budding attempts to exemplify this principle. In other words, only in light of the above ecumenical maxim is part III of this volume rightly understood.

Ending this chapter, I would like to venture in a direction where angels might not dare to tread and formulate the thesis that in a world of modernity that increasingly privatizes the Christian faith, the church's public character is reclaimed only and precisely by overcoming the internal splits and by (re-)creating a truly catholic and evangelical church and theology — I should better say, by praying for the Holy Spirit to do the overcoming and creating. Or, to intensify the thesis: The obvious internal failure of the Western church in modernity can be rightly understood as God's judgment on the church's unfaithfulness and unwillingness to take up the way of the cross in the violent religious struggles of the sixteenth and seventeenth centuries (with the notable exception of most of the left wing of the Reformation and the monastic communities). Thereafter, only the privatization of the Christian faith could allow a "peaceful" public to be envisioned and constructed.[72] This "Babylonian exile" of the church into privacy needs to be reclaimed by the church as "church history" in the fullest theological sense. The church's eclipse as a public in its own right in modernity will not be overcome by reactively opposing modernity (Peterson) or by willingly succumbing to it (Harnack). Rather, the church's eclipse as a genuine public in its own right will be overcome only when we let ourselves be overcome by the Holy Spirit, namely, through repentance on all relevant sides and through the healing of the split in the Western church and between West and East. An eschatological perspective? — Exactly!

3. The Knowledge of the Triune God: Practice, Doctrine, and Theology

The goal of this chapter is to retrieve an understanding common to almost all Christians until roughly two hundred years ago: *that the church is the location where we come to know God, surely not in every possible way, but in the one decisive way, namely, as the One who saves us and draws us into the fullness of the divine life — all of this through faith in the crucified and risen Jesus Christ.* The church itself is nothing other than the thankful creature of God's saving work, not a proud executor but a glad recipient. Yet this receiving embodied in practices is precisely the way in and through which the Holy Spirit works the saving knowledge of God. For this very reason not only the Catholics but also the Reformers could call the church the "mother of faith."[1]

Yet the great schism of the Western church, with its ensuing religious wars and mutual doctrinal condemnations, opened the door to a profound skepticism about the very possibility of coming to know the triune God in and through the church's practices and teachings. As a result, the intellectual avant-garde of the seventeenth and eighteenth centuries felt forced to fall back onto a rational knowledge of God that could be metaphysically warranted and assured. Both the late medieval developments in rational theology and the increased retrieval of antique thinking during the Renaissance facilitated this move considerably.[2] Yet a metaphysically assured knowledge of God itself proved to be unstable. It was the very project of Kant's critical philosophy to show that the existence and knowledge of God can in no circumstances fall under the competence of a rational metaphysics.[3] Rather, the idea of God is a necessary consequence of the human being as moral agent. Another "Copernican revolution" of sorts was at hand: the human subject became the fixed point for whom the idea of God is a necessary working hypothesis of practical reason.[4] What is the point of the church under these radically changed circumstances? The church as pure aggregation is the location for moral motivation and improvement, with Jesus being the paradigm of perfect morality.[5] It was Schleiermacher's great achievement to overcome this radical reduction of the saving knowledge of God to a model of the moral life by establishing the category "religion" as an entity fundamentally different from metaphysics and morals and therefore immune to Kant's critical philosophy. Religion is rooted in a pre-reflective and ultimately ineffable feeling of radical dependence over against the universe in its totality as experienced by the subject.[6] The church is now the community of those religiously moved to express and communicate and thereby interpret and understand their ineffable religious experience. Jesus is now the paradigm of this very religiosity.[7]

What is significant is that in both the "Kantian church" of moral motivation and the "Schleiermacherian church" of religious communication, the moral and/or religious subject antecedes the church. The fixed point is the subject to whom the "church" stands in a functional relationship of service — be it of a moral or a religious kind. In other words, *the subject is the end of the church*. The result of this is nothing other than the modern "denomination" and the "service" jargon pervasive in contemporary church growth talk. And this is not surprising. Where the subject is the end of the church, the market becomes the means.[8]

The point of the following proposal is not to overcome this problematic by heralding some "postmodern turn" that might simply relieve us from our predicament. The postmodernity currently celebrated seems to be nothing less than an intensification of the very turn to the subject — with a concurrent loss of the utopian assurances once associated with the subject by the Enlightenment. The point, rather, is to undertake an exercise in theological remembrance in the face of the modern turn to the subject and its postmodern mass application. Nor is the point to suggest a return to "premodern" securities. Rather, in the context of a conflictual and thus critical relationship to modernity, the point is to attempt to remember theologically what is at stake in the church being the church for knowing the triune God. The church is gifted with a promise that it carries in its very way of being the church. This promise is nothing less than a knowledge of God that both saves and transforms. Yet it is a knowledge that depends on the church's practices and in this significant sense antecedes us as individuals. Only by being drawn into those practices that in their very core are the church's makeup do we come to a knowledge of God that we do not own — a knowledge that ultimately will own us. In this very specific way *the church will turn out to be the end of the subject* — precisely in its modern sense, where knowledge presupposes the subject's self-positing and, ultimately, the subject's will to power.

And what would it mean if theology were to be itself reconceived in light of this theological remembrance? What if theology were neither a hermeneutics of "values" to be distilled from the moral paradigm "Jesus" nor a description or reimagination of the religious subjectivity paradigmatically encountered in Jesus? Theology, I will claim, has to be understood as a distinct practice that comes necessarily with the church — yet without being constitutive of the church. As a church practice, theology precisely realizes the fact that the knowledge of God cannot be achieved "nakedly," be it in the form of the "thereness" of an "objective" knowledge (premodern metaphysics) or of "knowledge" that is the construct of the poietic subject (modern religiosity after Kant). Rather, Christian knowledge of God can be gained only by suffering God's saving activity as it engages us in word and sacrament as well as the rest of the church's core practices and as it commits us to preaching and teaching *(doctrina evangelii)* through those normative formulations *(doctrina definita;* doctrine) that help us hold on to the gospel in the face of its distortion. In other words, if the church is the end of the subject because the Holy Spirit becomes the agent of the triune God's knowledge through the church's core practices and teaching, "to do theology" appropriately means to do it in relation to both the church's core practices and to doctrine. This claim is clearly an affront if we assume that the subject is the end of the church. Yet under the presupposition here entertained, that the church is the end of the subject, this understanding of theology is its necessary implication.[9]

I. Naked "Knowledge of God" and the Modern Dilemma: God "Reified" or God "Construed"

Before we move into more explicitly theological considerations, we have to realize what the specific dilemma is under which we encounter the question of the knowledge of God in modernity: "Knowledge of God" is an oxymoron as long as we understand it strictly along the lines of "knowledge of something as acquired according to the universal standards of knowledge." Under the epistemological conditions of modernity, essentially two dominant ways out of this oxymoronic situation were developed.

First, since God is not a part — or even the totality — of that which can be "known," that is, of the created world, God cannot be known in the strict sense at all. All we can do is consciously construe similes or metaphors that most accurately reflect our pre-reflective and essentially ineffable experiences of the transcendent and communicate them to others. This communication is essential for a full development of human selfhood in relation to others and to the transcendent. The estrangement inherent in this kind of "knowledge of God" is transparent in the poietic nature of theology's "similes" for the ineffable "mystery" of the divine. Thus the oxymoronic situation is solved by giving up the expectation of a genuine knowledge in relation to God. There might be intimations of the divine as poietically construed by the pious consciousness, but there is no genuine knowledge of God.[10]

Second, since God is to be understood as the omnipotent creator of the world, it is quite conceivable that God has established ways that allow for a genuine knowledge of God under the conditions of a created world, be it via human reason's immediate participation in divine reason or via a particular corpus of divinely inspired texts or via a particular deposit of faith that potentially contains all the knowledge of God to be unfolded and mediated by an infallible magisterium. Here there is a form of "worldly knowledge" to be acquired under the conditions of the world, as any other knowledge is acquired. Some particular aspect of the created world has to be claimed so that God can be known "univocally," that is, under the general conditions of knowledge as constitutive of this world.[11] "God" becomes a "thing" to be "known." Thus the oxymoronic situation is solved by getting rid of "God" in relation to knowledge. There is knowledge of a "God" who has essentially ceased to be God.[12]

An earlier attempt at overcoming this modern dilemma was Hegel's speculative sublation of the two alternatives in the human spirit's participation in the absolute Spirit: knowledge of God is attained insofar as we participate, via speculative reflection, in God's own self-knowledge. The decisive problem in this still deeply influential way of thinking is that the radical difference between Creator and creature is erased in the (self-)movement of spirit. The "knowledge of God" is saved by Hegel in and through the human spirit's reflective activity completed from the standpoint of absolute Thought.[13]

II. Karl Barth's Solution and Its Pneumatological Instability

One of the lasting achievements of Karl Barth and the theological movement he initiated was to keenly see this modern dilemma and at the same time not succumb to the Hegelian temptation, namely, to ultimately identify the human mind's self-reflexivity with God's self-knowledge, or at least a genuine moment of it. The crucial insight that allowed Barth to stay free from the Hegelian temptation was his awareness of the noetic effects of human sin. *Post lapsum,* not only has humanity lost any genuine community with God that might allow for a participatory knowledge of God, but humanity finds itself in a position of radical estrangement from and even enmity toward God — a situation in which knowledge of God can be experienced only as a radical judgment of the human knower and, at the very same time, a radical justification "in Christo" of this very knower.[14] Therefore, the knowledge of God is possible only as God's self-giving knowledge.[15] Barth had to develop the knowledge of God as God's self-communication *in actu* in order to preserve God's freedom from the modern claim to the self's epistemic primacy (Kant)[16] or supremacy (Fichte).[17] At the same time, Barth integrated genuine concerns of modernity into his account by construing human selfhood and freedom relationally so that in the encounter with God's self-communication the human is not only judged and justified in Christ but also genuinely set free in relationship to God, the enactment of which are faith and witness. "In" this knowledge of God *in actu* this "freedom as relationship," to which humanity was destined from the beginning, is both fully revealed and restored.[18]

But how, we might ask, is *theology* being construed from this perspective in relation to the knowledge of God? For Barth, theology is the dialectical practice of reflecting on the witness of God's past self-communication in constant expectation of God's future self-communication. Being stretched out between memory and hope, between the witness of Scripture and the mandate of proclamation, theology critically examines the church's performance of witnessing to God's self-communication by preaching the gospel.[19] Barth deployed the philosophical concept of a "realist actualism"[20] as a way of overcoming the modern dilemma in regard to the knowledge of God. This concept allows Barth to differentiate categorically between God and God's act of self-communication on the one hand and all "traces" of this self-communication in humanity's witness to it on the other, be they in Scripture, the acts of baptism and the Lord's Supper, church doctrines, or the teachings of the church fathers and later theologians. Insofar as they are faithful witnesses, they are to be taken seriously. But since they are just that, witnesses, the danger of reification, of mixing up God with one of the reflections of God's self-communication can thereby be avoided.[21] On the other hand, Barth's concept allows him to keep in check any modern claims to the poietic primacy (or supremacy) of the knowing subject.

Yet Barth has to pay a high price for his intricate way of coping with the modern dilemma of the knowledge of God. His "actualistic" solution imprisons as much as it liberates. Why? Because it leads to the eclipse of the distinct economy and mission of the Holy Spirit. Barth understands the Holy Spirit as God's self-enactment or, better put, as the enacted relationship, first, as the inner-trinitarian relationship between Father and Son and, second, as the actualization of God's self-revelation in the human being, thus setting him or her free to be a believing and responding agent.[22] What is lost in this pneumatological account is, first, the Holy Spirit as distinct trinitarian "identity" (*hypostasis*)[23] and, second, the Spirit's distinct economy as enacted through the Spirit's work.[24]

The severe limitation of Barth's pneumatology is mirrored in the very way his concept of the knowledge of God and of theology finally is unable fully to overcome the modern dilemma. Barth's central concept of "actualism" makes the dialectical discourse of theology a *conditio sine qua non* for avoiding the unhappy choice between human reification and construction. Only the ongoing dialectic of the theological discourse itself keeps the witness (Scripture, church doctrine, theological teaching) "fluid" (i.e., preserves it from becoming a reified knowledge of God) and at the same time resists theological poiesis by committing and submitting the theologian to the ongoing discourse with all the significant interlocutors (Scripture, church doctrine, theological teaching).[25] This is the reason the *Church Dogmatics* is essentially a discourse without beginning or end.[26] In the very enactment of a discourse, the dialectical theologian practices a subtle sublation of both ends of the modern dilemma. Yet Barth achieves this only by means of a sleight of hand. The one who practices the dialectic of sublation, the ongoing suspense for the sake of the ever new inbreaking of God's self-communication, is the individual theologian in the enactment of an ongoing theological discourse. While thus the noetic primacy (or supremacy) of the human might be held in check, the primacy of the human as the condition for the possibility of practicing the ongoing suspense of theological discourse is implicitly but de facto reaffirmed in Barth's concept.[27]

One way out would be to succumb again to the Hegelian temptation and claim that the discourse itself reflects the Spirit's self-enactment in history, which would only deepen the question of how to achieve a knowledge of God that is not primarily self-knowledge. Yet both Kierkegaard and Barth make a serious return to this path impossible. Another way out would be to rethink the question of how the knowledge of God and theology relate by rethinking the interconnection between the church's practice, doctrine, and theology. The guiding concept would be *pathos* in its original meaning: being formed and thus qualified by the knowledge of God as embodied in the church's core practices and in doctrine — both of which would have to be understood as the Spirit's work. In the following, we will take this course.[28]

III. The Holy Spirit's Economy and the Knowledge of God

It is necessary to approach the question of the knowledge of God — following Barth's initial direction — by starting from a much more substantive pneumatology, one that takes the Holy Spirit's distinct economy into account. Following the lead of Eastern Orthodox theologians,[29] this move will allow us to understand the church's existence and mission in the closest connection with the Holy Spirit's person and mission. In addition, it will enable a pneumatological notion of doctrine that will allow us to understand the knowledge of God as a distinct *pathos*, a "suffering," through which the Spirit re-creates us and draws us into his sanctifying mission. My thesis is the following: *The knowledge of God is achieved in and through the reception of the gospel proclaimed and taught* (doctrina evangelii), *which takes place via the church's core practices and via doctrine* (dogma; doctrina definita). There might be potential and partial knowledge of God separate from these practices and from doctrine, yet saving knowledge of God — that knowledge that we suffer by being drawn into God's triune life — is the reception of the gospel through which the Holy Spirit re-creates us. Most crucial in this regard are (1) how the church, in its core practices, is to be understood as the Spirit's work, through which he fulfills his own sanctifying mission in the triune economy of salvation; (2) how doctrine, as it specifies the gospel, is to be understood similarly as the Spirit's work; and (3) how theology as distinct discourse practice of the church is completely informed by the Spirit's work, namely, by the church's core practices and by doctrine. The knowledge of God has to be understood as constituting theology's *pathos* in that theology's discourse is completely informed or, better, qualified by the core practices and the doctrine through which it receives the saving and sanctifying knowledge of the triune God. Thus theology's discourse depends upon the prior existence of the knowledge of God as it is embodied in the church's core practices and the gospel, as specified through doctrine. Its very *pathic* character reflects theology's complete dependence on the Spirit's work. As I claimed in chapter 2, this work constitutes the Spirit's own distinct public, whose telos is the fulfillment of the Spirit's sanctifying mission in the triune God's economy of salvation.

IV. Practice: The Knowledge of God Enacted

While it might be possible to draw upon a number of theologians at this point, it makes most eminent sense to return to Martin Luther. Not only is he the preeminent Reformer, acknowledged by both Melanchthon and Calvin as their senior and teacher, but more importantly, he offers an ecumenically as well as theologically helpful way of perceiving the church and its core practices as the Holy Spirit's work. In the third part of his treatise *On the Councils and the Church*,[30] probably the best summary of his mature ecclesiology, Luther develops a much richer and denser account of the relationship between the Holy Spirit and the church than we tend to find in the standard Protestantism of "word and sacrament." As I set forth in chapter 2, Luther identifies a set of particular practices as the church's constitutive marks. In them we encounter not only "church" but also the Spirit's concrete work, through which he fulfills his own sanctifying mission in the triune economy of salvation. These constitutive marks, or core practices, include the proclamation of God's word and its reception in faith, confession, and deed; baptism; the Lord's Supper; the office of the keys, or church discipline; ordained ministry; prayer, doxology, and catechesis; and the way of the cross, or discipleship. What we find in Luther's account is a way to conceive these distinct communal practices as concretely enacting and thus mediating the Holy Spirit's sanctifying work. For Luther, these practices not only identify the church but *make* it "church" in the strict sense. That is why I tend to call them "core" practices.

Yet how does this relate to the knowledge of God? In an immediate sense, as I will show: What is received and enacted in the church's core practices through the Holy Spirit's work is nothing less than the saving knowledge of God. It is the gospel proclaimed and taught, the *doctrina evangelii*. In the proclamation of God's word, in baptism, and in the Lord's Supper, the gospel addresses and claims us in tangible and specific ways; in ordained office, prayer, doxology, catechesis, and the suffering walk of discipleship, the gospel engages us in a personal, intellectual, and most deeply existential way. The gospel proclaimed and taught *(doctrina evangelii)* is the very point of the core practices, their telos. It is both the core practices' criterion and their justification for a faithful enactment and embodiment of God's redeeming and reconciling work, the economy of salvation.

Yet the gospel proclaimed and taught does not exist without its normative specification. Or, more strongly: Without its normative specification, the gospel could be neither proclaimed nor taught. Precisely because the gospel is a specific proclamation and teaching, it is open to manifold concrete misunderstandings and distortions. Thus precisely in order to hold on to and remain faithful to the gospel's proclamation and teaching, the church must specify it in a normative way — by offering definite formulations that concretely clarify particular misrepresentations and distortions.[31]

V. Doctrine: The Knowledge of God Specified

The formation of the biblical canon of Scripture[32] and the emergence of the *regula fidei*[33] and the creeds are reflections from early on of the necessity of the gospel's normative specification. This is the very task of doctrine *(doctrina definita)* or, in its specific ecumenically pronounced form, of "dogma" — with the biblical canon and the rule of faith as their earliest instantiations. The development of trinitarian, christological, and pneumatological doctrines, but also the development of the doctrines of *creatio ex nihilo*, of grace, and eventually, of justification by faith alone, as well as of Christ's real presence in the Eucharist, need to be understood in this light. Far from being an estrangement of the gospel, doctrine enables the gospel's proclamation and teaching![34] While doctrine always presupposes the gospel and continuously depends on it, there simply is no gospel without the doctrine of the gospel.

Thus it is crucial to differentiate between the gospel *(doctrina evangelii)* and doctrine *(doctrina definita)*. The gospel, in its core, is nothing other than Christ's own presence in the promise. Received in faith, Christ thus becomes faith's "form."[35] Traditionally put, in Christ as the "form of faith" both the content of faith *(fides quae creditur)* and the act of faith *(fides qua creditur)* are inseparably one. Faith's form, Christ's presence, realizes both together. This is the fundamental *pathos* of Christian existence — fully identical with the saving knowledge of God. What is most crucial is that faith's "form" cannot be isolated either from the church's core practices or from doctrine, since such an attempt would mean to abstract Christ's presence in the believer from the Spirit's work, from the Spirit's means of conveying and enacting this qualification that *is* the gospel proclaimed and taught. Christ's saving presence cannot be separated from the Spirit's sanctifying mission as enacted through his particular work. This is why doctrine needs to be carefully distinguished from the gospel yet cannot be separated from it, because the latter is secured through the specifications of the former. In other words, doctrine is another form of enactment of the gospel in analogy to the church's core practices — yet under a different aspect: doctrine's *pathos*, its own qualification through the gospel, is constituted by the binding formulation of the gospel's proclamation and teaching in the context of its internal challenge, distortion, or rejection. Doctrine is thus completely qualified by the gospel in committing itself in a binding way to a distinct teaching and by distinctively rejecting a particular theological teaching or set of teachings. Thus the saving knowledge of God, the gospel proclaimed and taught, is mediated and specified both by the church's core practices and by doctrine.[36]

Yet another important distinction needs to be made in order to fully unpack the relationship between the church and the knowledge of God. Not only is doctrine *(doctrina definita)* to be distinguished from the gospel *(doctrina evangelii)*, it also needs to be distinguished from any given particular consensus of theological teaching *(dogmatics)*, which is a phenomenon that belongs to the ongoing church practice of theology. While this distinction is crucial in that the latter *(dogmatics)* is not binding, the former *(doctrina definita)* cannot exist independently from the latter. Doctrine is in constant need of reappropriation, of reinterpretation, and of recommunication lest it become a reified quasi knowledge of God that substitutes for the gospel itself.[37] This task of preventing doctrine from turning the saving knowledge of God into an ossified, formulaic knowledge shapes theology as a distinct church practice. Yet it is important to understand that there is no transference of "accumulative effect" from theological teaching or dogmatics to doctrine/dogma. In other words, no theology as such, even if it finds widest acceptance and is deeply formative, becomes thereby "doctrine" or "dogma" — not even the theology of an Augustine, Aquinas, or Luther! The latter requires a distinct and always new "the Holy Spirit and we have decided . . ." (Acts 15:28), in other words, a binding confession of faith of the whole church through its appropriate channels. This always and only occurs as a reaffirmation of the one gospel *(doctrina evangelii)* under the conditions of its serious challenge, distortion, or rejection *inside* the church.[38]

While particular theologians have had, either directly or indirectly, a decisive influence on the shaping of doctrine, the authority of their respective theologies is categorically different from the doctrines/dogmas they were formative in shaping. In other words, the authority of the theology of the Cappadocians Basil the Great, Gregory Nazianzen, and Gregory of Nyssa is categorically different from the Creed formulated at the Second Ecumenical Council (Constantinople 381), the authority of Augustine's theology from the twenty-five canons of the Synod of Orange (529), the authority of Luther's and Melanchthon's theology from the Augsburg Confession (1530) and the *Book of Concord* (1580), the authority of Calvin's theology from the Synod of Dort (1618/19), and the authority of Barth's theology from the Barmen Declaration (1934). To illustrate the most recent: While Barth's theology is not doctrine (*pace* some Barthians!), the Barmen Declaration (the drafter of which was Barth) *is*, because it was accepted as such by the subscribing Confessing Churches as a way to hold on to the gospel, thereby being completely qualified by the gospel, while at the same time rejecting a distinct set of heretical teachings promoted by the so-called German Christians.

Let us summarize: The gospel is the saving knowledge of God received in word and sacrament. Each of the church's core practices (as the Holy Spirit's work) enacts and embodies the gospel, in a particular way, "pathically": participating in these practices provides the ongoing occasion for "suffering" the Spirit's sanctifying work, for growing in faith. *Doctrine reflects its own distinct pathos by holding fast to the gospel in the binding character of its concrete affirmations and rejections.*

Thus saving knowledge of God entails being engaged and transformed by the Spirit's sanctifying work and thereby increasingly drawn into God's triune life. There is no immediate knowledge of the God of the gospel in abstraction from being engaged by and drawn into the church's core practices and being kept accountable by doctrine. Yet both, the core practices and doctrine, are in need of another particular practice: theology. While not constitutive of the church, theology is integral to the church's being that public through which the Spirit's sanctifying mission is fulfilled.

VI. Theology: The Knowledge of God Unfolded

Next to its core practices, each distinct public is characterized by a unique *discourse practice* that in an ongoing way thematizes the public's defining telos in relation to its core practices and underlying convictions. Each public needs its own discourse practice in order to remain faithfully oriented to its telos. While this discourse practice is in a unique way "critical" in that it consciously thematizes the public's telos — its practices and convictions in relation to its performance — the discourse practice is in no way a neutral arbiter independent of the core practices and binding convictions of the respective public. Rather, its being completely informed by the public's distinct telos constitutes its precise freedom in relation to both the core practices and the binding convictions. In other words, the "critical" attitude of theology as discourse practice of the church rests in the concreteness of its freedom in relation to the core practices and to doctrine. The freedom of theology is precisely constituted and shaped by the same telos that informs the core practices and doctrine. Thus, the critical nature of theology as church practice remains concrete and limited by its own accountability to the gospel and to doctrine. In this regard, theology as discourse practice of the church is distinct from the abstract and negative freedom that modern theology characteristically has claimed for itself over against the core practices and the doctrine of the church.

Therefore, as long and insofar as the church exists as a public in its own right, the teaching and the theological exploration of those practices and convictions that constitute it will continue. The discourse practice of theology is a practice of the church as public only insofar as it is bound to those rules and convictions that constitute it as a public. This is precisely why theology makes sense only as a church practice bound to those norms (doctrines) that constitute the public that is the church.

The practice of theology in relation to doctrine is crucial because it is doctrine that relates normatively to the core practices — not theology itself (*pace* many contemporary theologians!). Theology as discourse practice of the church, rather, is the occasion of bringing the core practices and doctrine into that kind of interface where they constructively and critically inform each other, since *both* are ways through which the saving knowledge of God is mediated. And they need each other, or, to put it technically: the relationship of "lex orandi, lex credendi" is a two-way street.[39] Yet doctrine, insofar as it is itself normed by and accountable to the witness of Scripture, has the right-of-way in this mutual traffic managed by theology as church practice.

Despite this important role, theology is in no way the final arbiter between practice and doctrine. Rather, theology is itself nurtured and formed through the church's core practices. Without being rooted in the very life of these practices, theology becomes a stale enterprise cut off from its living subject. Without being kept accountable to doctrine, theology becomes in all of its interpretive, imaginative, and speculative moves a free-floating enterprise — in other words, a bad form of philosophy. In both cases, theology loses its vital contact with its subject matter, the saving knowledge of God, the gospel proclaimed and taught *(doctrina evangelii)*.

So far we have been sketching an alternative route for the Christian knowledge of God under the conditions of modernity, an alternative that will both avoid the temptation of reification and construction and avoid the pneumatological instability of Barth's still eminently significant proposal for overcoming the modern dilemma about the knowledge of God. This other "way out" has been to approach the question of the knowledge of God by rethinking the relationship between church, doctrine, and theology under the aspect of *pathos* — of being formed and thus qualified by the knowledge of God as embodied in the church's core practices and in doctrine, both of which are developed as the Spirit's work.

It has become clear that the *pathos* of theology as church practice consists precisely in the circumstance that the knowledge of God cannot be achieved "nakedly," whether in the form of the "thereness" of an "objective" knowledge or in the form of that knowledge that is the construct of the poietic subject. Christian knowledge of God can be gained only by suffering God's saving activity as it engages us in word and sacrament as well as the rest of the core practices and as it commits us to the gospel's proclamation and teaching *(doctrina evangelii)* through doctrine *(doctrina definita)*. In other words, our knowledge of God is subject to the same *eschatological condition* to which our whole being is subject. We find ourselves engaged by and in the Spirit's beginning and increasing work *(opus inchoatum)* of sanctification.[40] The knowledge of God we are thereby drawn into is saving, yet not total; concrete, yet not complete; distinct, yet not comprehensive; "clothed" by embodied practices and normative doctrine and thus perceived "in a mirror, dimly," yet still not "face to face." It is not insignificant that the last practice Luther enumerates as mark of the church is the way of the cross. The knowledge of God that we suffer in faith — embodied in and lived through the core practices — as the Holy Spirit's sanctification can ultimately be reflected only in a theology of the cross. Because only here, in the cross of Christ, do we find the immovable difference secured between the love that is God's full knowledge of us, achieved in Christ's cross — when we were still sinners, radically estranged from God — and our love, the full knowledge of God that is the completion of the Spirit's sanctifying work.

To use a biblical analogy: The core practices and doctrine surround us like a tent. By being engaged in them practically and intellectually, we find ourselves "clothed" with the knowledge of *God for us* in Christ. But being clothed in this way, we long for the full knowledge of God that completely transforms us into the likeness of the One who is the knowledge of God and who fully knows us, since he took our human lot upon himself. Through his crucifixion and resurrection we have the promise of "suffering" a last knowledge of God, namely, of being "clothed with our heavenly dwelling."[41]

The Spirit and the Spirit's work are precisely the guarantee that the knowledge of God, which we suffer by being engaged by them, is a knowledge neither at our disposal nor of our making, but the beginning of a final "clothing," a last "suffering," that will include that knowledge of God of which the Apostle Paul says: "Then I will know fully, even as I have been fully known" (1 Cor 13:12).

4. Hospitality and Truth: The Disclosure of Reality in Worship and Doctrine

The practices of hospitality and honoring the truth are generally held in the highest regard. While, to be sure, not universally enacted, they are at least broadly acknowledged as central to human life.[1] Yet we hardly think about these practices at the same time. Indeed, for most of us, they seem to be fundamentally unrelated. It is the task of the present chapter to show that they are in fact deeply interrelated — to the point of being mutually dependent. Yet that is not all. I will also argue that Christian beliefs disclose reality to be such that practicing hospitality and honoring the truth in their integral relation correspond most accurately to the way things are. The Christian faith is capable of doing this because it is itself the result of God's own practice of hospitality, in and through which we receive the truth that is the triune God as the communion of the Father with the Son in the Holy Spirit; thus also are we called to share in the triune God's hospitality and truth.[2]

Yet how are we connected to and drawn into this disclosure? This occurs, I will argue, through two modes of reception: *worship* and *doctrine. In worship we continuously receive the very hospitality of God's truth, and in doctrine the very truth of God's hospitality.* Worship thus relates in a fundamental yet complex way to the practice of hospitality, and doctrine in an equally fundamental yet complex way to the practice of honoring the truth. Making my case would, of course, require far more space than one chapter allows. Therefore, instead of arguing the case at length, I will only sketch the contours of such an argument in the course of rereading two theologically pregnant stories, one fictional and one biblical: C. S. Lewis's *The Great Divorce* and the Emmaus story, as found in the twenty-fourth chapter of the Gospel of Luke.

I. Beginning with a Story: C. S. Lewis's *The Great Divorce*

Stories often capture the hidden interrelationships that make up our world with greater clarity and nuance than our conscious reflection is able. C. S. Lewis's allegorical recasting of heaven and hell depicts the countercultural commerce between practicing hospitality and honoring the truth in a surprisingly powerful way.[3]

As you may remember, the story begins in a gray and rainy place at what seems to be dusk. "Time seemed to have paused on that dismal moment when only a few shops have lit up and it is not yet dark enough for their windows to look cheering" (p. 1). Our protagonist, identified only as the narrator's voice, finds himself at a bus stop in some forlorn section of a sprawling metropolis. The place is more than a little reminiscent of London. Yet, as the description unfolds, this city — let us call it Twilight City for convenience' sake — differs from London in being surprisingly devoid of people. As our protagonist eventually hears from another passenger on the bus, the city is constantly expanding ad infinitum into the dusk. Later he will learn that this expansion is in reality a form of negativity, a gradual implosion into nothingness. As it turns out, Twilight City is a place of increasing emptiness caused by its inhabitants' becoming more and more isolated from themselves and from each other.

It is hardly surprising that the practices of hospitality and honoring the truth are glaringly absent in this place of impending nothingness. Yet it is interesting that their very lack seems to be connected with the city's endless growth. Somewhat later, our protagonist's co-traveler on the bus describes this growth:

> As soon as anyone arrives he settles in some street. Before he's been there twenty-four hours he quarrels with his neighbour. Before the week is over he's quarrelled so badly that he decides to move. Very likely he finds the next street empty because all the people there have quarrelled with *their* neighbours — and moved. So he settles in. If by any chance the street is full, he goes further. But even if he stays, it makes no odds. He's sure to have another quarrel pretty soon and then he'll move on again. Finally he'll move right out to the edge of the town and build a new house. You see, it's easy here. You've only got to *think* a house and there it is. That's how the town keeps on growing. (pp. 8-9)

It is clear that in their constant quarreling the inhabitants of Twilight City do not practice hospitality. Yet it is less clear how they do not honor the truth. The quarreling might give us a clue. Left to their emptiness and to the endless rewinding of their self-indulgent and thus precisely self-deceptive memories,[4] they cannot stand their own company. And because they cannot bear their own company, they are unable to bear the company of anyone else and therefore quarrel and move ever farther away from others. Being able to bear and actually enjoy one's own company presupposes the ability to face and thus honor the truth of one's own life. As we will see later in the story, it is precisely acknowledging and thus receiving the truth of whose and thus who we are that liberates us for genuine hospitality. Yet because the inhabitants of Twilight City lack this truth, they are completely absorbed by themselves — the self-absorption of a void in search of a substance. They want to grasp and own what can only be received as a gift: a self that is transparent to the truth that it owes its existence not to itself but to the Giver of Life. Honoring this truth in its constant reception is what forms a self that is open to the other, to genuine hospitality. Yet being completely curved in upon themselves, the inhabitants of Twilight City can neither offer themselves to others nor welcome others into their own lives — there simply is nothing to offer and nowhere to invite into.

Moreover, as our protagonist quickly finds out, this place is not hospitable to the truth. Questions pertaining to the future (and thus, by implication, to the nature) of Twilight City are not to be raised. Answering these questions would require its inhabitants to face the truth about this city's precarious predicament on the very brink of utter darkness. Having nevertheless raised such a politically incorrect question, our protagonist finds himself subjected to an "enlightening" discourse from one of Twilight City's many intellectuals:

> There is not a shred of evidence that this twilight is ever going to turn into a night. There has been a revolution of opinion on that in educated circles. I am surprised that you haven't heard of it. All the nightmare fantasies of our ancestors are being swept away. What we now see in this subdued and delicate half-light is the promise of the dawn: the slow turning of a whole nation towards the light. Slow and imperceptible, of course. . . . A sublime thought. (pp. 14-15)

Interestingly, there still seem to exist loose intellectual circles where the possibilities of change, improvement, and transformation of life in Twilight City are discussed. Yet in their inherent instability, their lack of relevance, and their abundant self-deception about the truth of the common predicament, these circles are only a lively witness to the degree to which the practices of hospitality and honoring the truth are indeed absent from Twilight City. Interpreting the twilight as the beginning of a great "enlightenment" only works as a loan on the truth by allowing for a semblance of meaningful intellectual interaction: a discourse among shadows, the whole point of which is the endless deferral of the truth — that they are nothing but shadows.[5]

Conspicuously absent from Twilight City are both real, existing persons and real, existing relationships, both of which — as will later become clear — are the gift of truth and can only be acknowledged by honoring the truth. Indeed, it is the truth that makes it possible to be hospitable to the presence of other persons. Without truth, space and time — instead of being the rich ground of endless occasions of hospitality fueled by the acknowledgment of the truth — become endless wastelands of negativity, dramatically pictured by Lewis as imploding into nothingness.[6]

Yet in a completely random spot somewhere in this vast desert of gray inhospitality and self-deception covered by dusk and drizzling rain — or, to be precise, "thousands of miles from the Civic Centre where all the newcomers arrive from earth" (p. 9) — there is a bus stop. From there, once a week, a bus takes anyone who wants (that is to say, who is able to "stand" for long enough all the others waiting in line) up to heaven for free, in and of itself already an overabundant act of hospitality. On this day, after a significant number of people drop out of line because of ongoing quarreling, our protagonist and a few others manage to get on the bus. And after an "enlightening" flight — the ever intensifying heavenly light increasingly revealing the passengers' true ghostlike condition — the bus lands on a grassy plain under a penetrating blue sky.

In profound contrast to Twilight City, life on the light-bathed green plain, the "beginning" of heaven, is characterized by moving acts of hospitality and of honoring the truth. And as it quickly turns out, both hospitality and truth are inherently linked to the practice of forgiveness. On leaving the bus, the passengers from Twilight City are welcomed by delegates from heaven and invited in. Hospitality to these lost souls, to these strangers to heaven, is obviously essential to the character of heaven.

Yet accepting heaven's hospitality turns out to be a deeply painful affair. Why is that, we might ask? Hospitality — which is fundamentally different from paternalism, even heavenly paternalism — presupposes real, existing persons who are capable of personal relationships. Yet being a person and thus being capable of personal relationships depends on the gift of truth in and through which one's own personhood is received; this reception is actively acknowledged by honoring the truth. Heaven's hospitality turns out to be painful because it does not trade truth for hospitality — the former *in* its hospitality simply being heaven's identity. Hospitality can only be truthful and thus true hospitality if it does not betray the nature of the host and so does not undercut the truth that presupposes a personal relationship. Thus heaven's light, true to its own nature, unavoidably reveals the truth of the passengers as they increasingly enter the abode of its hospitality. Precisely because of its very nature, the light at first has a striking resemblance to *in*hospitality.

> It was a cruel light. I shrank from the faces and forms by which I was surrounded. They were all fixed faces, full not of possibilities but of impossibilities, some gaunt, some bloated, some glaring with idiotic ferocity, some drowned beyond recovery in dreams; but all, in one way or another, distorted and faded. One had a feeling that they might fall to pieces at any moment if the light grew much stronger. (p. 16)

As it turns out, not only the light but also the very solidity of the grass and everything else on the green plain are hard for the ghostlike passengers to stand. Heaven's hospitality hurts, because the passengers from Twilight City are not — yet — real enough to be taken in and to fully participate. So even walking on the grass hurts like being pricked with needles. And reality, as it turns out, is a matter of truth — the truth that makes us a person and thus real. Yet acknowledging this truth means encountering the sum of our deeds and sufferings, the innumerable ways we have failed others and others have failed us. Thus receiving the truth about ourselves decisively implies our asking for forgiveness as well as our granting forgiveness and thereby actively acknowledging and thus ultimately receiving our own personhood and that of others. The challenge each passenger faces is to become hospitable to the truth and thereby to be transformed into the person he or she is meant to be.[7]

What is of crucial importance now is that heaven's hospitality is practiced and sustained by a truth that fundamentally shapes both the hospitality of the welcomers and their own truth-telling. It is here that the "disclosure" of the practices of hospitality and honoring the truth begins to emerge.

The persons who extend heaven's hospitality of forgiving truth to the passengers from Twilight City are not random characters. Rather, they play a key role in understanding the truth of the very lives of the shadow-persons whom they welcome. As it turns out in the unfolding dialogues, accepting heaven's hospitality is identical with being willing to receive the truth about our own lives — a truth that always includes the recognition of our need to be forgiven as well as our readiness to forgive, well illustrated in the following dialogue between a ghostly passenger from Twilight City and his heavenly greeter.[8] Particularly interesting in this exchange is that the ghostly passenger uses "rights" language, which, we could argue, is a way of asking for "truth." Yet here the very nature of truth is at stake in the manner of its sharing. Having a "right" to the truth establishes a claim of ownership that antecedently precludes reception of the truth — a reception that can only be acknowledged in honoring the truth. And thus also the hospitality that the truth makes possible cannot be claimed as a right but only asked for as "Bleeding Charity."

> "Only be happy and come with me."
> "What do you keep on arguing for? I'm only telling you the sort of chap I am. I only want my rights. I'm not asking for anybody's bleeding charity."
> "Then do. At once. Ask for the Bleeding Charity. Everything is here for the asking and nothing can be bought."
> "That may be very well for you, I daresay.... I don't want charity. I'm a decent man and if I had my rights I'd have been here long ago and you tell them I said so."
> The other shook his head. "You can never do it like that," he said. "Your feet will never grow hard enough to walk on our grass that way. You'd be tired out before we got to the mountains. And it isn't exactly true, you know." (pp. 26-27)

Refusing heaven's hospitality also means refusing heaven's truth — which is first of all nothing other than the truth about oneself and one's need to receive and grant forgiveness. An unforgiving spirit simply cannot bear the sheer brightness of heaven's penetrating reality — a reality that is constituted by real, existing persons and their perfect intersubjectivity — and thus the ghostly passenger eventually flees back to the bus in order to be embraced again by the implosive void of nothingness.

> "I'd rather be damned than go along with you. I came here to get my rights, see? Not to go snivelling along on charity tied onto your apron-strings. If they're too fine to have me without you, I'll go home.... I didn't come here to be treated like a dog. I'll go home.... That's what I'll do.... Damn and blast the whole pack of you...." In the end, still grumbling, but whimpering also a little as it picked its way over the sharp grasses, it made off. (pp. 28-29).

The ghostly passenger shuts himself up against the truth that can only be received as a gift and is impossible to claim as a right. Because he cannot receive the truth, the hospitality that rests in the host's very identity and the process of transformation from shadow into the person that the shadow implies seem simply too painful to bear.

II. The Countercultural Commerce between Hospitality and Truth

In his allegory of heaven and hell, Lewis offers us a narrative account of the deep theological reason why the practices of hospitality and honoring the truth mutually depend on each other. He achieves this insight by approaching them from a perspective that allows him to perceive them first of all as God's practices. In the course of this "disclosure," he shows that our very capacity to practice hospitality and to honor the truth presupposes that we first receive the hospitality of God's truth — which at one point in the story is called "Bleeding Charity" — and then, in turn, be transformed by it so as to live in the truth of God's hospitality. Thus *The Great Divorce* ever so gently prepares us for the crucial insight that the triune God is both truth and host in one. In his self-giving in Christ — the Bleeding Charity — God offers radical hospitality to a humanity hopelessly entangled in practices and habits of sin. God's own distinct and radical hospitality culminates in opening Israel "for the many" — through Christ's eucharistic self-giving (Mark 10:45; 14:24) — and thus in welcoming the Gentiles into God's own household through and in the body of the crucified and risen Christ (Eph 2:11-22). If this is indeed true about the gospel, then we should rightly expect that the gospel — precisely in its particularity — should disclose the very web of creation, should offer us particular insights into the way things are. Thus we will take as our guide God's saving work in the life, death, and resurrection of Jesus Christ, God's Bleeding Charity, as we now ask how two particular practices that are known among virtually all of humanity fundamentally depend on each other.

Lewis's allegorical account helps us begin to discern the hidden but profound forces in and among ourselves that militate against genuine engagement in the practices of hospitality and honoring the truth. Let us first consider two basic impediments to these practices and then, with Lewis, the essential interdependence that becomes apparent when the two practices are genuinely pursued.

Probably the most significant impediment to the practice of hospitality is *uncharitableness*. Our lack of self-giving, our failure to share ourselves with others, results in a hospitality that is nothing more than "entertaining." We present an appearance that is estranged from ourselves; that is, we do not give ourselves as persons. Rather, we offer inauthentic selves as a means to self-serving ends. Our hospitality becomes a "commercial exchange," undertaken to gain some advantage — often, to satisfy our deep-rooted need to please others in order to be liked in return.[9] Such uncharitable hospitality betrays both our own personhood and the personhood of those whom we thus use.

The second impediment, the most significant to the practice of honoring the truth, is *self-deception*,[10] the self-protective reaction caused by the convicting work of conscience when we are forced to face the truth without the gift of forgiveness. Self-deception protects us from the prospective final conviction through strategies of tacit self-justification, too subtle even to rise to the level of consciousness. And it is precisely these strategies that make it effectively impossible to receive the forgiving truth that would allow us to fully honor the truth in the first place. Unable to accept the truth about ourselves, we have no means of sharing ourselves with others, of giving ourselves away in authentic personhood — in short, no means of practicing hospitality in any authentic sense.

Not so on the green plain. Hospitality is extended at the same time that the truth is honored because those who practice heaven's hospitality by greeting the passengers from Twilight City know that all that they are — and all that those they welcome are — rests ultimately in God's forgiving grace. The hospitality of heaven's truth requires and effects a transformation that amounts to nothing less than becoming "real," being filled with heaven's truth and thus receiving a gloriously imperishable body — an irreversible personhood that is capable of giving and thus also of extending true hospitality.[11] As a result of participating in this reality, heaven's greeters can honor the truth without falling into uncharitableness and self-deception and thus can extend a hospitality that is genuine and substantive.

As Lewis's story brings out so clearly, the practice of hospitality is the very training ground for that of honoring the truth.[12] Only by letting ourselves be welcomed by the greeters of heaven and by ultimately welcoming them, by accepting heaven's hospitality and by extending it, can the truth about our own lives and pasts be truthfully faced — and thus forgiven. In welcoming others into our lives, especially strangers and the needy, we have to face the truth about distinct persons, about the state of the world and society, and — not least — about ourselves. Practicing true hospitality is challenging, demanding, stretching, and threatening — as, indeed, is honoring the truth that such hospitality uncovers. Yet from the very difficulty of genuine practice we develop distinct virtues: courage, patience, hope, humility, prudence (in the classical sense), self-restraint, and the readiness to be out of control.

Honoring the truth starts with the reception of the very truth about ourselves. Yet it does not end there. Honoring the truth occurs always in specific relationships of responsibility and accountability.[13] One of the most pervasive temptations to "manage" the truth is to abstract it, to distance it from distinct moral settings. To abstract the truth, however, is to betray it.[14] In our concrete, specific relationships of commitment, duty, and office we are called to honor the truth in concrete and specific ways. It is precisely the "hands-on" character of practicing hospitality that prepares us for the "hands-on" entailment of honoring the truth.

Lewis's story teaches as well that the practice of honoring the truth is itself a significant way of practicing hospitality. Since truth is not produced but acknowledged, honoring the truth cannot be anything else but inviting others into the same acknowledgment. This is the very life of the greeters of heaven: only by first having been guests of the truth can they become its hosts in the practice of honoring it and extending it to others in truthful speech. Moreover, the practice of hospitality is itself a significant way of honoring the truth. It is in the course of acknowledging the truth that our personhood is received. Thus the practice of hospitality — the giving of ourselves as persons to other persons and the receiving of others as persons — points to the fact that truth entails mutual participation as persons. Finally, participation in the truth as persons is possible only because the truth itself is a Person who gives himself in an encounter of which he simultaneously is the host and the gift. Jesus is truth's hospitality and hospitality's truth in one, as is strikingly evident in the Emmaus story.

III. The Truth Comes as a Stranger:
Hospitality and Truth in the Emmaus Story

Quite a number of biblical stories display the fundamental link between hospitality and honoring the truth (e.g., Abraham and the three messengers at the tree of Mamre in Gen 18:1-15). Yet none does so in as striking a way as Luke 24, the Emmaus story.[15]

The context of events in which Luke offers his account of the Emmaus story is highly dramatic and deeply perturbing. Only two days before, Jesus has died the death of a criminal, punished by the Roman means of executing noncitizens: crucifixion. Yet on the morning of the third day after his death and burial — the first day of the week according to the Jewish counting — "the women who had come with him from Galilee" (Luke 23:55)[16] find the tomb's stone rolled away and the grave empty. Even more disturbing than that, "suddenly two men in dazzling clothes" appear beside them, informing them that "he is not here, but has risen" (Luke 24:4-5). After Peter confirms the witness of the women by going to the empty grave himself, the scene changes.

Two disciples are on the way to the village of Emmaus, "about seven miles from Jerusalem." We do not learn why they are going there. But they are deeply immersed in a conversation, discussing the events of the last three days. The next thing we know is that Jesus "comes close" (ἐγγίσας) and accompanies them on their walk. Yet their eyes, as our text puts it in a curious way, are "kept from recognizing him" (Luke 24:16). Our text fails to tell us whether they are actively prevented from recognizing him or whether it is a matter of their own perception. The latter is suggested by the fact that all the other post-resurrection encounters begin with the disciples' nonrecognition and continue with Jesus' self-identification (Luke 24:36-43; John 20:14-16, 19-20). Something beyond ordinary vision seems to be necessary for recognizing the risen Jesus. What seems to be required is the acknowledgment of who he is. In other words, after the resurrection, the recognition of his person can no longer be separated from the reception of the truth of his identity. Now recognizing Jesus means recognizing him as who he truly is.[17] What enables this reception and recognition?

Interestingly, Jesus first explains the Scriptures to the two disciples. In this way he again offers himself as the exegete of the Father (John 1:18), as the one who interprets the Scriptures' promises while effectively embodying their fulfillment. Yet most surprisingly, the two disciples do not yet recognize Jesus in light of his own exegesis. The referent to whom Scripture's promises point and in whom — in this very moment — they are fulfilled remains concealed from their eyes. The fulfillment remains hidden even in its advent.

The situation obviously summarizes the very nature of Jesus' earthly ministry. After all, exegesis of this kind was what Jesus did all the time during his proclamation of the reign of God on the way to the cross. The disciples did not understand then — and they do not yet understand now. Jesus is a stranger who is practicing truth-telling yet remains strange, unrecognized in the very telling of the truth. The prophetic word interpreted even by the one in whom it has been fulfilled does not bridge the gap between its utterance and its reception.

Only a twofold act of hospitality fundamentally changes this situation of truth spoken but not understood, of truth present but not received. Jesus' words seem to have a consoling effect. The way the disciples address the stranger, offering their hospitality, makes the veil of nonrecognition almost transparent: "Stay with us, because it is almost evening and the day is now nearly over" (Luke 24:29). Yet all by itself, even this act of hospitality does not disclose the truth, namely, the identity of the crucified Jesus, whom they followed, as the resurrected, who is with them now.

It is only Jesus' own act of hospitality, his self-giving in the breaking, the blessing, and the giving of the bread that reveals the truth. The truth of the resurrected grants itself only in the course of his self-giving. Only in light of the very hospitality that summarizes, epitomizes, and fully re-presents Jesus' mission and self-giving "for the many" are their eyes opened, do they finally understand the truth. They suddenly "see," because now they participate in the truth in the very event of its donation. The referent of the scriptural utterance has granted his presence in his self-giving.[18]

Jesus vanishes from their sight in the very moment of recognition. The reception and the recognition occur in one and the same instance: Jesus' giving of himself in the breaking of the bread. The broken bread now not only signifies but also embodies Christ's self-giving "for the many." Christ is thus the host in precisely its double sense: he hosts the meal in which he gives himself, and he is the host that is received in his self-giving.

Are there lessons to be learned from the Emmaus story? Let us address first the most likely kind of lesson that might be drawn from this narrative account. While it follows the most common path taken in the contemporary religious culture of educated doubt, it is precisely not the way to Emmaus. This quite popular — but false — approach would suggest that our story functions as a "myth," as the narrative rendering of a universal moral truth.

For our story the lesson would be the following: Practicing hospitality to the stranger will help us encounter the truth. If we want to encounter truth beyond our preconceived notions, we need to be hospitable to what seems at first sight to be strange. Thus on a fundamental epistemological as well as moral level hospitality emerges as the program for the reception of truth under pluralistic conditions. The more radically and comprehensively we practice hospitality to everyone and everything strange, the more closely we will approximate the truth.

Following this line of reasoning often reflects the attempt to do justice to three assumptions deeply held in contemporary educated culture: *First,* to the postmodern dogma that "truth" is both ultimately elusive and always profoundly "other." "Truth" can only be approximated in and through being relentlessly hospitable to the possibility of its emergence precisely in what we encounter as "strange." Yet precisely this mandates truth's infinite deferral. *Second,* to the inner mandate of a late modern pluralistic society that everyone we encounter is fundamentally a stranger in need of due recognition and therefore has the inalienable right to some form of hospitality. And *third,* to the notion of our moral sovereignty — that increasing or decreasing hospitality is ultimately a matter of our moral will, its inner resolve and its outer endurance. Failure to offer constant moral hospitality is a reflection of willful omission.

Even if we were to grant some nuanced merit to one or another of these broadly held assumptions, the Emmaus story clearly resists such a universalizing exegetical strategy. At the same time, it inverts the universalistic purchase attempted through its reading as myth in a threefold way: *First,* we do not know what honoring the truth fundamentally is without the truth being granted itself and being continuously received in its self-giving. *Second,* if there is any truth per se at all, it is the identity of the crucified with the resurrected, the "icon of the Father." *Third,* we do not know what hospitality fundamentally is without God's having offered his own ultimate hospitality to us, a hospitality that is continuously received in Christ's eucharistic self-giving.

Thus our narrative points to the fact that, while very well being able to perceive intimations of a deep interplay between the practices of hospitality and honoring the truth, we are unable to grasp what ultimately is at stake in them. This is also the reason that the very concept of "practice" requires its own theological "conversion." While we seemingly can practice hospitality and honor the truth in our own truth-telling, the very facility of this assumption hides the fact that in both practices our own humanity is at stake — and this on a level that is beyond our own grasp.[19]

The disciples (as much as Abraham) practice hospitality to the stranger, not randomly or habitually, because it seems to be the decent thing to do, but precisely because of who they are. Because they already are on a journey with God, they are willing to practice hospitality to the stranger and they precisely thereby receive the hospitality of God's truth — as did Abraham (Gen 18:1-15). In other words, there is no other way to give a fundamental account of the practices of hospitality and honoring the truth than to see them rooted in God's own particular dealing with creation and humanity. With this realization, it is no longer surprising to find it already foreshadowed in the virtually universal character of both practices. Yet this universal character can only be accounted for rightly in light of the particular One in whose own self-giving hospitality we come to know the truth.

IV. The Disclosing Nature of the Christian Faith

As we come to see, what emerges in the course of a deeper questioning of precisely why each of these practices needs the other is the disclosing nature of Christian beliefs. Furthermore, as *The Great Divorce* and the Emmaus story so convincingly display, in light of these Christian beliefs, both practices are eventually "disclosed" and thereby actually received in their fullness. Instead of being just at the center of human life in general, they turn out to have a much deeper presupposition: they form the very center of God's own dealing with humanity and the world. If the latter indeed holds, these practices imply much more than they themselves are ever able to convey. They bring us into touch with the way things really are and thus beg for their very disclosure.

How would the Christian theological tradition have put this matter? Very likely in the following way: According to the Christian faith, truth does not rest in the dead abstractness of contingent correspondences.[20] Rather, truth rests in the threefold identity and agency of the triune God as these identities unfold in creation, the election of Israel, the life, death, and resurrection of Jesus Christ, and the calling of the many into a communion in the life of the triune God through the Holy Spirit.[21] This calling restores full and genuine humanity yet has a superabundant end in humanity's everlasting participation in God's love.

The practice of hospitality is therefore rightly both a reflection and an extension of God's own hospitality — sharing the love of the triune life with those who are dust. At the very center of this hospitality stands both a death and a resurrection, the most fundamental enactment of truth from God's side and therefore the threshold of God's abundant hospitality.[22] The truth that needs to be not only spoken but concretely judged, concretely undone in and through the full bearing by One (and once) for all, is that humanity is radically estranged from God because of a fundamental betrayal of God's original truth-telling and hospitality.

Precisely the One who does not participate in this predicament but is the embodiment of God's truth is therefore able to restore God's hospitality. Yet this occurs through a judgment, a death sentence, that we receive as our forgiveness. The truth and thereby the condition for reentering God's hospitality can be spoken only through God's own embodiment and self-abandonment in Jesus' death on the cross. We receive this death ("given for you") as the gift of forgiveness, the one particular truth of God's abundant, costly, and holy hospitality on the grounds of which we can welcome the company of ourselves and others and therefore overcome the urge for self-deception and the desire to please and to be liked, both of which decisively undercut the practices of hospitality and honoring the truth.

Worship: Receiving the Hospitality of God's Truth in Christ

We have expressed in briefest terms the voice of the Christian theological tradition on the nature of God's hospitable truth and truthful hospitality in Christ. Now we are more than ready to ask how we in fact concretely receive the hospitality of God's truth. It is by no means accidental that the broad stream of the Christian tradition has pointed to "word and sacrament" for an answer. From its very beginning, the central elements of Christian worship have been gathering for table fellowship with the risen Christ, reading the Scriptures together in light of his cross and resurrection, praying the prayer that Jesus taught his disciples, and, in and through worship, receiving the Spirit that rested on Jesus.[23] It is in worship itself that the hospitality of God's truth in Christ is continuously received.

The German word for worship — *Gottesdienst,* "service of God" — conveys this in a striking way. In worship we receive God's service in Christ. Christ humbles and empties himself (Phil 2:5-11) for our sake by becoming our servant. (Our service of God, in contrast, does not occur in worship but in what St. Paul calls "spiritual [or reasonable] worship," namely, "to present your bodies as a living sacrifice, holy and acceptable to God"; Rom 12:1.)[24] The two central loci of receiving God's service in Christ are word and sacrament: Christ is the host who proclaims his self-giving in the word and enacts it in the Eucharist.

It is well known that the Reformation tradition emphasizes the sacramental character of the word and the word character of the sacrament, while the Roman Catholic tradition emphasizes the prophetic character of the word and the participatory character of the Eucharist. Yet underlying both emphases is the distinct location of word and sacrament within worship. There is no reduction of the one into the other. In the proclamation of the word, the hospitality of God's truth in Christ is announced and promised; in the celebration of the Lord's Supper, this hospitality is concretely remembered and tangibly received. God's own truth grants itself, enacts its own hospitality, whenever the gospel is proclaimed and the Lord's Supper celebrated. They point to each other. The one cannot exist without the other: the one announces and effectively promises the hospitality of God's truth in Christ; the other executes it. In both, Christ gives himself to and in faith. Yet word and sacrament are by no means to be isolated from the rest of worship.

Rather, we need to understand worship as a rich web of activities, among which some are so important that they constitute what worship is all about. I call these distinct activities "core practices."[25] At their center, undoubtedly, we find the proclamation of the gospel and the celebration of the

Eucharist. Yet of great importance also are baptism, confession of sin and absolution, and binding and loosing (church discipline).[26] For some traditions, the practice of footwashing belongs to this list; for others, also confirmation, Christian marriage, priestly ordination, and the last unction.[27] For a long time this was an open list in the Christian tradition; it has become a hotly contested issue only since the Reformation and Counter-Reformation in the sixteenth century.

In and through these core practices the hospitality of God's truth in Christ is both actively received and announced in word and witness. Only on the grounds of this receiving does the fundamental connection between our practicing hospitality and our honoring the truth become clear. That is, only in retrospect do we come to understand how much we indeed depend on both the hidden and the revealed ways of God's practicing hospitality and honoring the truth in his simply being the truth. Yet once having received the hospitality of God's truth explicitly, we cannot but recognize our prior and full dependence on the truth of God's hospitality — as the Gospel of John puts it: "You have already been cleansed by the word that I have spoken to you. Abide in me as I abide in you. Just as the branch cannot bear fruit by itself unless it abides in the vine, neither can you unless you abide in me. I am the vine, you are the branches. Those who abide in me and I in them bear much fruit, because apart from me you can do nothing" (John 15:3-5). Worship is the original location in which the grapes receive their strength from the vine, where they continuously become part of the vine. Worship is therefore the fundamental setting in which, again and again, we receive the hospitality of God's truth and thereby the "reasons for hope" that will enable Christian living to make its way into a future that otherwise seems so profoundly uncertain.[28]

Doctrine: Receiving and Honoring the Truth of God's Hospitality in Christ

A question less often asked yet equally pressing is how we receive and continue to hold on to and thereby honor the truth of God's hospitality in Christ. This is what is at stake in a claim of St. Paul, one that is quite disturbing to modern sensibilities: "If you confess with your lips that Jesus is Lord and believe in your heart that God raised him from the dead, you will be saved" (Rom 10:9). What do we need to profess and teach under all circumstances and in every context in order to receive and continue to hold on to the truth of God's hospitality in Christ? This is what is at stake in "doctrine" — and, if ecumenically ratified, in "dogma."

Yet approaching doctrine and especially dogma in these days of late modernity is far from easy. The reservations against it are too deep seated, the resentments too pervasive. Are doctrine and especially dogma not the very contradiction of whatever we might associate with hospitality and truth? Is dogma not the very enemy of hospitality and truth?

First, regarding truth: Under the powerful influence of the Enlightenment, Christianity in many of its Protestant strands became nondogmatic and even antidogmatic. Dogma was seen as an ossified and reified set of propositions that oppressed the free and critical thinking of individuals in search of the living truth as it emerged in the context of an unencumbered inquiry into the world. Dogma thus came to stand for everything backward, outmoded, and inimical to new and critical insights. In other words, dogma was — and still pervasively is — seen as the very enemy of truth.

Second, regarding hospitality: Since the time of the Inquisition and the religious wars, doctrine and dogma have carried the connotation of intolerance, exclusion, and, worse, persecution. As a result, dogma was — and still today often is — feared as the very enemy of hospitality.

As alleged enemies of truth and hospitality, doctrine and especially dogma seem to be nothing less than the archenemies of true humanity itself. So the stakes are high for those who continue to oppose "doctrine" and "dogma" on these grounds, and the prospects dim for those who consider their rehabilitation long overdue. Yet if we at all agree that in Jesus Christ's life, death, and resurrection the truth of God's hospitality is at stake, then next to worship, nothing matters more than doctrine and dogma. Why?

Because the very point of doctrine is to both receive and hold on to the truth of the gospel's hospitality. But why not, instead of the gospel's hospitality, the hospitality of a "love" or "tolerance" that only excludes the excluders? What is at stake in receiving and holding on to specifically the gospel's hospitality? Only the gospel's hospitality assures us in no uncertain terms that reality is such that practicing hospitality and honoring the truth in their integral relation correspond most accurately to the way things are. The truth of the gospel's hospitality thus carries with it a reality-claim that simply has no equivalent in a hospitality that is based on anthropological principles such as "tolerance" or sentiments such as "love." What is at stake in the truth of the gospel's hospitality is a claim about reality as it is constituted by "the end of the world and the ends of God." God's love and humanity's calling is what is at stake in specifically the truth of the gospel's hospitality and consequently what doctrine both receives and holds on to.

V. The Practice of Theology between Doctrine and Worship

All Christians are called to be theologians in the sense enjoined by the writer of 1 Peter: "Always be ready to make your defense to anyone who demands from you an accounting for the hope that is in you" (1 Pet 3:15). Sometimes we demand such an account from ourselves; sometimes our children, our spouses, our friends, our neighbors, our colleagues, or some stranger will demand such an account from us. As soon as we begin to formulate and give our account, we are beginning to be theologians and to practice theology.

Yet the account we might be asked to give pertains not only to the form and content of our faith, its inner coherence, and how it might relate to other things we take to be true. It pertains as well to the way we live our lives, or fail to do so; to the way we engage the world in which we live, or fail to do so. Moreover, it pertains to the way "the hope that is in us" shapes our way of life and the practices that are involved in it, or fails to do so.

For a variety of complex theological, historical, and cultural reasons not to be pursued here, there emerged in the church the vocation of the "theologian," whose task it is to engage in a distinct reflective and discursive practice in service to and for the sake of the Christian community at large. While this practice involves a variety of linguistic, hermeneutical, and conceptual skills, it does not distinguish itself fundamentally from "doing theology" in the larger sense. Nor is it meant to replace the doing of theology in the larger sense. Rather, theology engaged as a vocation is practiced in service of the whole church and for the sake of enabling all Christians to offer an account of the hope that is in them.

Let me give you an example. If I am expected to be able to practice a certain craft or art, I need to learn it; and in order to learn it well, I need to be taught. Yet my teacher must be someone who has gained a degree of excellence in this craft or art, who has mastered it. It is only this mastery that allows other practitioners to see what is possible in this craft or art, to benefit from its best insights, and to improve it in unexpected ways. Mastery of this kind tends to require a lifelong and full-time dedication to its subject matter. It is along these lines that we need to think if we want to understand rightly the practice of theology as engaged by academic theologians in colleges, seminaries, and university faculties — and in the pastor's and the bishop's study.

What shape does the practice of theology take if my hypothesis is correct, if practicing hospitality and honoring the truth stand at the very center of God's dealing with humanity — if, in other words, Emmaus is the founding location for the practice of theology? If this is in fact the case, theology needs to be deeply informed by both doctrine and worship. In other words, the practice of theology needs to reflect doctrine's way of holding on to and honoring the truth of God's hospitality, as well as the hospitality of God's truth as we continually receive it in worship. Continuing to unfold my hypothesis, in the following sections I will consider, *first*, the ways in which theology inescapably remains accountable to doctrine and, *second*, the ways in which worship inescapably remains the root from which this practice draws its inner strength.

Theology and Doctrine:
Honoring the Truth of God's Hospitality

There are at least three central aspects that strike me as necessary when we consider the practice of theology in its relationship to doctrine.

There is, *first*, the task of reappropriation *(fides quaerens doctrinam)*. Doctrine itself cannot fulfill its own task of holding on to the truth of God's hospitality in Christ if it is not constantly tested and reappropriated theologically.[29] When particular doctrines, once well established, fall out of use from ecclesial or theological amnesia, the churches tend to be haunted by teachings — destructive to the very core of the Christian faith — that these doctrines were originally meant to forestall. Yet theologians can never successfully undertake this task without simultaneously attending to another.

That is, *second*, the task of reinterpretation, of perceiving and judging how specific doctrines inform particular contexts *(fides quaerens locum)* and what kinds of challenges particular contexts raise for the communication and presentation of particular doctrines.[30] What this complex task specifically entails — and its wider ramifications for the way theology, more broadly conceived, is to be practiced — can only be intimated in this chapter.

And there is, *third*, the task of recommunication, of constantly re-presenting the gospel. This recommunication has two elements: *catechesis*, the teaching of the faith that is informed by the core practices, by doctrine, and by location, and *ad hoc apologetics*, the tactical defense of the faith by engaging the intellectual context of a given time and location. Neither element should be underestimated — as in fact is the case in most of contemporary academic theology, especially regarding catechesis. There is currently no more urgent task for contemporary theology than to develop a genre of catechesis that is accessible, challenging, and sophisticated. Yet, again, this task will be successfully accomplished only as long as theologians simultaneously attend to the other two.

Fulfilling these three tasks in their inherent interrelationship requires both *discernment* and *judgment*. We need to be able to discern a particular context in light of doctrine, and vice versa, and in the course of that, we need to be able to assess unrepeatable particulars in order to arrive at a theological judgment. It is of utmost importance that we arrive at such a theological judgment, since without it we are not able to hold on to and therefore honor the truth of God's hospitality in Christ. Recasting doctrine with respect to the perceived needs of a particular context suffices as little as the dead repetition of an ossified teaching — even be it a "dogma." What is called for, rather, is a practice of theology that is equally faithful as it is rigorous in its discerning and judging. What is called for, in other words, is a renewal of the old, venerable tradition of "dogmatics."

It strikes me that part of the misery from which "constructive theology" currently suffers is that it cannot practice dogmatics joyfully.[31] In light of the above, practicing dogmatics joyfully means nothing less than taking the exhortation of 1 Peter to heart in searching constantly and patiently for what needs to be said under all circumstances in light of God's abundant hospitality in Christ.[32] Only in light of continuously discerning what needs to be maintained under all circumstances is it possible to arrive at concrete judgments when we reflect in the daily Christian life about the shape and direction of particular practices.[33]

But why "joyfully"? Is that not asking too much? Precisely not. If dogmatics is practiced by giving an account for the hope that is in us, it is God's very hospitality in Christ that grounds and gives reason for this hope. And in light of this grounding and reason, dogmatics ultimately can only be a joyful undertaking — or it is not dogmatics at all.[34]

Theology and Worship:
Practicing the Hospitality of God's Truth

Thus the practice of theology is not only important and complex but vulnerable to all kinds of distortions as well. There is first of all the imminent danger of misunderstanding our own theological position as doctrine — or even worse, as "dogma" — and anathematizing any divergent perspective simply for the reason that it differs from our own. In this — admittedly none too rare — misuse of theology, the deep reservations many hold against "dogmatics" find their legitimate object. It is precisely the practice of hospitality that corrects this distortion of practicing theology. "Making room" for different theological concerns, for different theological voices and their particular truth-claims, and consequently for letting ourselves (particularly the blind spots of our own theological field of vision as well as our own most cherished assumptions) be scrutinized, criticized, and questioned, keeps the practice of theology truthful. For we are constantly in need of being reminded of the difference between our own theologizing and doctrine.[35]

Yet another danger is as imminent — and in these days of celebrating plurality and difference, maybe even more so. It is the danger of doctrinal indifferentism. Not responding to this danger will only result in the unavoidable decline of theological hospitality into "entertaining." We only "entertain" the proposals and interventions of those who, while different from us, are nice to us, so that we in turn may be nice to them.[36] In the course of such entertaining, we cease to reflect God's costly and holy hospitality in Christ. Rather, we come to reflect the late modern, mainline Protestant celebration of the "nice god" and this god's "cheap grace": Because god is nice to me, I am nice to you so that you may be nice to me in return — grace as the economy of nicety.

Augustine's passion, Luther's rudeness, Teresa's intensity, Kierkegaard's irony, and Barth's sharpness are only famous reminders of what is at stake for all of us in practicing theology: the triune God's abundant, costly, and holy hospitality in Christ. It is the practice of honoring the truth in doctrine's enactment of truth-telling that keeps the practice of theology accountable at this point, keeps theology's hospitality truthful and prevents it from declining into the intellectual death of uncommitted nicety.[37] In short, it gives theology no choice but to openly admit its true nature as "dogmatics."

So it seems that we have returned to doctrine and dogma. Yet only in order to keep the second danger in check. And that is not the last word. While in doctrine we honor and hold on to the truth of God's hospitality in Christ, it is in worship that we first and foremost receive the living and tangible reference of this hospitality. Worship is the context where we — precisely as theologians — confess our sins and receive forgiveness, where we share the peace of Christ, where we hear the living promise of God's hospitality in Christ, and where we share this costly hospitality in table fellowship with the crucified and risen Christ. In these and other core practices, we again and again receive the framework that enables us to learn how to practice the hospitality of God's truth rightly in the course of doing theology — or, dare I say, "dogmatics."

All practitioners of theology — and it is irrelevant whether they practice it simply on the grounds of their baptism or more specifically as a distinct vocation — are continuously in need of forgiveness (the latter only more so) because of the fallible nature of their theological discernment and judgment. Pride, anger, sloth, impatience, thoughtlessness, and a whole range of other vices are constantly bent on distorting our discerning and judging theologically. Undoubtedly, the critical intervention of other theologians will help in confining the destructive effects of our failings. Yet all too often these interventions only result in the *rabies theologorum,* the "rage of theologians," a term that the Reformation theologian and humanist Philipp Melanchthon coined as he suffered greatly under it.

It is, rather, the ongoing intervention of God's own hospitality as, again and again, it reaches out to us in worship where the space for repentance, forgiveness, and reconciliation is opened up. And these three are continuously needed so that God's hospitality in Christ may be rightly honored in our practice of theology. This insight sometimes comes late, but in light of God's own hospitality, it can never come too late.

It was precisely in the context of worship that a recent, highly significant act of theological repentance occurred — an event whose significance is still just dawning upon most Christians and theologians. I am referring to the Pontifical Mass from March 12, 2000, in the papal cathedral of St. Peter's. Pope John Paul II, together with select members from the College of Cardinals, offered a prayer of repentance and forgiveness, unique in its kind in the history of theology. Under the heading of "Confession of sin in the service of truth," Cardinal Ratzinger, head of the Congregation for the Doctrine of the Faith, addressed the particular sins committed in the context of discerning and judging theologically, especially when done in the service of the Church's *magisterium.* "Let every one of us arrive at the insight that in their necessary engagement of protecting the truth also members of the Church have, from time to time, relied on methods that do not correspond to the Gospel."[38] In acts, maybe not as momentous as this particular one, but analogous to it, the practice of theology is renewed by being grounded again and again in a repentance that asks for that forgiveness that we find at the very core of God's hospitality in Christ.

Only in worship can we expect to continuously receive the forgiveness that will allow us to honor the truth of God's hospitality rightly in the course of carrying out this fragile but irreplaceable practice of theology. It is thus only on the grounds of the forgiveness received in worship that we can hope to both forgive and be forgiven and thus become able to go on with the practice of discerning and judging theologically — in short, with "doing dogmatics."

VI. Instead of a Conclusion

It was the task of this chapter to suggest that honoring the truth and practicing hospitality are deeply interrelated — to the point of mutually depending on each other. Yet more important was the task of arguing that nothing less than the core of the Christian faith discloses their integral relation by disclosing reality to be such that practicing hospitality and honoring the truth in their integral relation correspond most accurately to the way things are. The Christian faith is capable of doing this because it is itself the result of God's own practice of hospitality, in and through which we receive the truth that *is* the triune God as the communion of the Father with the Son in the Holy Spirit; thus also are we called to share in the triune God's hospitality and truth.

We are connected to and drawn into the Christian faith's disclosure of the triune God's hospitality and truth through two modes of reception: worship and doctrine. In worship we continuously receive the very hospitality of God's truth, and in doctrine the very truth of God's hospitality. Ultimately, it is this "disclosure" of hospitality and truth as enacted in worship and doctrine that shows us what is fundamentally both necessary and at stake in practicing hospitality truthfully and in honoring and thus being hospitable to the truth.

With these reflections I have obviously not answered why it is that in the past and in the present many Christians (and I mean here those who regularly participate in worship and hold on to doctrine) fail to practice hospitality and to honor the truth — and why at the same time we find many practitioners of hospitality and of honoring the truth who do not share the Christian confession of Christ as Lord. While significant, these questions ultimately point beyond this chapter and invite further theological exploration, some of which I undertake in part II, "*Eleutheria* — or, Free to Live with God." At this point, however, I would suggest that they teach us at least three things: *first,* that there is a knowledge of created goods dispersed among all humanity; *second,* that worship and doctrine obviously do not "function" *ex opere operato,* that is, what has been received does not transpose itself, machinelike, into a way of life; and *third,* and most important, how utterly serious it is and how deeply it questions the reality-claims of the gospel when Christians fail to practice hospitality and to honor the truth.

5. Karl Barth's "Dialectical Catholicity": *Sic et Non*

Let me begin with a question:

> I would like to ask in all seriousness whether Protestantism can be a real answer to anyone to whom Catholicism never should be a real question. Whether we still have any real business with the Church of the Reformation if in the meanwhile we should have indeed left alone the counterpart with which it struggled. And I would like to give warning of the unhappy awakening which might some day follow such detachment. Those who know Catholicism even a little know how deceiving its remoteness and strangeness are, how uncannily close it is to us in reality, how urgent and vital the questions it puts to us are, and how inherently impossible the possibility is, not to seriously listen to them after one has once heard them. . . .[1]

This question is mine only in a secondary way. It is, of course, a quote from the theologian whom I plan to engage in the following pages. As I will show, for Barth the vitality of the Reformation never meant anything less than to still have real business with the church of the Reformation. And the real business of the church of the Reformation was, according to Barth, its struggle with its counterpart, the Roman Catholic Church. The issue at stake for both sides was and is true catholicity. Yet for the Reformation churches, if they do not continuously engage Roman Catholicism both critically and constructively, the claim to catholicity remains empty. Barth's own theology from the mid-1920s on is exemplary in exercising this insight.[2] I will call this particular form of engagement, which is Barth's unique way of displaying the Reformation's vitality in his own work, his "dialectical catholicity." Instead of giving an advance definition of what Barth or I might precisely mean by "dialectical theology," I prefer to let this term unfold itself in the course of this inquiry — an inquiry that will begin with the end of Barth's career.

I. Evangelical Catholicity: *"Ad Limina Apostolorum"* — or, "The Pope Is Not the Antichrist"

Despite an official invitation to attend the last sessions of Vatican II as an observer, Barth was unable to make the trip because of prolonged hospital stays. By then, Barth was in his late seventies. When his health had stabilized, he paid a private visit to the Vatican, in September 1966, after having studied the documents of Vatican II all summer and having prepared a list of detailed questions on most of its constitutions and decrees. They were, interestingly, more "questions for clarification" than "critical questions." How did Barth come away from this unique experience of close dialogue with high Vatican officials and theologians and a private audience with Pope Paul VI? I will let him speak for himself:

> As a result of the trip I gained a close acquaintance with a church and a theology which have begun a movement, the results of which are incalculable and slow but clearly genuine and irreversible. In looking at it we can only wish that we had something comparable, if it could avoid a repetition of at least the worst mistakes we have made since the sixteenth century. I would be happy to see the words "Protestant" and "Protestantism" disappear from our vocabulary. . . . The Pope is not the Antichrist! The apparatus of all the anathemas directed at us by the Council of Trent is now to be found, with all sorts of other old weaponry, only in the Denzinger. *Ultra montes* I met so many Christians with whom I could not only speak candidly and seriously, but also join in hearty laughter, that I could not think without pain of certain dwarfs in our own theological backyard. Any optimism about the future is automatically excluded. But calm, brotherly hope is called for, together with a willingness in the meanwhile to conduct in both great and small affairs a thorough housecleaning of our own. "Conversions" from us to the Roman Catholic Church or from there to one of our churches have as such no significance *(peccatur intra muros et extra!)*. They can have significance only if they are in the form of a conscientiously necessary "conversion" — not to another church, but to Jesus Christ, the Lord of the one, holy, catholic and apostolic church. Basically both here and there it can only be a matter of

each one heeding in his place in his own church the call to faith in the one Lord, and to his service.³

We might be tempted to wonder whether — intoxicated by the luring songs of the Roman sirens — Barth might have turned overnight into a crypto-Catholic. He might have worried about this possible impression himself. Maybe it was in order to regain the right balance in his dialectical relationship to Roman Catholicism that a bit further down in his account, in reference to his critical remarks on the Mariology of a Roman Catholic colleague, he said: "Anxious souls on our side may here at last see that I returned from Rome just as stubbornly evangelical — I would really rather say, evangelical-catholic — as before."⁴ At the very end of his career, one year before his death, we find the drafter of the Barmen Declaration describing himself as "evangelical catholic" and as someone who would like to see the terms "Protestant" and "Protestantism" disappear from our theological vocabulary! Obviously, the term "evangelical catholic" had taken on a new and quite positive meaning for Barth. Yet this was by no means always the case. In 1924 he used it to distance himself from the high church movement in post–World War I Lutheranism in Germany and could speak of "mystical, High-Church, Evangelical-Catholic, dilettantism."⁵

We can make one rather obvious observation that some might think undercuts the force of the late Barth's self-description as "evangelical catholic." After all, Barth faced Paul VI in Rome, not John Paul II. He encountered a church in the morning breeze of optimism and renewal right after Vatican II, not in the context of hierarchical reassertion and doctrinal retrenchment, as some might describe the Roman Catholic Church in the later years of John Paul II's pontificate. Yet this objection fails to recognize that Barth met with the conservative party in the Vatican as well.⁶ He was quite aware of the conservative interpretation of Vatican II. And it is nothing else but the conservative interpretation of Vatican II that we encounter in the pontificate of John Paul II. Yet much more decisive is the fact that long before Vatican II we find Barth saying things about Roman Catholicism that were highly surprising, not to say shocking, for many Protestant ears. Let us therefore turn from the end of Barth's journey to its beginnings.

II. Dialectical Catholicity: Barth's "Discovery" of Roman Catholicism

Yet instead of turning to his early days as a student in the centers of *Kulturprotestantismus* or as a dialectical theologian wrestling with Paul's

Epistle to the Romans in Safenwil, I shall focus on the beginnings of Barth's teaching career, in Göttingen. As soon as Barth had to teach theology and, in the course of his preparations, to seriously study and engage Reformation theology (especially that of Calvin), he began to engage Roman Catholic theology as a decisive counterpart. We can observe already in Barth's earliest lectures on dogmatics, his so-called Göttingen Dogmatics, two crucial moves. *First,* retrieving Reformation theology for contemporary dogmatic reflection would not work for Barth without the engagement of Roman Catholicism. *Second,* the formal structure of his dialectical catholicity was already in place before his serious encounter with "flesh and blood" Catholics.[7] Yet it was only this latter encounter that turned the tentative and nonpublic probing of the Göttingen lectures on dogmatics into an urgent and public concern. I shall therefore focus on the second phase of his beginnings as a professional university theologian, his tenure at the University of Münster from October 1925 to March 1930, which was the intermediate station on his journey from Göttingen to Bonn.[8] This particular phase of his development as a university theologian is significant, because it was precisely during this period that Barth encountered for the first time Roman Catholicism both as a highly competent conversation partner and as a live and, in fact, majority phenomenon. We should not forget that three out of the four universities where Barth studied theology — Berne, Berlin, and Marburg — had only Protestant theological faculties and were in either completely Protestant areas or those where Protestants constituted the overwhelming majority.[9] It is safe to say that before Barth's arrival in Münster, Roman Catholicism really did not exist in his world. Münster changed this dramatically. The Roman Catholicism of this corner of Germany was and is a formidable and deeply rooted reality. Beyond that, the Roman Catholic faculty at the university was much larger and older than the Protestant one, and it attracted and still attracts many more students.[10] Here Barth encountered another "strange new world." His essay "Roman Catholicism: A Question to the Protestant Church," from the year 1928, gives a lively witness to this circumstance.[11] In addition, it is one of the earliest documents in which Barth's dialectical catholicity is displayed extensively and in full force.[12] What is remarkable about this essay is that it was originally given to three Protestant audiences,[13] urging them to reexamine critically their own Protestantism and to take seriously Roman Catholicism as a challenge that was by no means overcome.

Before addressing the two central questions he sees put before Protestantism by Roman Catholicism, Barth dismisses three possible objections that are all too likely to come from the Protestant camp: *First,* Roman Catholicism does not really present a challenge to us. It is a phenomenon too distant, strange, and unrelated to our concrete thinking and feeling for us to be concerned with what we might be asked from there.[14] *Second,* "good, serious, convinced Protestantism" consists in the fact that it has settled, once and for all, the question of Catholicism.[15] And *third,* Catholicism does not acknowledge the commonality of the space it inhabits with us and does not take the question seriously that Protestantism represents for itself. Why, then, should we listen to and take its question seriously?[16] Obviously, all three claims are still very much alive in contemporary Protestantism. And thus Barth's vehement rejection of each is still equally pertinent. Yet we cannot focus on them in detail at this point.

Much more decisive are the two central questions that Barth sees put before the Protestant church by Roman Catholicism and the way he characterizes those questions: "First, the Protestant Church is asked by Roman Catholicism whether and how far it is a *church.*"[17] It is liberal Protestantism's turn to the individual and his or her piety or faith as the center point of Christianity and the church as an aggregation of believers — in other words, liberal Protestantism's complete failure to give a theologically substantive account of the church as church — that Barth sees addressed here.

> Catholicism becomes this question to us because in its presuppositions for the Church, in spite of all contradictions, it is closer to the Reformers than is the Church of the Reformation so far as that has actually and finally become [Neo-Protestantism].[18] It becomes this question to us because, if any of the concern of the Reformation is still ours in spite of [Neo-Protestantism], we cannot deny that we feel more at home in the world of Catholicism and among its believers than in a world and among believers where the reality about which the Reformation centred has become an unknown or almost unknown entity.[19]

In addition, it is precisely also liberal Protestantism's view of the Reformation, that is, its self-legitimation through its reading of the Reformation as leading precisely and unavoidably to liberal individualism, that Barth challenges head-on in a famous — and, for some, rather infamous — footnote:

> It perhaps will make for clarity if I state explicitly one implication of this sentence. If I today became convinced that the interpretation of the Reformation on the line taken by Schleiermacher-Ritschl-Troeltsch (or even by Seeberg or Holl) was correct; that Luther and Calvin really intended such an outcome of their labours; I could not become a Catholic tomorrow, but I should have to withdraw from the evangelical Church. And if I

were forced to make a choice between the two evils, I should, in fact, prefer the Catholic.[20]

There is only a very small step, if any at all, from this warning signal of the early Barth to the self-description of the later Barth as an "evangelical catholic." Yet despite his clear emphasis on "catholicity," the "evangelical" pole is not lost.

The *second* question with which Barth sees Roman Catholicism confront the Protestant church is "whether and in how far it is a *Protestant Church*."[21] Here the dialectical nature of Barth's encounter with Roman Catholicism comes clearly to the fore. He turns the normative nature of what constitutes the church as church against both neo-Protestantism and Roman Catholicism by reaching back to the Reformers themselves:

> The Reformation restored the Church as the Church of the Word. Word is the revelation and self-mediation of another person, a person who meets us. And if this person is the person of God, his Word is the expression of his authority; not of his domineering over us, but of his Lordship over us. God encounters me in his Word, and this means that he directs me through his commands and through his promise; that I am to believe him and obey him. These categories differ fundamentally from other categories. By them is declared and established . . . the immutable subjectivity of God, the freedom of God above all instruments, the uniqueness of God's authority. To declare and establish this truth is the business of Protestantism. We cannot see that this is really done in the Catholic teaching.[22]

It becomes quite clear from this quote and from Barth's overall argument in his lecture from 1928 that *dialectical catholicity* is his fundamental strategy to steer a course between neo-Protestantism on the one side and Roman Catholicism on the other. The goal of this strategy is precisely to reconnect contemporary Protestantism with the church of the Reformation and thereby to make it again "genuine." The unique argumentative force of this dialectical catholicity allows him to avoid, on the one side, the Scylla of a Protestantism that has settled with the modern turn to the self and given up on the priority and gift of the gospel's *ad extra* and, on the other side, the Charybdis of placing the church above the gospel and thereby turning the gift into a given that is managed and organized as a human institution. This strategy can be observed throughout the opening chapters of his *Church Dogmatics* I/1[23] and can be described as a fundamental characteristic for the way he shapes the basic theological landscape of the *Church Dogmatics* in its entirety.

Yet it is important to understand that Barth's dialectical catholicity is by no means a balanced system in which both neo-Protestantism and Roman Catholicism are held at an equally critical arm's length. While Barth in the end maintains his distance also from Roman Catholicism, he consistently prefers it in comparison to the neo-Protestant alternative. One last example from the *Church Dogmatics* points to this particular trait in Barth's dialectical catholicity. It is from *Church Dogmatics* II/2, paragraph 36, "The Command of God and the Ethical Problem." After giving an outline of the unique Roman Catholic coordination of moral philosophy and moral theology, Barth states:

> We hardly need compare this construction with the uncertainty and confusion of the corresponding Neo-Protestant proposals to be forced to acknowledge that what we have here is on any count a very imposing, indeed in its way a classical, attempt at a solution. . . . And if we were compelled to choose between the Neo-Protestant and the Roman Catholic solutions, in this as in so many other questions we should have no option but to prefer the latter.[24]

But then Barth continues, of course: "Yet in spite of all this we cannot really be satisfied with it."[25] The reason is that ultimately not only neo-Protestantism but also Roman Catholicism fall behind the truth in principle, the first by placing the modern religious subject at the center of the religious universe, the latter by granting a human institution a semidivine function. Both install principles that ultimately undercut God's sovereignty, and it is precisely the church of the Reformation that offers Barth the *critical* principle to unmask both aberrations — with neo-Protestantism as the clearly worse and by far more serious one. Thus Barth has to encounter and engage both aberrations constantly in order to remain faithful to his own project. He knows that there is no way to face the challenge posed by neo-Protestantism successfully without being in a constant and serious engagement of Roman Catholicism. And it is precisely this side of the lesson of Barth's dialectical catholicity about which contemporary Protestant theologians are remarkably forgetful.[26] If this forgetfulness had a principle, it would need to be called by the old, well-known Protestant maxim *Catholica non leguntur* — "Catholics are not read." Among the few leading contemporary Protestant theologians whose own work strikingly reflects Barth's insight are, on the European side, Wolfhart Pannenberg and (to a lesser degree) Eberhard Jüngel and, on the American side, George Lindbeck,[27] Robert Jenson,[28] and Stanley Hauerwas.[29]

Yet the methodological strategy of dialectical catholicity not only represents for Barth the crucial way to continue what he calls "mature Protestant thinking" in the line of the Reformers; it is also of central importance for an accurate reading of Barth's own theology. The failure to recognize Barth's dialectical catholicity as the fundamental methodological strategy of his theology — and the consequent failure to interpret Barth's relationship to neo-Protestantism in light of his continuity with the Reformers as well as his conversation with Roman Catholicism — unavoidably results in a severely truncated reading of Barth's theology. It is precisely Barth's running dialogue with and engagement of Roman Catholic theology that saves him from what he would regard as neo-Protestantism's dead-end, namely, its almost exclusive focus on the modern predicament as its privileged point of reference. In other words, a reading of Barth's theology as primarily a running dialogue and controversy with neo-Protestantism and a testing and deepening of "the fundamental insights of the Reformation in face of the development of modernity"[30] reflects a limited, one-dimensional understanding of Barth's project.

Yet we need to ask more specifically now whether Barth's distinct methodological strategy of engagement, his dialectical catholicity, actually constitutes a sustainable approach, a paradigm for an ongoing critical and constructive engagement of Roman Catholicism. Might it not all too easily turn into an endless dialectical play, a ceaseless critical oscillation between neo-Protestantism and Roman Catholicism, a way to gesture toward a third option that is precisely in need of this ongoing dialectical movement in order to stabilize itself?[31] Might dialectical catholicity not become a recipe for a theology without any tangible ecclesial roots, especially if it is practiced by less gifted and ecclesially committed apprentices of the great master of theological dialectics? Or might already Barth himself be playing theological "hide and seek" in his engagement of Roman Catholicism? Does his theology become ecclesially concrete so that also he himself could concretely be engaged by Roman Catholicism? The latter strikes me as being the only test for a successful *theological* "catholicity" that truly is in touch with the church of the Reformation.

III. "Genuine Protestantism" as Critical Principle

In order to approach an answer to the question just raised, we need to first ask, *What is it that makes this engagement of Roman Catholicism in Barth's theology both possible and necessary?* In his essay "Roman Catholicism: A Question to the Protestant Church" Barth employs an interesting metaphor that might provide a clue to the answer: the "occupation of a common room"[32] by

Roman Catholics and Protestants. The metaphor is more important than we might assume at first sight. Only if one occupies a "common room" can the other *become* a question to oneself; only if one continues to occupy a common room will the other *continue* to be a question to oneself. In his essay from 1928 Barth never grants the term "church" to Roman Catholicism but keeps it strictly reserved for Protestantism. Nevertheless, Roman Catholicism clearly has for him so much ecclesial substance that it can and does amount to a question for the Protestant church. How so? In order to find an answer we need to turn to the nature of the "room" that Barth assumes is occupied by both Roman Catholics and Protestants. What is the theological nature of this "room" that it can be occupied by both?

Here we approach the very root of Barth's ecclesiology. In order to find it fully fleshed out we have to turn to volumes II and IV of his *Church Dogmatics*. It will become clear that by moving ahead in Barth's development and writing, we are not doing him any injustice, because he remains fully consistent with his central theological principle.

In *Church Dogmatics* II/2 we find remarkable evidence for both his ecclesiology and the possibility of his dialectical catholicity:

> Anthropological and ecclesiological assertions arise only as they are borrowed from Christology. That is to say, no anthropological or ecclesiological assertion is true in itself and as such. Its truth subsists in the assertion of Christology, or rather in the reality of Jesus Christ alone.[33]

Barth's ecclesiology is a function of his Christology, and the nature of the relationship between the two is fundamentally determined already in his doctrine of election.[34] It therefore comes as no surprise that to a large degree both the nature and the problem of his dialectical catholicity can be found in his doctrine of election. Barth's distinctive way of developing the doctrine of election — the centerpiece of his theology, as Hans Urs von Balthasar has rightly observed[35] — involves a radical subsumption of election under the particularity of the gospel. From eternity God elects in Christ to take the condemnation for human sin upon himself and to grant to humanity, for Christ's sake, the love of the Father for the Son. In this way, Barth clearly revolutionizes the traditional accounts of election. Yet more importantly, he secures the gospel protologically, not as an unavoidable expression of God's nature, but as the free eternal decision of God's will to determine all of the triune God's activity in time through the election of Christ. The eternal reality of this election is mirrored by a community in which God's act in Christ becomes public for all humanity and whose vocation is nothing less — and nothing other —

than witnessing to God's election in Christ by communicating it to all the world through word and witness.[36]

The theological root of Barth's dialectical catholicity and its inner problematic can be traced to the fact that there exists an inner dialectic in the elect community, in the people of God, itself. There is both a witness to God's act of election in Christ and a witness to God's judgment, a judgment that is internal to God's election. The church is that segment of the elect community that witnesses to the former; Israel, that segment of the elect community that witnesses to the latter. Both election and judgment are strictly divine acts, internal to the triune God, embodied in Christ's cross and resurrection, with the judgment being taken strictly upon God in Christ's cross. The vocation of both communities is strictly one of witness. In their unity and differentiation, they both correspond to the inner unity and differentiation of God's action in Christ.[37] Thus Israel in and of itself is clearly not rejected.[38] Yet in its way of existence, in not accepting Christ as its Messiah, Israel witnesses precisely to the rejection and condemnation that God took upon himself in Christ's cross.[39]

There is undeniably a catholicity in Barth's way of seeing Israel and the church together as the one elect people of God called to witness to nothing other than the very dialectic of God's saving activity itself through Israel's election and Christ's incarnation, life, crucifixion, and resurrection that for Barth always is at once grace and judgment, salvation and condemnation. And the distinct dialectic inherent in God's own encounter with a sinful humanity finds its precise reflection in Barth's dialectical distinction between Israel and the church in regard to the particular nature of their respective witness. But since for Barth judgment is grace and grace is judgment, both witnessing communities belong inherently together. They are differentiated only in regard to their particular vocation of witness. In other words, they both occupy together the "one room" of election! Thus we can see that the theological root of Barth's dialectical catholicity is to be found in the nature of God's election in Christ. While the identity of the elect community rests in the election of Jesus Christ, the inner dialectic of this election can only be expressed through an internally differentiated witness in the elect community.[40] And it is precisely this differentiating dynamic between "identity" and "difference" that finds its continuation in Barth's later ecclesiology as well. It is the very point of what I call Barth's "genuine Protestantism" as a critical principle. In the doctrine of election "church" is only "church" under very precise conditions that differentiate it within the elect community from Israel. And it comes as no surprise that also here in the community that witnesses specifically to the grace of God's election in Christ we can find the differentiating dynamic of dialectical catholicity at work. For it is through this differentiating dynamic that the critical principle of "genuine Protestantism" is applied.

But first we need to see how this differentiating dynamic plays itself out in Barth's ecclesiology in the doctrine of reconciliation, where he treats ecclesiology in much greater detail. The one true church can only exist as an event in which, through the Holy Spirit's action, the human witness fully coincides with its referent, God's graceful election in Christ. Yet this event occurs, under the condition of time, provisionally and periodically, "again and again." Only eschatologically in the full consummation of all will the church coincide perpetually with its referent. And that is precisely when the church as a distinct community of witness will disappear, because its vocation of witness will have ended.

In the provisionality of human life under the condition of time, every witness is a limited witness, every witness is an approximation, every witness is just that, a witness. As such, the witnessing community completely depends on the Holy Spirit's activity for each individual act of witness to be completed in the recognition of those who perceive it. The church as such has no signifying power, no communicative potency whatsoever. Only the Spirit's act links the sign with its referent, God's grace in Christ. Only the Spirit, as the link between the Father and the Son, bridges the infinite abyss between a creaturely witness and its divine referent. For Barth, "genuine Protestantism," namely, Protestantism that is still in touch with the church of the Reformation, approximates this truth most closely, because it is constituted by the awareness of its character as witness, its inherent frailty, and its complete dependence upon God's initiating and completing activity. Both Roman Catholicism and neo-Protestantism precisely lack this ecclesial self-understanding. "Genuine Protestantism" as a *critical* principle practices in its dialectical catholicity the distinction between the church's identity, which rests in God's reconciling activity in Christ, and the difference of human witness from that activity. It is precisely this fundamental difference that allows for differences among the witnessing communities. In all concrete ecclesial communities there is a mixture of clear and muddled witness, all to be found in the "one room of election." "Genuine Protestantism" is the critical principle that offers a normative account of the nature and form of any genuine ecclesial witness. The deep problem now is that Barth's "genuine Protestantism" cannot really exist in an ecclesially embodied form. "Genuine Protestantism," for Barth, rather serves as a critical theological principle to be employed over against all real, existing churches. Dialectical catholicity is the concrete strategy through which this critical principle takes shape in light of the opposing principles of neo-

Protestantism and Roman Catholicism. Yet it is precisely in its very dialecticity that this principle has to remain abstract from each concrete ecclesial body. Why? Because critical principles by definition cannot be embodied but are to be applied in relation to concrete embodiments.

The critical principle of "genuine Protestantism," embodied in Barth's practice of dialectical catholicity, constitutes the inner self-reflexivity of his distinct theological program that attempts in its dialectical movement to witness to God's sovereign freedom over against the individual and collective ecclesial communities.[41] The identity of the church rests, according to Barth, precisely in God's freedom and faithfulness, which is nothing other than the identity of God's election in Christ, something that the church receives provisionally and periodically, "again and again," something that in no way and to no degree subsists in the real existing communities of witness and service. And precisely because the church's identity is not at hand for the church, the difference between the churches is ultimately a preliminary and a relative difference. In addition, it is the ineffable inner dialectic of God's activity in Christ that necessitates a differentiated witness in the one "room of God's election." The differences of witness are to be understood in light of the identity that rests in God's self-giving in Christ, something to be had only *in actu*. Yet let us understand clearly: Barth does not regard the divisions between the churches as differences of this kind. The disunity, the division in faith, is mysterious and ultimately inexplicable. It is a division necessitated precisely by faith, precisely by the church's identity in Christ.[42]

Let us turn again to one central quote from Barth's early essay "Roman Catholicism: A Question to the Protestant Church":

> The Reformation restored the Church as the Church of the Word. Word is the revelation and self-mediation of another person, a person who meets us. And if this person is the person of God, his Word is the expression of his authority; not of his domineering over us, but of his Lordship over us. God encounters me in his Word, and this means that he directs me through his commands and through his promise; that I am to believe him and obey him. These categories differ fundamentally from other categories. By them is declared and established . . . the immutable subjectivity of God, the freedom of God above all instruments, the uniqueness of God's authority. To declare and establish this truth is the business of Protestantism. We cannot see that this is really done in the Catholic teaching.[43]

Ecclesial difference does not matter as long as the nature and location of the identity of God's activity and of Christ's body is rightly understood. And the prerogative Barth claims for the church of the Reformation that comes to self-reflexivity, that is, to the full self-awareness of its nature in Barth's critical principle of "genuine Protestantism," is precisely the truth about the theological relationship between ecclesial identity and difference. What makes neo-Protestantism and Roman Catholicism, according to Barth, theological and especially ecclesiological heresies is their profound confusion about the relationship between identity and difference in relation to the body of Christ. For neo-Protestantism, the location of identity is the individual's religious awareness of oneness with the divine; the location of difference, the varieties of individual and collective expressions of this awareness. For Roman Catholicism, the location of identity is the identification of the body of Christ in the Roman Catholic Church; the location of difference, all those Christian communities that are not in communion with Rome. What makes Barth's dialectical catholicity *conceptually* superior is its inherent power to situate, criticize, and overcome both alternatives with an ecclesiological account that is self-transparent in its reflexivity because it is a *critical* account of all possible ecclesial communities. Thus Barth's dialectical catholicity has to be understood as the practice of "transcendental ecclesiology," as circumscribing the conditions for the possibility of "church" to be transparent to and self-reflexive of its nature as a "sign" of God's grace. Yet the conceptual superiority of the "transcendental ecclesiology" that is "genuine Protestantism" is bought at a high price, namely, the loss of the church's concreteness that does not rest in our witness but is precisely God's own work. In the next and final part, I want to suggest that the Reformers, especially Luther, were working with a "concrete catholicity," rooted in distinct practices that were understood as the Holy Spirit's work. In contrast to Barth's disembodied pneumatology and critical ecclesiology, this strategy allowed for an embodied pneumatology and a concrete ecclesiology. And the latter is a sine qua non for a lasting theological engagement of Roman Catholicism.

IV. *Sic et Non* — or, Dialectical versus Concrete Catholicity

In my eyes, the distinct abstractness of Barth's ecclesiology, which precisely makes his dialectical catholicity possible, comes out most clearly in his doctrine of election — in his deeply problematic treatment of Israel in relation to the church. Or, to put it differently and more starkly: A closer inspection of Barth's dialectical catholicity reveals a much larger issue — the relation of the church to Israel.[44] Nicholas Healy states the matter well when he observes: "Scripture locates the spiritual and the theological not apart from, but as identifiable with and through the material. Try to think of an invisible yet 'real' Israel distinct from its socio-cultural identity; the notion strikes one immediately as quite odd. Israel's identity is constituted by its distinctive beliefs, practices and valuations developed within the narrative of what Israel construes as its dealing with God in history."[45] I think Healy is right. To think of Israel and the church dialectically as the two communities that mirror, in their existence together, the inner dialectic of God's election in Christ means unavoidably to turn concretely embodied ways of life and belief into abstract principles. One might want to argue that Barth makes major efforts in *Church Dogmatics* IV to overcome the danger of abstraction by offering a denser and more concrete ecclesiology.[46] But as Healy has shown, it is precisely the bifurcation in Barth's ecclesiology between the church as God's act, the true church, and the human witness to God's act, the *Scheinkirche*, and the dialectical relationship between the two, that undercuts any possibility of offering a denser account of the church.[47] Barth's late ecclesiology, rather, has to be understood as a further development of his critical ecclesiological strategy of dialectical catholicity, now offering in detail the *conditions* under which a concrete witness is faithful to the nature and vocation of the church and to its referent. In other words, Barth's approach to ecclesiology remains ultimately transcendental.

Therefore, Healy's trenchant remark regarding Israel holds even in light of Barth's late ecclesiology. As much as Israel, the church is first of all *a way of life*, that is, a distinct set of practices interwoven with normative beliefs, concretely and distinctly embodied. And interestingly, understanding the church primarily as a concrete way of life in analogy to Israel is much closer to both Roman Catholicism and the church of the Reformation, at least to Luther, than is Barth's account.[48] For Luther, the best case can be made on the grounds of his mature ecclesiology as developed in the treatise *On the Councils and the Church*. Recall that in this treatise Luther names a distinct number of practices through which God's saving economy instantiates itself. He regards them as constitutive of the church — that is, wherever they are practiced, there the church of Christ is, and wherever they are not practiced, there the church of Christ is not. These practices are the proclamation of God's word and its reception in faith, confession, and deed; baptism; the Lord's Supper; the office of the keys; ordination and ordained office; prayer, doxology, and catechesis; and the way of the cross.[49] What is also remarkable about Luther's account in contrast to Barth's is that Luther understands these practices as the church's marks. They are the "holy things" *(Heiltümer)* through which the Holy Spirit enacts his regenerating and sanctifying work. Instead of pointing as witnesses to the Holy Spirit's activity, these practices rather embody the Holy Spirit's work. The result of this "concrete pneumatology," to borrow a term from David Yeago and Joseph Mangina,[50] is at least twofold.

First, the Spirit has a salvific economy in his own right, to which the church's constitutive practices are central. Therefore, Barth's claim that "the world would not necessarily be lost if there were no Church"[51] is a claim in starkest contrast to the church of the Reformation and to Roman Catholicism. It also shows most clearly that for Barth "the church's sole distinguishing characteristic is its knowledge"[52] about Christ, given by the Spirit, while for Luther the church's distinguishing characteristics are its constitutive practices, through which the Spirit does his sanctifying work. In this sense, for Luther at least, the church is both an embodied and an indispensable reality.

Second, the catholicity implicit in Luther's account is an undialectical and concretely embodied catholicity. It refers to the people of God as marked through specific practices, a distinct people that can be localized and identified. For Luther, the ongoing engagement of the church of Rome was a given, but that was because there was a concrete and tangible theological and ecclesial conflict. It was not an alternative fundamental "principle" that was at stake.[53]

It is Luther's account of the church's marks as constitutive practices, together with his understanding of the Holy Spirit's doing his work precisely in and through them, that allows Luther to begin ecclesiologically with the concrete — yet without becoming a sectarian. Rather, his ecclesiology opens up a horizon of catholicity that focuses on the concreteness of practices and beliefs that transcend the particularities of specific communions. And it is precisely Luther's unique "pneumatological ecclesiology" that enables such a perspective.

But is Barth not known, we might ask, for his notorious insistence on beginning with the particular? Does Barth not explicitly claim: "It is not the general which comes first, but the particular. The general does not exist without this particular and cannot therefore be prior to the particular. It cannot, then, be recognized and understood as the general prior to it, as if it were itself a particular. Thus we cannot move from the general to this particular, but only in the opposite direction — from this particular to the general."[54]

While this move is definitely characteristic of Barth's theology, his rule of particularity extends only to Christ. Precisely because Barth renders Christ's particularity as an essential "over againstness" to all ecclesial acts of witness to him, the church only "is" in its distinct acts.[55] And these acts can only be accounted for by describing their possibility and its guiding principle — in other words, by a transcendental account. While for Luther the Holy Spirit becomes "embodied" in particular practices (and therefore, for him, a beginning with the concrete practices is also possible in his ecclesiology),[56] for Barth the church's practices remain, as witnessing responses, radically distinguished from the Holy Spirit's activity. This leads unavoidably to what Healy rightly calls Barth's "bifurcated ecclesiology," which precisely functions as a transcendental account of all possible acts of witness. Therefore, Barth's catholicity must unavoidably be dialectical in nature: neo-Protestantism and Roman Catholicism represent alternative ecclesiological principles that need to be constantly engaged in order to be critically overcome through a transcendental critique that is reflective of the sovereignty of God's activity in Christ.

Thus we need to distinguish between two closely interwoven aspects of Barth's theology: on the one hand, Barth's crucial theological insight that real business with the church of the Reformation requires an ongoing serious encounter with Roman Catholicism; and on the other hand, Barth's critical principle of "genuine Protestantism," which was put into practice through the specific methodological strategy of dialectical catholicity. Barth is right in emphasizing the importance of continuing to seriously engage and be engaged by Roman Catholicism in order to remain in contact with the Reformation's vital concerns. This insight — including the important claim that Roman Catholicism represents a much more substantive and serious challenge than neo-Protestantism — is evident throughout the *Church Dogmatics*. Yet Barth's dialectical catholicity as a distinct and pervasive methodological strategy turns out to be a deeply problematic and ambiguous phenomenon, one that is inherently linked with his disembodied pneumatology and therefore bifurcated ecclesiology. In other words, if we want to be true to Barth's deep theological concern to still have real business with the church of the Reformation, we are forced to question his own performance, namely, his dialectical catholicity.

One major challenge for us is to understand the Spirit and the church in a way that avoids transcendental moves by giving due account of the Spirit's embodiment in distinct practices, and thereby the church's concreteness, yet also of the church's brokenness. Only a return to concrete ecclesial traditions, doctrines, and liturgical, communal, and moral practices will allow us to address each other concretely and to face the concrete, pressing nature of the brokenness of Christ's body in this world. No evasion of the brokenness can be allowed — by rendering it irrelevant (because, after all, the church is just a replaceable tool) or trivial (because, with some simple good will, we could all be one) or abstract (because the one true church, as God's act, is wholly distinct from a plurality of witnessing communities).[57]

Karl Barth was the most important Protestant theological voice of the twentieth century. And we should continue to learn from him this decisive insight, even if it is only a *particula veri*. Moreover, it is precisely our greatest teachers from whom we can also learn what not to do and where not to follow. Barth's dialectical catholicity, as I have tried to show, while very tempting in its *conceptual* force and central for a full understanding of his theology, should not be followed — precisely in order to stay in touch with the concrete catholicity of the church of the Reformation.

6. Beyond Dialectics: *Est* and *Esse*

The Affirmative and the Negative in Theological Discourse

The following considerations are an exercise in *theological* reflection upon the affirmative and the negative moments in theological discourse. While they draw upon the resources of philosophical theology, these considerations rest squarely upon the normative implications of the *doctrina evangelii*. Their goal is to specify the proper location of negative theology in the overall matrix of theological discourse. Hence, they do not focus on the historical genealogy of negative theology.[1] Nor do they engage the kind of negative theology that constitutes the proper telos and therefore genuine fulfillment of philosophical theology at its most reflective stage.[2] Nor do they pursue the present interest in a relentlessly negative philosophy, a philosophy of *différance,* and ask the obvious question whether negative philosophy is at variance with or tacitly draws upon the tradition and logic of negative theology.[3] While all these investigations are indeed worthy, they do not address the important question, Why and in what way does negative theology constitute a necessary moment in proper theological discourse?

Hence, the question at stake is not whether mystical theology, or apophaticism, is a legitimate form of Christian theology;[4] rather, the question concerns negative theology as a necessary moment in the discourse of Christian theology. The thesis I wish to advance is the following: Negative theology, far from being an accidental, ultimately extrinsic, and even intrusively neoplatonic element of Christian theological discourse — and therefore allegedly foreign to the nature of the Christian gospel and its Hebrew roots — must rather be understood as a necessary moment, albeit not the primary moment, of proper Christian theological discourse itself. The very necessity of negative theology as an intrinsic moment of theological discourse arises from the specific conceptual limitations entailed in any affirmative theology as the discourse of creatures. Without the corrective dynamic of negative theology, affirmative theology continuously stands in acute danger of succumbing to the subtle dynamic of conceptual idolatry.[5] This truism loses its obviousness as soon as a contemporary, primarily historically oriented philosophy of religion reconstructs the inner logic of negative theology by projecting backwards the uniquely modern distinction between theology and philosophy. Such a reconstruction tends to draw exclusively on the negative theology of the neoplatonic tradition or of German Idealism (those being part of genuine "philosophy") without explicitly considering the fact that this kind of negative theology does not at all depend on the antecedence of God's salvific economy as reflectively unfolded in the affirmative discourse characteristic of Christian theology. A proper consideration of negative theology in all its respects thus entails the question whether negative theology is indeed a necessary moment of theology proper.

A memorable statement from Maximus the Confessor, himself a master of both affirmative and negative theology, makes clear the character negative theology assumes in Christian theological discourse: "If you theologize in an affirmative or cataphatic manner, starting from positive statements about God, you make the Word flesh (cf. John 1:14), for you have no other means of knowing God as cause except from what is visible and tangible. If you theologize in a negative or apophatic manner, through stripping away of positive attributes, you make the Word spirit as being in the beginning God and with God (cf. John 1:1): starting from absolutely none of the things that can be known, you come in an admirable way to know Him who transcends unknowing."[6]

Maximus here elucidates a conceptual distinction more fundamental than that between the affirmative and the negative moments of theological discourse. It is the distinction between *oikonomia*, God's creative and saving economy, which centers in Christ's incarnation, and *theologia* as pertains to what can be said of God irrespective of the economy (usually referring to the mystery of the triune God), a distinction common to most of the Greek Fathers and to the tradition of Byzantine theology. Vladimir Lossky, one of the most significant Russian Orthodox theologians of the twentieth century, himself steeped in the Byzantine tradition, reminds us that "[i]n order to reach this 'theology' properly so-called, one therefore must go beyond the aspect under which we know God as Creator of the universe, in order to be able to extricate the notion of the Trinity from the cosmological implications proper to the 'economy.' To the economy in which God reveals Himself in creating the world and in becoming incarnate, we must respond by theology, confessing the transcendent nature of the Trinity in an ascent of thought which necessarily has an apophatic thrust."[7] It is (negative) *theologia* in its inherent relationship to an antecedent *oikonomia* that will occupy us in the following considerations.[8]

I. The *Est* of the Economy: Affirmative Theology, or Cataphasis

Et verbum caro factum est, et habitavit in nobis: Et vidimus gloriam eius, gloriam quasi unigeniti a Patre plenum gratiae et veritatis.
(John 1:14)

Owing to the nature of its unique subject matter, Christian theological discourse has to begin as affirmative discourse, lest Christian theology simply betray its subject matter. Precisely because of the economy of God's self-manifestation in the history of Israel and in the life, death, and resurrection of Christ, theology is mandated to speak of God in specifically affirmative ways that reflect the definite nature of that self-manifestation as it is articulated in the canonical narratives that recollect and definitively pronounce it. Hence, Christian theology *must* be a theology of the *est* in that it reflects God's definite and irreversible activity, God's economy of salvation.[9] Yet it is important to understand that the *est* on which the fundamental and unceasingly affirmative character of Christian theological discourse rests is not self-produced. Rather, while having its constitutive center in Christ's hypostatic union, the economy's *est* occurs continuously in specifically structured activities, analogous to practices, that mediate the kerygma itself; that is, the *est* occurs first and foremost in the proclamation of the gospel and the celebration of the Eucharist.[10] It is crucial that in both cases the human activity, while instrumental in the kerygma's performative proclamation as well as its sacramental enactment, is not constitutive of their respective efficacy. Yet in both cases there occurs a fundamental identification between the divine and the human activity. The divine activity is not only announced but also performed in the latter to the degree that we have to speak of a strict identification between a particular human activity and the divine self-manifestation. This is expressed in the eucharistic identification "hoc *est* corpus meum," announced and thus enacted by the celebrant, as well as in the Reformation axiom "praedicatio verbi divini *est* verbum divinum,"[11] which unambiguously identifies the proclamation of the gospel with God's word itself.

Undoubtedly, the very scandal of the kerygma is this *est*, the strict identification of a creaturely activity or substance with God's agency and being. Yet this identification, once established, almost immediately entails a further identification, one that emerged very early in the church: the ongoing normative interpretation of the economy's *est* in communally binding doctrinal specifications.¹² The entailment is of utter importance, since this latter identification draws out the conceptual implications of the *est* itself. There are two sides of which to be aware. On the one hand, it is only on the basis of the *est* of word and sacrament that theological doctrine and eventually dogma can be dared and — indeed — are mandated. Without the former, the latter would be just an act of foolish conceit. Yet on the other hand, without the latter, the former would eventually be voided. It is only in the latter that the *est* is reflectively as well as normatively maintained with the increasingly precise formulation of its conceptual implications.

In its most extreme, affirmative theology can thus become just the ongoing interpretation of the fundamental normative affirmation of dogma. It was Erik Peterson who, with characteristic consistency, once carried this position to its extreme conclusion. God has assumed human speech in Christ, and there is therefore a continuity of human speech in Christ's stead and on the basis of the presence of the Spirit's guidance: this is the very presupposition of dogma, or ecclesial doctrine.¹³ Extrapolating from Peterson's understanding, there would be only one task left for theology, namely, to function as the affirmative interpretation and defense of the prior and normative affirmation of dogma. Following this trajectory, we would have to conclude that theology rests exclusively on the *est* as its antecedent datum and unfolds the affirmative dynamic of the *est* in all its conceptual and interpretive moves.

Yet we must ask, is this notion of an exclusively affirmative dogmatic theology desirable or even defensible? Indeed, it seems neither desirable nor defensible, as will soon become clear. With the help of concept and narrative, affirmative theology reflectively follows the specific contours of the history of divine self-manifestation as canonically witnessed and recollected. Yet in that self-manifestation, God is not exhaustively disclosed so as to become accessible to, and thus an object of, human comprehension or possession.¹⁴ Rather, it is precisely in God's self-manifestation that God remains incomprehensible, that is, irreducible mystery.¹⁵ The very dialectic of the giving and withholding, or, to say it with Karl Barth, of the "unveiling and veiling," of the name in Exodus 3:13-14 reflects this fundamental dynamic.¹⁶ Affirmative theology draws upon the definite character of this self-manifestation and the definitive character of the promises and mandates that come along with it. In this way, as the conceptual unfolding of God's economy, affirmative theology has a fundamentally narrative structure and logic that in explicating withdraws from explication.¹⁷ Yet in what particular conceptual way would theological discourse appropriately take account of the fact that its cataphatic *est* has the structure of an interpenetrating giving and withdrawal in the self-manifestation of the One who remains inexhaustibly transcendent to his own manifestation and revelation and therefore preempts the ostensibly comprehensive and hegemonic grasp of the concept *(Begriff)* by which everything is "at hand"?[18] It is this danger of the "at hand," the danger of the univocalistic fallacy that would equate the *est* of the divine self-manifestation with the divine *esse* (as inherent in the dynamic of the *Begriff*)[19] — that would move from God's self-manifestation *sub conditione creaturae* to the Creator *in se* — that requires negation as a necessary moment within Christian discourse.

It is to be immediately said, however, that Christian theology's negative moment must not be understood as canceling the affirmative. More properly, negation helps identify and thereby bring into relief the creaturely contours of the affirmative discourse. Put differently, the very logic of the *oikonomia* and its ensuing affirmative discourse requires a *theologia* with its ensuing negative discourse. The reason for this is that the God revealed in the history of Israel and in the person of Christ, on the one hand, and the God who is Creator, on the other, indeed are one. Yet the latter case, wherein God is Creator, presses Christian theology to conceive God in ways that take full account of the difference in category between creation and Creator. In other words, the negative moment in theological discourse becomes dogmatically necessary as soon as the doctrine of *creatio ex nihilo* is entailed by an affirmative discourse that is prepared to reflect explicitly upon itself as a creaturely discourse attending to the Creator.[20] If this particular and, indeed, crucial difficulty is not fully appreciated and sufficiently addressed or, worse, is simply not understood, theological discourse, by relentlessly unfolding the *est*, runs the risk of committing the univocalist fallacy — that is, of being caught unawares in the conceptual cage of the univocity of being by interpreting the *est* of the divine economy ultimately in the conceptual horizon of the *ens commune*. The ontological difference would then be obscured: the Creator would become a conceptual moment within the thought of creation, if not an ontological moment of its unfolding.

Thus we confront the necessity of apophasis for cataphasis: the deconstruction of the conceptual idol created by a theology of the *est* that is conceived as sheer positivity. That positivity can take three basic forms. Two belong to the discourse of the *oikonomia*, and one belongs to the discourse of *theologia* proper. The first form is a "conceptual biblicism" that would unfold the canon of Scripture as a narratively coherent matrix of propositions; the second, a "conceptual traditionalism" that would unfold dogma and ecclesial doctrine as a notionally coherent matrix of propositions. The third form, which pertains to *theologia*, is the new "natural theology" that emerged in the wake of the metaphysics of early modernity (Suarez, Leibniz, Wolff, et al.), a metaphysics that adopted the Scotist univocity of being as its central tenet.[21] All three forms are characterized by a distinct "positivity," with a distinct "givenness" *(Gegebenheit)* conceptually at hand.

Characteristically — and problematically — in the metaphysical discourse about God, as constitutive of this third form, the very location *sub conditione creaturae* of this conceptually affirmative discourse is lost. Yet a discourse that conceives of God under the conditions of the univocity of being and thereby obscures the Creator/creature difference produces only a conceptual idol that instantaneously calls for its own metaphysical deconstruction. And since modern metaphysics was understood largely as an enterprise dependent upon this conceptual idol, the latter's deconstruction increasingly and consequently turned into the deconstruction first of classical modern metaphysics and eventually of metaphysics per se. Thus one way to appreciate postmetaphysical thinking is to understand it as a thinking after the death of the conceptual idol. As exhaustively documented in recent research, the deconstruction of this kind of metaphysical theology, "ontotheology," was initiated by Kant's *Critique of Pure Reason*,[22] culminated in Heidegger's interpretation of Nietzsche's finalization and ultimate "overturning" of metaphysics,[23] and continued in Derrida's ongoing deconstruction of logocentric strategies.[24]

Thus when the *est* that utters the mystery of the economy is drawn into the explicit or implicit hegemony of a metaphysics of essence, that is, an onto-theology, it inevitably calls for the deconstruction of the conceptual idol it unavoidably produces — unless negative theology offers the necessary reflexive correction and critique. Lest the definite character of the economy's *est* be itself criticized as an instantiation of "positivity" (in the course of such a critique, most likely drawing upon Bonhoeffer's often abused descriptor *Offenbarungspositivismus,* "revelation positivism"), it is important to remember at this point a fundamental distinction entailed in the very logic of the economy — the distinction between the essentially performative God-talk of liturgical recollection and proclamation and the reflective God-talk of theological discourse (affirmative as well as negative). As argued above, the definite *est* of the primary, ecclesially enacted God-talk[25] would eventually be voided without its specific reception in modes of *doctrina,* first in the canon of Scripture and the *regula fidei,* and eventually in dogma and ecclesial doctrine.[26]

It is solely in the conceptual interpretation and unfolding of the canon of Scripture as well as of dogma and ecclesial doctrine (in distinction from the primary, ecclesially enacted God-talk) that the danger of a conceptual idolatry that distorts affirmative discourse can occur. And it is precisely this danger that is addressed by the corrective move of negative theology, a move that can be undertaken in at least two ways.

The first is to reintegrate the canon of Scripture and dogma into the dialectic of revelation, which is the dialectic of the divine veiling in the unveiling. This was the path taken most energetically in the twentieth century by Karl Barth, who "splits" the economy's *est* into the event of divine self-revelation, which occurs "again and again," and the human witness to it. Consequently, Barth understands the corrective moment of negative theology to be an integral moment in the movement of affirmative theology itself, thereby turning theological discourse into an essentially dialectical enterprise. While this strategy successfully overcomes the danger of construing conceptual idols, through a ceaseless dialectical self-correction of each particular affirmation, the force of the dialectic falls back onto the proclamatory and liturgical enactment of the economy's *est*.[27] Precisely because Barth's strategy splits the *est* into event and witness, it ultimately undermines the economy's concrete, historically embodied *Widerständigkeit*, its "resistancy."[28] Yet that said, dialectical theology still remains the best option available under the conceptual condition of the univocity of being. Indeed, any attempt to overcome the problematic implications of dialectical theology would need to reconsider the *analogia entis*, the analogy of being[29] — that is, specifically, as an analogy of participation.[30]

Thus we turn to the second way of undertaking the corrective move of negative theology. This way does not attempt to overcome the definite character of the economy's *est* as such. Rather, it corrects and thus brings into strongest relief the situatedness of the affirmative discourse *sub conditione creaturae*.

II. The Difference between *Est* and *Esse*: Negative Theology, or Apophasis

> *Deum nemo vidit umquam: unigenitus Filius, qui est in sinu Patris, ipse enarravit.* (John 1:18)

We will in no way be able even to begin to do justice to the rich and complex history of negative theology in the following short remarks. Rather, all we shall focus on here are two distinctions crucial for understanding negative theology as a necessary and intrinsic moment of the theological discourse: (1) the distinction between (a) the category of sin and (b) the category of creation, each entailing a distinct negative moment of its own; and (2) the distinction between (a) a reflection upon the difference between Creator and creature that is grounded in the economy and (b) a seemingly similar reflection on this difference that does not give antecedence to the economy.[31] In the first instance of this second distinction (2a), negative theology, while gesturing toward the ineffability of the divine *esse*, always remains embedded in and arises from the economy's *est* and therefore leads to what I will call "iconic theology." In the second instance (2b), negative theology develops the potential of "erasing" affirmative theology as such and consequently facilitates the ultimate erosion of the economy's *est*.

First, the distinction between sin and creation. Sin is to be understood as the incurvature of the creature upon itself and therefore the radical estrangement of the creature from the Creator.[32] According to the inner drama of the economy, God enters this comprehensive horizon of sin in a form that radically negates the logic incessantly produced by sin itself, the logic of "wisdom and signs"; that is, God negates the very framework that aims at ascertaining God under the condition of sin and therefore at enfolding God into the incurvature of sin.[33] This is the dynamic most radically addressed in a theology of the cross and its ensuing negative discourse.[34] Yet it is of crucial importance to understand that the negative discourse of a theology of the cross is nothing other than the precise form of affirmative theology in which the economy's *est* is articulated *sub conditione peccati*, that is, as negating the negativity of sin itself. The negation proper to the theology of the cross therefore is not the negation of a prior given. Rather, it is the appearance of the kerygma's affirmation as the negation of the negativity that sin itself is.

Negative theology as *theologia*, in contrast, considers and corrects the nature of theological discourse, which, insofar as it reflects the economy's *est*, is not determined anymore by the sinner's incurvature[35] but nevertheless remains a discourse *sub conditione creaturae* — a condition that is not overcome and never, in principle, will be. Therefore, it is profoundly misleading to play off against each other a "negative theology" of the cross and a "negative theology" that brings the nature of theological discourse *sub conditione creaturae* into the strongest relief. Even if not completely unheard of, the identification of creatureliness with sin has always been renounced by Christian orthodoxy as a Manichean heresy. As long as the illegitimacy of this identification is acknowledged, the negativity of a theology of the cross and the apophasis inherent in the discourse of *theologia* should be understood as fundamentally different yet fully compatible moments of theological discourse.

Before we turn to the second critical distinction, we need first to register two central points about the basic strategy of negation that was put in place for the Christian tradition of apophaticism paradigmatically by Denys the Areopagite. Denys Turner characterized the strategy with exemplary clarity: "It is of the greatest consequence to see that negative language about God is no more apophatic in itself than is affirmative language. The apophatic is the linguistic strategy of somehow showing by means of language that which lies beyond language. It is not done, and it cannot be done, by means of negative utterances alone which are no less bits of ordinarily intelligible human discourse than are affirmations. Our negations, therefore, fail of God as much as do our affirmations."[36] It matters crucially from what source the affirmative language in use arises, whether from the economy's *est* or from the *theologia* that intends God solely on the basis of the Creator/creature difference. In each case, the cataphatic takes on a very different character. If it is essentially one of two strategies of negativity in *theologia*, negative propositions belong essentially to the cataphatic, as Turner rightly emphasizes: "For there is a very great difference between the strategy of *negative propositions* and the strategy of *negating the propositional;* between that of the *negative image* and that of the *negation of imagery*. The first of each of these pairs belongs to the cataphatic in theology, and only the second is the strategy of the apophatic."[37]

Yet in Maximus we encounter a slight but decisive variance with respect to Denys. Because of his central focus on the incarnate Word, Maximus roots the cataphatic christologically, that is, in the economy's *est*.[38] Hence, he comes to regard the distinction between the cataphatic and the apophatic as reflective of the distinction between *oikonomia* and *theologia* — in spite of his own otherwise strong indebtedness to Denys's apophatic theology.[39]

We have come, then, to the second critical distinction. While the distinction in its actual use might not be as clear as the systematic theologian would wish, we nevertheless have here two different theological strategies of the cataphatic: one starts from the plenitude of names (cataphasis) called forth by the ascending move of *theologia*, driven by the Creator/creature distinction and complemented by the negation of all imagery, including negative images (apophasis); the other understands cataphasis as the very unfolding of the economy's *est*, having its center in the incarnation.

This difference carries significant theological consequence. For if the cataphatic arises from the economy's *est* and the apophatic move of *theologia* intends the divine *esse* as the Trinity (the way Lossky insists), negative theology is salutarily prevented from developing a dynamic that would ultimately erase the affirmative, giving rise to an ultimate *Verstummen*, "falling silent," before the ineffable mystery.[40] The knowing silence of the apophatic correction, rather, remains inherently linked to the economy's *est* such that the end of the apophatic correction always remains the definitive, albeit incomprehensible, subject of *theologia,* and therefore also of the *oikonomia* — the triune God.

Yet we might ask, what if the affirmative moment is indeed genuinely located in the *theologia?* In this case, affirmative theology is nothing other than that mode of the cataphatic naming that draws upon the Creator as the cause of all creatures, a mode that ultimately needs to be overcome by its apophatic negation, especially when the triune God fails to be the specific "end" of *theologia* but comes to function as a moment of theological naming to be negatively transcended in the apophatic ascent beyond all names.[41]

In short, if both the affirmative and the negative are indeed just that, strategies of the negative discourse of *theologia,* it will always be the case that the negating force of the apophasis will eventually erase the cataphatic. This is because here cataphasis is isolated from the very particularity of its self-affirming subject (matter) in the economy's *est* and rests solely on its conceptual reservoir *sub conditione creaturae.* But this means that cataphasis rests finally on its own finitude and on the univocity of being, which both are in need of apophatic overcoming in the ascent of *theologia* as it intends divine *esse.* In other words, this kind of abstractly affirmative theology, precisely because of its necessarily onto-theological mode of operation — abstractly, we can only affirm what is given to us *sub conditione creaturae* — indeed calls for its apophatic annihilation. Yet insofar as affirmative theology is concretely affirmative in arising from the economy's *est,* the affirmative moment is not a speculative and therefore conceptually driven characteristic. Rather, the affirmative moment is of a derivative and secondary nature that depends on the contingently yet de facto antecedent reality of the kerygma, its proclamatory and liturgical enactment in the eucharistic worship, and its normative formulation in dogma and ecclesial doctrine. Hence, only by relying upon and assuming the threefold affirmative character of the *est* does Christian theology develop an affirmative discourse. The apophatic moment, on the contrary, is a purely reflective phenomenon set into motion by conceptually attending to the unfathomable difference between Creator and creature. As such, it necessarily negates affirmative theology's conceptuality *sub conditione creaturae,* and indeed, precisely this is its therapeutic task. Yet in accomplishing this task, negative theology can never erase the very source from which affirmative theology incessantly arises, that is, the particularity of the economy and its liturgical recollection.

Taking this peculiar asymmetry between affirmative and negative theology into account, we are led to the conclusion that there indeed also occurs an asymmetrical "negation" of negative theology. This negation obviously does not occur simply in the form of a renewed affirmation, just on a higher level of synthesis, that sublates, as it were, the negated affirmation and the negation that achieved it — a synthesis merely waiting for a superior negation. Rather, in proper Christian theological discourse, negative theology finds itself interrupted, as it were, again and again by the ongoing gratuitous self-giving of the gift — in short, by the economy's *est*. For negative theology, as a moment of proper Christian theological discourse, cannot remove itself from the very originating location of this discourse in its liturgical recollection nor absent itself from its normative rendition in dogma and ecclesial doctrine. In other words, even while Denys or, later, Cusanus locate the cataphatic squarely in the strategy of *theologia*, it is this latter feature, their commitment to the doctrinal and liturgical implications of the economy's *est*, that fundamentally distinguishes even their negative theologies from the kind of radical apophasis advanced by Fichte in his second *Wissenschaftslehre* from the year 1804 or by Derrida in various of his works.[42] Because of their varying strategies of obliterating the concept, Fichte as well as Derrida have to annihilate the affirmative moment — without an economy to fall back upon.

III. The Icon: The Negation Christologically Assumed and Transfigured

> *Qui est imago Dei invisibilis, primogenitus omnis creaturae.*
> (Colossians 1:15)

The ultimate reason for the difference between the two kinds of negative theology rests therefore in Christology. The critical question is whether negative theology itself is christologically configured or whether it is conceptually abstracted from Christology. In other words, either Christology itself creates a difference in the negative dynamic of *theologia* so that the latter remains an intrinsic moment of Christology, or negative theology remains purely bound to the Creator/creature difference but internally undifferentiated in a way that leads the apophatic eventually to erase the cataphatic.

The christological difference in this regard is the following: the negation of negative theology is not a new affirmation that in an ascending move sublates the prior affirmation and its negation. Rather, the negation of negative theology occurs in the form of its ongoing interruption through the continuous granting of the economy's *est*, the incarnation of the Word. Yet how should we conceive of this distinct christological negation of negative theology? Lossky points in the right direction when he states: "The apophatic element, as the consciousness of intellectual failure, is present in various forms in most Christian theologians (exceptions are rare). We can say as well that it is not foreign to sacred art, where failure of artistic means of expression, deliberately conspicuous in the very art of the iconographer, corresponds to the learned ignorance of the theologian. However, just as iconographic 'antinaturalistic' apophaticism is not iconoclasm, so also the antirationalistic negative way is not gnosimachian: it cannot result in the suppression of theological thought without detriment to the essential fact of Christianity: the incarnation of the Word, the central event of revelation, which makes iconography as well as theology possible."[43]

Precisely because of its essentially christological character, the icon can serve as the appropriate analogy for the proper relationship between affirmative and negative theology as they together arise from the economy and, most eminently, from its christological center.[44] In its very intentional artistic schematism, the icon assumes the negative moment christologically. It is precisely the acknowledgment of the inexhaustible divine *esse* in and behind the *est* of God's incarnation in Christ that not only makes the icon possible in the first place but first and foremost grants it its *eikon*, its image (Col 1:15).

Thus the icon is to be understood as the artistic rendition of a peculiar dynamic between the ineffable and incomprehensible divine *esse* and the economy's *est*. Without the schematic negation of the *est*, the icon would simply render an idolatrous depiction that a spectator could "seize" and thus "comprehend" with his gaze. And an ensuing iconoclasm would be the requisite equivalent to a negative theology, annihilating idolatrous pictorial transgressions *sub conditione creaturae*. Yet the icon's schematism does not merely prevent any objectifying comprehension by way of situating the *est* of the economy in the golden horizon of the unfathomable divine *esse*. Rather, it is the latter's unique fusion with the particularity of the icon's *est*, often creating an inverted iconic perspective, that also draws the spectator into the icon's own gaze.[45] Thus the icon holds the divine *esse* and the economic *est* in a dynamic yet specific relationship such that the divine *esse* manifests itself in the *est* of its *eikon* yet remains in its self-manifestation the manifestation of its incomprehensibility. The primacy of the icon's sheer givenness over against its corrective, quasi-negating schematism precisely reflects the continuous dependence of the negative moment of theological reflection upon the economy's antecedence. Most crucially, the *est* is *eikon* only insofar as it participates fully in the divine *esse*, and it is only on the grounds of this participation that the *est* matters, first of all in word and sacrament, and then, somewhat removed from it but nevertheless in clear proximity, also in dogma. Moreover, it is the very dynamic of participation that ultimately accounts for any inversion of the speculative gaze in the encounter with an icon, as also for the inversion of one's own being in the encounter with word and sacrament.

It is only appropriate that our reflections about the proper location of negative theology in the overall matrix of theological discourse end with the question of the conceptual icon and thus lead into asking for the distinct discursive practice in which the economy's *est*, undergirded by the *est* of creation, is conceived as participating in the divine *esse* itself. Iconic theology entails a dynamic in which the ascent from an *est* that comprises both creation and economy christologically to the divine *esse* is rooted in an antecedent participation caused and sustained by the divine *esse* itself. Yet precisely because of its inexhaustibly causative antecedence, the divine *esse* remains incomprehensible, that is, in no way conceptually "at hand." At the same time, the economy's *est* is preserved from its conceptual reification, because it "is" for us only insofar as it participates in the divine *esse* and is perpetually given to us as a gift from it; hence, while being received *sub conditione creaturae*, the *est* cannot be conceptually fixed within the univocal horizon of the *conditio creaturae*. Rather, the *est*, while offering itself definitively in dogma to the concept, arises inexhaustibly from the divine *esse*, thereby incessantly calling forth the apophatic correction while constantly interrupting it. The dynamic that holds these two moments together *is* the analogy of participation.[46]

II. *Eleutheria* — or, Free to Live with God

7. (Re-)Forming Freedom: Freedom's Fate in Modernity and Protestantism's Antinomian Captivity

What Is Freedom?

If we had to name the one idea that encapsulates for most Protestants what was fundamentally at stake in the Reformation, the clear winner would be *freedom*. Surely the Reformation was all about freedom. And certainly Protestantism is all about freedom. Yet interestingly, and most disturbingly for those who regard Protestantism as the religion of freedom, Pope John Paul II's 1993 encyclical *Veritatis Splendor/The Splendor of Truth*[1] is also all about freedom. This surprising alliance obviously begs the question, What is "freedom"?

As soon as we begin to seriously attend to this question, we will understand why the French philosopher Jean-Luc Nancy recently observed: "If nothing is more common today than demanding or defending freedom in the spheres of morality, law, or politics . . . , then nothing is less articulated or problematized, in turn, than the nature and stakes of what we call 'freedom.'"[2] Because this is arguably the case, many take it for granted that all we can say is that freedom is "polyvalent" — and accordingly, the very essence of what "postmodernity" is all about. Though the latter is not beyond dispute, it is hard to deny that we had to debase freedom before we could "discover" its polyvalence. This was observed more than one hundred years ago by John Henry Newman in his prophetic indictment of what "freedom of conscience" has come to mean:

> If conscience has its rights, it is because duties are implied. But in our day, in the minds of a great number of people, the rights and freedom of conscience serve only to dispense conscience. They would like to ignore the

Lawgiver and Judge, and be free of all interior obligation. . . . In former times, conscience was a strict counselor. Nowadays it has yielded its place to a sham unheard of in eighteen centuries, which would never have taken people in if they had known of it: the right to do as you please.[3]

Like a coin handled for too long by too many hands, "freedom" has lost its clear imprint. We still circulate the coin — the more quickly and the more frequently the less it is worth. Yet we no longer know what "freedom" means. Is it what is realized when we create the meaning and the values of our own lives? Is it what is brought about when we exercise the right of making our own choices without being answerable to anyone? Is it what is mandated by political liberation and self-determination? Is it what is presupposed by moral responsibility? Is it what comes about when we receive the gospel of God's free grace? Is it several of these? Or all of them? Or is "freedom" simply an equivocal term that covers fundamentally different and ultimately incompatible things? Not only many coins in various currencies — polyvalent freedom — but next to coins, tokens and chips of all sorts?

What makes the encyclical *Veritatis Splendor* such a significant document is that here we deal with one coin only and, moreover, with a coin that suddenly shows again a clear and distinct imprint. Gone is the ambiguity, the polyvalence that haunts the late modern coinage of freedom. Moreover, "after *Veritatis Splendor*," Protestantism — for many the religion of freedom — faces the question whether it is ready to handle the coin offered in the encyclical, with its renewed, distinctly visible and distinctly challenging imprint. The challenge represented by this imprint, which already resided in Newman's words, consists in the intrinsic relationship between freedom and law. This challenge, immediately alarming to late modern sensibilities about freedom, is what I wish to address.

Three Times Freedom and Its Opposite

Yet before moving on we must briefly recall the ways in which the concept of freedom is most commonly employed. In order to do this, we can best concretize the term "freedom" by relating it to its opposite — a clear sign of its multifaceted and almost intractable nature.

There is, *first*, freedom versus interference. The latter can appear in varying degrees as restraint, coercion, or, worse, bondage. Here freedom denotes the absence of interference by others. Usually called "negative freedom," it constitutes the core of the venerable Anglo-Saxon tradition of political liberty and has made its way from there into modern political liberalism.⁴ Its driving force is humans' contingent and boundless willfulness, which consequently calls for an external limitation: the law. The law serves to curb this intrinsically interfering willfulness for the sake of protecting everyone else's negative freedom. Freedom and law are related, yet in a completely extrinsic and antagonistic way: the law is negative freedom's termination.

There is, *second*, freedom versus determination. Here freedom stands for "free will" and refers to our capacity of initiating actions that are described by our intentions.⁵ Modernity typically has considered the source and condition of free will to be the "positive freedom" of self-determination and its driving force to be reason legislating itself as the will's law.⁶ Consequently, the law appears as the internal form of reason that continuously directs the will. Positive freedom thus amounts essentially to rational self-mastery, an idea in which Western philosophical thought has been passionately invested. Since the Enlightenment, freedom in this sense constitutes the core of moral agency and responsibility; moreover, it forms the very basis on which rest the claim and legitimation of ordinary humans' rational self-government.⁷ Rational law thus becomes the medium in and through which freedom realizes — that is, socially embodies — itself.⁸

And there is, *third*, freedom *schlechthin*, freedom as such. It is the constitutive absence of its opposite that characterizes this fundamental concept of freedom. When its opposite is absent, freedom can only be an attribute of that which is its own origin, that is, precisely, the unoriginate origin. The Christian tradition therefore has always considered freedom in this sense to be nothing other than a necessary divine attribute and as such to be strictly distinguished from created freedom — the latter being a divine gift that has its own created form.⁹ The "law" of this freedom, that is, divine freedom, can only be God's triune life itself and this divine life's "being": love.¹⁰

As soon as we lose this distinction between *uncreated* and *created* freedom — and the latter's ongoing dependence on the former, the gift on the Giver — both negative and positive freedom as articulated above become questionable.¹¹ Both negative and positive freedom presuppose the prior reality of created freedom. And precisely here the nature of freedom itself is ultimately at stake. On this level, freedom is not determined by its opposite but by the fundamental relationship between freedom and truth, that is, between the gift of created freedom and its divine Giver.¹² Therefore, in the following discussion, *genuine freedom denotes the truthful enactment of created existence*. Because this enactment continuously depends on its source, the gift on the Giver, genuine freedom must be understood most fundamentally as a *receiving*. The truthful enactment of created existence — genuine freedom — thus completely depends on its prior receiving. Yet a receiving of what, we might ask. Suffice it to say that genuine freedom understood as "receiving" will open the avenue for a fundamental rethinking of the law in relation to freedom.

The Argument

My argument will unfold in four steps. *First,* I will sketch in broad strokes the way the modern notion of freedom has set the stage on which now also Protestantism moves. If we want to grasp the sweeping theological intervention of *Veritatis Splendor,* we need to understand the claim that is encapsulated in the modern notion of freedom. It is the freedom of the self that demands a position of sovereignty in relation to the body and the natural world — in short, the freedom of the *Promethean self.* It is the self for whom freedom has ultimately come to mean *autopoiesis,* self-creation: I am genuinely free only if my identity is the creation of my own will. Everything that might bind me, that might restrict me, that might direct me without myself having chosen the direction is regarded by the Promethean self as estranging and oppressive — whether bodies, laws, traditions, conventions, or something as simple as taxes. Yet this modern daydream of Promethean freedom is producing its own "postmodern" nightmare: systemic control and the pervasive feeling of freedom's being eclipsed by anonymous forces in politics, economics, and everyone else's will to power, masked as freedom. The modern daydream and the postmodern nightmare belong inherently together: license produces its own other — legalistic and systemic enforcement.

To be clearly understood: The target of my criticism is not the modern concept of autonomy in the rigorous way Kant defined it.[13] Yet neither do I regard that concept as defensible on its own terms. While undoubtedly rigorously argued and heroically conceived in its own way, Kantian "autonomy" depends on presuppositions inherently beyond its grasp, and it is by no means just a regrettable accident that autonomy thus conceived has declined into its late modern distortions of individual sovereignty, will to power, and license. These three, rather, are "preprogrammed" in the very concept of autonomy itself because, despite its impressive internal coherence, the ethics of autonomy depends on resources it ultimately cannot account for.[14]

The *thesis* guiding this first section will be this: When the ethics of autonomy construes freedom to be the very core of subjectivity, it eliminates from the very outset the law's otherness and therefore reception. In order to secure the fundamental principle of subjectivity, the ethics of autonomy has to conceptually subordinate the law to freedom. It does so by developing the concept of the law from the concept of freedom. It is thus freedom's own law that is being conceived. At the same time, the ethics of autonomy cannot see created freedom as genuinely received freedom. Therefore, the freedom grounding the principle of subjectivity has to turn into an unoriginate origin that ultimately absorbs the law. Yet without the law as its received form, freedom turns out to be the will that only wills itself. This is why autonomy based on the single principle of subjectivity must ultimately decline into those substitutes that today reign under the name of autonomy: individual sovereignty, will to power, and license.

Against the background of this problematic I will, *second,* consider the vision of freedom put before us in *Veritatis Splendor,* a vision in which Christ, God's goodness as the human's ultimate end, and our created embodiedness form a dense and rich matrix of participatory freedom. To this vision of genuine freedom the encyclical most importantly links God's law in a way that is as compelling as it is complex.[15] Intimately connected to the way the encyclical conceives freedom in relation to the law is one particularly controversial teaching. This connection has rarely been recognized but is, in my eyes, crucial. I am speaking of the encyclical's teaching on "intrinsically evil acts," acts that are wrong per se and that, in their enactment — while asserting the freedom of indifference — precisely undercut and destroy genuine freedom. While I will argue that this teaching is inherent in the encyclical's concept of freedom, I will not offer the kind of argument necessary to fully substantiate this claim. That would require a chapter of its own.

Rather, I will, *third,* turn to Protestantism "after *Veritatis Splendor*" and argue that *Veritatis Splendor*'s vision of freedom brings into clear relief what I shall term the antinomian captivity of contemporary Protestantism. Yet instead of chasing down this unself-conscious and therefore elusive phenomenon in contemporary Protestantism, I will look at the outspoken antinomian movement as it emerged in the very center of the Lutheran Reformation in Wittenberg. Surprisingly, it is *Veritatis Splendor*'s pressure on this issue that offers fresh access to Luther's largely unknown and therefore regrettably unappreciated opposition to antinomianism.[16] Together with other less known elements of his thought, Luther's unequivocal rejection of antinomianism offers a richer and more nuanced picture than the standard Protestant account of Luther, which all too often has only served to justify the regnant antinomian leanings. To some it might thus come as a surprise that Luther, no less than Aquinas and Calvin, would prohibit any antinomian displacement[17] of the law in the Christian faith. While Luther and *Veritatis Splendor* clearly disagree on some central issues of the way freedom and law relate, we will appreciate Luther's own insistence on the law's ongoing importance much more after having been exposed to the challenge of *Veritatis Splendor*'s teaching on freedom and law.

Finally, I will pose ten theses "after the Promethean self" that point out the way freedom will need to be theologically rethought in order to overcome the antinomian captivity of contemporary Protestantism. And yes — the subtext of these considerations is a variation on a theological theme that regrettably seems to have become the special preoccupation of Lutheran theology: *law and gospel.* I regard it, nevertheless, as a theme that all of Christian theology has to come to terms with in one way or another. When we repress this theme by prematurely announcing its demise, we only continue to be haunted by it unawares.[18] Moreover, my drawing upon the thought of the "late Luther" in order to address Protestantism's antinomian captivity "after *Veritatis Splendor*" might suggest to some readers that the following considerations are of real concern only to Lutherans. Yet nothing would be further from the truth. To the contrary, the diagnosis in the first section, the engagement of *Veritatis Splendor* in the second, and the prescription of Luther's "late" theology in the third are pressingly relevant for mainline Protestantism across the board. The antinomian captivity is anything but a strictly Lutheran prerogative. It is a phenomenon of ecumenical dimensions.

I. Modernity's Daydream and Postmodernity's Nightmare

Modernity's central protagonist, undoubtedly, is freedom. Hegel once observed that "world history is progress in the consciousness of freedom, a progress that we have to understand in its necessity."[19] His famous pronouncement documents in striking ways how deeply modern philosophy is absorbed with its main protagonist. If we wanted to give a full account of freedom's fate in modernity, it would have to be a novel — a late modern novel, of course — complex, melancholic, and ultimately tragic in the modern sense of inconclusively open-ended and unfulfilled.[20]

It is precisely freedom's unhappy fate in modernity that creates the backdrop for *Veritatis Splendor*'s teaching on freedom. Indeed, there is no way to fully comprehend *Veritatis Splendor*'s sweeping reconceptualization of freedom (in which the encyclical moves far beyond the in-house battles with certain schools of Roman Catholic moral theology) unless we appreciate this larger problem that the encyclical presupposes. It would, of course, be quite impossible to offer here an even remotely satisfying account of such a complex and highly contested phenomenon. After all, modernity's nature itself is at stake in the very narration of freedom's fate.[21] Instead of the comprehensive narrative the topic clearly demands, I will have to settle for a representative typology that only intimates the tragic rise and fall of a freedom that conceived itself as unoriginate origin — constitutive of the subject's subjectivity and, identical with it, reason's original spontaneity.

For this limited purpose, the following typology will fuse two images of classical mythology: Icarus and Prometheus. It is modernity's sense of moral sovereignty and self-sufficiency that Prometheus — challenger of Zeus and benefactor of humanity — so strikingly reflects. With his poem "Prometheus," Goethe sets him a memorable monument that elevates him into the paradigm of what modern freedom is fundamentally about. "Here I sit, forming men / In my own image, / A race, that is like me, / Made to suffer, to weep, / To take pleasure and to enjoy itself, / And to pay no attention to your kind, / Like me."[22]

The very fate of modernity's Promethean claim of freedom, in contrast, is captured by Icarus's fall. King Minos of Crete, so the archaic story goes, imprisoned Daedalus, a legendary inventor and craftsman, together with his son Icarus, for the help that Daedalus had rendered to Minos's wife, Pasiphaë. In order to escape, Daedalus constructed two pairs of artificial wings, and he and his son Icarus flew away. Yet despite his father's warnings, Icarus soared too high and thus approached the sun too closely so that the wax of his wings melted and he drowned in the sea.[23]

The typology will take its structure and inner dynamic from the three stages of the Promethean self's Icaric flight: a state of uneasy and laborious suspension, a steep, soaring ascent, and an eventual stalling and fall. When in the following I identify each stage of the flight of freedom with a particular thinker of overarching significance, I of course do not wish to imply that this philosopher's thought "caused" in any direct sense one distinct way of conceiving modernity's protagonist. Nor do I want to suggest that each of these thinkers just happens to be the societal "product" of a certain notion of freedom. Obviously, the multiple ways religious, philosophical, cultural, political, and economic factors interrelate are far more complex than that. Yet my typology does imply the following minimal claims: *first*, that ideas matter in the way cultures and societies configure themselves and, *second*, that false ideas ultimately have destructive consequences.[24]

That said, I will briefly identify the three stages of my Icaric typology: freedom's uneasy suspension *(Kant)*; its rising and soaring *(Fichte)*; and its stalling and subsequent fall *(Nietzsche)*.[25] The body, society, and the world take their revenge by announcing not only the fall but also the end of the Promethean self as the "death of the subject." Yet the ghost of modernity's daydream of Promethean freedom still haunts the late modern scene enough to cause postmodern nightmares of intractable fragmentation, plurality, porosity, and indeterminacy.[26] This, of course, is a highly contested but far from indefensible reading.[27]

Kant's Uneasy Suspension

As has often been observed, Kant's philosophy completes the "Copernican turn" to the subject initiated by Descartes.[28] Yet in Kant's transcendental idealism, the subject's creative intellectual powers finally gain a constitutive role in the way knowledge about the world is construed. Because of reason's new constructive capacity, the human becomes sovereign in the *noumenal* world, the world of pure reason, and is precisely thereby promoted to Promethean status. Unsurprisingly, freedom occupies the very center of Kant's critical philosophy.[29] Yet this center is concealed, since — for profound reasons — it remains inaccessible to the self-reflective grasp of reason. Pure reason, as Kant argues in the famous third antinomy of his *Critique of Pure Reason,* while it is unable to disprove the possibility of freedom, can conceive only determination.[30] In other words, freedom cannot be the possible object of scientific or critical "metaphysical" knowledge. Rather, as Kant claims in his *Critique of Practical Reason,* freedom must be conceived as the fundamental postulate of practical reason — which is nothing other than pure reason in its practical intent.

The argument goes like this: Pure reason in its practical intent finds in itself a structure of reasonable willing. This "fact of reason" is the moral law that reason in its practical intent itself legislates.[31] Yet the very possibility of this presupposes freedom, which thus becomes the fundamental postulate of practical reason. As such, freedom cannot be conceived but must be presupposed as the "unoriginate origin"[32] of the pure spontaneity of reason (in its speculative as well as its practical respect).

Yet as Kant continues to work out the concept of freedom in *Religion within the Limits of Reason Alone,* freedom carries in itself the fundamental split between the freedom of indifference *(Willkür)* — pure spontaneity — and the freedom of reason *(Wille).* Kant identifies concrete, finite freedom with the will's operation, which, in turn, is identical with reason in its practical capacity.[33] Therefore, concrete freedom is always realized in the moral act. Its "ground" remains hidden in the mystery of the transcendental ego, which — because it is the spontaneity of thinking itself — cannot grasp itself in thought.[34]

Kant's Promethean self is embodied, yet tragically so. While Kant is able to overcome the heteronomy of the law in his account of autonomy, the body becomes the locus of heteronomy per se.[35] The body's ongoing "otherness" is clearly betrayed by Kant's account of virtue. For him, virtue is the will's capacity to subject all incentives of sensibility to the demands of the moral law, that is, to the will's own legislation and concrete enactment of autonomy. In marked contrast to Aristotle and Aquinas, for Kant the body does not participate in the person's enactment of freedom but remains endlessly contrarian. And precisely this is the human as Promethean self: being a "resident alien" in an essentially foreign environment in which the only means of self-assertion is to overcome again and again and eventually to bring into submission the unthematized other, the body. Under these conditions, concrete freedom is exercised as the rational self realizes itself in the course of virtuously ruling its bodily acts — that is, through the power of the will as guided by reason. The unoriginate origin of freedom is therefore realized, *first*, in the self's rule over the body, the unruly other; *second*, in the self's legislative activity of maxim-forming according to the categorical imperative; and *third*, in the creation of a society and eventually a world in which the rule of the moral law becomes the constitutive matrix of all human interactions.[36]

The Promethean self has taken off on its Icaric flight. Yet it is by no means an easy flight but rather an uneasy suspension — the powerful pull of the "earthly" other beneath and the open universe above, with the moral law as the only compass. Is this the realization of freedom, this laborious, endless flapping of the wings of virtue, always in danger of being pulled down by powerful incentives, and only sustained by the ideas of practical reason: freedom, immortality, and the rewards of happiness granted by an omniscient, omnipotent, and just deity? Will it not eventually be necessary to stabilize this flight by overcoming its uneasy and laborious suspension? — by seizing the opportunity of a powerful upward current, soaring to heights that might put the self irrevocably beyond the reach of the ceaseless gravitational pull of bodily incentives? If the ground of freedom can be conceived, might this not revolutionize the gravitational forces working on the Promethean self? Might, then, the self not be irresistibly pulled upward into absolute freedom? This is precisely the pathos that drives Fichte's fundamental inquiry into the idea of freedom.

Fichte's Soaring

In Kant's thought, there is a complex system of checks and balances that limits and constrains the Promethean self in relation to reality's objectivity.

Yet his most ingenious student, Fichte, the father of German Idealism, removes these checks and balances; consequently, the daydream of the Promethean self soars to dizzying heights. While for Kant reason plays a constitutive role in cognition, understanding still depends on the fundamental input of the senses. The "thing-in-itself" secures, so to speak, reality's irresolvable otherness and objectivity — to be sure, construed and thus fundamentally mediated by reason's faculties, but ultimately still "given."[37] Yet a consistent conception of the unoriginate origin of freedom, as Fichte undertakes it, makes this assumption impossible.[38] Moving beyond Kant, Fichte's goal is to "break the enslaving chains of the thing-in-itself and develop a system in which freedom [is] absolute."[39] In order to achieve this goal, he has to demonstrate the exclusive causality of freedom by way of epistemologically deriving the world as a whole from freedom. Therefore, in his *Science of Knowledge* Fichte argues — contra Kant — that no analysis of the components that establish self-consciousness is able to account for its reality. Rather, self-consciousness presupposes the pure activity of the absolutely unconditioned I. As Dieter Henrich has shown in detail, Fichte's fundamental insight is his recognition of the I as self-positing.[40] For Fichte, self-positing is the fundamental act of production that grounds all other acts. In other words, it is the very act that grounds freedom. It does not come as a surprise that in the course of his argument Fichte fundamentally revises reason itself, namely, as creative positing, as imaginative making, as "poiesis."[41]

It would lead too far afield to expand on Fichte's hermetic but ingenious epistemological reflections at this point. Yet we need to attend to one important distinction he makes in his early *Foundations of the Complete Science of Knowledge* (1794) that gives his concept of freedom its decisive dynamic — a dynamic that was crucial for his influence on political utopianism.[42] Although Fichte construes the I as the original one substance, the I is clearly limited by the not-I.[43] So he sees himself forced to distinguish between the absolute and the finite I.

> Insofar as the I is limited by the not-I, it is finite; as such, i.e. as it is posited through its own absolute activity, it is infinite. Both moments of it, its infiniteness and its finitude, need to be united. Yet such a union is impossible per se. For a long time this argument can be appeased by mediation: the infinite limits the finite. Yet finally, as the complete impossibility of this union becomes clear, the finite as such needs to be abolished; all the limitations must disappear; the infinite I needs to remain as the One and All.[44]

Of greatest interest to us here are not the epistemological but the moral and the political implications of this fundamental claim. And Fichte cannot be blamed for leaving them obscure. Since freedom needs to be understood as the fundamental act of the I's self-positing, it becomes the project of the I's ongoing self-realization in the world. In his *Science of Ethics,* Fichte puts the central issue in this way:

> As has often been said, independence [*Selbständigkeit*] — which is our ultimate goal — consists in the fact that everything depends on me and I depend on nothing; that what I will occurs in the complete world of senses [*Sinnenwelt*], that it occurs absolutely and merely through the fact that I will it — in the same way that it occurs in my body, the starting point of my absolute causality. The world has to become for me what my body is to me. Although this goal cannot be reached, I have to continually approximate it, i.e. to treat everything in the world of senses such that it becomes a means for reaching this final goal. This approximation is my final goal.[45]

It is crucial to keep in mind that Fichte does not intend this approximation to be understood in a transmoral way. Yet the moral principle, conscience,[46] becomes dangerously subjective for Fichte and ultimately unable to contain the finite I's will to approximate complete independence. It is also important to realize, as Friedrich Mildenberger rightly points out, that Fichte is hiding an equivocation in the startling claim "the world has to become for me what my body is to me."[47] The "me" in Fichte's statement is not identical with itself. Rather, the I of the ultimate goal is the absolute I — spirit — or freely willing humanity as such; the I of the finite goal is the individual, embodied person. The difference between the two is freedom's endless task. "I am to *act free* in order to *become free.*"[48] Thus freedom's upward soaring is a never-ending movement, as Gillespie aptly states: "For Fichte . . . the human will can change the world, and moral satisfaction thus comes only from the constant use of one's freedom to effect such a transformation. The end of this transformation is the completion of freedom, that is, the liberation of the empirical I from all constraints. Because this goal can never be attained but only approached, striving always has a moral goal. Fichte's thought thus establishes an ideal that can never be attained as a spur to an activity that can never be completed."[49] Icarus cannot become one with the sky.

While it cannot be argued here, I think it is possible to make a reasonable case for reading the late Fichte, the late Schelling, and Hegel as different attempts to get a controlling grasp of this all too dangerous soaring of the

Promethean self's daydream of freedom by rethinking freedom first of all in relation to the divine — although they are in their own ways deeply problematic speculations.[50] Yet these attempts come too late. The powerful turn to the subject cannot be overcome by higher synthesis. While Kierkegaard forcefully reasserts the principle of subjectivity "after Hegel," the "young Hegelians" only reinforce the gravitational pull of the body (Feuerbach) and of the socioeconomic structures (Marx). Not the sky but the earth becomes the end of the Promethean self's Icaric flight. Yet Fichte's utopian logic, freedom as fundamental self-positing and ultimate self-realization, still shines through in the early Marx:

> A being is truly independent when it stands on its own feet, and it only stands on its own feet when it owes its existence to itself. A human being, which lives from somebody else's grace, sees him- or herself as dependent being. Yet I fully live from somebody else's grace when I not only owe to him my life's support but when he, in addition, has created my life, when he is the source of my life. And my life necessarily has such a ground outside of itself as long as it is not my own creation.[51]

And Marx is not the only inheritor of Fichte's radical, poietic concept of freedom. While Marx turns it ultimately into a utopian political project that is more in debt to Hegel's speculative account of a world historical process, there is another inheritor of Fichte's willful freedom: Friedrich Nietzsche.

Nietzsche's Stalling and Subsequent Fall

Nietzsche fuses the Fichtean will of freedom — mediated by Schopenhauer[52] — with the post-Hegelian reemergence of the body. His goal is to put human beings finally on their own feet as *Übermenschen* (i.e., via self-overcoming) and to reintegrate them fully into the totality of nature. The truly pure human being will thus find a second, childlike innocence (to which atheism belongs): "The human being is in the middle of nature always the child as such. This child may very well from time to time dream a deeply fearsome dream; yet when the child opens its eyes again, it always finds itself again in paradise."[53]

There are two moments in Nietzsche's thought that need to be distinguished. *First*, Nietzsche "stalls" the Promethean self's soaring flight of freedom by radically rejecting the traditional understanding of freedom as connected with the substance-subject notion: "There is no 'being' behind doing, being active, becoming; the 'agent' is a mere fabrication added to the doing — the doing is all."[54] Nietzsche ceaselessly unmasks this fabrication by identifying the "will to power" as the basis of everything. And so, consequently, the Promethean self dissolves into the flight itself. The difference between the finite and the absolute I disappears — the will to power is all there is.

This leads, *second*, to an inevitable fall: the Promethean self dissolves into the will to power, into sheer self-assertion. Even more so, the will to power manifests itself in and through the body, which becomes probably the most important weapon in Nietzsche's fight against all dualisms. Against his Platonic, Christian (i.e., Augustinian), and Idealist enemies, Nietzsche wants to conceive the body in a way that would irreversibly overcome the dualisms of body and spirit, of immanence and transcendence, of life and morality.[55] For Nietzsche, this overcoming is irreversibly secured in the "eternal return," which effectively undercuts any eschatological, teleological, or ontological resolution (and thus a return to what, for Nietzsche, amounts to only various forms of Platonism).[56] In the eternal return, freedom is both ultimately achieved and utterly lost. Thus the Promethean self reunites with both sky and earth, and the finite will to power — the body — with the absolute will.

Yet this forceful fusion was not meant to last. Already during Nietzsche's lifetime, the two poles (absolute freedom and radical determination) that he attempted to force together in the endless becoming of the will to power and the eternal return of things fell apart into the fragmented assumptions of late modernity. The revolutionary insights of Darwin, Freud, and Marx suggest freedom to be but the benign illusion of a being ultimately determined by biological, psychological, social, and economic forces. Yet at the same time, the Promethean self's daydream of freedom (as fundamental self-determination, as autocreativity, and more recently, simply as license) celebrates a surprising comeback in Western societies, both on the popular level and in the discourse of philosophy.[57]

And so, after Kant, Fichte, and Nietzsche on the one hand and Marx, Darwin, and Freud on the other, we find ourselves as late moderns caught on a manic-depressive roller-coaster ride between the ghost of the Promethean daydream of freedom, by now turned desperate and therefore dreaming of autocreativity[58] — that is, of designing our bodies, of choosing our gender, our values, and our destinies freely according to our idiosyncratic likings and longings — and the Hades-like nightmare of endless victimization by "the system" — by anonymous economic, political, and cultural power structures, by our own genetic makeup, and by the will to power of everyone else around us. So it happens that our late modern lives oscillate between the dream-ghosts of freedom's Promethean expansion and the nightmare of freedom's total eclipse.⁵⁹ And, of course, both are nothing other than the two sides of the coin that has lost its clear imprint, of freedom that has lost its distinct gestalt and embodiment. This predicament is the setting we need to keep in mind as we now turn to the second stage of the argument.⁶⁰

II. *Veritatis Splendor:* God's Law and Participatory Freedom

The encyclical meets the modern double phenomenon, the Promethean expansion *and* the total eclipse of human freedom, with a thesis as striking as it is untimely. According to *Veritatis Splendor,* genuine human freedom is attained on the path of and is formed by God's law. It is God's law — identical with God's goodness — that liberates and forms human freedom and thus prevents it from its Promethean expansion as well as its ensuing eclipse. The encyclical thus challenges conventional modern wisdom in a twofold way: *First,* freedom is not a *given* but a *gift.* And *second,* the relationship between freedom and law is teleological: genuine human freedom is the very telos toward which the law is ordered.⁶¹

God's Law: The "Limit" of Genuine Freedom (Genesis 2:16-17)

In order to establish the fundamental role of God's law for human freedom, the encyclical builds upon what we might call God's original address to humanity in the second chapter of the book of Genesis: "Of the tree of the knowledge of good and evil you shall not eat" (Gen 2:17). Human freedom

> must halt before the "tree of the knowledge of good and evil," for it is called to accept the moral law given by God. In fact, human freedom finds its authentic and complete fulfilment precisely in the acceptance of that law. . . .
>
> . . . God's law does not reduce, much less do away with human freedom; rather, it protects and promotes that freedom. (*VS* 35)⁶²

Here we already encounter what the encyclical claims about the nature of freedom, a thesis as provocative as it is profound. *Human freedom finds fulfillment as genuine freedom only when it receives its limit, a limit that both grounds and forms it.* And this limit is not so much a border, a form of negativity, of imposition against which to rebel. Nor is it a "known" limit that is already crossed in the very knowledge of it by having to conceptualize the limit's other side in order to conceive the limit itself. Rather, God's law as the limit of genuine freedom stands for both form and fulfillment. Freedom's form is neither "discovered" (in that we eventually find out about it on our own through bad experience) nor "known" (in that we fully understand and therefore ultimately impose the limit on ourselves). Rather, it is *received* in the original encounter with God as God's commandment. Thus God's commandment inherently belongs to what the witness of Scripture conceives as the relationship between Creator and creature in the state of integrity. Here, freedom is gracefully prevented from emancipating itself from its creaturely abode precisely by continuously receiving — that is, by living in ongoing obedience to — God's original commandment. At the same time, freedom is affirmed and promoted as that very medium of their relationship with God in which humans are neither angels nor creatures of the field — but genuinely human.

Yet we might want to ask immediately, How is God's law[63] accessible to humanity now, under the condition of sin? Here *human reason* — modernity's other protagonist — comes into the picture, and the encyclical takes an approach similar to its approach to freedom. First, the encyclical affirms the active role of human reason in the finding and applying of the moral law: "[T]he moral life calls for that creativity and originality typical of the person, the source and cause of his own deliberate acts" (*VS* 40). At the same time, it emphasizes that the truth and authority of human reason are rooted in the eternal law, which is identical with God's own wisdom: "The rightful autonomy of the practical reason means that man possesses in himself his own law, received from the Creator" (*VS* 40). Thus the autonomy of human reason is to be understood not as sovereign, as being a *creator* of "values" and "norms," but as *participatory*, as partaking in the divine Creator's and lawgiver's wisdom: True moral autonomy consists in the free submission under and obedience to God's moral law.[64] Thus in clear contrast to the modern concept of moral autonomy, as especially developed by Kant, reason is not constitutive of the moral law.[65] Rather, reason participates in the law by acknowledging its truth and submitting to its authority. Yet, to be clear, this submitting is *intrinsic* to the participation, not extrinsic. God invites and calls humanity to participate via reason in the unfolding of God's providence — reason being guided in the right direction by practical reason's natural light.[66]

The "New Law": The Spirit's Self-Enactment

Yet by observing the natural law via reason, humans enact their freedom only in a very incipient and fundamentally incomplete way.[67] This creaturely reality under the condition of sin is met with a new divine initiative that the encyclical regards as essential for achieving genuine human freedom (*pace* the *opinio communis* of the natural law philosophers): God's revealed law in the economy of salvation. Israel received the Torah as a gift and a special sign of its divine election and of the covenant. And this gift of God, according to the encyclical, continues to play a central role in the church, yet now in a new, pneumatological horizon:

> The Church gratefully accepts and lovingly preserves the entire deposit of Revelation, treating it with religious respect and fulfilling her mission of authentically interpreting God's law in the light of the Gospel. In addition, the Church receives the gift of the New Law, which is the "fulfilment" of God's law in Jesus Christ and in his Spirit. This is an "interior" law (cf. *Jer* 31:31-33), "written not with ink but with the Spirit of the living God, not on tablets of stone but on tablets of human hearts" (2 *Cor* 3:3); a law of perfection and of freedom (cf. 2 *Cor* 3:17); "the law of the Spirit of life in Christ Jesus" (*Rom* 8:2). (*VS* 45)[68]

The encyclical draws at this point upon Thomas Aquinas's influential teaching on the gospel as the "new law."[69] For Aquinas, the "new law" encompasses both justification and sanctification[70] and ultimately stands for the Holy Spirit's presence in the believer. As uncreated grace, the "new law" is the Holy Spirit's self-enactment in the believer's life. The Lutheran theologian and noted Aquinas interpreter Ulrich Kühn aptly puts it the following way:

> One needs to emphasize first of all that the term "new law" in the *Summa theologiae* has primarily nothing to do with a legally posited, external precept. Rather, one must think of grace, which is being discussed by Thomas at length at a later point in the *Summa* and which essentially consists in a supernatural *habitus*, which is infused into the soul and which raises it toward God. Thomas interprets this grace as the grace of the "Holy Spirit," whereby its nature as rooted in God and as "uncreated" is emphasized, and at the same time, he evokes a whole range of biblical reminiscences. Thomas himself refers especially to Romans 8, which prompts us to take the beautiful comments into account which he offers on this passage in his *Romans Commentary* regarding the term "lex spiritus." According to Thomas, "lex spiritus" refers to the Holy Spirit residing in the soul, who teaches the human about right action and guides him or her to it. In addition, "lex spiritus" refers to the closest and most genuine effects of the Holy Spirit in the

human being: to faith active through love, a faith which itself again teaches inwardly about what is to be done.[71]

Thus we need to understand the notion of the "new law" in a fundamentally pneumatological way. For Aquinas, the new law refers to the genuine and fully realized freedom in the Holy Spirit: "Ubi Spiritus Domini, ibi libertas" ["Where the Spirit of the Lord is, there is freedom"].[72] Yet the freedom that *is* the Spirit's presence does not lead away from God's will as expressed in God's commandments. Life in the Spirit does not mean that the Decalogue as received in Israel's Scriptures is abolished.

The Path of the Law — or, "Life with God": The Creaturely Shape of Freedom

Rather, according to *Veritatis Splendor*, the freedom in the Spirit has a concrete *creaturely shape*: it is "life with God," a concrete way of life in God's commandments as embodied in the Decalogue, the key of which is the first commandment. "*The good is belonging to God, obeying him, walking humbly with him in doing justice and in loving kindness (cf. Mic 6:8). Acknowledging the Lord as God is the very core, the heart of the Law,* from which the particular precepts flow and towards which they are ordered" (*VS* 11). Here we are reminded of Martin Luther, who remarks in his *Large Catechism* regarding the Decalogue's first commandment: "[I]f the heart is right with God and we keep this commandment, all the rest will follow on their own."[73] And the fulfillment of the first commandment, according to Luther, is of course faith — that in which genuine freedom is made concrete.

Only in fulfilling the commandments of the Decalogue do we, according to *Veritatis Splendor*, remain in the presence of the Good and thereby genuinely free.[74] Therefore, the relationship between human freedom and God's explicit commandments is *ideally* — similar to the relationship between natural law and human freedom — not one of estrangement, of heteronomy. Rather, because the commandments contain the Good, toward which human freedom is ordered, our practice of them fulfills our human vocation in relation to God, to neighbor, and to ourselves. In short, human freedom comes to itself only in the practice of the commandments. With its strong emphasis on the *human good*, which is the very foundation of God's commandments, the encyclical attempts to overcome the deeply modern antinomy between the sovereignty of the human agent and the heteronomy of any external, randomly imposed law.[75]

In sum, the encyclical operates with a comprehensive paradigm of "law" in which God's creative and salvific activities penetrate each other in an essentially harmonious way. The origin and goal of this activity is humanity's destiny "to be conformed to the image of [God's] Son (*Rom* 8:29)" (*VS* 45) — that is, on the path of observing God's law, only and precisely by which genuine human freedom is achieved. Thus in clear contrast to the modern self-understanding, genuine human freedom is not a *given*, a starting point, but a *gift*, to be received on the path of following God's commandments.

> They are the *first necessary step on the journey towards freedom*, its starting-point. "The beginning of freedom," Saint Augustine writes, "is to be free from crimes . . . such as murder, adultery, fornication, theft, fraud, sacrilege and so forth. When once one is without these crimes (and every Christian should be without them), one begins to lift up one's head towards freedom. But this is only the beginning of freedom, not perfect freedom. . . ." (*VS* 13)[76]

Yet following this path is not at all simply doing what lies within us, a *facere quod in se est*, as Protestants might be quick to suspect. Rather, following this path to conformity with Christ is enabled by the Spirit of the triune God, in whom the gift of freedom is an ever present reality. In other words, freedom and law are mediated both christologically and pneumatologically. But how exactly do the gift of freedom and the path of God's commandments look as a coherent reality?

"The End of the Law": Christ's Paradigmatic Example

The encyclical takes Christ to be "the end of the law" — not in the sense of overcoming and abolishing the law but rather in the sense of being its living fulfillment — in accord with St. Ambrose's dictum "Plenitudo legis in Christo est." "*Jesus himself is the living 'fulfilment' of the Law* inasmuch as he fulfils its authentic meaning by the total gift of himself: *he himself becomes a living and personal Law,* who invites people to follow him; through the Spirit, he gives the grace to share his own life and love and provides the strength to bear witness to that love in personal choices and actions (cf. *Jn* 13:34-35)" (*VS* 15).

Having fulfilled the law completely and in the very core of its intention, Christ becomes the paradigmatic example, the most genuine witness of the law's truth.⁷⁷ The *koinōnia* between Christ's example and the witness of the faithful occurs precisely in the Spirit. Genuine freedom is thus nothing less than life in this *koinōnia* of the Spirit.⁷⁸ As Livio Melina rightly observes, "In this way the dialectic of autonomy and heteronomy is also surpassed." He continues:

> "In Christ" the law is perceived as the expression of the will of the Father and embraced in a filial way; in the Spirit, while remaining *heteron* (something other) with respect to God, we are assumed gratuitously into a filiation that makes us also *heteros* (someone other). In the Spirit, the Christological commandment is interiorized and becomes the new law of love, without, however, completely eliminating on earth the exterior elements (cf. VS 53), which are nevertheless subordinated in function to the interior element *(lex nova Spiritus Sancti)*.⁷⁹

Here we encounter what looks like an obvious tension between the encyclical's focus on Christ and the Spirit and its focus on human reason's participation in the "eternal law" via the natural law. Why is it that we need Christ's example and, in addition, the Spirit's presence in us so that through the law's fulfillment we become conformed to Christ's image? Why do we need "to go to the heart of the Gospel's moral teaching and grasp its profound and unchanging content" (*VS* 8), if "[i]t follows that the natural law is *itself the eternal law*, implanted in beings endowed with reason, and inclining them *towards their right action and end*" (*VS* 44)?

Practice of the Law: The Path to Genuine Freedom

The answer to this question is at the same time the encyclical's most penetrating critique of the modern daydream of Promethean freedom. Human freedom — *post lapsum* — is only inauthentic freedom, because it is turned in upon itself, into its own self-sufficient ground and principle, which ultimately assumes the identity between the transcendental subject and God.⁸⁰ This very core of the Promethean self's daydream stands in fundamental opposition to the first commandment of the Decalogue. By attempting to secure itself on its own instead of receiving itself as the gift of faith, "natural" freedom constantly misses itself. Only when it is liberated can freedom receive itself, can *liberum arbitrium* turn into *libertas*. Before the painful process of liberation has started, we do not even know how deeply we are entangled in the web of sin.

> St. Augustine, after speaking of the observance of the commandments as being a kind of incipient, imperfect freedom, goes on to say: "Why, someone will ask, is it not yet perfect? Because 'I see in my members another law at war with the law of my reason.'... In part freedom, in part slavery: not yet complete freedom, not yet pure, not yet whole, because we are not yet in eternity. In part we retain our weakness and in part we have attained freedom.... Therefore, since some weakness has remained in us, I dare to say that to the extent to which we serve God we are free, while to the extent that we follow the law of sin, we are still slaves." (VS 17)

Precisely because humans are embodied beings living under the condition of sin, beings with desires, dispositions, and habits, the encyclical points out, it is necessary to concretely retrain and redirect our desires, dispositions, and habits.[81] Only by learning the alphabet of freedom do we learn what it means to be God's creatures called to genuine freedom. This happens by engaging in those activities and practices that God's revealed law circumscribes and commands and refraining from those activities and practices that it forbids. As MacIntyre aptly puts in reference to *Veritatis Splendor* 52: "Obedience to these negative precepts is, then, enabling, both individually and communally. It frees us from a variety of hindrances and frustrations that would otherwise bring to nothing the pursuit by each of us of our own positive good and that of others."[82] Both the positive and the negative commandments engender those actions and practices through which we are liberated to genuine freedom, that freedom whose paradigm and ultimate gestalt is Christ himself.[83]

Witness to the Law: Martyrdom as the Crown of Freedom

After having learned the alphabet of freedom, we are able to read the text of self-giving love, of genuine freedom itself.[84] In a most untimely and provocative way, *Veritatis Splendor* suggests that the crown of genuine freedom is martyrdom. "Martyrdom, accepted as an affirmation of the inviolability of the moral order, bears splendid witness to both the holiness of God's law and to the inviolability of the personal dignity of man, created in God's image and likeness. This dignity may never be disparaged or called into question, even with good intentions, whatever the difficulties involved" (VS 92).

Surprisingly, for *Veritatis Splendor* the very focus of martyrdom is God's law — and not the confession of Christ and the gospel as the *Catechism of the Catholic Church* instructs: "Martyrdom is the supreme witness given to the truth of the faith: it means bearing witness even unto death. The martyr bears witness to Christ who died and rose, to whom he is united by charity. He bears witness to the truth of the faith and of Christian doctrine. He endures death through an act of fortitude" (#2473).

Yet when the encyclical emphasizes the law as the subject of the martyr's witness, it remains wholly consistent with its own Christology. Because Christ *is* the paradigmatic example of God's law, fulfilled in love, he is the true *hermeneute* of God's will. Therefore, witness to the truth of God's law implies witness to Christ — and vice versa, one might assume, even if this is not the encyclical's immediate concern. Rather, the encyclical's burning concern is the relationship between freedom and law in Christ. And so the focus of the ultimate act of freedom, martyrdom, is on the witness to the law's truth. "*When it is a matter of the moral norms prohibiting intrinsic evil, there are no privileges or exceptions for anyone.* It makes no difference whether one is the master of the world or the 'poorest of the poor' on the face of the earth. Before the demands of morality we are all absolutely equal" (*VS* 96).[85]

Thus when the encyclical identifies martyrdom as the crown of freedom precisely in its witness to the law, it brings into strong relief the crucial sticking point of the concept of freedom.[86] The law performs a limiting service that protects genuine freedom from being reinterpreted as license and thus from losing the good by defining good and evil itself and consequently losing itself.[87]

The Limiting Authority of the Law: Intrinsically Evil Acts

This limit to which the martyr witnesses consists in the so-called intrinsically evil acts, acts "which *per se* and in themselves, independently of circumstances, are always seriously wrong by reason of their object" (*VS* 80). Admittedly, this teaching is highly complex and, among Roman Catholic moral theologians, somewhat controversial, especially the question of how the "object" of the act is to be understood in relation to the act's intention.[88] Nevertheless, the encyclical's insistence on intrinsically evil acts and their role in its way of conceiving martyrdom strike me as crucial for the encyclical's vision of genuine freedom. While it would lead too far afield at this point to unfold the complex issues involved in the teaching of intrinsically evil acts, there are at least two implications of this teaching that are central for the encyclical's concept of freedom.

First, this teaching undercuts the moral subjectivism that misconceives freedom as the sovereignty of indifference by claiming the moral nature of the agent's acts to be precisely a function of freedom's unoriginate origin.[89] In this way, the encyclical exposes the false poietic presumptions entertained by the Promethean daydream of freedom: the self as constitutive and creative of moral meaning and value.[90] Rather, as Cardinal Avery Dulles points out: "Far from being an exception to the general rule that freedom is oriented toward objective truth, the experience of conscientious decision-making confirms the rule that . . . the freedom of conscience is never freedom from the truth but always and only freedom in the truth (VS 64)."[91] In this way the teaching of intrinsically evil acts explicitly challenges the modern self's hermeneutic hegemony, namely, that the moral meanings of my acts are controlled by me and me alone.[92] This leads, consequently, to the questioning of the formal self-sufficiency that the modern notion of freedom secures in the moral realm (assuming that subjectivist sovereignty is rejected): freedom has its inner compass in the structure of practical reason (Kant) or in conscience (Fichte) and is therefore fully self-sufficient.

In contrast, the teaching of intrinsically evil acts implies that genuine freedom remains dependent on the precepts of the moral law, with the exceptionless negative precepts precisely identifying those kinds of acts that would undermine genuine freedom itself.[93] We need to see this in close connection with the way *Veritatis Splendor* implicitly builds its case on Aquinas's teaching: because the natural law has been almost completely obscured under the condition of sin, the revealed law *(Decalogue)* needs to recover it in the form of an *anamnēsis*. Thus genuine freedom depends on a contingent reality completely outside the scope of its main modern routes of access, Kantian reason or Fichtean conscience.

The *second* implication of this teaching for the concept of freedom is that it undercuts the radical postmodern claims about the self's "multiplicity, heterogeneity, difference, and ceaseless becoming, bereft of origin and purpose"[94] — claims that intend to intensify freedom by liberating agents from the burden of continuity with and responsibility for their own past.[95]

In sum, this teaching belongs intrinsically to *Veritatis Splendor*'s concept of freedom, as the latter intends to overcome both the modern expansion of freedom and its late modern eclipse. Without this teaching, *Veritatis Splendor*'s vision of freedom would clearly lose its cutting edge. To acknowledge the nature and reality of these acts is to acknowledge the creaturely finitude and therefore also the concrete form of human freedom. To withdraw this teaching would be to open the very concept of freedom precisely to both its Promethean expansion and its total eclipse.

Even so, I surely do not want to downplay the inner complexities that burden the concept of intrinsically evil acts. I rather agree with Stanley Hauerwas, who has recently pressed the point that it is important not to get distracted by what one might call a "metaphysics of intrinsic evil." Following Martin Rhonheimer's interpretation, he rightly emphasizes the agent's perspective and the importance of the virtues — a theme we have not been able to sufficiently address in the present deliberations on freedom and law. What is finally most decisive in the teaching of intrinsically evil acts, according to Hauerwas, is that there exist descriptions for particular acts that can never be overwritten by further descriptions and further ends justifying these acts.[96]

Moreover, I have no interest here in mounting a substantive defense of this teaching in one of its present forms. Rather, I regard it as important not to dodge the question whether, indeed, genuine human freedom as restored in Christ can be gravely endangered, deeply distorted, and ultimately destroyed by particular kinds of acts.[97]

The Question to Be Raised

Might it be that contemporary Protestant theology lacks the very conceptuality even to recognize this question as a challenge, since it lacks a theology of the law that would complement and shape the inflated and rarely reflected upon use of the notion of "freedom"? In short, could it be that much of contemporary Protestantism is unable even to recognize that there is a challenge, because antinomianism has become so thoroughly taken for granted that any self-awareness — not to mention *critical* self-awareness — of its deeply ingrained antinomian commitments has been lost?

Precisely because of its largely unthematized character, this antinomianism is a complex and multi-stranded phenomenon. One thread can be traced to the fact that Protestantism was and still is actively and passively involved in modernity's daydream of Promethean freedom.[98] Another, related thread originates in a long liberal Protestant tradition of fundamentally displacing the law and of combining this tendency with a relentless polemic against Roman Catholic "legalism."

Untangling and rightly identifying these strands would require an inquiry far beyond the scope of what is possible in this place. Yet I will at least gesture in this direction by attending to the very setting in which Protestant antinomianism first emerged: Martin Luther's own Wittenberg. In light of *Veritatis Splendor*'s teaching on freedom and law, we will be able to appreciate in a fresh and relevant way Martin Luther's own vehement opposition to the antinomians of his own day and context. Moreover, rereading Luther "after *Veritatis Splendor*" will offer us some clues to the source of the antinomian fallacy that haunts Protestantism today.

III. After *Veritatis Splendor:* The Antinomian Fallacy of a Protestantism without the Law

Martin Luther's epochal significance for modernity, especially viewed through the lens of his famous stance at the Diet of Worms in 1521, has typically been related to the idea of "freedom of conscience." Yet what might seem to be a consensus has by no means led to a unified interpretation of Luther's historical and political significance. Rather, each epoch has created a Luther of its own. Since the Reformation — and already even during its course — he has been claimed by progressives and revolutionaries as well as conservatives and reactionaries in Germany's troubled political history. Certainly most damaging has been his (ab-)use in support of Nazism. Yet no less problematic was the (ironically supportive) counterpropaganda in the Allied countries that construed a "line of inheritance" from Luther via Frederick the Great and Bismarck to Hitler. It is therefore not surprising that in reaction, German Protestantism (especially liberal Protestantism) and American Lutheranism have reemphasized the deep links between Luther's theology, the Reformation, and modernity's fundamental concern — that is, freedom. Yet this apologetic way of presenting Luther as "father of modernity" has resulted in bringing into too close proximity, or even equating, Luther's account of the freedom of a Christian with the freedom of sovereignty and indifference that *Veritatis Splendor* so clearly is bent on correcting and overcoming.[99]

Only quite recently have fresh readings of Luther challenged this apologetically accommodating picture. He now looks much more like an anticipatory critic of modernity, much more like a prophet who could see looming on the horizon the specter of both modernity's daydream and late modernity's nightmare.[100] In recent years, we have come to appreciate again from Luther's *Bondage of the Will*[101] that *libertas*, genuine freedom, is first and foremost a predicate of God. Luther consequently would regard the modern daydream of the Promethean self and the postmodern nightmare of freedom's eclipse as the two sides of the one bondage we rebel against yet cannot escape. We have also come to appreciate again from Luther's *Treatise on Good Works* and from his *Large Catechism* that he does not hesitate to put forth the Decalogue as the blueprint for the gestalt of Christian freedom.[102] And we have come to appreciate again from Luther's *On the Councils and the Church* the intrinsic connection between the freedom in the Spirit and the gestalt of this freedom in distinct practices of redemption — practices not of *effecting* redemption but of *actively receiving* redemption.[103] Moreover, in the same treatise Luther gestures toward practices through which creation is continuously sustained. What is most significant in this regard is that Luther relates both sets of practices to the Decalogue's two tables and understands both sets as the Spirit's work through which the Spirit sanctifies the Christian people.[104] This should make evident that it would be indeed erroneous to place Luther's and *Veritatis Splendor*'s visions of freedom into a facile fundamental opposition.

Yet to be clear, there remain significant differences that need to be identified and critically explored. Those I have elaborated in other places.[105] In a nutshell: They touch, *first,* upon the primacy of Christ as gift over against Christ as example; *second,* upon the difference between law and gospel and the encyclical's underplaying of the unmasking and convicting character of God's law; and *third,* upon the woundedness of human reason itself to the point that the rational capacity to discern God's law is more severely limited than the encyclical allows for. *Fourth, Veritatis Splendor* — especially in its middle section — tends to read Thomas Aquinas on natural law, revealed law, and grace through a chiefly neo-scholastic lens instead of allowing its formulations on freedom and law to be shaped by the recent recovery of Aquinas as a genuinely theological and even christological thinker.[106]

Yet instead of returning to these important differences, I would like to focus on the one issue that — if we look at contemporary Protestant belief and ethos — is put into starkest relief by the encyclical. What starts to stand out in light of *Veritatis Splendor* is the pervasive *antinomian* character of contemporary Protestantism, its unique way of oscillating between the modern daydream of Promethean freedom and the postmodern nightmare of freedom's eclipse. The concept of freedom embedded in contemporary Protestant belief and ethos tends to expand ghostlike into thin air in the attempt to embrace and accept everything — and then to collapse into the most surprising legalisms.

Faced with the challenge of *Veritatis Splendor,* contemporary Protestantism will have to relearn that *without a theology of the law, there is no basis for a theology of freedom.* Without a developed and compelling theology of the law, Christ himself, his atoning work, and the knowledge of God's will in light of which Christ *is* God's forgiving and saving grace evaporates into the sentimentality of a god whose job it is to forgive — as Voltaire once put it so aptly. In order to develop a theology of freedom, antinomianism is exactly the wrong answer. Yet that is precisely the fallacy of much contemporary Protestant belief and ethos: *less law, more freedom; no law, all freedom.* When we reflect thoughtfully on the modern daydream and the postmodern nightmare as well as on the teaching of *Veritatis Splendor,* quite another relationship between law and freedom impresses itself on us: *less law, less freedom; no law, no freedom.* And it is again Luther who is ahead of us here in one of the two best-kept secrets among his writings, his *Theses against the Antinomians,* buried in the Weimar edition,[107] and his late *Lectures on Genesis,* which until recently Luther scholars had by and large ignored.[108]

Law and Gospel in Luther's Theses against the Antinomians

Let us turn first to Luther's *Theses against the Antinomians.* After a short general introduction we are confronted with the following startling theses: "(1) The law is not worthy to be called word of God. (2) If you are a fornicator, a criminal, an adulterer or a sinner in some other way and have faith, you are walking on the path of blessedness. (3) If you stick to the highest in sin and remain in it, and you believe, so you are right away in blessedness. (1) The Decalogue belongs in the city hall, not in the pulpit. (2) All who deal with Moses have to go to the devil; to the gallows with Moses. . . . (8) As soon as you think, such and such should it be among Christians, they should be fine, honorable, disciplined, holy, and chaste people, so you have already given away the Gospel."[109] Could these statements, somewhat modernized in wording and content, not have come, mutatis mutandis, as a sincere summary of contemporary Protestant belief and ethos — assured of its genuine "Protestant" character? It must come as nothing less than a deep shock to this kind of contemporary Protestantism to realize that Luther lists precisely these particular theses as worthy of unequivocal theological condemnation. In other words, the above theses were theological claims — allegedly or truly — propagated by the so-called antinomians and quoted by Luther in sharp disapproval. What they reveal most clearly is the deeply law-displacing character of the antinomian cause. The Decalogue as the law's center has no ongoing role among Christians qua Christians. The law of Moses is not fulfilled in Christ so that it has reached its telos in him; rather, it is radically abrogated and abolished in the sense that it no longer belongs in any form to Christian preaching and teaching.[110]

While I cannot unfold here the complex textual and historical issues involved in the antinomian controversy, it is important at least to explicitly acknowledge Luther's clear awareness of how radically the context in the course of the Reformation problematic changed from anxiety-driven works-righteousness to self-confident moral libertinism and indifferentism:

> True it is that at the early stages of this movement we began strenuously to teach the gospel and made use of these words which the Antinomians now quote. But the circumstances of that time were very different from those of the present day. Then the world was terrorized enough when the

pope or the visage of a single priest shook the whole of Olympus, not to mention earth and hell, over all which that man of sin had usurped the power to himself. To the consciences of men so oppressed, terrified, miserable, anxious, and afflicted, there was no need to inculcate the law. The clamant need then was to present the other part of the teaching of Christ in which he commands us to preach the remission of sin in his name, so that those who were already sufficiently terrified might learn not to despair, but to take refuge in the grace and mercy offered in Christ. Now, however, when the times are very dissimilar from those under the pope, our Antinomians — those suave theologians — retain our words, our doctrine, the joyful tidings concerning Christ, and wish to preach this alone, not observing that men are other than they were under that hangman, the pope, and have become secure, froward, wicked violators — yea, Epicureans who neither fear God nor men. Such men they confirm and comfort by their doctrine. In those days we were terrorized so that we trembled even at the fall of a leaf. . . . But now our softly singing Antinomians, paying no attention to the change of the times, make men secure who are of themselves already so secure that they fall away from grace. . . . Our view hitherto has been and ought to be this salutary one — if you see the afflicted and contrite, preach grace as much as you can. But not to the secure, the slothful, the harlots, adulterers, and blasphemers.[111]

Luther's burning concern here is the security of a false freedom, the security of a freedom that is seized as our own, that makes us rest securely in ourselves — a freedom that ultimately rests in the self's sovereignty and is lived out as license. Precisely this freedom seized is freedom lost, and it is nothing other than God's law that unmasks the pretension of the self-seizing and the bondage of a license in which we are seized by powers beyond our control. Thus God's law awakens us from both the daydream of Promethean freedom — by exposing our entanglement in sin — and the nightmare of freedom's eclipse — by precisely holding us accountable for our deeds. Consequently, the law remains important and valid, both as the other in light of which the gospel's grace is unequivocally forgiving (effected in the fact of its fulfillment) and as that in light of which human freedom comes into view as realized through the gospel but given shape by the law's intention. And this is precisely why Luther assumes that the law will remain in eternity. It is in its essence, after all, the law of God's love: "Therefore the law will not be abolished in all eternity; rather, it will remain — with the condemned as one to be fulfilled, with the blessed as fulfilled one."[112]

Following Luther, therefore, the task before us is to conceive freedom and law — as fulfilled, not abolished — together, yet without fusing them into one and without turning one into the other. Precisely for this reason, *Veritatis Splendor*'s teaching on freedom makes us appreciate Luther's struggle against antinomianism in fresh and surprising ways. The difference between Luther and *Veritatis Splendor* notwithstanding, the two are still closer to each other than either is to contemporary Protestant antinomianism. According to Luther, in the law we encounter God's will, and in doing away with the law, we do away with God's will. And while doing away with God's will might be seen as a final liberation of humanity to genuine freedom — this is precisely the core of the modern daydream of the Promethean self — Luther insists that it actually results in freedom's total eclipse. The first six theses from Luther's sixth and last series of disputation theses against the antinomians[113] will illustrate the point:

1. ... Where there is no law, there is no trespass, not only in a theological sense but also in a political sense, and naturally then, it [the trespass] is good.
2. ... Where there is no sin, there is neither punishment nor remission.
3. ... Where there is neither punishment nor remission, there is neither wrath nor grace.
4. ... Where there is neither wrath nor grace, there is neither divine nor human governance.
5. ... Where there is neither divine nor human governance, there is neither God nor human.
6. ... Where there is neither God nor human, there is nothing other than the devil in full strength.

In these theses, Luther does not mention the word "freedom." But what is lost with the elimination of God and human, of divine and human governance, is precisely the possibility of a creaturely, Christlike freedom in communion with God under God's governance, as well as human freedom under human governance. What is left, of course, is nothing other than a ceaseless oscillation between the daydream of Promethean freedom and the nightmare of freedom's eclipse. The reason for this is that genuine freedom under the ongoing condition of sin continuously needs a point of reference that critically unmasks freedom's self-deceptions and offers a clear criterion for freedom's exercise. Yet why, we might ask, can this not be freedom's own "inner law," as Kant argued about 250 years after Luther? In his ironic résumé of the antinomian position, Luther might not have done full justice to his opponents. Yet he clearly anticipated the very core of modernity's daydream of freedom: a self beyond the grasp and the ongoing power of sin, transparent to itself, all spirit, and therefore in full control of its thoughts and its body:

> But it is no use — we are so secure, without fear and concern; the devil is far from us, and we have none of that flesh in us that was in St. Paul and of which he complains in Romans 7[:23-24], exclaiming that he cannot deliver himself from it as he would like, but that he is captive to it. No, we are the heroes who need not worry about our flesh and our thoughts. We are sheer spirit, we have taken captive our own flesh together with the devil, so that all our thoughts and ideas are surely and certainly inspired by the Holy Spirit, and how can he be found wanting? Therefore it all has such a nice ending — namely, that both steed and rider break their necks.[114]

God's law reminds us continuously how utterly fragile, how continually assailable, how ultimately communal is the gift of genuine freedom. When we thus put law and gospel into a relationship where the latter fundamentally displaces the former, we achieve nothing for genuine freedom. We rather abolish freedom itself. Like freedom, the law is fundamentally an attribute of God, originally *for* the human, and only under the condition of sin *against* the human. And here Luther emerges as one of modernity's strongest anticipatory critics and therefore remains an ongoing cause of offense to modern sensibilities: his theology of freedom, as well as his theology of the law, remains resistant to the all-absorbing embrace of the modern theory of subjectivity. Genuine freedom remains God's gift and therefore participatory.[115] The law remains God's law and therefore always, as "lex aeterna," an "alia lex,"[116] namely, identical with God's own being — and therefore not something humans simply share with a possible deity because both supposedly belong to the moral community of all rational beings.[117] So we have to conclude (*pace* liberal Protestantism) that Luther (and thereby the very *initium* of the Reformation movement) is fundamentally at odds with a modernity that, at its very best, can only fathom "law" as freedom's internal rational structure.

Yet there conceivably are theologians — especially Lutheran theologians — who, while agreeing with my conclusions so far, would still want to argue for a fundamental and principled difference between Luther and *Veritatis Splendor* at this point. They would want to emphasize Luther's strong focus on the theological use of the law (to unmask and convict of sin) in an ongoing and basically static dialectic of *simul iustus et peccator*, at the same time righteous and a sinner. This they would want to contrast in the strongest terms with what they would regard as a synthesis of law and gospel in *Veritatis Splendor*. The argument would go like this: While Luther might still strongly support an ongoing negative function of the law (in a way deeply at odds with modern sensibilities), he would not support a positive function of the law in relation to genuine freedom, a freedom attained only through faith in the gospel. In contrast to Catholics, Calvinists, and — worst of all — Melanchthonians, Luther would let freedom be genuinely free; that is, genuine freedom would displace any notion of commandment or law.

Law and Gospel in Luther's Lectures on Genesis

In order to meet this objection, we need to turn to Luther's late *Lectures on Genesis,* delivered during and in the aftermath of the antinomian controversy. His interpretation of Genesis 2, the human in the state of original grace, is of special interest to our concern:

> And so when Adam had been created in such a way that he was, as it were, intoxicated with rejoicing toward God and was delighted also with all the other creatures, there is now created a new tree for the distinguishing of good and evil, so that Adam might have a definite way to express his worship and reverence toward God. After everything had been entrusted to him to make use of it according to his will, whether he wished to do so for necessity or for pleasure, God finally demands from Adam that at this tree of the knowledge of good and evil he demonstrate his reverence and obedience toward God and that he maintain this practice, as it were, of worshipping God by not eating anything from it.[118]

It might come as a surprise to many, but clearly Luther assumes the original unity of gospel and law, of a freedom in communion with God that is practiced in obedience to God's commandment and thereby precisely receives its creaturely form. As David Yeago observes:

> [H]ere Luther is describing a function of divine law, divine commandment, which is neither correlative with sin nor antithetical to grace; indeed, it presupposes the presence of grace and not sin. This function of divine commandment is, moreover, its original and proper function. . . . The fundamental significance of the law is thus neither to enable human beings to attain righteousness nor to accuse their sin, but to give concrete, historical form to the "divine life" of the human creature deified by grace.[119]

Genuine freedom — freedom in the "state of paradise,"[120] so to speak — receives its creaturely form in practicing God's commandment. It is not at all accidental that Luther lets Adam proclaim God's word from under the tree of the knowledge of good and evil.[121] Luther is keen on emphasizing how genuine freedom is concretely embodied in the very practice of obeying the commandment, a practice that constitutes the framework in which God's goodness is received and proclaimed.

Precisely in breaking God's commandment, in leaving the mode of reception by abandoning the practice and thus the obedience in and through which freedom is received, the original communion with God is lost — and with it the original righteousness, the very source of genuine freedom. Human willfulness consequently seeks to secure itself by endeavoring to become the self-originating origin, a self in need of no reception. Only now does God's commandment, originally freedom's form, turn into the law that both constrains (*usus politicus legis,* the political, or "first," use of the law) and unmasks and convicts (*usus theologicus legis,* the theological, or "second," use of the law) the human pretension to self-grounding.

Because the law is fulfilled once and for all through God's own costly intervention in Christ, Christ, for Luther, is incredibly good news — gospel. In Christ the triune God restores the original communion as gift to all nations through a self-donation in love that fulfills the law in an exemplary way and grants life in God's spirit of love. The law is abrogated through Christ insofar as it constrains, unmasks, and convicts the sinner.[122] Yet the law's substance is restored to its original intent as the genuine expression of God's will: the law of love.[123] It provides the creaturely gestalt of genuine freedom, the freedom of communion with God as received by faith. Now it is God's own law of love received in Christ, a "law" therefore welcomed with delight: *"Whenever there is this delight, it does what God commands. Then the law does not cause a guilty conscience, but causes joy, because one has become another person already."*[124] Only when the gift itself becomes the very essence and horizon of the freedom received can this reception be enacted and thus actively received in freedom's form, delight in the law.

What might first have seemed to be a somewhat tedious Luther-exegesis has turned out to be a necessary exercise. The reason is simply that on the grounds of Melanchthon's or Calvin's theologies of the law, antinomian Protestantism can never legitimate itself. Only a particular way of interpreting "law and gospel" in Luther offers such a legitimation, an interpretation that turns Luther's unequivocal prioritizing of the gospel into a radical displacement of the law. In order to overcome the antinomian captivity of contemporary Protestantism, it is necessary to show that Luther's writings resist such a legitimating interpretation. Admittedly, all of this will eventually require a much more substantiated account.[125] Yet by rereading Luther "after *Veritatis Splendor*" we are able at least to put the ax to the very root out of which the legitimation of antinomian Protestantism grows. The following theses partially summarize my reflections and partially indicate the course toward further displacing the law-displacement as practiced by antinomian Protestantism.

IV. After the Promethean Self — beyond the Antinomian Fallacy: Ten Theses for Theologically Rethinking Freedom and Law

1. It is not just ten rules for decent behavior that Israel receives in the Decalogue. Rather, the Decalogue's preamble unequivocally claims Israel and in so doing constitutes the form of Israel's way of life with the God who "raised Israel from Egypt."[126] As Frank Crüsemann has argued, this way of life, being always directed to its source, constitutes the form of Israel's freedom.[127] For Israel, the nature of positive freedom is thus irreversibly defined: freedom is "life with God"[128] and as such is actualized in the course of continuously meditating on and enacting God's commandments — which precisely is the way of continuously receiving them. Practicing the form of this freedom is therefore the very mode of its ongoing reception. We find a paradigmatic witness to this mode of continuous reception in Psalm 119. Israel's life of faith, as witnessed to by the Scriptures, documents most clearly that this continuous receiving occurs only in community, a community shaped by practices of remembrance and discipleship.

2. Yet since this way of life depends on a source that is intrinsically beyond its reach, it inevitably leads to its own crisis.[129] Were it not for its prophetic indictment, this crisis would not necessarily be visible by itself. Rather, it emerges in full clarity only in light of its resolution. While "the law is holy, and the commandment is holy and just and good" (Rom 7:12), it cannot achieve its own end, fulfill its comprehensive reception. This fulfillment remains God's own eschatological act that imparts the messianic gift of reception in the form of God's own self-giving. In Christ's life, death, and resurrection, this mode of reception is fundamentally fulfilled "for the many" and offered to all the nations as gift and as example. Thus ultimately, it is for Christ's sake that the law is continuously present in the church. Without God's law continuously being taught, we cannot understand what it means that Christ fulfilled God's law *pro nobis*, that Christ is the gift of fulfillment, and that we al-

ways remain in need of Christ's fulfillment of the law.[130] In other words, only in light of the law's ongoing presence does Christ remain "the unsurpassable exegesis of the law" as well as its ongoing fulfillment.[131]

3. In Christian catechesis, the Decalogue circumscribes the practices in which creaturely freedom is genuinely received and therefore continuously practiced, and continuously practiced and therefore genuinely received. The fundamental mode of reception is faith, precisely because the first commandment can be fulfilled only by faith. Yet "faith" is nothing other than the receiving of Christ. It is thus always something less and other than genuine faith if it is not active, living faith. Therefore, genuine creaturely freedom exists only insofar as it is fully received in the form of — and thus in being formed by — God's commandments. And this form is precisely their faithful enactment.[132]

4. If, indeed, genuine freedom receives itself always together with its form, which itself continuously remains in the mode of reception,[133] then humans cannot realize freedom on their own, nor can they conceive freedom as self-originating origin without continuously failing freedom. Nor can humans give themselves the law in the course of whose practice genuine freedom is realized.[134] This law can only be received — and so cannot be a human law. Rather, it must be the gift of the One whose creatures humans are. And if it is to be received as the Creator's gift, it must ultimately be reflective of the Giver *(lex aeterna)*.[135]

5. We do not find a displacement of the revealed law in Aquinas, Luther, Melanchthon, and Calvin. Because they presuppose the law's paradigmatic fulfillment in Christ, they are able to posit a differentiated reception of the law that still deserves to be seriously considered. In its fundamentally contingent reception (Decalogue), the law remains authoritative as the revealed summary of the *natural law*. What, in contrast, concerns Israel as a contingent political reality finds its equivalent in *human law* (Aquinas) or the *Sachsenspiegel* (Luther). And what, finally, concerns Israel as God's holy people, *purity law* and *sacrificial law*, is not abolished but rather is received — as fulfilled in Christ — through baptism and the Lord's Supper.[136] Though this traditional way of differentiation is far superior to the roundabout way of displacing the law in liberal Protestantism, it very likely will not be the last word on this matter.[137]

6. The antinomian displacement of the law undercuts the notion of freedom as gift that — in its very enactment — needs to remain in the mode of reception (i.e., continuously connected to the Giver) precisely in order to remain genuine freedom. It is the utter dependence of genu-

ine freedom on God's redeeming and restoring self-giving in Christ that the law's critical function continues to press. Yet at the same time, the mode of reception is continued in the very form of freedom's enactment — in the practice of God's precepts, or commandments.

7. Genuine freedom, therefore, presupposes communal practices of ongoing reception that include practices of remembrance, instruction, interpretation, discernment, discipline, and discipleship.[138] What *Veritatis Splendor* points to only tangentially, and what antinomian Protestantism has lost sight of, is most crucial: the enactment of genuine freedom presupposes and requires the existence of distinct communities in which these practices of reception concretely occur.

8. These "communities" are to be conceived neither as aggregations of like-minded individuals for limited purposes nor (as is occurring most lately) as a panacea for the loneliness, isolation, and inner emptiness of the late modern individual. Oddly enough, these communities cannot be called for as another thing to be done, achieved, and put into place — managerially, so to speak — but can only be received as the result of a continuing conversion.

9. If, indeed, freedom's form and fulfillment, its redemption from the "fall" into individual sovereignty, will to power, and license, is to be received "on the way," is to be learned by participating in the practices of reception, then the self's late modern problematic of ceaselessly oscillating between the daydream of Promethean freedom and the nightmare of freedom's eclipse is irresolvable on its own terms.

10. Precisely because freedom is fallen, positive freedom (as the freeing of freedom in and through the practices of its reception) must ultimately also be able to account for the rudiments of negative freedom (as protected by a "law" that equally recognizes the fundamental dignity of all human beings qua human beings).[139] Yet what is crucial and what is not understood in most of liberal theory is that negative freedom itself rests upon the freeing of freedom as its ongoing reception — lest negative freedom be deconstrued as a decisionist fiction.[140] In order to avoid this deconstruction, the law of negative freedom must itself be received. Yet this reception depends internally on the reception of that law that is both the fulfillment and the form of genuine freedom. In other words, political liberalism depends on resources that are intrinsically beyond its grasp — and antinomian Protestantism is precisely not one of them.

8. Freedom and Commandment: The Twofold Center of Christian Ethics

In this chapter I will entertain the following thesis: *There is no way to address what Christian ethics should look like in the contemporary matrix of the Western world without considering and correcting the deeply problematic opposition that is widely assumed to exist between freedom and law.* Because "freedom" most often is understood as the license of autarky, any concept of "law" must be seen as random legislative imposition. Yet if "freedom" is understood as the movement of the human toward good — any good, but especially toward God — "law" can be seen as the external principle of action that gives shape and form to this freedom in its directedness toward both God and created goods.[1] I will give a brief historical account of the contemporary perspective and then flesh out a vision of what overcoming the opposition between freedom and law might presuppose and entail.

Instead of unfolding the above thesis in an abstract and purely formal way, I will develop it by recovering the twofold center of Christian ethics — freedom and commandment — via an evangelical catholic reading of the Reformation tradition.[2] I will do this in six interconnected steps. First, I will address the modern theological impoverishment of Protestant ethics. Second, I will identify three twentieth-century movements that have aimed to overcome it. And third, I will turn to a short remembrance of Luther's theology of Christian freedom. In a fourth section I will sketch out five aspects of how God's "law," God's commandments, must be understood as the very path of Christian freedom, and on this ground, in a fifth section, I will develop a notion of "re(dis)covering" the natural law under pluralistic conditions. Finally, I will return to the underlying theme of "law and gospel."

I. The Modern Theological Impoverishment of Protestant Ethics

Before considering again the theme of chapter 7, that is, the inherent interrelationship between Christian freedom and God's "law," God's commandments — how this freedom *is* the embodiment of practicing these commandments as a way of life — we need to ask why it seems necessary to press the obvious by reintroducing this positive and substantive notion of Christian freedom. The reason is that in modern Protestant ethics, "freedom" has come to be understood primarily as negative freedom: freedom "from" and not freedom "for." Two complex developments contributed to the notion of this deeply problematic dichotomy between a purely negative freedom and its archenemy — indeed, its *termination* — a law that is understood as purely legislative and enforcing.

The first development is broadly associated with an outcome of the "Luther renaissance" that emerged toward the end of the nineteenth century and dominated the Luther-research of most of the twentieth. Besides rediscovering the centrality of the doctrine of justification by faith alone, this movement sought to construe "Protestantism" generically as an imprincipled alternative to "Roman Catholicism," both theologically and ethically. This was a misguided enterprise that eventually overstretched and thereby misapplied the central doctrine as the formal, defining principle of Protestantism.[3]

The second development is associated with the overarching significance that Kant's philosophy gained for modern Protestant ethics, especially his concepts of "freedom" and "law." It is largely because of the way Kant was received in Protestantism that modern Protestant ethics understands "freedom" as primarily negative, as freedom "from," and "law" either as heteronomous and thus as threatening to autonomy or as mediated through autonomy and thus as purely formal.

Luther's Sola Fide

If there exists one decisive fallacy of modern Protestant ethics, it is the broadly shared assumption that what makes a Christian ethics recognizably "Protestant" is the conviction that everything must ultimately be framed by and derived from the one central article of Protestantism, namely, justification by grace through faith alone.[4] I do not intend to challenge the very centrality of this doctrine; rather, I intend to safeguard it from misapplication beyond, and thereby against, the Reformers' intention. The fallacy of modern Protestant ethics is not its insistence on the centrality of the doctrine of justification by faith alone but its regard of this doctrine as a ceiling that has to cover everything instead of the very floor on which we stand. Instead of simply and precisely describing what God has done and still does for us through Christ's incarnation, death, and resurrection, the doctrine of justification was turned into a systematic principle with the purpose of governing and controlling every other element of the Christian faith. One product of this development was an understanding of the doctrine of justification in exclusively forensic terms, which eclipsed Luther's other emphasis, namely, the very presence of Christ in faith.[5] The surely unintended consequence was, *first*, that "justification" became a purely external, formal, and juridical transaction whose only immediately tangible effect was freedom, in faith, "from" the law's unmasking and convicting force. This meant, *second*, that "law" came to be seen as relevant only in this unmasking and convicting use (its "second," or *theological*, use, through which it prepares us for the gospel's word of forgiveness). In fact, God's law came to be simply identified with this use, so that "law" took on a pervasively negative connotation. While this negative law clearly continued to serve a constructive purpose *theologically*, it could not possibly continue to matter *ethically*. Seen only from the perspective of its unmasking and convicting function, God's law had to be kept at all costs from becoming ethically relevant and thereby once again threatening to the newly won freedom "from."

The focus on an exclusively forensic understanding of justification fostered the assumption that the gospel had nothing but a negative relationship to God's law. This negative relationship, of course, had inherently antinomian consequences.[6] If the gospel is interpreted as radically opposed to the law, the freedom that results in the gospel's acceptance can only be construed as negative freedom, as freedom from any alienating, authenticity-inhibiting restrictions. The law — and not humanity, under the condition of sin, faced by God's law! — becomes the essential problem.[7]

Kant's "Freedom" and "Law"

While this is not the place to discuss Kant's ethics, we do need to see how modern Protestantism superimposed its own agenda on Kant's framework. What is crucial about this framework is that God matters in the realm of reason only as a transcendental idea that accounts for human moral agency. The idea of God safeguards the agent's freedom and thereby his or her moral responsibility. Kant's framework had two critical implications: First, any externally encountered law would undercut the self-legislative nature of human freedom and thus had to be rejected as heteronomous. Second, the only place left for the gospel was its "effect" on the agent, namely, making the freedom of the moral agent possible by redefining the agent and liberating him or her from all heteronomy. This tendency later encouraged the exclusively forensic understanding of the doctrine of justification in the "Luther renaissance." By becoming an abstract condition of the believer's constitution as moral agent, the gospel is reduced to the point of its forensic message, which the believer, once justified, always "knows": We are radically and unavoidably accepted by God. The "life in faith" that brings forth good works and is directed toward the neighbor's service is now defined by the logic of "motivation" and "effect." Yet this service has to remain completely abstract in its description because the gospel-based "freedom" is caught in its purely negative relationship to the law (heteronomously understood). Any definite shape and form in which the end of our acceptance (communion with the triune God) might be embodied must be rejected because of the allegedly ever present dangers of legalism and works-righteousness.

On the one side, both developments converge in a radical eclipse of the "first" use of the law, namely, the encounter of humans with a *moral order* that represents the ordinance of a divine lawgiver. According to the first development, the ordinance is seen only as convicting and unmasking and thereby irrelevant for the moral conduct of humanity *post lapsum*. According to the second development, the first use of the law is unavoidably heteronomous and therefore a threat to human "autonomy," since in the external encounter with God's law the self-legislative nature of practical reason seems to be displaced. Yet precisely because of human estrangement from God, God's law *does* have a deeply heteronomous quality. In other words, in the shadow of both developments, the insight has been lost that it is not God's law but human life under the condition of sin that is the archenemy of genuine human freedom, of "libertas."[8]

On the other side, both developments converge in a primarily negative understanding of human freedom. Freedom is not allowed to have a substantive gestalt, an orderedness through distinct practices that draw it ultimately into the divine communion, which is the only source of genuine freedom. The first development, because of its focus on justification as purely forensic, would see this gestalt as a new, more sophisticated form of works-righteousness; the second development would see it as contradictory to the self-legislative nature of human freedom. There is no place for a gestalt because there is no substantive place for Christ in the concept of freedom. In the first case, justification works only by imputation and not also by Christ becoming the very form of faith. In the second case, faith is reduced to the "gnosis" of radical acceptance manifested only in its effect on the agency of the believer. While Christ is the medium of acceptance, he remains essentially to be "known," not to be grasped by faith as the very gestalt of a particular way of life.[9]

In the framework of this negative freedom, the gospel becomes the impetus for a "utilitarianism of love" directed to an abstract neighbor. Again, the problem is the formalization of both "love" and "neighbor" that results from the eclipse of the first use of the law — which could give substance to both the love that is called for in particular settings and the neighbor that is encountered in morally distinct relationships. Instead, specific determinations and questions are replaced by abstract calculations of what kinds of acts might best serve my neighbor in the sense of the agape-love to which the gospel so unavoidably motivates.[10] This explains the strong need for ethical analyses of the political, social, and economic life, which give these utilitarian calculations their necessary framework.[11] Such analysis most often depends completely on the ethicist's personal political preferences and his or her identification with one or the other ideological wing of the divide between "progressives" and "conservatives," a divide that itself is constitutive of modernity.

This is the light baggage with which a significant segment of contemporary Protestant ethics that wants to be intentionally "Protestant" travels: a motivating, gnostically understood gospel of radical acceptance, a broadly conceived tendency of utilitarian thinking oriented to somehow enhance or enrich the neighbor's life, and a loosely knit set of framing analyses of the political, social, and economic life. Compared with the rich, dense, and complex tradition and discourse of Roman Catholic moral theology and social teaching,[12] this kind of Protestant ethics seems indeed emaciated. Yet according to our Protestant fallacy, this ethic is one of the supposedly crucial points of the Reformation's rediscovery of "Christian liberty." Christians act freely, spontaneously, and lovingly out of the gospel in light of the challenges they face.

The core assumption of this "radically Protestant" — that is, "radically modern" — reading of Luther and the Reformation is that the gospel makes possible this new moral subject. We are set free to do what we want, as long as we have a "good will" (are motivated by the "gospel") and thereby intend "something good" in what we do. Insofar as our doing is sinful — and, after all, all our doing is sinful in the ambiguity of life and action under the condition of sin — it is already forgiven by that radical acceptance that constitutes our existence as believers. With this worry out of the way, we are radically set free as moral agents to act on behalf of the gospel in the service of the neighbor and therefore — to use one of the Protestant fallacy's favorite formulas —

"to sin boldly": we do not let ourselves be inhibited by moralistic scruples. As long as our intentions are well meaning, we can do what is necessary and anticipate God's forgiveness for our moral failures.

Any additional baggage, such as concrete commandments, binding and — God forbid — even exceptionless norms, orienting and ordering goods, and formative virtues, can only serve to infringe upon the precious freedom to which we are called and can only tempt us to the one unforgivable double sin in Protestantism: legalism and works-righteousness. If there is one thing modern Protestant ethics is — with a very good conscience — *dogmatic* about, it is the protection of human freedom from the dangers of legalism and works-righteousness.

In our increasingly post-Christian environment in the Western world, this "Protestantism lite" turns out to be fatal. Why? Because in our late modern sentiment, freedom and law, freedom and binding obligation, freedom and the encounter of an unambiguous commandment, have become mutually exclusive. From the original heroism of Kantian autonomy — freedom ultimately consists in giving oneself the law[13] — things have boiled down to the popular conviction that freedom means doing our own thing without being accountable to anyone but ourselves. The moral law has been replaced by the law of our unexamined desires. Because "Protestantism lite" has given up the substantive notion of freedom, it has lost all critical perspective on its own inflated notion, which it has — blindly — presumed to champion as genuine "Christian freedom." While in traditional Protestant ethics "freedom" and "law," or the "Christian life" and "God's commandments," were regarded as mutually dependent on and presupposing each other, in modern Protestant ethics they have increasingly become mutually exclusive because of the fallacy described above. The result is that modern Protestant ethics has become thoroughly antinomian and — at the same time — extremely legalistic about particular "correctnesses" that are reflective of distinct social and political agendas. What has happened?

Instead of Luther's "happy exchange" between the person's sin and Christ's righteousness, during the last two hundred years there has been a quite "unhappy exchange" between God and the self-sufficient subject. God is no longer the defining horizon of the human good, the end of all things, and present in the conscience. In other words, the eschatological horizon of life with God, God's utter proximity in his commandments, has slowly but increasingly turned into life according to the methodological procedure of modern science: *etsi Deus non daretur,* as if God did not exist. Thus the thinking and judging individual subject has become the central focus in theories of ethics and in the practical ways of going about our moral lives.

Freedom and Commandment

Yet for Luther, Calvin, and the other Reformers — together with the whole Catholic tradition — the Christian life (and any theological reflection upon it) hinges first and foremost on God's future with and for us: the resurrection of the dead, the last judgment, and the everlasting enjoyment of the triune God. Second, it hinges on God's past with and for us: the creation of the contingent world we know, the election of Israel, and the life, death, and resurrection of Jesus of Nazareth, God incarnate in human flesh. And third, Christian life hinges on God's presence with and for us: in God's word proclaimed, in baptism and Holy Communion, in the ongoing presence of Israel and the tangible body of Christ, the church, and in God's ongoing and sustaining care for creation and all creatures, human and nonhuman. Three times God, and each time irreplaceably constitutive of the Christian life.[14]

As the remembrance of God's sustaining and redeeming past with us becomes less and less crucial, and as the expectation of God's future with us becomes less and less sure, why should the notion of God's presence with us still matter for the Christian life? As God has ceased to be the present One in the Christian life, we have turned to a willing substitute, eager to step in: we ourselves. As a result, both the past and the future have been reconstituted through the centrality of the human agent. In historicism and utopianism, both past and future have become human constructs, no longer received through remembrance and expectation.[15]

Modernity has been constituted by a Copernican revolution in the moral universe. It has moved from the theocentricity still characteristic of the Reformation to a new, radical anthropocentricity: God becomes a transcendental idea necessary to secure the inner stability of the moral agent.[16] While Kant was quite serious about God as transcendental idea, we would look in vain for this idea even among Kant's most popular disciples in contemporary ethics, the school of discourse ethics.[17] Presupposing the radical critique of Marx, Nietzsche, and Freud, this neo-Kantian school fully operates from the axiom *etsi Deus non daretur,* as if God did not exist. The human agent might need to be extended intersubjectively, but God no longer matters at all for most of contemporary ethics.[18] And a significant stream of Protestant ethics in the nineteenth and twentieth centuries has claimed the Kantian tradition as the best of Protestantism, a Protestantism free of the baggage of metaphysics on the upward road of seemingly inevitable moral, political, and scientific progress.

Yet the killing fields of World Wars I and II, the Holocaust, the Vietnam War, the collapse of the colonial empires (including the Soviet Union), and a sustained and sharp critique of all forms of Eurocentrism have shattered the self-confidence of modern Protestantism in the line of Kant and the neo-

Kantians. As a result, three broad movements in Protestant ethics have challenged the Kantian paradigm and thereby begun to overcome the Protestant fallacy.

II. Overcoming the Protestant Fallacy: Three Twentieth-Century Movements in Protestant Ethics

In the *first* movement, which arose after World War I, "dialectical theology" and later the "theology of the word of God" sought to *decenter the moral agent*. One of the early battle cries of this movement was Karl Barth's claim that "the general concept of ethics interestingly coincides exactly with the concept of sin."[19] With this widely misunderstood statement Barth was not arguing against "ethics" but was attacking all forms of Kantian ethics, in which the human agent and his or her practical reason constitute the very center of the moral universe. For Nietzsche, it was only a small step from the human agent as center to the human agent as the measure of the law of practical reason, of good and evil — a step from moral autonomy to moral sovereignty. In identifying this ethics with original sin, Barth was attempting to decenter the human being as the ethical subject, to remeasure the moral agent as finite creature, mortally wounded by sin. God, the only good One, the only free One, again became the center of Christian ethics, often with a strongly christological emphasis, as in the later Barth and in Bonhoeffer's ethics.[20] Not surprisingly, God's commandments reemerge as a theme in this movement in close connection with the way Christian freedom is conceived.

A *second* important movement in Protestant ethics, which originated in the 1970s and 1980s in the United States, has sought to *differentiate the moral agent*, to show that the moral agent is a much more complex reality than the mathematical point to which it had shrunk in the wake of Kantian ethics.[21] Centrally, this movement has recovered the concepts of character and the virtues for Protestant ethics. Here the Protestant rediscovery of Aristotle and Thomas Aquinas has helped significantly. The notions of character and the virtues are essential in showing how particular goods and practices can direct and form the agent's character in both positive and negative ways. Freedom is concretely enabled by particular virtues, such as prudence, justice, or courage, and hindered by particular vices, such as greed, pride, or impatience. Thus character- and virtue-ethics give flesh and bones back to the Kantian moral agent, who had been rarefied to the "punctual self" of reason.[22]

A *third* broad movement in recent Protestant ethics has focused on overcoming the abstract universalism of modern ethics by seeking to *recontextualize the moral agent*. This has occurred through two theological foci: *creation* and God's *economy of salvation* as concretely embodied in Israel and the church. With respect to *creation,* liberation theology has reemphasized the sociopolitical location of the agent as a critical aspect of his or her identity and struggle.[23] Feminist theology has sharpened our eyes to the world of gender differentiation as crucial for an embodied moral agent,[24] and the emerging eco-ethics and animal ethics have strongly pressed the embeddedness of the human agent in an intricate network of natural habitats on earth, of which the human is only one.[25] The focus on God's *economy of salvation* in recent Protestant ethics has emphasized the communal existence of Christians and the ecclesial character of Christian ethics. It reflects on the morals, practices, and activity of a certain people, namely, God's people as a particular community of moral discourse and witness.[26]

We might ask whether it is really helpful to lump liberation ethics and ecclesial ethics together as two modes of recontextualization. The very way it is done here begs the question of how I understand "context." At first glance, this grouping might seem to be heuristically helpful for describing their common opposition to abstract universalism. But is that sufficient to make them credible as parts of a single broad movement? Of course not. There is obviously a deep and critical tension between the way "context" is understood and framed by the two modes, and I will attempt to show that it can be settled only in light of a constructive interrelationship of freedom and law.

Undoubtedly, all three movements are of great significance for Protestant ethics in overcoming its colonization by the Kantian paradigm and its confusion by the closely related Protestant fallacy. Yet I would argue also for a *fourth movement,* one that challenges head-on the widespread antinomianism of contemporary Protestant ethics — its sheer indifference toward and even open rejection of the notion that God's commandments are of central, unnegotiable importance for Christian ethics and, more crucially, for a substantive notion of Christian freedom. In other words, Christian freedom, the true freedom of the Christian moral agent, and thereby genuine human freedom, is fatally misconstrued in the absence of a serious consideration of God's commandments. The initial challenge in this regard has been posed by Martin Luther himself. In his thought on Christian existence and the moral life, we find an anticipatory critique of modernity's misconstruals of both freedom and law.[27] This critique points us toward a "decentered self" that understands itself as essentially gifted and its freedom as inherently relational. The decentered self is shaped by a way of life whose end is good works and whose form is God's commandments.

III. Luther's Theology of Christian Freedom

How does a theology and ethics rooted in the Reformation tradition respond to this challenge? Does Lutheranism promote a "freedom without the law"? Are Lutherans, as "Catholics of the Augsburg Confession," responsible for the flat notion of autonomy characteristic of late modernity, in which the autocratic self is free to define its own value sets so long as the majority-defined rules are not breached? What is authentic human freedom? Is it in principle a freedom without the law, so that on its basis we have license to avoid paying serious and sustained attention to God's law? How are Christian freedom and God's commandments related? Does the former need to exclude any reference to the latter in order to avoid even the slightest danger of works-righteousness or legalism? Does any reference to the latter irretrievably destroy the precious good of the former? In addressing these questions, it seems wise to turn directly to the treatise of Luther's to which the Protestant fallacy most often refers — that is, refers rhetorically, without fully taking into account all aspects of this rich and dense text.

Luther's magna charta of the Christian life, his treatise *The Freedom of a Christian* (1520), is still one of the most decisive and foundational texts for Christian ethics in the Reformation tradition. The text opens with this dramatic dialectic: "A Christian is a perfectly free lord of all, subject to none. A Christian is a perfectly dutiful servant of all, subject to all."[28] The sad story of this formula is that the dialectic has not been maintained. Either its first half has been emphasized and its second half forgotten, which has led directly to our late modern notion of the moral autocracy of the independent self, or its second half has been emphasized and its first half forgotten, which has led to the notorious Lutheran subservience to all kinds of political authorities guided by a very problematic notion of Christian obedience. A third error has been to dichotomize the two statements: freedom for the "inner" (spiritual) life, and uncritical acceptance of all the *Eigengesetzlichkeiten,* the intrinsic "mechanisms" and "dynamics," of the "outer" (political and economic) life.[29]

Any attempt to claim anything less than the whole radical dialectic is a fatal mistake. What Luther has to say in two sentences, what cannot be said in one, is the one dynamic of the Christian life in faith, life in union with Christ, as part of his body. Insofar as we become one with Christ in faith, this dialectic of freedom in faith and service in love expresses God's own freedom in love.

Having laid out the dynamic of salvation (focusing on the image of the "happy exchange" of attributes between Christ and the sinner),[30] Luther zeroes in on his main concern, the telos of it all, namely, the Christian life, in which this faith is embodied in love. How is this life of evangelical freedom in

Christ to be understood and grasped? Luther makes two telling biblical references at this point.

One is Philippians 2, where we find the christological hymn.[31] Here Luther, with St. Paul, points to Christ's and, in the most radical sense, God's own humility in the very economy of salvation. This is the embodiment of God's freedom in love, which we are called to emulate in our own lives in faith. Here is our evangelical paradigm, the overarching model of our Christian freedom. In this model, love — God's self-giving love — is the effective and the final cause, and service, the very shape of this freedom in humility.

Christians are perfectly free lords over all things in creation. Justified by faith, all idols before which we would justify ourselves and our deeds have been unmasked as false gods. Only insofar as they serve God's sustaining and redeeming activity do they have authority over us. This authority is significantly limited by and completely derived from the One who authorizes them. Yet "in faith," in union with Christ, Christians participate in God's own freedom, the inner dynamic of God's triune love, which — through Christ and the Spirit's mission — aims to draw all of creation into communion with the triune God. Christian freedom is our participation in this very mission through our loving service to the neighbor.

But doesn't this sound like the very "Protestantism lite" I chastised above? Obviously, this life of freedom seems to spring from the free spontaneity of Christian faith and love and to be otherwise guided only by the needs of the neighbor, by the concrete situation — in other words, by that utilitarianism of love for which modern Protestant ethics is so notorious. It seems as if the person living in faith has no need of God's commandments.[32]

Precisely at this point, however, we need to consider the other of Luther's telling biblical references about freedom in the life of faith, his reference to Genesis 2:

> We should think of the works of a Christian who is justified and saved by faith because of the pure and free mercy of God, just as we would think of the works which Adam and Eve did in Paradise, and all their children would have done if they had not sinned. . . . The works of a believer are like this. Through his faith he has been restored to Paradise and created anew, has no need of works that he may become righteous; but that he may not be idle and may provide for and keep his body, he must do such works freely only to please God.[33]

Luther claims that "in faith," that is, in union with Christ, the Christian is restored to the original state of prelapsarian life with God. As I argued extensively in chapter 7, there is a way of life proper to that state of being. *Sola gratia* and *sola fide,* the Christian is back in that righteousness that God's commandment presupposes and to which God's commandment gives creaturely form. This is precisely why for Luther the "freedom of a Christian" never contradicts God's commandments and never comes without them but rather rejoices in them and welcomes them as creaturely ways of embodying our love of God and love of neighbor. Receiving the law as an external code is typical of sinful humanity.[34] According to Luther, both the law of Moses and natural law are subject to this distortion *sub conditione peccati,* under the condition of sin, where we have lost the original grace of humanity created in the image of God. Yet God's grace received in faith rectifies this distortion by restoring believers to the state of paradise, "drunk with joy towards God." Now the original, spiritual understanding of the law is again accessible. As David Yeago aptly puts it:

> This means that one who understands the law spiritually remembers that all God's commandments presuppose a subject deified by grace, a human being who is drunk with joy toward God and rejoices in all God's creatures. This is, after all, precisely what Jesus teaches: the law and the prophets hang on the double commandment of love, the commandment to love God with all our heart, soul, mind, and strength and our neighbor as ourselves.[35]

Thus according to Luther's eschatological understanding of faith, when Christ himself, the new Adam, is present in the believer, there is no difference anymore between God's gospel — God's forgiving, restoring, and sanctifying activity in Christ — and God's commandments, the creaturely form of freedom. Hence, Christians now know God's law in a new way, that is, as "the law of Christ," the form of which, Luther says, is faith,

> that living and spiritual flame inscribed by the Spirit in human hearts, which wills, does, and indeed *is* that which the law of Moses commands and requires verbally.... And so the law of Christ is properly not teaching but living, not word but reality, not sign but fulfillment. And it is the word of the gospel which is the ministry of this life, reality, and fulfillment and the means by which it is brought to our hearts.[36]

IV. The Path of Christian Freedom: God's Commandments

How does this reading of Luther's *Freedom of a Christian* connect with our first part, with the Protestant fallacy and the modern notion of freedom without the law? I will sketch here five points, which allude to the ongoing importance of God's commandments for Christian ethics — and not only in the Reformation tradition. These points will draw heavily on the "ethics" of Luther's *Catechisms* to underscore the fruitfulness and constructive potential of being continuously engaged by the Decalogue so that Christian freedom may find its appropriate gestalt.[37]

1. God's commandments have to be understood as that *shape and form of our life with God* that corresponds to us as creatures. God's commandments allow us to embody our obedience to God and our service to humanity in concrete historical practices and distinct activities. God's commandments are a welcome help in forming the freedom of the Christian life. The remembrance of God's commandments, their interpretation and application, and the discernment of reality in light of them are worthy and important themes for Christian ethics. This is especially true for a Protestant ethics that is interested in overcoming contemporary impoverishments and in continuing the fullness of the Reformation tradition. Most crucially, the first commandment undercuts the operative axiom of modernity, *etsi Deus non daretur,* as if God did not exist. It invites us to the lifelong practical training of learning how to embody the first article of the Creed, that is, how to be a creature, how to trust completely in God as our ultimate good, and how to remain vulnerable in our dependence upon God's gift of sustenance and communion. Luther puts it the following way:

> Thus you can easily understand what and how much this commandment requires, namely, that one's whole heart and confidence be placed in God alone, and in no one else. To have a God, as you can well imagine, does not mean to grasp him with your fingers, or to put him into a purse, or to shut him up in a box. Rather, you lay hold of God when your heart grasps him and clings to him. To cling to him with your heart is nothing else than to entrust yourself to him completely. He wishes to turn us away from everything else apart from him, and to draw us to himself, because he is the one, eternal good.[38]

Christian freedom finds its gestalt most fundamentally in learning how to embody this most simple and yet most difficult fact of our human lives. According to Luther, it is wrong to assume that this simplicity is "at hand." Our radical estrangement from God, our bondage to sin, keeps this simplicity hidden from our gaze. Humans need to be liberated through God's grace from the force of sin in order to learn the radical simplicity of fulfilling the first commandment by faith alone. Stanley Hauerwas calls this "learning to be a sinner";[39] Martin Luther would have called it "learning Christ's lordship." He explains it in a way that is offensive to our modern sensibilities: "What is it 'to become a lord'? It means that he has redeemed and released me from sin, from the devil, from death, and from all misfortune. Before this I had no lord or king, but was captive under the power of the devil. I was condemned to death and entangled in sin and blindness."[40]

2. To overcome the abstract universalism of modern ethics and the Protestant complicity in it, God's commandments are in need of a concrete community of remembrance and interpretation. In other words, we do not encounter God's commandments in an abstract way and an empty space but in a concrete ecclesial context, in a dense web of relationships and in light of particular challenges. God's commandments are not encountered via solitary introspection but via an *ecclesial hermeneutics* in which they are constantly remembered, interpreted, and enacted in faithful service. Let me be clear: Ecclesial hermeneutics must not mean that the church becomes the "master" of God's commandments, that we bend them to our purposes, that we streamline them according to the requirements of the Zeitgeist, that we curtail them according to our small visions and our great anxieties.[41] Instead, ecclesial hermeneutics means that through the faithful remembrance of God's commandments in concrete ecclesial contexts we are stretched, challenged, and kept accountable by those commandments.[42] Received as a naked, external code, they are terrifying and deadly; received as the form of faith, they are breathtaking — exciting and exhilarating. But one thing they surely are not — namely, "at hand" for casual or self-interested examination by a sovereign moral subject. Luther's urgent invitation in regard to the first commandment extends to all of them:

> Let each and everyone, then, see to it that you esteem this commandment above all things and not make light of it. Search and examine your own heart thoroughly, and you will discover whether or not it clings to God alone. If you have the sort of heart that expects from him nothing but good, especially in distress and need, and renounces and forsakes all that is not God, then you have the one true God. On the contrary, if your heart clings to something else and expects to receive from it more good and help than from God and does not run to God but flees from him when things go wrong, then you have another god, an idol.[43]

Christian freedom is embodied in this ongoing ecclesial hermeneutics of remembering God's commandments. Otherwise, it is not Christian freedom. Embodied in this ecclesial hermeneutics, Christian freedom becomes concrete as a spiritual discipline in concrete practices such as meditation on Scripture, the ongoing exegesis and examination of God's commandments, and the continuing explication and application of the Decalogue.[44]

3. Part of this spiritual discipline of remembering God's commandments is to learn *how to see, to perceive, rightly.*[45] The first question of Christian ethics should be not, What ought I now to do? but, How does the world really look? In other words, "situations" are not just static, objective realities that we simply encounter. Rather, the description of a situation is everything; it is the situation itself. It is in the description of a situation that the morally decisive moves for choices and decisions are already made. Being shaped by the spiritual practice of ceaselessly remembering God's commandments means being faced with God's constant critical intervention in our construals of reality. God's commandments thus help us avoid being trapped by false necessities and givens. They free us from becoming victimized by the power of facticity, which ceaselessly presses in on us to submit us to its alleged necessities. God's commandments represent the Creator's and Redeemer's counterfactual, wholesome claim on us, which keeps those powers and principalities in check that wish to control our ways of seeing how things really are. In the kabbalistic tradition, the Hebrew word for evil, *rah*, is interpreted to actually mean "to see, to perceive, badly." This is the point: The double love commandment and the Decalogue, the one positively and the other negatively, teach us how to be a neighbor to others, to pay attention, to care. By helping us to see rightly, God's commandments protect and concretely enable Christian freedom to fulfill its calling, to be free *from* our self-absorption *for* the worship of God and the service of God's creation. The fundamental commandment that points to that practice in and through which we learn "to see rightly" is the third commandment (according to Luther's counting), the sanctification of the holy day. This might come somewhat as a surprise, but "seeing rightly" presupposes having acquired a character formed by the ongoing encounter with God's word. To learn how to be a creature and a neighbor happens precisely in those practices through which we sanctify the holy day — first of all, by common worship. Through word and sacrament we are "neighbored to" by God in Christ and thereby "re-created" through the Spirit. Luther reminds us that this holy encounter with God's word is not limited to the worship for which we might gather once a week: "Truly, we Christians ought to make every day such a holy day and devote ourselves only to holy things, that is, to occupy ourselves daily with God's Word and carry it in our hearts and on our lips."[46]

4. One of the most serious blind spots in contemporary ethics is the critical and constructive treatment of *human desire*. Yet if there is one force that drives the relentless growth and dynamic of the modern market economy and modern technology, it is unexamined and unchecked human desire. What makes human desires so fatally dangerous is that they have tacitly occupied and claimed the notion of human freedom for their insatiable purposes. In the context of late modernity, freedom means happiness, and happiness is unfortunately defined as the fulfillment of desires. Coveting — the endless, limitless, ceaseless desiring of "things," of pleasures, of experiences — is the fuel that runs the engine of our consumer-oriented and therefore supposedly "free" global market economy. Yet each thing acquired, each pleasure fulfilled produces only the thirst, the desire for more.[47]

In this context the relevance of God's commandments becomes starkly clear: they stubbornly keep our desires directed toward God. Desire as such is *not* the problem; it is *not* "bad." Indeed, we are created as creatures with desires; to be human is to be desiring. Yet all of our desires were created to come to a rest in their one ultimate good, communion with God. Augustine's famous sentence from the *Confessions* — "[Y]ou have made us and drawn us to yourself, and our heart is unquiet until it rests in you"[48] — expresses how only in God do our desires find rest and fulfillment. If other created things are elevated to the position of the ultimate good in ceaseless exchange, coveting is the unavoidable result, since none of these created things will ultimately bring our desiring to a rest. Without desire we would cease to be human; without God as desire's ultimate end, we cease to be humane. Therefore, Christian freedom has to be precisely understood as true *askesis*, or chastity,[49] that is, letting all our desires be ordered by and fulfilled in the communion with God that has begun in our grasping of Christ in faith. Instead of being governed by the insatiability of our desires seeking ultimate fulfillment in finite goods, we become free to desire our ultimate good. In communion with that good, we receive the finite goods of creation that we also desire.

Positively, the Decalogue can and should be summarized in the double love commandment; negatively, it can be summarized in the stark commandment Thou shalt not covet — that is, Do not submit yourself to the insatiable thirst of your desires directed toward the world: wealth, power, ownership of truth, control of the neighbor and all the goods of the world.[50] Misdirected, our desires completely distort any serious notion of authentic freedom by subtly redefining freedom as the potential to fulfill whatever we desire. Freedom as slavery to our desires is the result of life in the absence of God's wholesome commandment Thou shalt not covet. This commandment directs our desire to the first commandment, the one source that can bring all our desires to their rest and fulfillment. The fulfillment of the first commandment through faith opens us to the presence and the need of the neighbor.[51]

5. Life according to God's commandments, with its center in the first commandment of the Decalogue, is Christian freedom. It is life with God, our being drawn into the very freedom of God's own inner-trinitarian life of love. Participating in God's very freedom, we walk the walk that God has walked for us already. "For we are what he has made us, created in Christ Jesus for good works, which God prepared beforehand to be our way of life" (Eph 2:10).[52] Good works, according to the Reformers, are nothing other than the shape of Christian freedom as informed by God's commandments; they are a participation in the freedom of the one who has already prepared, in triune love, these good works. To put it differently, by pointing to the gestalt of Christian freedom, God's commandments are in their deepest sense "transmoral"; they are actually "beyond good and evil." They do not thrive on the distinction between and thereby the reproduction of "good" and "evil" *post lapsum* by offering a map on which we can mark out "good" and "evil" according to our knowledge.[53] Rather, they point to those intrinsically good acts through which Christian freedom is exercised.

V. God's Commandments and the Natural Law

There are two important reasons why this account in itself is not fully sufficient, reasons that lead us back to the tension between a creation-centered ethics and an ecclesially centered ethics.

First, the church occupies concrete space in the world, which means that the gestalt of Christian freedom will encounter and relate to other ways of life and other ways of thinking about morality. The church has done so from its inception. Yet in its knowledge and confession of God as the Creator of the universe, the church also assumes and expects that it will find traces of a knowledge of God's will in its encounter with non-Christians. Therefore, the account just sketched of how the commandments guide us on the path of freedom is anything but a "sectarian" way of life of some ghettoized community. Rather, in our highly pluralistic society, it amounts to a particular witness with universal implications. It is a particular, embodied argument with universal intent. It is a particular, embodied universality — not one of abstract procedures.[54]

Second, one of the most deep-seated assumptions of modernity is that human practical reason is unimpaired and can, through the transparency of its own reflection, come to certain results. To a certain degree this seems possible. The phenomenon of the *human conscience* points to this fact. Thomas Aquinas has given classical expression to the way it dominates Roman Catholic understanding. According to this understanding, humans are aware of basic moral principles. Conscience is the judgment of practical reason as it brings these principles to bear on particular moral issues.[55] The broad acceptance of this phenomenon is reflected in the Roman Catholic Church's traditional teaching that one must always obey one's conscience. Yet in contrast to this notion of conscience, which does not pay explicit attention to the human condition *post lapsum,* Luther distinguishes sharply between a "conscience before the people" and "conscience" in a theologically more substantive and finally transmoral way. The latter is where we are radically addressed and questioned by God's word and exposed to God's judgment.[56] Here faith, the very acceptance of God's judgment in Christ's cross and resurrection, *is* the good conscience. "[O]nly Christ belongs in the conscience. The person God intends is the person of faith who is one person, 'one cake,' with Christ."[57] Without faith conscience remains anxious, exposed to the pressing onslaught of the law's continuous unmasking of our radical estrangement from God.[58] In an anticipatory critique of modernity, Luther identified the theological quality of conscience, the very "blind spot" concealed by its primarily moral character.

The Enlightenment assumption of an unimpaired practical reason thus conceals the very fact that because of our estrangement from God we are battlefields of conflicting forces and desires. The claim of moral sovereignty and autocracy leads only to enslavement by our unexamined wishes, desires, and anxieties. Equally problematic as the blind spot itself is the assumption of modernity's self-critical turn, namely, that this blind spot can be examined and thus mastered by reason itself, be it via psychoanalysis, a phenomenology of existence, a hermeneutics of suspicion, or deconstruction. The soteriological offense remains: the law's second use remains intact, constantly convicting us as curved in on ourselves. This is equally true of Christians, since the struggle between our renewal through the Spirit of Christ and our sinful habits, involvements, and practices is not yet over (Gal 5:17).

Therefore, there is no path "upward" from a stable, unimpaired, practical rationality toward the theological horizon that this rationality always already presupposes and on which it always already depends. Rather, natural law constantly needs to be "discovered" and "recovered."

Interiorization and Memorization: Shaping the Intentionality

The Decalogue is the "foundationless beginning" of our practical thinking, its "efficient cause," so to speak, the beginning from which it always starts anew. The Sermon on the Mount is its "final cause," the promise of the embodied ultimate good as circumscribed by the practices toward which the Decalogue always is directed. The beginning takes a concrete form in the ever new meditation on the Decalogue. This inward training in God's commandments from the Decalogue toward the Sermon on the Mount shapes the way human intentionality gives gestalt to Christian freedom.

Remembering: Natural Law as Particular Discourse Tradition Summarized in an Interpretation of the Decalogue

There has been from antiquity a tradition of basic axioms, a "natural law discourse," that was appropriated by the patristic fathers, is part of the tradition's consensus,[59] and makes up a great portion of the concrete substance of the "universal" ethics of the Enlightenment.[60] This particular tradition of natural law discourse needs to be understood as part of an ongoing remembering and recovering of the natural law that has been submerged and forgotten under the condition of sin. This is where a constructive awareness of historical change, experience, and growth in the tradition of the natural law discourse has to take place — an awareness in the sense not of a historicist critique but of an *anamnēsis* and a growth of insight into both the nature of the natural law axioms and the breadth of their application. Yet it is crucial to understand that this ongoing remembrance and recovery of the natural law in the form of an ongoing discourse is not to be divorced from the church's way of life embodied in its practices. As soon as it is turned into an "independent" secular enterprise, into a discourse of "nature" and "law" divorced from a substantively Christian theology, it becomes open to historicist, genealogical, and ideological criticisms, as, indeed, is amply evidenced by the secular natural law discourse of modernity.

Witnessing to and Arguing for the Decalogue as Summary of the Natural Law

Christians individually and the church corporately do not have any privileged, detailed knowledge in practical moral matters. They find themselves bound, however, by the perspectives and insights of a path that God has willed for all humanity. The way of the commandments as human freedom in communion with God is the path on which re(dis)covery of the natural law takes place. In a time of rampant individualism in so-called private moral matters, and equally rampant commodification of humans on a global scale, the church witnesses to and argues for natural law. It does so when it reminds humans of those limits to power and license that demarcate the path of God's commandments. There are no simple, fixed answers, but there are unquestionable limitations to which all humans are bound; that is the double-edged nature of God's commandments. On the one hand, they point out freedom's gestalt in communion with God, the intrinsically good works of faith. On the other hand, they identify what have often been called "intrinsically evil acts." They do so by circumscribing the most essential moral notions: dishonoring our indebtedness, unjust killing (that is, murdering), stealing, lying, coveting what is not our own, and — most fundamentally — failing to acknowledge the very source of our being as creatures.

Re(dis)covering the Natural Law in Concreto and under the Conditions of Pluralism

This is not a theory to be applied but a particular practice that involves both theoretical and practical reasoning. It is bound to a way of *theological* thinking that *presupposes*, first, God the Creator and Redeemer, who unmasks and judges humans' estrangement from the divine origin, from each other, and from creation and who calls humans into the communion of the divine life; second, a created order and a "way of life" willed for all humans; and third, a practical reason that is neither unimpaired nor fully transparent to itself but rather wounded and obscured by sinful desires, habits, and practices.[61] Natural law is not something "out there" that we eventually stumble across if we search long enough; neither is it to be found written in our genes or in the stars. Nor is it to be understood as a means of a priori access to the moral universal. While some principles of practical reason are accessible to all of us, the natural law in its fullness is not simply inscribed in our minds. Instead, diverse practices and traditions that structure human society present a matrix of contingent and unpredictable resonances with the divine purpose for humankind as articulated in the narratives of Israel and Jesus. In particular structures of responsibility (vocations), Christians have to discern and judge the resonances and dissonances in light of God's commandments. Where we recognize a significant and broadly based correspondence between God's law and these traditions and patterns of human society, there natural law has been re(dis)covered. This can happen in a variety of ways. Particular "heroes"[62] and their distinct activities can make us "see" things that we otherwise would not have seen. We might think of Martin Luther King Jr., Mahatma Ghandi, Mother Teresa, or innumerable local figures who are less well known. It can happen through thoughtful public discussions of particularly pressing questions that lead to an extension or change of positive laws — the civil rights and environmental movements, for example. It can occur through symbolic witness and protest against existing laws that contradict both the Decalogue and the natural law tradition — nonviolent demonstrations against laws legalizing abortion, euthanasia, or distinct forms of discrimination, for example. Re(dis)covery can also occur through ongoing discernment and discourse about complex social and cultural phenomena that need to be sorted out. An obvious example pervasive in Western society today is the broad insecurity and variety of options and issues related to human sexuality outside the Christian vocations of heterosexual, lifelong marriage and celibate singleness.

Yet we must not assume that this approach might work as a "method" to be applied irrespective of and independent from the church's faithful witness to and teaching of God's law. Modernity's project of accessing the natural law as something "at hand" for human reason in isolation from a *theology of the natural law* produced its own most radical critique in Nietzsche's deconstruction of these assumptions. That critique created the basis for postmodernity's celebration of the ultimately plural, pragmatic, and political nature of any kind of "law" and "morality."

VI. Law and Gospel — or, Redeemed Life "Already and Not Yet"

I pointed earlier to a significant tension in the way I grouped a primarily creation-focused ethics (liberation ethics and feminist ethics) and a primarily ecclesially focused ethics as two modes of recontextualizing the moral agent. I asked whether such a grouping is helpful or appropriate and whether it might not conceal the significant differences in how these two distinct approaches understand and use "context." Yet I also claimed that we can make sense of and settle this tension in light of the constructive interrelationship between freedom and law. God's commandments encompass both sides. They presuppose the ecclesial context of particular practices in and through which God's economy of salvation is communicated and embodied — first of all, in word and sacrament. Through these distinct ecclesial practices the Decalogue points us to those intrinsically good acts (the "good works" of faith) in which Christian freedom has its gestalt. While this gestalt is rooted in the primary context of the ecclesial practices, it is by no means *limited* to them. Rather, it is coextensive with our scope as human agents and primarily directed to the concrete creaturely contexts in which we find ourselves.

Here we share a whole range of determinations, qualifications, and conditions — inklings of the natural law — with people who do not share our ecclesial vocation. In these contexts the Decalogue helps us re(dis)cover the natural law more fully. Particular creaturely contexts frame the way in which our moral imagination is challenged by God's commandments. In light of hunger and poverty, the fourth, fifth, and seventh commandments (Luther's counting) imply a radical social and economic critique. They demand just economic structures that effect, if not the complete fulfillment of these commandments, at least a genuine challenge by them. In light of the ecological crisis, God's commandments demand a radical questioning of the unexamined ways of life intrinsic in an excessive and destructive consumer culture. Yet these contexts that Christians share with all humans *post lapsum* are in tension with the context in which the gestalt of Christian freedom takes shape in accordance with the commandments. As long as the church takes up space in the world, this tension will remain. Attempting to overcome it from the one side results in the eclipse of Christian freedom and its unique gestalt, the negation of the difference that the church's unique vocation creates. From the other side, it results in another form of Constantinianism, the church's succumbing to the temptation to make history come out right. As Stanley Hauerwas recently put it: "[A] true and proper understanding of nature cannot be had apart from a true and proper understanding of the politics of God's rule. Any discussion of natural law which excludes or omits its ecclesial dimension is therefore bound to be distorted. The converse is also true: any understanding of ecclesiology which occludes its 'natural' dimension is likewise skewed. In short, because the God who exercises 'grace-full' dominion over creation (nature/human nature) is the same God who has revealed himself in Jesus Christ, it follows that such a self-disclosure entails the eschatological necessity (though perhaps not the temporal permanence) of the church."[63]

The first commandment lays bare the inner dialectic of our condition: We are created toward God, to desire God, yet we have lost the original communion with God. Nevertheless, we are commanded to attend to God before and above all other things — especially even before ourselves — and to fulfill this commandment only through the gift of faith. For now, the tension of this dialectic is held in suspense. To put it differently, the tension is the substance of the "law and gospel" dialectic, the final resolution of which we entreat in the petition "Thy kingdom come."

VII. The End

A Christian ethics in the Augsburg Confession's Catholic tradition, in short, an evangelical catholic ethics, serves the remembrance of God's commandments and the interpretation of the innumerable challenges, complexities, and perplexities that we encounter in our world in the critical and wholesome light of God's commandments. Such an ethics should, of course, always end with praise of God's commandments. Luther, the teacher of Christian freedom, wished that every student of theology — and what Christian is not always also a student of theology? — would read, meditate on, and scrutinize Psalm 119, the praise of God's commandments, on a daily basis.[64]

I began my reflections on Christian freedom and God's commandments with the assumption that the themes of "commandment" and "law" are not popular today. Yet, following the advice of Martin Luther, I end with the words of the psalmist who wrote Psalm 119 with the clear belief that there could hardly be anything more exciting than to be graciously addressed by God's commandments:

> Your decrees are wonderful;
>   therefore my soul keeps them.
> The unfolding of your words gives light;
>   it imparts understanding to the simple.
> With open mouth I pant,
>   because I long for your commandments.
> Turn to me and be gracious to me,
>   as is your custom toward those who love your name.
> Keep my steps steady according to your promise;
>   and never let iniquity have dominion over me.
> Redeem me from human oppression,
>   that I may keep your precepts.
> Make your face shine upon your servant,
>   and teach me your statutes.
> My eyes shed streams of tears
>   because your law is not kept. (Ps 119:129-136)

9. The Fallen Tongue and the Freedom of Praise: The Three Voices of the Eighth Commandment

"You shall not bear false witness against your neighbor." As do the other commandments of the Decalogue's second table, the eighth commandment pertains to a particular bodily member of the human being. It takes hands to kill and to steal, eyes to covet, and sexual organs to commit adultery — except adultery in the heart, for which the eyes suffice.

The eighth commandment focuses our attention on another part of the body: the tongue. The tongue is the organ par excellence of human intersubjectivity. With the tongue we praise and we curse, we speak truth and we lie. In his *Large Catechism,* Martin Luther ends the exposition of the eighth commandment with a pertinent remark in which James 3:5 strongly resonates: "There is nothing around or in us that can do greater good or greater harm in temporal or spiritual matters than the tongue, although it is the smallest and weakest member."[1] This all too well known intersubjective liability of the tongue would be a trivial matter and a concern only for social and political engineering if the human being were indeed just an accident of evolution. However, if the world — in and through the process of its distinct becoming — is understood as God's creation, everything in general and everything about the human in particular must be understood in light of God's providential intention and care. And if indeed the tongue must thus be understood as subject to divine providence, this smallest and weakest member acquires significant theological and metaphysical weight. For the tongue is the organ of speech, and the point of speech is nothing less than truthful communication — from the simple "Watch your step" to the significant "I love you."[2] Truthful communication is of profound importance to the intersubjective world.

Accordingly, Thomas Aquinas discusses the vice of lying in his *Summa*

The Fallen Tongue and the Freedom of Praise

theologiae in the context of those virtues that sustain and edify the life of the human community. For Aquinas, the intersubjective vice of lying is opposed to the intersubjective virtue of truthfulness, or veracity.[3] And it is Calvin who, in his *Sermons on the Ten Commandments,* most explicitly and forthrightly articulates the intersubjective character of truth-telling:

> Now if we want to observe what this text contains, we need to consider a higher principle, that is to consider why God created our tongues and why he gave us speech, the reason being that we might be able to communicate with each other. Now what is the purpose of communication if it isn't our mutual support and charity? Consequently, then, it is essential for us to learn to bridle our tongues to the extent that the union which God commands us may constantly be nurtured as much as possible. And that is why Saint James employs such vehemence when he speaks of evil reports. He says that the tongue, which is such a little member, or such a small piece of flesh, can start such a fire as to ravage the largest forest of the world. Therefore let us come back to our principle knowledge that God provided us with a unique gift when he gave us a means of being able to communicate with each other. So, on the one hand, men's affections may be hidden, but on the other the tongue exists to reveal our hearts. Therefore let us be encouraged to use such a gift and not to soil it with our vices and deplorableness. And seeing that God has given it to us for the purpose of nurturing tender love and fraternity with each other, may we not abuse it in order to gossip and bustle about here and there, so perverting our speech as to poison ourselves against each other.[4]

It seems that everything worth saying on this topic Calvin has said in his sermon on the eighth commandment. But it only seems so. To be sure, in the sermon passage just quoted Calvin touches upon all the topics that we rightly should expect from a catechetical sermon on the eighth commandment. However, in the following remarks, I do not want to simply expound upon extant interpretations of the eighth commandment, even such influential ones as Luther's or Calvin's. Nor do I want to belabor the classical and by now outworn philosophical debate about lying that has preoccupied deontologists and utilitarians for so long.[5] Rather, I want to focus on the way in which the eighth commandment encounters *us*. That is, I want to pay attention to the distinctly *theological* dynamic of this commandment as we find ourselves addressed by it. For we all too easily forget that we do not meet the Decalogue as abstract modern subjects on some "insulated" neutral ground. To the contrary, the Decalogue encounters *us* in a highly charged theological context.

I. The Fallen Tongue

This theological context has a surprising and deeply disquieting contour, although it appears in a narrative clothing that is seductively familiar. According to the biblical witness, and more precisely, according to Genesis 3, mendacity already emerges in the garden of Eden, that is, in the state of original human righteousness before God. And what is even more significant, it emerges not just somehow but in precise relation to God's commandment "You may freely eat of every tree of the garden; but of the tree of the knowledge of good and evil you shall not eat, for in the day that you eat of it you shall die" (Gen 2:16-17).[6] As we know all too well, Eve's interlocutor, the serpent, deconstructs this unequivocal commandment as a concealed way of protecting divine self-interest: "God knows that when you eat of it your eyes will be opened, and you will be like God, knowing good and evil" (Gen 3:5).

When Adam and Eve subsequently disobey God's original commandment, their eyes are instantaneously opened to their profound estrangement from God. It is not that they are naked but that they *feel* naked — exposed, because estranged. Eve, being asked by God to account for her act of disobedience, responds with "The serpent tricked me, and I ate" (Gen 3:13). We must grant that Eve's insight into the serpent's activity is perceptive and accurate. Having been tricked means having been lied to — this Eve now understands. And her understanding matches exactly what Thomas Aquinas understands to be the perfection of a lie, namely, a successful deception.

Three things need to come together, according to Aquinas, to constitute a lie in all respects: first, falsehood of what is said; second, the will to tell a falsehood; and third, the intention to deceive.[7] While on the matters of the serpent's will and intention the narrative account of Genesis 3 remains explicitly silent, the serpent's lack of any attempt at a defense and, moreover, his punishment are more than telling. All three conditions, then, must have been constitutive of the serpent's communication with Eve. According to Aquinas, deception is a perfection of the species of lying, and it is precisely the perfection of this vice that we see for the first time in Genesis 3. From here on, things decline rapidly and dramatically to Cain's murder of his brother Abel in Genesis 4. Interestingly, the first blatantly explicit lie from a human in relation to God occurs immediately after the first homicide. I do not need to remind you that according to the narrative account of Genesis 4, God asks, "Where is your brother Abel?" and Cain answers, "I do not know; am I my brother's keeper?" (Gen 4:9). In this lie that is as short as it is insolent, we discover the intimate commerce between mendacity and murder. Coveting, lying, and murdering emerge as fundamental and ultimately lethal contours of a life profoundly estranged from God, a life under the condition of sin.

It is telling that right after the first homicide has been committed and the first blatant human lie has been told, the NRSV introduces a heading that suggests a transition in the Genesis narrative: "Beginnings of Civilization." While the committee of translators of the NRSV might not have intended it, this heading suggests that the distinct brew of mendacity and murder narrated in Genesis 4 forms the secret underground, the repressed past, the concealed core of every civilization, past, present, and future. It took a René Girard to remind us of this fact.[8]

This, in brief, is the theologically charged context in which the eighth commandment encounters and addresses us — as human beings under the condition of sin. Estranged from God and afraid of each other, we turn to lying as a mode of survival. Being truthful can be dangerous — indeed, suicidal — and lying, in contrast, useful — even beneficial — or so it seems in a world full of potential competitors and enemies. And, indeed, if God did not exist and if every human just acted according to the laws of self-preservation and self-enhancement (or, in the logic of contemporary sociobiology, in order to expand his or her own genetic pool), truthfulness and lying would be nothing other than functions of such self-interest.

No one has seen the profound implications of radical sociobiological reductionism more clearly than Friedrich Nietzsche in his early essay "On Truth and Lies in a Nonmoral Sense." Just one short sampling will suffice:

> What then is truth? A movable host of metaphors, metonymies, and anthropomorphisms: in short, a sum of human relations which have been poetically and rhetorically intensified, transferred, and embellished, and which, after long usage, seem to a people to be fixed, canonical, and binding. Truths are illusions which we have forgotten are illusions; they are metaphors that have become worn out and have been drained of sensuous force, coins which have lost their embossing and are now considered as metal and no longer as coins.[9]

Nietzsche draws out the ultimate consequence of a knowledge of good and evil that is severed from its root, obedience to God's original commandment. Truthfulness and lying become functions of personal or collective utility and thus contingent aspects of the endless play of the human will to power, which claims to stand beyond good and evil. And Nietzsche says it straightforwardly in a note published posthumously in the volume *The Will to Power*: "If the morality of 'thou shalt not lie' is rejected, the 'sense for truth' will have to legitimize itself before another tribunal: — as a means of the preservation of man, as *will to power*."[10] And while Nietzsche seems right, especially in light of the terrors that the twentieth century brought upon humanity, not least by Nietzsche's own fatherland, he is nevertheless wrong. The reason is simple, to be found right here in the narrative of Genesis 4. While God punished Cain, God did not abandon him so that he too might perish by being murdered. Rather, God protected Cain in and under the condition of his punishment. Similarly, God does not abandon humanity. Rather, God gracefully sustains humanity even under the condition of profound estrangement from and outrageous rebellion against God. Nietzsche seems right in so much of what he wrote because he was so acutely aware of a part of the theological context we inhabit: the history of human sin finds its expression in the form of *ressentiment* and the *will to power*.

Yet because Nietzsche got only part of the theological context right, he had to reinterpret the history of human misery and rebellion for it to read as a genealogy of morals, thereby giving voice only to his own deep longing for empowerment and his own deep-seated *ressentiment* against the Christian faith. For Nietzsche was fully aware that the Christian gospel claims unequivocally to disclose the theological context in which the Decalogue addresses us. In light of the narrative account of Genesis 3 and 4, and resonating James 3, I shall characterize this context with the appropriate abbreviature, namely, the "fallen tongue." Having served as the catalyst for the first, aboriginal sin, mendacity has become a characteristic expression of life under the condition of sin. Although mendacity is caused not by the tongue but by the intention to deceive, we still most appropriately name the lie after the organ that initially carried out, and in most instances still carries out, this intersubjective vice. Hence, in the following remarks the "fallen tongue" shall designate the theological context in which the eighth commandment encounters and addresses us.

II. The Three Voices of the Eighth Commandment

The commandment's encounter and address occurs, I will argue, in a threefold way. First, as a heuristic device, pointing out to us what is "natural" according to God's good creation and what therefore needs to be morally demanded and even legally enforced in order to sustain human life under the condition of sin. In the Lutheran tradition this is called the "first," or political, use of the law. Here the commandment speaks in the voice of "You shall not lie."

The commandment encounters us, second, by holding a mirror before our faces and thereby unmasking and convicting us as its violators. In the Lutheran tradition this is called the "second," or theological, use of the law. Here our commandment speaks in the voice of "You must not lie." The Letter to the Hebrews gives us an idea of how deeply in this unmasking and convicting encounter God's word cuts: "Indeed, the word of God is living and active, sharper than any two-edged sword, piercing until it divides soul from spirit, joints from marrow; it is able to judge the thoughts and intentions of the heart. And before him no creature is hidden, but all are naked and laid bare to the eyes of the one to whom we must render an account" (Heb 4:12-13).

Third, and now in a fundamentally different and completely new voice, one never before heard, the commandment encounters us by teaching us the genuine gestalt of the life with God in faith. In this form, the commandment announces the future of the life with God that already becomes present in the life of faith. Hence, the commandment takes on the voice of a parenetic prophecy: "You will not lie." In contradistinction to the disciplining and enforcing political use and the unmasking and convicting theological use of the law, some Lutherans have called this voice the "second," or parenetic, use of the gospel,[11] while Calvinists have tended to call it the "third," or genuinely spiritual, use of the law.

The First Voice: A Schooling in the "Grain of the Universe"

In its first voice the eighth commandment works heuristically. That is, it functions as an explicit reminder of something humanity should and indeed can know in light of the "grain of the universe,"[12] what is "natural" to creation. And, sure enough, it is not difficult to find thinkers in antiquity who concerned themselves with the destructive character of lying and the constructive and edifying character of truthfulness, thinkers such as Aristotle and Sallust.[13] Precisely in light of the largely correct but also largely ineffective moral insight of ancient sages, however, Christian theologians from Ambrose and Augustine on maintained that the continuously bad habits of mendacity had rendered humanity's collective memory about truthfulness as natural to creation more and more unreliable. In short, despite the individual insight of some sages, humanity in general was increasingly in need of an explicit divine reminder of what is natural to human creatures in relation to God and neighbor. Hence, the classical Christian tradition, which includes Aquinas and Luther, understood the Decalogue as God's condensed salutary reminder to humanity, given first of all, yet not exclusively, to the particular people that God had chosen as his witness of holiness to all the nations. As God's revealed reminder to humanity, the Decalogue amounts to the "ultimate" clear and authoritative summary of the natural law, readily grasped and easily memorized by the common person. In a most straightforward and condensed form, the Decalogue points out what is natural to God's good creation and what temporal guises of moral demand and legal enforcement the commandment must assume in order to sustain human life under the condition of sin.

Regarding the eighth commandment, we find this heuristic function well reflected in the old German proverb "Lügen haben kurze Beine" ["Lies have short legs"]. That is, lies will always eventually be outrun by the truth. Lies are parasitical on truth; they depend on the ontological as well as the communal primacy of veracity. The proverb itself thus echoes what humanity should and can know about veracity and mendacity in light of creation's inner law. Life in community can be sustained only on the basis of an ongoing practice of truth-telling that is habitualized in the virtue of veracity, or truthfulness. Every basic communication, every basic economic interaction, every basic political act is built upon trust, a trust that in turn presupposes truthfulness. Every act of public mendacity has an immediate destructive effect on the community at large. When, for example, lying occurs on a large political scale of national or even international dimensions — and especially when corruption becomes a way of life among a political elite — it poisons the political culture, encourages a pervasive hermeneutics of suspicion by the electorate, and thereby undermines the basic trust necessary to uphold and sustain a body politic.

The heuristic of the eighth commandment thus helps us see the ways in which this particular commandment has salutarily encountered us long before, in the guise of laws that prohibit and legally prosecute all forms of giving false witness that undercut or damage the common good, as do such things as perjury, defamation, tax evasion, and fraud. In the body politic, in the economy, in the church as an institution of law and public accountability, and wherever else justice and the common good are at stake, lying must be denounced and appropriately punished in order to undercut and deter all habits and structures of mendacity and in order to promote and sustain the veracity necessary to the flourishing of human life together. The fallen tongue and its concomitant vices are a deadly danger for any human community. If mendacity takes over and gains broad public acceptance, it will eventually destroy human community — a lesson easily learned from history.

But if indeed it is the case that lies have short legs and are always eventually outrun by the truth, why worry about the fallen tongue and its destructive consequences? Doesn't God's sustaining rule of creation always eventually let truth win over? Doesn't God assure that the ontological primacy of truth will always assert itself sooner or later? Why do we need the heuristic of the eighth commandment to point out the temporal guises of legal enforcement in which it has always already encountered us? Here we need to understand that what is natural to creation is not a quasi-physical, self-sustaining mechanism. That is, God's providential political use of the law does not work like a law of physics; rather, it draws upon the experiences and the reasoning capacity of human beings. We come to (re-)appreciate the ontological and communal primacy of veracity only after we have suffered under the destructive consequences of mendacity. A society in which political and economic mendacity take over the public life will eventually collapse, disintegrate, or be taken over by others — or that society will recover on the grounds of a collective repentance initiated by a sustained witness to truthfulness.[14]

Teaching the Decalogue to all the faithful and, moreover, witnessing to the Decalogue as God's revealed reminder to all humanity are therefore crucial services the church must offer to every society in which it dwells. For the eighth commandment does not belong exclusively to Judaism and to the church. Rather, it declares unequivocally what is natural for all human beings as God's creatures. Therefore, every society is in need of being reminded most sharply and forthrightly of what it should and indeed can know on its own. In the long run, veracity — habitual truthfulness — is not only politically and economically beneficial; it is the very lifeblood of human community.

The Second Voice: A Schooling concerning Sin

God's commandment not only reminds us of what is natural to humanity as God's good creation. In its second voice, the commandment unmasks the sin through which we fail God and God's creation. It addresses us individually and directly as those who are affected by the rule of the fallen tongue. Here neither the common good nor justice is at stake. Rather, what is at stake now is the source from which all lies well up: the human heart, as that unfathomable depth of the human being from which our thinking and willing are troubled and directed in ways we are hard pressed to account for. The fallen tongue is fed by a fearful heart that is not at rest in its true source, its Maker and Redeemer, but is restless and unsettled, perpetually in search of some semblance of security.

How easy it is to point to fraudulent CEOs and corrupt politicians and at the same time to forget how extremely widespread among all citizens is the willingness to commit tax evasion or insurance fraud whenever possible with impunity! Who does not know the temptation to commit the small fraud that no one will ever find out about? Whence do these temptations arise but from our restless hearts that are disclosed to none besides our own troubled consciences — and God?

The eighth commandment encounters us here in the form of the theological use of the law. It unmasks and convicts us by holding a mirror in front of our faces so that we may come to the awareness that we of all people are its violators. In the reflection of this mercilessly clear mirror, we are confronted not only with our actions but also with the mendacious thoughts and intentions that well up from the depths of our hearts. By speaking in the absolute voice of "You must not lie," the commandment convicts my own heart. I indeed live under the power of the lie insofar and as long as I am cut off from the truth to which I owe my existence and which alone can liberate me to live a life free from mendacity and free for truthfulness. In this way, the eighth commandment turns us back to the first commandment. Only when my heart comes to rest in God can I afford the truth about myself. Cut off from its ground, the truth is too hard to bear. My utter contingency and vulnerability, reaching their apogee in my mortality, my dependence upon and consequent indebtedness to others — all of this becomes unbearable.

It is this very inability to face the truth of our own lives that gives rise to the mendacity of moral euphemisms that are so pervasive in our contemporary culture. What do I mean by "moral euphemisms"? I have in mind the subtle form of euphemistically redescribing the moral character of what we are doing or neglecting to do. And precisely because moral description is the first act of moral judgment, these euphemisms are inherently mendacious. Let us call them the phenomenon of moral *newspeak*, ingeniously anticipated in Aldous Huxley's *Brave New World* and in George Orwell's *1984*. Instead of committing tax fraud we simply keep what is our own. Instead of killing in war we gain ground; instead of killing embryos for scientific purposes we do consumptive research; instead of having an abortion we terminate — or, worse, simply interrupt — a pregnancy; instead of fornicating we engage in premarital sex; instead of committing adultery we have an affair. Only in the case of divorce has the moral notion itself turned into the moral euphemism! That is, getting a divorce is still called getting a divorce, but it has become as morally significant as having a tooth pulled — uncomfortable, possibly painful, but morally neutral. These and endless other moral euphemisms allow us to practice a form of moral mendaciousness without explicitly lying about anything. As soon as we come to appreciate the depth of the collective complicity in the practice of moral euphemization, we come to understand how our society collectively violates the deep sense of the eighth commandment — and each one of us is unmasked as at least a potential violator. Our fearful hearts and our fallen tongues betray us, and our consciences, faced with the mirror of God's law, convict us.

The Third Voice: A Schooling in the Freedom of Good Works

However, while unmasking and convicting us, the law cannot transform our hearts; it only locks us more and more deeply into our violation of the law. Only God, touching us directly through his Spirit, can transform our hearts. Only when God's Spirit is poured out over all human beings do we receive new, living hearts to replace our rebellious hearts of stone. The Spirit's eschatological earnest is faith, the faith that is the fulfillment of the first commandment. And while God's Spirit rested upon the patriarchs, prophets, and saints of Israel, his full and unequivocal coming is intrinsically linked to the mission of Christ. The Father's Spirit, who is sent by the Father and the Son, re-creates our ossified hearts so that they become temples of the Spirit that rejoice in God through Christ. Now reconciled with the Father through Christ, new creations through the power of the Spirit, we have become, Luther would say, new persons, who now can delight in God's law because we now hear it in a completely new way, fundamentally different from its first, demanding and disciplining voice and its second, unmasking and convicting voice.

There are those who insist that there can be no third voice to God's commandment because where the Spirit is, there is freedom. And the genuine freedom of the Spirit is in no need of any commandment or guidance. It acts completely spontaneously, motivated exclusively by love. However, this is an antinomian and ultimately gnostic misunderstanding of genuine creaturely freedom, an understanding that mistakes the human being for an angel. Whoever yearns for a freedom without its gestalt yearns for a disembodied existence, for the sovereign self that instead of being embodied uses the body as its primary tool of self-realization. The gestalt of freedom is the link between the liberating truth and the path on which genuine freedom is exercised as a reconciled life with God.

Hence, we need first of all to appreciate that the very core of any positive freedom — not freedom "from," but freedom "for" — is the truth. If it is the case that Christ is the truth, as the whole Gospel of John ceaselessly confesses, then it is the case that those who have received Christ in faith and therefore continue in his word are free in the most profound sense: "You will know the truth, and the truth will make you free" (John 8:32). The positive character of freedom becomes concrete only if it receives a gestalt that enacts as well as protects it. Without its embodied gestalt this freedom would actualize itself only punctually and hence would come under the sovereignty of the self that interprets itself by spontaneous acts of freedom. The freedom of the truth that sets us free, however, is the freedom that is actualized in the life with God. And as a continuous reality, this freedom must be received together with the peculiar gestalt appropriate to the creature's finite and embodied nature. It is this peculiar received gestalt that enacts as well as protects the truth that set us free in the first place. How does the commandment do this?

In its third voice, the commandment announces the future of the life with God that already has become present in the life of faith. Hence, the commandment takes on the voice of parenetic prophecy: "You will not lie." The disciplining, enforcing, unmasking, and convicting voices have vanished. And if we understand "law" to be just that — disciplining, enforcing, unmasking, and convicting — it is indeed the case that wherever the Spirit of Christ has set us free, the law has passed away. Yet what cannot and will not pass away is the prophetic announcement and parenetic teaching of the very gestalt of the reconciled life with God. We find this voice most beautifully expressed in Psalm 15:

> O Lord, who may abide in your tent?
>   Who may dwell on your holy hill?
> Those who walk blamelessly, and do what is right,
>   and speak the truth from their heart;
> who do not slander with their tongue,
>   and do no evil to their friends,
> nor take up a reproach against their neighbors;
>   in whose eyes the wicked are despised,
> but who honor those who fear the Lord;
>   who stand by their oath even to their hurt;
> who do not lend money at interest,
>   and do not take a bribe against the innocent.
> Those who do these things shall never be moved.

Psalm 15 offers a prophetic parenesis of what the eighth commandment looks like when it completely shapes the way of a reconciled life with God — in short, what it looks like when the eighth commandment is fulfilled. Moreover, in Psalm 15 we see a reconciled intersubjectivity, because the tongue has been restored to its original purpose. As the psalmist puts it: "Those who . . . speak the truth from their heart [and] do not slander with their tongue."

What is natural to God's good creation encounters us here in the mode of fulfillment: no perjury, no fraud, no corruption, no slander are committed. This is why those who are freed by the truth do not need a law. They know what is natural to God's good creation because they walk in the freedom of the children of God. Yet this freedom is precisely free for the joyful embodiment of the creaturely gestalt that God has granted this freedom. This is the true sense of torah, the telos and fulfillment of which is Christ and his messianic announcement of God's reign as embodied in the Sermon on the Mount.

Luther and Calvin perfectly understood this aspect in their respective interpretations of the Decalogue by turning the commandment around, by turning it from an unequivocal prohibition into a limitless invitation to good works. Concerning the eighth commandment, then, from Luther's *Large Catechism:* "Rather, we should use our tongue to speak only the best about all people, to cover the sins and infirmities of our neighbors, to justify their actions, and to cloak and veil them with our own honor."[15] And Luther concludes his exposition of the eighth commandment thus: "This commandment, then, includes a great many good works that please God most highly and bestow abundant blessings, if only the blind world and false saints would recognize them."[16]

III. The Freedom of Praise

Our exploration of the third voice of our commandment is almost complete. Almost, but not quite. For in a final step we need to ask whether there is a specific characteristic of the tongue that is restored to its original purpose and glory, whether there is a practice that circumscribes its restored splendor. And indeed there is. The practice that embodies the tongue's restored splendor is praise, or adoration. Drawing upon an extraordinary insight from St. Augustine, Paul Griffiths puts it the following way: "The only possible response is praise. As Augustine says, 'non solum non peccemus adorando, sed peccemus non adorando.' Not only do we fail to sin by adoring, but we sin by failing to adore. . . . If you are not adoring God, you are sinning; lying is incompatible with the adoration of God."[17] Turned around positively into the voice of parenetic prophecy, St. Augustine's insight means that the tongues of those who have become a new creation in Christ will no longer lie, because they have been restored to their primary and original vocation, that is, ceaseless praise.

In Psalm 119 we find a stunning example of this ceaseless adoration, in praise of the glory of God's word:

> I rejoice at your word
>   like one who finds great spoil.
> I hate and abhor falsehood,
>   but I love your law.
> Seven times a day I praise you
>   for your righteous ordinances.
> . . . .
> My lips will pour forth praise,
>   because you teach me your statutes.
> My tongue will sing of your promise,
>   for all your commandments are right. (Ps 119:162-164, 171-172)

Luther insisted that every student of theology should meditate on Psalm 119 once a day, and of course, this psalm is sung daily in the monastic liturgy of the hours. Adoration directs our tongue primarily and ultimately toward God as the giver of all intersubjectivity. All creaturely intersubjectivity is received gratuitously. Living truthfully and hence freely means that all our relationships must be transparent to their gratuitous reception. This is why worship — "Seven times a day I praise you for your righteous ordinances" — is the most important and primary context in which our tongues are healed and trained in the truthfulness that grows out of adoration.

We need to end our meditation on the three voices of the eighth commandment with a cautionary note — a note intended to prevent the subtle self-deception of a realized eschatology in matters of speaking truthfully and lying. If we think the three voices amount to an irreversible narrative of progression from external compliance to crisis to spiritual fulfillment, if we therefore think that the third voice amounts to a precise description of our present state of being, we deceive ourselves and the truth is not in us. Forces of sin still oppose the power of the Spirit from without and within. External and internal tribulations *(Anfechtungen)*, temptations of fame and wealth, unrestrained passions such as anger and fear, and the seductive lullabies of a false security continually lure us toward violation of the eighth commandment. We need only to ask ourselves honestly: Do we Christians always speak truthfully? Do we give a truthful witness to the gospel? Do we cut through the cloud of moral euphemisms? Are we free of flattery, gossip, and backbiting — not to mention flat-out lies? Because the report will be very mixed at best, collectively as well as individually, and because we know that we are in ongoing need of forgiveness, Christians still need to hear the eighth commandment in its first and second voices, disciplining and unmasking us in light of what is natural to God's good creation.

The Fallen Tongue and the Freedom of Praise

We live by the trust in God's assurance that because of the power of God's Spirit working in our lives, the third voice will increasingly become a solo, while the two other voices will recede more and more into the background and eventually fade away. Yet as long as the power of sin is still active, as long as we feel the pull and lure of the power of the lie, it is crucial that the church proclaim and teach the eighth commandment in all three voices — lest our very proclamation and catechesis violate the eighth commandment. As Stanley Hauerwas and Will Willimon have so perceptively put it: "But to go to church on a summer Sunday, to settle down for a pleasant hour with people like us, planning to be soothed by the music of the organ, lulled by the mellifluous words of the preacher — then to be told the truth, and to be told it straight, thereby to discover we are called to truthful witness, is grand."[18] The third voice of the eighth commandment announces the freedom from which free and truthful speech arises: it declares that aspect of *eleutheria* that sets us free for *parrhēsia*, speech that ends in the freedom of praise.

III. *Parrhēsia* — or, Free to Speak Ecumenically

10. Christian Unity and the Papal Office

On the Encyclical *Ut Unum Sint/That They May Be One*

At the dawn of the third millennium, the world has very nearly closed in on us. Some speak in terms of a "global ethos" and others of "globalization"; our perceptions and experiences of the world have shifted almost entirely to a global horizon. At the same time, the horizon of the church has taken on a global dimension, which, in its own way, has reshaped and resituated the ecumenical dialogues. This circumstance is reflected in the document that is the only papal encyclical to date on the theme of ecumenism: *Ut Unum Sint/That They May Be One*. In 1995, looking ahead to the approaching millennium, Pope John Paul II established worldwide Christian unity as the theme of his encyclical and the goal of his ecumenical efforts.

To say the least, "unity" is a difficult subject. The call to unity is one thing; the concrete reality of reunification is quite another. As Christians and as theologians, we experience a deep tension between the call to unity and the fear of the unforeseeable with regard to reunification. We know that the call to unity is a binding given for the church to be church. We yearn for reconciliation and concord in worship, in doctrine, and in witness. But at the same time, we shrink back from unity again and again, because it is quite possible that unity could come as a form of reunification in which we would lose our very ecclesial identity. The compelling alternatives seem to take this form: *Unity at the cost of identity, or identity at the cost of unity.* This tension dominated the recent intra-Lutheran controversy about the joint Lutheran–Roman Catholic declaration on the doctrine of justification.[1] And, indeed, a similar tension seems to arise in the encyclical on ecumenism.

Apart from the fact that we have before us a teaching document from "the least" *(servus servorum)* of all the servants of the Roman Catholic Church, what is it that makes this encyclical worthy of serious engagement?

First, the timing. The generation of the ecumenical movement, characterized and inspired by the advent of the World Council of Churches, the Faith and Order proceedings, Taizé, the bilateral dialogues, and not least by Vatican II, is now moving into retirement. Gone is the sense of theological excitement over ecumenical themes: much of the conversation has become staid truism, whether good or bad. Gone as well is the sense of urgency: scarcely anyone now has sleepless nights over stagnating ecumenical dialogue. And precisely at this moment comes an encyclical in which the ecumenical task is proclaimed as belonging to the very essence of being Christian — indeed, of being Catholic — and, further, as unfinished business that still lies before us. At the very time when the ecumenical movement seems to have lost steam, the pope has made ecumenism determinative of the life of faith.[2] *Second,* the content. The encyclical is a threshold document. On the one hand, it is quite clearly "of the past," rooted in a conservative interpretation of the ecclesiology of Vatican II. On the other hand, with respect to its pastoral and prophetic intensity in challenging every ecclesiastical status quo, it is a document of the future, a text with passages that already speak of "tomorrow."

My dialogue with *Ut Unum Sint* will proceed in four steps. Because of the particular argumentational slant of the encyclical, this dialogue must focus from the outset on ecclesiology, and particularly on the papal office and the claim and contradiction inherent in that office.[3] First, I will recapitulate the encyclical's line of argument. Second, I will categorize the questions and doubts it calls to mind from an evangelical catholic point of view. Third, I will look at the challenge it raises for the churches of the Reformation and their ecumenical understanding. Finally, taking up this challenge, I will propose an alternative approach to ecumenism that holds out the possibility of a concrete — christological — reality of ecumenical unity.

I. The Call to Unity

In his theologically and pastorally charged introduction, the pope renews the summons to all Christians for unity issued by the Second Vatican Council. In this call, we immediately encounter the pope's conviction that the martyrs of this century, believers in Christ from within and outside the Catholic communion, have by the complete sacrifice of their lives borne witness that the schism of the church is already overcome. For according to the pope, they are confessors of the cross of Christ in a manner that is true for all Christians. In this way, right at the outset, *the motif of a theology of the cross* gains preeminence over all other motifs: "If [believers in Christ] wish truly and effectively to oppose the world's tendency to reduce to powerlessness the Mystery of Redemption, they must *profess together the same truth about the Cross*."4 Further, the pope emphasizes that the commitment to ecumenism must be based upon the conversion of hearts and upon prayer. In other words, ecumenism at its core is either a spiritual reality or no reality at all. Ecumenism must, according to the pope, concern itself with overcoming complacency, indifference, and insufficient knowledge of one another and with the "purification of past memories" (*UUS* 2) through mutual reexamination of long-standing misgivings and prejudices. At Vatican II, "the Catholic Church committed herself *irrevocably* to following the path of the ecumenical venture" and, in the years since, has become "even more profoundly aware of her identity and her mission in history" (*UUS* 3). Looking toward the new millennium, the pope speaks of petitioning the Lord to "increase the unity of all Christians until they reach full communion" (*UUS* 3) — the explicit goal of this encyclical. Finally, the pope underscores once again the specific ministry of the bishop of Rome as an office of the unity of the church. We will have to return later to this point, which is complex yet central to the encyclical, for it is precisely here that the churches of the Reformation encounter the stumbling blocks that seem most difficult to overcome. But it is here as well that we find the encyclical's most surprising and perhaps even most helpful allusions.

Chapter 1, "The Catholic Church's Commitment to Ecumenism," is theologically and strategically the decisive section. Here everything shifts gears — or precisely doesn't. Proceeding from Jesus' prayer in John 17, the encyclical develops first a christological-ecclesiological groundwork for the unity of the church. Jesus' plea for the unity of his disciples is interpreted as unity already given and received, established in the will of God, whose expression is the church.5 Immediately thereafter, the encyclical identifies the two fundamental ecclesiological pillars between which its discourse — in a tension-filled dialectic — will move. On the one side, there is the root axiom of Roman Catholic self-understanding, namely, that the church of Christ "subsists in the Catholic Church, which is governed by the Successor of Peter and by the Bishops in communion with him" (*UUS* 10).6 On the other side, there is the recognition that "many elements of sanctification and of truth can be found outside her visible structure. These elements, however, as gifts properly belonging to the Church of Christ, possess an inner dynamism towards Catholic unity" (*UUS* 10).7 This fundamental tension finds eloquent expression in what immediately follows: a conditional confession of guilt, which in one breath attributes to the Roman Catholic Church some responsibility for a divided Christianity but in the next breath claims the Roman Catholic Church's unbroken unity of and continuity with the complete fullness of all of God's gifts and graces. Thus the following picture emerges: "The elements of this already-given Church exist, found in their fullness in the Catholic Church and, without this fullness, in the other Communities, where certain features of the Christian mystery have at times been *more effectively* emphasized" (*UUS* 14; my emphasis).

Chapter 2, "The Fruits of Dialogue," is to be read as the historical narration of the first chapter, that is, as a brief and general story of the ecumenical achievements of this century, told from the Roman Catholic perspective.[8] The body of the text develops a detailed presentation of the restoration of extensive communion with the Eastern Orthodox churches and of relations with the ancient churches of the East, which had not agreed to the Councils of Chalcedon and Ephesus (*UUS* 50-63). If scope and manner of presentation may be understood as an ecclesio-political signal, then we have before us a clear indication that the restoration of communion with the Eastern Orthodox churches is of primary significance for Pope John Paul II. Chapter 2 of the encyclical ends with a comparatively brief presentation of the ecumenical dialogues with other churches of the West (*UUS* 64-73). In spite of a few specific references, such as those concerning the work of the Commission on Faith and Order of the World Council of Churches, the encyclical remains disappointingly vague in its treatment of this topic. We would look in vain, for example, for a precise naming of the national and international bilateral dialogues with the Lutherans, the Reformed, the Anglicans, and the Methodists, to name only the most important. There is general reference to these dialogues (e.g., *UUS* 69), but in light of the detailed treatment of the renewed relations with the ancient churches of the East, this displays a remarkable imbalance.

Chapter 3, "Quanta Est Nobis Via?/How Long Is the Way That Lies before Us?" once again takes up the theological thread of chapter 1 in its ecclesiological dialectic. First, the pope identifies those theological themes that must be studied more deeply in order to achieve consensus of faith: (1) the relationship between Scripture and tradition, (2) the Eucharist and the real presence of Christ in the Lord's Supper, (3) the office of ministry, in its structure and as sacrament, (4) the magisterium of the church and the primacy of the bishop of Rome, and (5) Mariology (*UUS* 79). He makes no mention of the bilateral dialogues between Catholics and Lutherans in the United States in which these themes have been handled thoroughly and with far-reaching convergence.[9] But the pope *does* emphasize the necessity of a comprehensive reception of the results of bilateral dialogues in *all* the churches. He underscores this necessity in summoning all Christian communities, Catholics first of all, to a spiritual ecumenism that is grounded in a "dialogue of conversion" — a serious examination of conscience before God, an earnest search for and confession of sin (*UUS* 82). This acknowledgment of sin creates an "interior spiritual space" in which Christ — the source of the church's unity — can effectively act (*UUS* 82; cf. 35). For John Paul II, a full and perfect communion is already present in the fellowship of martyrs and, indeed, of the saints from all Christian communities, "who, at the end of a life faithful to grace, are in communion with Christ in glory." The radiance of their testimony is to be seen as "proof of the transcendent power of the Spirit," which can enable all Christian communities "to 'be converted' to the quest for full and visible communion" (*UUS* 84). This substantial prophetic thrust is followed by a long discourse on the office of the bishop of Rome as a ministry of unity that is absolutely integral to the church and by the assertion that the communion of all particular churches with the church of Rome is an "essential requisite" for unity (*UUS* 88-97). Yet the pope *also* emphasizes in this section that the ministry of Peter is "a ministry of mercy, born of an act of Christ's own mercy" (*UUS* 93).[10]

In a closing parenetical section, the pope recalls that Christian unity, in the final analysis, is a gift of God — to which, nevertheless, our whole endeavor must be directed. The encyclical closes with a call to unity and the exhortation of St. Cyprian, which he spoke in his commentary on the Lord's Prayer: "God does not accept the sacrifice of a sower of disunion, but commands that he depart from the altar so that he may first be reconciled with his brother. For God can be appeased only by prayers that make peace. To God, the better offering is peace, brotherly concord and a people made one in the unity of the Father, Son, and Holy Spirit" (*UUS* 102).[11]

II. The Problem: Unity as Reunification and the Question of the Papal Office

In spite of the admission of Catholic co-responsibility for the Western schism and in spite of the affirmation "It is not that beyond the boundaries of the Catholic community there is an ecclesial vacuum" (*UUS* 13), the encyclical frames the issue in such a way as to render genuine *ecumenical* encounter virtually impossible. The question of the catholicity of the church is already decided from the outset,[12] since according to both the encyclical and Vatican II, the unity of Christ's church already subsists in the Roman Catholic communion. The ecumenical problem, according to *Ut Unum Sint,* is that not all participate in this unity. Even granting that certain gifts of the Spirit not only may occur in other communions but also may occur with greater effect than in the Roman Catholic Church, the latter is considered in no way deficient. *Considered strictly on the basis of the encyclical's ecclesiological core thesis — that the primacy of the bishop of Rome in its present form represents the condition for the possibility of Christian unity — visible Christian unity can mean only one thing: "redintegratio," that is, reunification with the Roman Catholic Church understood in terms of absorption.* This ecclesiological formulation of possible Christian unity is, however, impracticable, for it represents for the churches of the Reformation an ultimately unacceptable demand — namely, to admit that they suffer from an essential ecclesiological deficiency.

Naturally, the papal office in its present form is trapped precisely in this logic and is not at all free to leave itself and its defining conciliar texts open to possible revision. If the papal office of ministry in its present form, characterized by post-Tridentine and Vatican I confessionalism, *must* present itself as the condition for the possibility of the unity of the church, does it not de facto represent precisely, to quote Pope Paul VI, "the biggest obstacle on the road to ecumenism"?[13]

Some of John Paul II's remarks in the encyclical indicate that he is well aware of this contradiction. Even in the introduction he hints at a possible new perspective, one that lies beyond the horizons of both Vatican I and Vatican II. The pope asserts that "[i]n our ecumenical age, marked by the Second Vatican Council, the mission of the Bishop of Rome is particularly directed to recalling the need for full communion among Christ's disciples" (*UUS* 4). Then he continues as follows: "The Bishop of Rome himself must fervently make his own Christ's prayer for that conversion which is indispensable for 'Peter' to be able to serve his brethren. I earnestly invite the faithful of the Catholic Church and all Christians to share in this prayer. May all join me in praying for this conversion!" (*UUS* 4). Does this summons to prayer not allow for a glimpse of *a post-confessional* ecumenical understanding of the office of ministry of the bishop of Rome that might truly serve to strengthen *all* brothers and sisters in the faith?

At this point we might ask which aspects of the Christian mystery are, as it says in the encyclical, "more effectively emphasized" in the non-Catholic churches. It is significant — although surely not what the pope had in mind — that next to their confession of Jesus Christ as their sole Lord and Savior, all these churches have in common the absence of a papal primacy exercised by divine right in the narrow sense of Vatican I. We might ask whether the encyclical itself does not at least allow for the possibility of reform with respect to the papal office, for it emphasizes that Vatican II lays out the clear connection between *renewal, conversion,* and *reform* and says, "Christ summons the Church, as she goes her pilgrim way, to that continual reformation of which she always has need, insofar as she is an institution of human beings here on earth," asserting in closing, "No Christian Community can exempt itself from this call" (*UUS* 16).

There are two other remarks in the encyclical that point toward the possibility of a reform of the papal office: the plea for forgiveness for the particular exercise of the primacy that inflicted pain on Christian communities no longer in fellowship with Rome (*UUS* 88) and the explicit acknowledgment of the request from many communities "to find a way of exercising the primacy which, while in no way renouncing what is essential to its mission, is nonetheless open to a new situation" (*UUS* 95).[14] On these admittedly limited grounds for a reform perspective on papal primacy in *Ut Unum Sint*, we may now proceed to risk the next step.

III. The Challenge: Mutual "Dialogue of Conversion"

What question is raised by the encyclical for the churches of the Reformation, and how do these churches fend off the very fact of the ongoing existence of the Roman Catholic Church, which calls them into question? After all, the Roman Catholic Church continued to exist beyond the Reformation; indeed, it has grown into a worldwide communion. In recent years it has undertaken an internal process of reform. It rests, as it always has, on the common ground of the ancient ecumenical creeds. But since Vatican II, Scripture has played, in a new way, a central role in its dogmatic and moral theology. Moreover, in Vatican II the magisterium was explicitly placed under the authority of the word of God.[15] In the area of the doctrine of justification, the heart of Reformation theology, while there is not complete agreement, there is convergence, which suffices to certify that the truth of the gospel — that is, the biblical message of the sinner's justification by faith alone — has in the meantime been both permitted and recognized by the Roman Catholic Church.[16] In view of this situation, the temptation to find or invent ever new "basic differences"[17] that legitimate and sustain the schism of Western Christianity by considering it irreversible can only be viewed as a Protestant barricade against being called into question by the existence and internal transformation of the Roman Catholic Church. What would happen if the confessional rug were pulled out from under the feet of not only the Roman Catholic Church but also the churches of the Reformation? It is one thing to note that the pope has called the Roman Catholics to inward conversion while leaving little room for structural conversion — because without a new council, there can be no further redefinition. It is quite another thing to conceive a commitment to ecumenism for Lutheran and Protestant churches that both obliges them to hold fast to truth and at the same time directs them to ecumenical conversion. And precisely at this point the papal office becomes the ecumenical test case for the Western church, for Roman Catholic papalism and Protestant antipapalism correspond to one another in an ecumenically prohibitive way. The question is, What would happen if the papal summons to a "dialogue of conversion" were taken so seriously *on both sides* that new, formerly taboo questions were permitted to surface? Certainly, the crux of what up to now has been considered taboo is the office of ordained ministry. Since the Lima Declaration, *Baptism, Eucharist, and Ministry,* ecumenical efforts have come to a standstill precisely on this point. Serious consideration of the office of ordained ministry, which can no longer avoid the question of the papal office, is, as I see it, the greatest ecumenical challenge for the next generation.

IV. The Alternative: Unity as Living Concord

Would the Roman Catholic communion be prepared, in the framework of a Vatican III, to nuance or delimit its insistence upon the jurisdictional and doctrinal primacy of the bishop of Rome as a condition for mutual recognition and communion in faith and confession?[18] And on the other hand, would the churches of the Reformation be prepared to recognize an ecumenical primacy of the bishop of Rome that stood under the authority of the Scriptures, was post-confessional, and operated *iure humano* in service to the visible unity of all Christians?[19] We would do well to remember Melanchthon, who in his postscript to the *Smalcald Articles* of 1537 sent a signal that is decidedly both evangelical *and* ecumenical: "However, concerning the pope I maintain that if he would allow the gospel, we, too, may (for the sake of peace and general unity among those Christians who are now under him and might be in the future) grant to him his superiority over the bishops which he has 'by human right.'"[20] Melanchthon's postscript must be understood as an entirely proper use of Reformation ecclesiology. Precisely because the church stands or falls on the truth of the justification of sinners, she is *free* to recognize historically evolved structures and traditions and to affirm them as gift of the Holy Spirit to the church.[21] This recognition and affirmation is valid as long as these structures and traditions serve the proclamation of the gospel. Thus the church is *free* also to recognize and affirm an office of ministry understood as constituted by human right that both presides over and is in collegiality with the bishops and that serves the unity of the whole church.[22] Were the churches to pass this test case, it would leave open the possibility for a communio-ecclesiology perspective[23] in which unity did not necessarily flow out of an abstract *reunification* of the churches under the umbrella of a Tridentine-Vatican-ordered primacy. On the contrary, it would then be possible for Christian unity to be understood as a *concord of faith and confession in the Holy Spirit* that would reconcile the multiplicity of churches[24] and whose visible manifestation would be the common celebration of the Lord's Supper, at which the bishop of Rome could preside as *sign* of unity. However, the head[25] and center of this unity of concord would remain Christ alone, who is present in the word of promise and forgiveness and in the elements of the Supper. For only on the basis of *this* Center can the nature of the ordained office of word and sacrament manifest itself as an office of ministry to the proclamation of the gospel and, further, to the living concord of Christians in the local parish, as well as on the regional and indeed the universal level of the church.[26] According to Luther's ecclesiology, the test case of the papal office can hinge *solely* on whether the ordained ministry to the gospel *also* includes — and indeed, where possible, requires — a ministry of unity to all of Christendom.[27] If the papal office permitted itself to be understood as a ministry under the gospel, serving as a transforming — even re-forming — catalyst for the unity of the church, it would open the door to an ecumenically promising and, from the perspective of the Lutheran Reformation, permissible approach to the thorniest of all ecumenical dilemmas. After all, Luther himself asserted in 1531 that he "could kiss the pope's feet if he would permit the gospel."[28]

11. Freedom, Truth, and the Will

On the Encyclical *Fides et Ratio/*
On the Relationship between Faith and Reason

There are at least three ways of reading the encyclical *Fides et Ratio:*[1] First, as strictly magisterial, instructing Roman Catholic theologians and philosophers in matters of criteriology;[2] second, as pastoral-intellectual, urging all persons of good will toward a renewed faith in reason and bold and rigorous thought that is genuinely open to transcendence;[3] and third, as discursive, engaging theologians and philosophers in a specific theological argument about the proper relationship between faith and reason.[4]

Only by attending to all three ways of reading *Fides et Ratio* can we come to fully appreciate the encyclical's inner complexity. However, such comprehensive interpretation is beyond the scope of this discussion. Rather, I will focus exclusively on the third way of reading it, arguing that the encyclical both reveals and conceals a central problematic: the role that *libertas* and *voluntas*, freedom and will, play in relation to faith and reason. *Fides et Ratio* raises this issue explicitly in several prominent passages where freedom and truth are linked, which should be expected. For, after all, the relationship between freedom and truth is constitutive of the relationship in which faith and reason, theology and philosophy, find each other.[5]

I. *Fides et Ratio*

Raising the question of the role of the will in relation to faith and reason immediately averts the problematic move of treating *fides* and *ratio* as fundamentally extrinsic to each other or, worse, as fundamentally opposed — perpetually engaged in negotiation between sometimes peaceful and sometimes warring encampments. Rather, similar to complex force fields, *fides* and *ratio* constantly overlap and presuppose each other as a function of the will's central, if not constitutive, role in their respective operations. It is in two different, albeit related, instantiations of "faith" — faith *simpliciter* and faith *secundum quid* — that faith and reason incessantly interact. On the one hand, faith reasons in order to explore the reasons of faith *(fidei ratio)*.[6] Yet on the other hand, reason in its own comprehensive reaching toward truth constantly anticipates — in a kind of implicit faith *(rationis fides)* — an antecedent coherence of reality that is already presupposed in any process of inquiry.[7] As an inherently teleological activity, rational inquiry needs to anticipate the existence of the goal for which it aims (this goal being not a particular object but an insight in which the inquiry's investigative motion comes to rest). This primordial trust in the intelligibility of reality is the basis on which *Fides et Ratio* is able as well as entitled to encourage a "restoring [of] faith in reason."[8]

Reason's implicit faith, of course, differs fundamentally from the faith that ultimately is the gift of the Spirit. In its strict theological sense, faith *(fides)* must be clearly distinguished from reason's implicit faith, for faith is the active reception of an inexhaustible yet concrete personal truth, a reception in and through which the believer begins to participate inchoately in the divine life.[9] The reasoning of faith *(fidei ratio)* signifies faith's intellectual exploration of this received truth, an exploration that draws upon concepts forged by a reason that enacts its own implicit faith *(rationis fides)* in the prolepsis of the unity of truth.[10]

Fides et Ratio seems to assume that faith in the strict sense always encompasses as well as accounts for (through *fidei ratio*) reason's implicit faith. However, reason's implicit faith, if explicitly granted by those who engage in rational inquiry, might become open for moments of instruction by the latter. Yet how is the interrelationship between the two to be understood precisely, and more importantly, can this interrelationship be understood without addressing the question of the role of the will?

II. Reason's Implicit Faith and the Specter of the Will

It is safe to say that as long as the "will" remains unthematized, reason's implicit faith remains untroubled. But as soon as we attend to the will, the question of reason's liberation from the will's incurvature emerges with full force. The reason is this: The very fact that reason's implicit faith must anticipate the unity of truth that is the telos of any ordered inquiry entails the tacit assumption of the *liberum arbitrium*, that is, of a will that is fundamentally free in that it is reason's own capacity to choose not only the goal of inquiry but also all the means necessary to pursue it. And obviously, in the process of a rational inquiry, we are indeed free not only to attend to the way things are but, more importantly, to relate critically to the way we do things in the very process of inquiry. However, we are unable to relate freely to our critical relating — unless we are drawn into a freedom that allows us to do so by being shaped, rectified, and transformed in ways we could not even have anticipated without this liberation. Hence, reason's implicit faith operates on an assumption that transcends its capacity of anticipation and for which it cannot account: the freedom to choose the quality of its willing. Thus attending to the very dynamic of reason's implicit faith raises the specter of the will and the role of the will in reason's epistemic operations.

How does this problem affect *Fides et Ratio* as it presses for and encourages a "philosophia naturae *vere metaphysicae*" ["a philosophy of *genuinely metaphysical* range"] (*FR* 83) that does justice to the ultimate unity of truth? On the one hand, reason's implicit faith, by anticipating a teleologically structured order of reality as a function of reason's own analytic, synthetic, and intentional processes of inquiry, itself invites the rigorous pursuit of metaphysics. Yet on the other hand, precisely the same implicit faith of reason is constrained — bound to respond to the way things are "out there," and bound by the human condition itself and therefore the ways in which reason is shaped not only by humanity's practical needs but even more so by humanity's concrete existence under the condition of sin. Hence, while being substantively distinct from faith in the strict theological sense, reason's implicit faith cannot be regarded as a theologically indifferent and purely epistemological phenomenon. Rather, the very dynamic of reason's implicit faith raises the specter of the will and hence the question of how reason and will interrelate.

III. The Boldness of Reason and the Freedom of Faith

We find the dynamic of reason's implicit faith and the specter of the will most clearly entailed in the encyclical's central mandate: "Fidei parrhesiae respondere debet rationis audacia" ["The *parrhesia* of faith must be matched by the boldness of reason"] (*FR* 48). How so? If the freedom of faith is supposed to be matched by the boldness of reason, we must suppose that the "boldness of reason" emerges from rectitude of mind and not from reason possibly misdirected by a will that under the condition of sin is turned in upon itself. Otherwise, the boldness of reason could as well lead — and de facto did lead — to the hubris of a totalitarian grasp of reality exercised by a reason bent into a purely instrumental rationality or inflated into a quasi-absolute faculty, falsely assuming speculative self-transparency. In short, while the boldness of reason clearly seems to presuppose rectitude of mind, the question remains what precisely the will's role is in relation to rectitude of mind and, even more so, how the will's incurvature under the condition of sin might affect the boldness of reason.

Moreover, the encyclical's central mandate implies a dynamic relationship between the reasoning of faith and reason's implicit faith, since the *parrhēsia* of the former presupposes the rectitude of the latter, while the rectitude of the latter and its subsequent proper boldness presuppose the implicit horizon of the former. Yet again, what is the role of the will in this mutual dynamic implication?

Fides et Ratio does not address this question directly. Rather, it suggests an answer in the way it addresses the relationship between freedom and truth.

IV. Freedom and Truth

The fundamental relationship between freedom and truth emerges explicitly in the opening chapter, "Sapientiae Divinae Patefactio" ["The Revelation of God's Wisdom"], and carries the telling heading "Coram arcano — ratio" ["Reason before the Mystery"] (*FR* 13-15). Yet the text does not turn immediately to freedom. Rather, its theme is faith — to be precise, *oboeditio fidei*, the obedience of faith. This is the response that must be given to the revealing God, whose self-revelation is Jesus Christ (*Iesus Patris Revelator; FR* 7-12). The emphasis falls on obedient response[11] — thus already implying that it is an essentially free response in which humans acknowledge God in his supreme transcendence and freedom.[12]

At this point, two observations are in order: First, *transcendentia* and *libertas* are the only attributes of God that are addressed. Second, faith is understood as the obedient act of assent to God's self-revelation. Yet what is the cause of this obedient act of assent? And how does it differ from yielding to the logical force of a superior argument as well as from a non-engaged acknowledgment of a contingent fact? Does the gift, God's self-revelation, elicit this response; that is, does prevenient grace put humans, in the very encounter, in a position to respond freely, or do we respond on the grounds of a capacity that would allow us to respond irrespective of who invited the response — that is, "naturally"? In other words, is the notion of "response" simply formal, based on a transcendental account of freedom, or is the response (and the freedom presupposed in its act) enabled by the very nature of the encounter itself and thus "graced"? In short, how should we understand this "act of entrusting ourselves to God" (*actus ille, quo nos Deo committimus; FR* 13)?

Here we enter a highly charged theological ground, as is well reflected in the English and German translations of the encyclical. The English translation renders the act as ". . . a moment of fundamental decision which engages the whole person," while the German translation puts it as "ein grundlegender Entscheidungsvorgang . . . in den die ganze Person eingebunden ist." Yet interestingly, the Latin text offers the following: ". . . tamquam tempus habitus est cuiusdam electionis fundamentalis, qua tota involvitur persona." And the subsequent sentence gives us the key for what is intended with "tamquam tempus habitus": "Usque ad extremum intellectus ac voluntas exercent spiritualem suam naturam ut subiecto humano permittatur actum perficere quo uniuscuiusque libertas pleno modo vivatur" ["In that act, the intellect and the will display their spiritual nature, enabling the subject to act in a way which realizes personal freedom to the full"]. Both intellect and will exercise their spiritual nature in order to allow the human subject *actum perficere*, to accomplish the act in and through which freedom is lived to the fullest. A third observation is in order at this point: The term *libertas* is used not only in reference to God but also in reference to human beings. In other words, *Fides et Ratio* does not make terminological distinctions in this crucial matter.[13]

Yet let us return to the main line of the argument. *Fides et Ratio* becomes more specific: in faith, freedom is not simply "there"; it is not a given (*praesens*). Rather, freedom *postulatur;* it is called for, or, as the English translation puts it rather strongly and freely, "absolutely required." Even more so, *ipsa fides*, faith itself, seems to be that which allows human beings to best express their freedom. So freedom seems to be an antecedent capacity that is called for, claimed, and also best expressed in the very act of faith. Why is that? According to *Fides et Ratio,* it is because freedom does not come to its fulfillment *(impletur)* in decisions against God, since in God human beings encounter the reality that grants their full realization *(id quod sinit homines se totos explicare)*. Because the act of faith opens us to the very reality that enables our full realization, freedom is "realized" in that very act. Thus *Fides et Ratio* prepares us for the final encounter between freedom and truth: "Men and women can accomplish no more important act in their lives than the act of faith; it is here that freedom reaches the certainty of truth and chooses to live in that truth" (*FR* 13).

"Freedom" — at least in the English translation that I just quoted — has now advanced to the dignity of an agent and commands the role of a grammatical subject in this important sentence. Thus the English translation invites the following interpretation: freedom, being antecedently present and functional in an incipient way all along, reaches the certainty of truth in the act of faith and makes its ultimate decision, namely, to live in that truth in light of its very certainty.

V. The Hidden Will

The potential problem with this kind of reading is the following: Freedom could be seen here as hypostatized *potestas absoluta*, a freedom not constituted by the truth encountered (and even more importantly, not received in the encounter with the truth) but rather able to exercise a sovereign choice in light of the certainty of truth. We might wonder to what degree a Molinist account of human freedom lingers beneath the surface of a document that otherwise clearly favors Thomas Aquinas. However, we see that on closer inspection, this seems to be more the case with the English and German translations of the text. When we attend to the Latin text, the picture turns out to be more nuanced.

First, in the Latin text we find an agent, *voluntas*, that is suppressed in both the English and German translations. "Quomodo enim verus libertatis usus iudicari posset nulla sese aperiendi voluntas ad id quod sinit homines se totos explicare?" ["For how could it be judged as a true use of freedom for no will to be open to that which grants humans to fully realize themselves?"] (*FR* 13). Second, the term *libertas* does not appear in the most decisive — and potentially problematic — place: "Credendo namque persona humana actum suae vitae significantissimum complet; hic enim veritatis certitudinem adsequitur veritas in eaque vivere decernit" ["For in believing, the human person accomplishes the most significant act of his/her life, since here truth reaches the certainty of truth and he/she decides to live in it"] (*FR* 13). What has happened? In the Latin, the *persona humana* emerges as the decisive subject of the claim that connects freedom and truth. In the act of faith, human persons accomplish the most significant act of their lives. In faith — *credendo* — truth turns into certainty, and again *credendo* the human person decides to live in this truth. *Credendo* stands at the head of the sentence like a mathematical sign in front of a bracket that encloses everything else in the expression: in faith, which is an active reception, truth becomes certain (that is, it becomes determinative of who the person is and what he/she does — personal truth), and in this certainty, and still *credendo*, the person decides to live. Must this *credere* not already be conceived as the act of grace in which we are liberated to participate freely and thus "decide" not *for* grace but on the basis of grace and as moved by grace?

It is noteworthy, to say the least, that the official Latin text of the encyclical is much more nuanced than the English and German translations in setting up a complex relationship between *verus libertatis usus, voluntas, persona humana,* and *credere* as the *actus significantissimum,* a relationship that allows for various Augustinian construals of how faith draws upon as well as informs reason and will. What the Latin text clearly does not allow for is a reading of freedom as the capacity of an ultimate choice, as that abyss of willing out of which choices emerge sovereignly. Rather, the *verus libertatis usus* seems to depend on the *veritas* that can be seen only *credendo,* and in that, it becomes a certitude that precisely allows true freedom to occur.

However, FR 15 simultaneously affirms and questions this reading. How? "The truth of Christian Revelation, found in Jesus of Nazareth, enables all men and women to embrace the 'mystery' of their own life."[14] Yet in so doing, the truth of revelation acknowledges an antecedent reality in the creature: "As absolute truth, it summons human beings to be open to the transcendent, whilst respecting both their autonomy as creatures and their freedom. At this point the relationship between freedom and truth is complete, and we understand the full meaning of the Lord's words: 'You will know the truth, and the truth will make you free' (*Jn* 8:32)."[15] If the supreme truth sets free, then an antecedent bondage is implied. On the other hand, the supreme truth respects an antecedent human *autonomia* and *libertas.* What picture emerges if we assume both claims?

According to *Fides et Ratio,* created reason has the autonomy and freedom to investigate the mystery of human life. Yet as soon as this reason encounters the ultimate truth, it is obliged to open itself to transcendence and in that be truly liberated. Yet we might ask, liberated from what? *Fides et Ratio* would answer, from reductively immanentist limitations of the mind and constrictions of a technocratic logic.[16] But are those purely accidental deteriorations of reason's activity? Or could they possibly be the result of reason and will interacting in problematic ways? In other words, the question again arises of how the will affects reason and, more specifically, rational inquiry. This Augustinian question, intensified by Luther, is by no means an attack on reason or its capacities but rather a questioning of the tacit assumption that reason and will under the condition of sin are capable of sustaining a tradition of inquiry that would lead into a truthful investigation of the human mystery.

While *voluntas* emerges terminologically in a few places in the encyclical, the substantive issue remains hidden in the notion of a rightful *autonomia* and *libertas* of human reason that precede the encounter of faith. Yet how do the antecedent *autonomia* and *libertas* and the fullness of freedom cohere? The fullness of freedom seems to be received in faith. Freedom now takes full possession of our lives and follows the path of truth — both speculatively and practically. Yet an antecedent *autonomia* and *libertas* seem to allow reason to investigate on its own and to come to true results, that is, to achieve a truth of its own. However, since this *autonomia* and *libertas* are in need of liberation, the question arises, in what sense and to what degree can *autonomia* and *libertas* rightly be called such in the first place? If, indeed, reason's *autonomia* and *libertas* are in need of a liberation that is nothing less than fundamental, what is the point of *Fides et Ratio* in asking for a "philosophia naturae *vere metaphysicae*" (FR 83)? Would this metaphysics itself not need a kind of liberation? Would it not need to be enfolded in and guided by faith?

VI. Wisdom

Fides et Ratio offers an account of this tension after expounding "wisdom," the desire for and pursuit of truth (FR 16, 17). Here we find a balanced and integrated picture of faith and reason yet, interestingly, no thematization of *libertas* and *voluntas*. The very point of this transition is to illuminate the harmonious togetherness of faith and reason as reflected in the encyclical's opening picture of two wings carrying the human spirit to the ultimate truth.[17] Wisdom seems to be the very subject for which this picture actually fits, because wisdom — personified in the Logos — is identical with the ultimate good, the life of the triune God. Insofar as wisdom becomes a human attribute, it is that which is completely directed to and inchoately embraced by this ultimate good. We might wonder what a discussion of *libertas* and *voluntas* would look like in relation to wisdom — or better, why freedom and will might not need to be thematized explicitly in the context of wisdom. The end of FR 21 at least seems to suggest that freedom is "received" and thus identical with the teleological movement toward the beautiful, good, and true.

VII. The Will's Incurvature, the Wisdom of the Cross, and *Iudicium*

Yet *Fides et Ratio* moves beyond "wisdom" — into St. Paul's theology of the cross. Why? We might give the following reason: The end of FR 22 substantiates that to which the *Deo innixus,* the "leaning on God," at the end of *FR* 21 points. The cross stands for the ultimate and most radical questioning of any wisdom humans can muster. Simultaneously, the cross stands for the ultimate and most radical establishment of wisdom received in faith. And the reception of this wisdom entails the reception of a freedom in which the will is rectified and absorbed by its ultimate good, that is, conformed to God's will. This is the freedom in which reason can confidently develop again its genuine and original metaphysical range of inquiry. But how does this look in detail — and is this the way it really works in the encyclical?

According to *Fides et Ratio,* in Romans 1 Paul offers "[p]opulari sermone argumentationem quandam philosophicam" ["a philosophical argument in popular language"].[18] For *Fides et Ratio,* the upshot of Romans 1:20 is that "this important Pauline text affirms the human capacity for metaphysical enquiry" (*FR* 22).[19] However, is this alleged capacity not fundamentally undercut, or at least severely incapacitated, by the will's incurvature? According to *Fides et Ratio,* in an act of willful disobedience, *plena et absoluta libertate,* human beings opposed themselves to God, thus undercutting reason's original capacity *ad conditorem Deum revertendi,* to turn to God the Creator. Interestingly, *Fides et Ratio* turns to Genesis in order to expand St. Paul's account in Romans. The blindness of pride led the first human beings *ut se supremos esse crederent,* to assume themselves to be sovereign.[20] The grasp for sovereignty inflicts such wounds on reason *(atque rationi humanae vulnera intulerunt)* that reason eventually becomes a prisoner of its own: ". . . paulatim facta est ratio humana sui ipsius captiva" (*FR* 22).[21] Despite the obvious importance of the will for disobedience and pride, *Fides et Ratio,* in this crucial reflection on the condition of sin, abandons the notion of the will and the loss of its integrity in relation to reason's original capacity to know the truth.

Yet *Fides et Ratio* clearly emphasizes that only the coming of Christ redeems reason from its weakness and liberates it from its self-imprisonment. It is only through Christ, the very incarnation of wisdom, that reason's capacity to know the truth is restored. It is only in Christ, through faith, that participation in divine wisdom is restored. And by implication, I would argue, it is only in the context of this participation in Christ, the Wisdom, that the original metaphysical range of reason in *statu integritatis* is restored. *Fides et Ratio* acknowledges this fundamental limitation as *FR* 23 turns to St. Paul's theme of the opposition between the wisdom of the cross, God's wisdom, and the "wisdom of this world."

While a wide range of exegetical questions could be raised here, I will limit myself to two observations: *First,* "Non sane verborum sapientiam sed

Verbum Sapientiae Paulus recenset veluti veritatis regulam simulque salutis" ["It is not the wisdom of words, but the Word of Wisdom which Saint Paul offers as the criterion of both truth and salvation"] (*FR* 23). If we were to take *FR* 23 as the theological cornerstone of the encyclical and the above sentence as the very center of *FR* 23, what consequences would it have for the relationship between faith and reason? According to this reading, could the opening sentences of *FR* 34 — "Haec veritas, quam Deus in Christo Iesu nobis revelat, minime opponitur veritatibus quae per philosophiam assumuntur. Immo, duo cognitionis gradus ducunt ad veritatis plenitudinem" — still have been written in the same way? ["This truth, which God reveals to us in Jesus Christ, is not opposed to the truths which philosophy perceives. On the contrary, the two modes of knowledge lead to truth in all its fullness."] We do not need to question the rest of *FR* 34 in order to feel forced to see the relationship between faith and reason as much more complicated and strained as soon as we allow the full force of *FR* 23 and its key sentence to bear upon the issue. Following the inner thrust of *FR* 23's key sentence, faith must exercise discernment (Rom 12:2) by testing the results and implications of philosophical inquiry in light of the received *Verbum Sapientiae*.

And *second*, pointedly, *Fides et Ratio* exhorts us to employ precisely this discernment; for at the opening of *FR* 23, it calls for such a fundamental *iudicium*: "Postulat idcirco Christiani habitudo ad philosophiam fundamentale quoddam iudicium" ["This is why the Christian's relationship to philosophy requires thorough-going discernment"]. Chapters 4-7[22] can be understood as the application of a magisterial as well as an argumentative *iudicium*, especially in pointing both to exemplary theologians and to philosophers and in sketching a small syllabus of errors.

Yet the necessity of exercising *iudicium* in light of the word of the cross and on the basis of *FR* 22 and 23 creates a deep tension between the movement in chapter 2, "Credo ut Intellegam," and the movement in chapter 3, "Intellego ut Credam." We can see this tension emerge right at the opening of chapter 3, in *FR* 24. Quoting from the *Missale Romanum* a sentence reminiscent of Augustine's famous line from the opening pages of his *Confessions*, *Fides et Ratio* states that "in latebris cordis hominis flagrans Dei desiderium est seminatum" ["in the far reaches of the human heart there is a seed of desire and nostalgia for God"]. Yet it remains a disputable point whether — and if so, to what degree — that statement indeed entails the subsequent conclusion: "Iter igitur quoddam exstat quod homo sua ex voluntate emetiri potest" ["There is therefore a path which the human being may choose to take"]. Rather, in light of *FR* 22 and 23, there seems to surface a hiatus in the argument.

Let us briefly review the line of the argument that leads up to this point:

1. Natural desires for God are God-given.
2. God-given desires must be capable of satisfaction.
3. The power to satisfy desires does not lie with God alone.
4. Therefore, there must be some human *potestas* that can be turned to this purpose.

The hiatus seems to lie between this fourth step and *FR* 22 and 23. Let me put it in the form of a question: To what *potestas* can "sua ex voluntate" refer, and what kind of *iudicium* is called for in light of the "primal disobedience" in which all humans are caught up (*FR* 22)? How does this path of reasoning inquiry — which human beings can allegedly enter *sua ex voluntate* — relate to the vanity of human thoughts that *FR* 22 so strongly underscores?[23]

This tension, as created by the necessity of *iudicium* based on the word of the cross, carries all through chapter 3 and reaches its peak in *FR* 34, so that *FR* 34 comes to stand in an essential and perplexing tension with *FR* 23. While *FR* 23 assumes a requisite *iudicium*, *FR* 34 makes any *iudicium* unnecessary, since it claims a fundamental harmony where the Apostle Paul sees a fundamental opposition. While *FR* 23 would lead to a critical and theologically reflective relationship between theology and the traditions of philosophical inquiry, somewhat reminiscent of Augustine (e.g., *De Trinitate*, esp. book XV; *De civitate Dei*, esp. books I-X; and *Contra secundam Juliani responsionem opus imperfectum*), *FR* 34 echoes the pacified division of labor toward which first Wolffian and later, after *Aeterni Patris*, Thomist neo-scholasticism of the nineteenth century strove.[24] In short, the force of *FR* 22 and 23 is to press the following issues on chapter 3:

1. The identity of God as Creator and as Redeemer seems to stand as guarantee for the unity of truth that is the complementarity of two modes of knowledge. Yet in light of *FR* 34, reason is clearly privileged, because truth that comes from revelation is at the same time truth that needs to be understood by reason (après Hegel, raising *Vorstellung* to *Begriff*?). There is no bidirectionality here: the insights of reason are not to be tested and assessed in light of the truth of revelation. Yet this seems to be exactly what the *iudicium* of *FR* 23 would actually require.

2. Is it the case in *FR* 22 and 23 that faith and reason "encounter" each other? Is it not more the case that they constantly imply each other — that faith, as theology, always already reasons and in so doing, while also informing reason, always already draws upon reason's epistemic and logical capacity? And does philosophical reasoning not very often draw more or less im-

plicitly upon some religious roots[25] or at least presuppose a horizon of totality and transcendence in light of which the philosophical inquiry is intelligible?[26] Moreover, does philosophical reasoning, while eliciting important insights, not share, *post lapsum,* in the onerous opacity of a wounded reason and the intractable instability of a will curved in upon itself?

3. How do the *veritates quae per philosophiam assumuntur* in *FR* 34, the truths that philosophy perceives, *relate to the wisdom of the cross and the wisdom of this world in FR* 23? The account in *FR* 23 implies a concept of freedom and will, while the account in *FR* 34 does not. *Haec veritas,* the wisdom of the cross, is in no way an equivalent to any of the *veritates* of philosophy. Rather, the first is categorically different in that it concretely affects the will's restoration in the reception of freedom. It is also simply not clear what the *veritates* of philosophy are. To what truths do we come through philosophy? A phenomenologist will answer this question differently from a Kantian, a Hegelian, a Fregean, an Aristotelian, a Heideggerian, or a Nietzschean. And it is also clear that at least the Augustinian strand in Christian theology would like to reflect critically upon these *veritates* to which philosophers come in light of the reasoning of faith.

4. In *FR* 107 there seems to be a distinction between a philosophical search of an existential kind and various philosophical systems that actually have lured the human into thinking that "ipsum absolutum esse sui dominum, qui de fortuna sua deque eventura sorte per se decernere possit, sibimet ipsi suisque dumtaxat fidens viribus" ["they are their own absolute master, able to decide their own destiny and future in complete autonomy, trusting only in themselves and their own powers"]. Here the *iudicium* distinguishes between a legitimate search and the problematic, systematized outcomes of this search, between a search for *veritas* and the systematized *veritates* that falsify by premature closure. Yet what prevents the genuine philosophical search from leading again and again to new versions of premature closure — for *post lapsum* reason is its own captive, and the will, curved in upon itself — unless and until the human being "in veritatem se inseri eligit, sub Sapientiae umbra suum struens domicilium ibique inhabitans" ["in choosing to enter the truth (makes) a home under the shade of Wisdom and dwell(s) there"] (*FR* 107)? And to finish *FR* 107 with the English translation: "Only within this horizon of truth will people understand their freedom in its fullness and their call to know and love God as the supreme realization of their true self." This emphasis on restored reason is clearly consistent with chapter 2 and can be seen as completing the *iudicium* called for by *FR* 23.

5. Yet how does the "narrative" of reason offered in chapter 3, "Intellego ut Credam," fit into the overarching narrative begun in chapter 2, "Credo ut

Intellegam," and completed in *FR* 107? If Christ truly liberates reason, how can the search for truth take place as consistently as chapter 3 supposes? The framework that seems to emerge is that of answer-question. Only after the answer has been given do we come to better understand the consistency of the question: Christ's death on the cross offers the ultimate answer to which Socrates' death was the permanent question (*FR* 26, with its peak in *FR* 33).

At the center of the tension, created by the necessity of *iudicium*, between chapter 2 and chapter 3 and, most intensely, between *FR* 22 and 23 on the one hand and *FR* 34 on the other stands the largely unattended question of the relationship between *libertas Dei, libertas hominum, voluntas hominum,* and *ratio hominum*. Moreover, while the concept of freedom emerges in crucial instances in *Fides et Ratio*, freedom does not receive the focused discussion it deserves. This internal imbalance points to the unthematized "other" in the encyclical: *the will and its relation to reason.*

VIII. The Wisdom of *Philosophari in Maria*

As I see it, the key to the unattended problem of the will in *Fides et Ratio* is wisdom. Wisdom holds a place of such prominence in the encyclical that clearly the encouragement to reason authentically can pertain only to redeemed, liberated reason, not to created reason under the condition of sin. Let us remember that, according to *Fides et Ratio*, the telos of all human life is deification, participation in the life of the triune God (*FR* 7). The ultimate freedom that human freedom can receive is to be liberated in faith in order to participate in divine freedom by receiving the new telos of God's life.

It is thus by no means accidental that *Fides et Ratio* ends with a short meditation on *philosophari in Maria*, the "seat of wisdom" (*FR* 108). To repeat here an earlier point: for *Fides et Ratio*, wisdom, personified in the Logos, is identical with the ultimate good, the life of the triune God. Insofar as wisdom becomes a human attribute, it is completely directed to and inchoately embraced by this ultimate good. The will that is drawn to this good can lose itself in that embrace. Thus transformed, the will finds itself again as freedom received. Hence, true freedom stands for liberation from incurvature, in which the will asserts its own *libido dominandi* (the self-assertion of the subject and the subjugation of the world, be it by way of metaphysics or technology). *Philosophari in Maria* would seem to me to be able to think in the mode of *pathos*, in the mode of reception, in the mode of faith.[27]

Fides et Ratio's inner tension makes it amply clear that a reconsideration of the relationship between freedom and truth entails the question of the will's impact on the work of reason. *Post lapsum,* how does the will's *libido dominandi* affect reason such that reason's grasp of reality unavoidably ends in a knowledge that is nothing other than an extension of power? *Fides et Ratio* is clearly aware of the deeply reductionist tendencies that certain strands of post-Nietzschean and neo-pragmatist thinking involve, strands that can arguably be identified as voluntarist. I think it is right in light of these tendencies that *Fides et Ratio* reemphasizes reason's fundamental epistemic capacities and, by implication, its epistemic primacy over against the will. Furthermore, I regard it as crucial that the encyclical encourages a renewal of a philosophy of being.[28] Yet it strikes me as detrimental to the encyclical's fundamental concern — "fidei parrhēsia respondere debet rationis audacia" — to omit an explicit discussion of the will's relationship to reason and its role in considering the relationship between freedom and truth.

12. "In"

On the Declaration *The Jewish People and Their Sacred Scriptures in the Christian Bible*

I. The Problem: Denunciation or Dissociation

It is not at all rare that the most significant and groundbreaking documents are the ones that appear most quietly on the public stage. Thanks to their substance, they can forgo the usual assistance of spotlights, headlines, and three-point summaries. On the Feast Day of the Ascension 2001, the Pontifical Biblical Commission released such a document in the most inconspicuous way. The roughly hundred-page text, introduced by Cardinal Joseph Ratzinger, with the baroque title *The Jewish People and Their Sacred Scriptures in the Christian Bible (JPSSCB)* was originally composed in French[1] and first available only in an Italian translation. Unsurprisingly, therefore, the document resisted quick and easy consumption by the English-speaking media. Only quite recently, since an English translation[2] has become available, has the document begun to "exist" in the English-speaking world and, consequently, to make headlines. And indeed, there will be no haste in "being done" with it. Theological texts of this size and substance take time — time to compose and time to consume. It took the Pontifical Biblical Commission a number of years to produce this impressively comprehensive study, and anyone seriously interested in the topic it treats will need to invest in more than a brief scan of the introduction and conclusion in search of the paragraph that says it all. Beware — this document requires patient and attentive study and, more importantly, compels an even more patient and attentive (re-)reading of the Bible. Hence, just over two years after its release, the reception of this teaching document of the Roman Catholic Church has just begun. And any facile "situating" of the document will be resisted in a most salutary way by its immense range and nuanced argumentation.

Obviously, every Christian should care, if not about the document itself, at least about the topic it treats. Whether Christians like it or not, since the Shoah our very identity has been on trial, and the defendants' reaction has been vacillating between a stubborn supersessionism on the right and an equally "showy self-immolation"[3] on the left. In this situation, *JPSSCB* presses forward by returning to the canon of the Christian Bible and by offering a reading of it that is as comprehensive as it is nuanced, thereby moving beyond the intra-Christian stalemate between the quite different but equally tempting lures of supersessionist triumphalism and post-Holocaust self-negation.

Protestants especially should care about this document. Its primary impetus clearly was the Second Vatican Council or, more precisely, Vatican II's Dogmatic Constitution on Divine Revelation, *Dei Verbum*,[4] and its Declaration on the Church's Relationship to Non-Christian Religions, *Nostra Aetate*.[5] Yet even more important, by building upon the earlier, even more comprehensive 1993 teaching document of the Pontifical Biblical Commission, *The Interpretation of the Bible in the Church*,[6] *JPSSCB* offers a reading of Scripture that is as faithful to the rule of faith as it is receptive to the results of historical-critical research. American Protestantism finds itself thus confronted with the embodied suggestion, if not the evidence, that it might indeed require a church (and not merely a conglomerate of denominations) to overcome American Protestantism's seemingly interminable vacillation between a self-assertive biblicism and a hysterical critical historicism (the notable exceptions in contemporary Protestant biblical scholarship notwithstanding). And, having spent many summers in Germany, and having encountered shockingly few Old Testament readings in the local Lutheran worship services, I am especially receptive to the way Cardinal Ratzinger reminds the reader in his introduction to *JPSSCB* of the Marcionite leanings in much of modern Protestantism, especially in Germany. He helpfully quotes Adolf von Harnack, the *spiritus rector* of modern liberal Protestantism, to drive home his point: "The rejection of the Old Testament in the second century [an allusion to Marcion] was an error which the great Church was right in resisting; holding on to it in the 16th century was a disaster from which the Reformation has not yet been able to extricate itself; but to maintain it since the 19th century in Protestantism as a canonical document equal in value to the New Testament, that is the result of religious and ecclesial paralysis."[7] Undoubtedly, Protestant theology has come a long way since Adolf von Harnack published his *Marcion* (suffice it to mention his great antagonist Karl Barth),[8] and in the meantime, the following central claim of *JPSSCB* would find broad and unqualified acceptance among most contemporary Protestant theologians: "Without the Old Testament, the New Testament would be an unintelligible book, a plant deprived of its roots and destined to dry up and wither" (*JPSSCB* 84). Moreover, among the Protestant avant-garde of a radical post-Holocaust revisionism, this conviction already has given rise to a profound questioning of all the maximalist (not to say orthodox) Christian claims about Christ.[9] The outcome has been a Protestantism deeply torn between two forces: on the one side, the holdouts for a liberal, quasi-Marcionite "Israel-forgetfulness,"[10] eager to denounce the Old Testament and the religion of Israel as legalistic, materialistic, fixated on exteriority, and, worst, paying allegiance to a jealous — if not cruel — deity. On the other side, we find a post-Holocaust revisionism, equally eager to dissociate the New Testament witness from the trinitarian and christological dogmas of the ecumenical councils and to qualify and bracket as much as possible the maximalist claims about Jesus Christ put forth by the New Testament itself. What makes *JPSSCB* so significant for contemporary Protestant theology is its move beyond those stale alternatives to a constructive ecumenical challenge.

II. The Ecumenical Challenge: Mutual Indwelling

The way forward, I am convinced, consists in the bold and creative Christian syntax governed by the little word "in," which separates and connects the two parts of the document's title: *The Jewish People and Their Holy Scriptures **in** the Christian Bible* (my emphasis). There are two inseparable but distinct ways that *JPSSCB* renders the Christian syntax governed by this "in": first, the church "in" Israel; and second, Israel "in" the church. Hence, the document could arguably carry the simple title *In*. While the syntactic significance of "in" becomes explicit only at the document's very end — in the section "Pastoral Orientations" (*JPSSCB* 86-87), where Pope John Paul II is quoted — that small word nevertheless governs and structures the document's overall argumentation.

But first the catalyst: John Paul II. The document quotes him as saying in 1980, during a visit to the synagogue of Mainz: "The encounter between the people of God of the Old Covenant, which has never been abrogated by God (cf. Rm 11:29), and that of the New Covenant is also an *internal* dialogue in our Church, similar to that between the first and second part of its Bible" (*JPSSCB* 86). And in 1986, during a visit to the synagogue of Rome, he is quoted as saying: "The Jewish religion is not 'extrinsic' to us, but in a certain manner, it is *'intrinsic'* to our religion. We have therefore a relationship with it which we do not have with any other religion. You [Jewish people] are our favored brothers and, in a certain sense, one can say our elder brothers" (*JPSSCB* 86). What makes *JPSSCB* such a significant document is that it offers a wide-ranging reading of Scripture that shows in great detail exactly how the "intrinsic" and the "internal" must be understood: as a complex and manifold mutual indwelling of Israel and the church to which the canon of Scripture inexorably gives rise.

First, and most important, *JPSSCB* affirms the church "in" Israel:

> In the beginning, the apostolic preaching was addressed only to the Jews and proselytes, pagans associated with the Jewish community (cf. Ac 2:11). Christianity, then, came to birth in the bosom of first century Judaism. (*JPSSCB* 2)

> The New Testament never says that Israel has been rejected. From the earliest times, the Church considered the Jews to be important witnesses to the divine economy of salvation. She understands her own existence as a participation in the election of Israel and in a vocation that belongs, in the first place, to Israel, despite the fact that only a small number of Israelites accepted it. (*JPSSCB* 36)

If there is one thing new and groundbreaking in *JPSSCB*, it is that the teaching document allows Christians, as Luke Timothy Johnson felicitously put it, not to focus on "the question of how Christians think about Jews" but "to think of themselves with reference to Jews."[11] In consequence, the document offers a consistent historical genealogical reading of the church and its canon that shows that the church is simply unintelligible outside and irrespective of God's history with and promises to his people Israel. After all, "[i]n the New Testament, the validity of the promise made to Abraham is never called into question" (*JPSSCB* 55).

At the same time and less surprisingly, however, *JPSSCB* — impressively unimpressed by post-Holocaust political correctness — affirms Israel "in" the church:

> The Church is composed of Israelites who have accepted the new covenant, and of other believers who have joined them. As a people of the new covenant, the Church is conscious of existing only in virtue of belonging to Christ Jesus, the Messiah of Israel, and because of its link with the apostles, who were all Israelites. Far from being a substitution for Israel, the Church is in solidarity with it. To the Christians who have come from the nations, the apostle Paul declares that they are grafted to the good ol-

ive tree which is Israel (Rm 11:16, 17). That is to say, the Church is conscious of being given a universal horizon by Christ, in conformity with Abraham's vocation, whose descendants from now on are multiplied in a filiation founded on faith in Christ (Rm 4:11-12). The reign of God is no longer confined to Israel alone, but is open to all, including pagans, with a place of honour for the poor and oppressed. (*JPSSCB* 65)

The litmus test for this aspect of the "in" arises in the Christian hermeneutics of the Old Testament as practiced most extensively and rigorously in patristic exegesis:[12] "Christian readers were convinced that their Old Testament hermeneutic, although significantly different from that of Judaism, corresponds nevertheless to a potentiality of meaning that is really present in the texts. Like a 'revelation' during the process of photographic development, the person of Jesus and the events concerning him now appear in the Scriptures with a fullness of meaning that could not be hitherto perceived" (*JPSSCB* 64). Hence, *JPSSCB* in principle legitimates the practice of patristic exegesis as a continuation of the way the New Testament reads the Scriptures of Israel in light of the life, death, and resurrection of Christ — and vice versa. Yet in a very timely and appropriate way, the document distances itself from any anti-Jewish implications of such patristic readings:

> Although the Christian reader is aware that the internal dynamism of the Old Testament finds its goal in Jesus, this is a retrospective perception whose point of departure is not in the text as such, but in the events of the New Testament proclaimed by the apostolic preaching. *It cannot be said, therefore, that Jews do not see what has been proclaimed in the text, but that the Christian, in the light of Christ and in the Spirit, discovers in the text an additional meaning that was hidden there.* (*JPSSCB* 21; my emphasis)

Yet how are the two aspects of this "in" — the church "in" Israel and Israel "in" the church — related to each other? Clearly not dialectically, *pace* the claim in *JPSSCB* 19 ("However, there is a dialectical relationship between Old Testament and New Testament"), since they are neither to be sublated in the form of a higher synthesis nor to be kept apart in the "either/or" of an eternal disjunction. Nor are they related harmoniously as two complementary aspects of one organic unity. Rather, according to *JPSSCB*, the two moments of this "in" are related as promise is to fulfillment — eschatologically and mysteriously, to be seen only retrospectively and through the eyes of faith, that is, through a mirror dimly. They are related in the way the resurrection of Jesus is related to God's "[raising] Israel from Egypt"[13] and Pentecost is related to the spirit of Israel's prophets. From the perspective of history, we see surprise, discontinuity, and rupture. In retrospect, however, we see the continuity in God's surprisingly novel yet utterly faithful ways.[14] And *JPSSCB* implies quite clearly that what is true for the church in the way she was called into existence has also proved true for Judaism in the way it has continued in its existence and witness over the centuries. Historically, discontinuity and rupture dominate. But retrospectively, through and beyond the terror of the Shoah, the striking continuity of God's utter faithfulness to his people becomes apparent.

The mutual indwelling of Israel and church has its ground and source in the unity and faithfulness of God's salvific economy. And offensively — yet nonnegotiably — the "in" has for Christians an irreducible center in the concrete person Jesus of Nazareth. While he is the stumbling block and the great offense, he (and nothing else) is at the same time the one and only substance that justifies *JPSSCB*'s bold claim: "In the past, the break between the Jewish people and the Church of Christ Jesus could sometimes, in certain times and places, give the impression of being complete. In the light of the Scriptures, this should never have occurred. For a complete break between Church and Synagogue contradicts Sacred Scripture" (*JPSSCB* 85).

If we ask where this contradiction becomes most evident in the Scriptures, Romans 9–11 comes immediately to mind. It is no surprise that Paul's letter to the Romans is one of the most frequently cited texts in *JPSSCB*. And it is my modest thesis that the mutual indwelling of Israel and the church that is argued at length in this document should be understood as the grammar of an extended canonical catechesis — one in which we are taught how to read all of Scripture in light of Romans 9–11, and vice versa, in and through a "dynamism of love" (*JPSSCB* 86). The dynamism of love, quite transparent in Romans 9–11, also shines forth in the following passage of *JPSSCB*:

> In the Old Testament, the plan of God is a union of love with his people, a paternal love, a spousal love and, notwithstanding Israel's infidelities, God will never renounce it, but affirms it in perpetuity (Is 54:8; Jr 31:3). In the New Testament, God's love overcomes the worst obstacles; even if they do not believe in his Son whom he sent as their Messiah Saviour, Israelites are still "loved" (Rm 11:29). *Whoever wishes to be united to God, must also love them.* (*JPSSCB* 86; my emphasis)

In short, *JPSSCB* teaches us that Christians must learn to dwell patiently, faithfully, and humbly in the space of faith, hope, and love opened by the Apostle Paul in Romans 9–11, as the *ecclesia* remains a community on the way, sustained solely by God's promise — especially after the Shoah.

As *JPSSCB* carefully narrates, Christians have been quick to point out from quite early on that Israel by and large was not ready for who Jesus, her Messiah, was and is. Now, after the Shoah, Christians have to begin to learn the hard lesson that Christianity by and large has not been ready for who Jesus, her Messiah, is and was. But there is hope that our learning will not be in vain. "For God has imprisoned all in disobedience so that he may be merciful to all" (Rom 11:32 NRSV).

III. Theological Implications

The complex and manifold mutual indwelling of Israel and the church as pressed by *JPSSCB* arises inexorably from the anticipatory retrospective of the last things inaugurated by Christ's life, death, and resurrection (cf. Eph 2:11-22). However, the "in" is of equal importance for a range of theological matters next to the last, possibly "first things." I shall mention only four of them.

First is the matter of *contemporary biblical exegesis*. The deep tension that runs through *JPSSCB* is indicative of a profound methodological difficulty that can also be found at the very heart of the earlier *Interpretation of the Bible in the Church:* the quandary of how to relate premodern and postcritical exegesis on the one hand with historical-critical exegesis on the other.[15] This dilemma characterizes as well the best of present critical biblical exegesis that has not yet jettisoned its theological commitments. I shall formulate it as a question: How can we affirm at the same time the validity of patristic exegesis — let's say a christological reading of the Psalms — and the validity of the historical-critical method with its specific normative presuppositions? *JPSSCB* does not offer a direct, coherent solution. Instead, it offers a circumspect and nuanced approach toward such a solution. This approach rests on three interconnected principles. First, a retrospective reading from inside the eschatological horizon of fulfillment inaugurated by Christ necessarily opens up perspectives that transcend the original, literal meaning of Old Testament texts — without falsifying the original, literal sense. Second, at the same time, such a retrospective reading is made possible by a history to which the literal sense bears witness, giving the latter a non-substitutable priority over against retrospective readings. Third, historical-critical research must be guided by this bifocal hermeneutical horizon lest it deteriorate into a purely historicist exercise sustained by theologically unaccounted-for normative commitments.[16]

Yet significant pressure can be exerted upon any one of the three principles that constitute *JPSSCB*'s approach to the quandary's solution. If, indeed,

Christ is who the New Testament claims he is, as also affirmed by the ecumenical councils, must not the whole canon of Scripture be read first of all in light of and from the perspective of this truth? Is not patristic exegesis, insofar as it practices precisely this insight, the most appropriate Christian exegesis? To put it concretely: Is not St. Augustine's christological interpretation of the Psalms in his monumental *Enarrationes in Psalmos* the most fitting — if not the only correct — way to read the Psalms? Yet if, on the other hand, any retrospective reading depends upon a prior literal sense, must not a rigorous interpretation of this sense and the history to which it gives witness antecede and possibly determine any other reading? And how do text and community interrelate? Does the text create the community, or the community, the text? Moreover, how do the traditions of interpretation in Judaism as well as in Christianity render the literal sense of the canon, and vice versa? Should Christians indeed expect to learn from Jewish exegesis — and vice versa? And finally, what is the exact relationship between historical-critical research and the theological convictions and commitments to which the canon of Scripture gives rise? *JPSSCB* gives its own answer only indirectly, through its particular practice of reading that draws upon the insights of historical-critical research, privileges the literal sense, and offers a nuanced defense of a retrospective christological reading.[17] But irrespective of what can and must be stated about the historical-critical method, it seems clear beyond doubt that a document of such nuanced and differentiated hermeneutical and historical argumentation would have been unthinkable had not — somewhat clandestinely since the 1950s and in full force since Vatican II — the historical-critical method become a vital interpretive tradition among Roman Catholic biblical scholars. In short, without it, there would be no *JPSSCB* in its present form.

Precisely because of its obvious application of the historical-critical method and its simultaneous affirmation of the legitimacy of a retrospective christological reading, *JPSSCB* is situated uneasily between those who reject any theologically constituted hermeneutical horizon for historical-critical exegesis and those who eschew such exegesis as a modern heresy.[18] Yet, more significant, *JPSSCB* implies the overarching importance of those settings in which these difficult questions can be addressed and sorted out — while practicing the reading of Scripture.[19] Which brings me to my next point.

Second, the project of practicing *interreligious readings of Scripture,* as fostered by the Society for Scriptural Reasoning,[20] finds explicit support in *JPSSCB*:

> Christians can and ought to admit that the Jewish reading of the Bible is a possible one, in continuity with the Jewish Sacred Scriptures from the

Second Temple period, a reading analogous to the Christian reading which developed in parallel fashion. Both readings are bound up with the vision of their respective faiths, of which the readings are the result and expression. Consequently, both are irreducible. On the practical level of exegesis, Christians can, nonetheless, learn much from Jewish exegesis practiced for more than two thousand years, and, in fact, they have learned much in the course of history. For their part, it is to be hoped that Jews themselves can derive profit from Christian exegetical research. (*JPSSCB* 22)

Some readers will be quick to realize and criticize that Islam is not at all addressed by *JPSSCB*.[21] While politically incorrect, this omission is not without its canonically motivated theological reasons, reasons that implicitly raise salient questions for an enterprise that attempts to involve Jews, Christians, and Muslims in the practice of reading Scripture. However, it might be the case that ultimately only precisely such a triadic context, as challenging for Christians as it is for Jews, will prove what Christians can indeed learn from Jewish exegesis and vice versa!

Third, one of the most significant claims put forth by *JPSSCB* can be found in the conclusion to the central, painstakingly comprehensive yet still highly condensed exegetical tour de force "Fundamental themes in the Jewish Scriptures and their reception into faith in Christ." I shall quote it here for a second time: "In the past, the break between the Jewish people and the Church of Christ Jesus could sometimes, in certain times and places, give the impression of being complete. In the light of the Scriptures, this should never have occurred. For a complete break between Church and Synagogue contradicts Sacred Scripture" (*JPSSCB* 85). With this claim *JPSSCB* characterizes Judaism and Christianity in their present forms as the result of an *antecedent schism.* This bold claim is only the consequent entailment of the "in" implying, first, that Judaism and Christianity are not two completely different "religions"; second (and consequently), that the dialogue between them is not interreligious but ecumenical; and finally, that a "two-ways" settlement between Judaism and Christianity amounts to a false settlement into the antecedent schism. This is possibly the most radical entailment of *JPSSCB*'s insistence upon the mutual indwelling of Israel and the church — and for contemporary Judaism, in light of the deeply problematic history of Christian attempts at converting Jews, not to mention the pogroms, it is rightly the most troubling. Yet it is a theological entailment of the "in," christologically warranted, and is at the same time the best medicine against Christianity's chronic Marcionite ailments. *JPSSCB* thus opens a promising intra-Christian line of dialogue, a dialogue that should not neglect the theological legacy of the late Mennonite theologian John Howard Yoder, who insisted upon Christianity's identity as a Jewish sect.[22] In similar ways, the document supports a long-standing ecumenical effort by George Lindbeck, namely, to develop an "Israel-like understanding of the Church."[23]

Yet, *fourth,* this reader finds the document most impressive in its willingness to place itself squarely in the middle by rightly disappointing those Christians who expected a radical post-Holocaust revision of and departure from orthodox christological claims as well as those who tenaciously cling to silent supersessionist or moderately Marcionite convictions. The uncomfortable, painful, unfathomable, but ultimately hopeful insistence upon the antinomy of *continuity "in" discontinuity* and *discontinuity "in" continuity* — in light of the offensive claim of a fulfillment of God's promises inaugurated by Christ's life, death, and resurrection — plainly suggests that we are still traveling on the road mapped out by the Apostle Paul in Romans 9–11. *JPSSCB* interprets Paul's road map in such salient and salutary ways that one can only exclaim, *"Tolle, lege!"* ["Take and read!"]. And even a cursory reading will make it plain that this is a road that Christians can travel faithfully only in company with Jews. For "whoever wishes to be united to God, must also love them" (*JPSSCB* 86). Thus it seems that we are invited to start all over again. In uttering this intense invitation, *JPSSCB* gives new force to the words of George Lindbeck, written in 1990: "We are now better placed than perhaps ever before to retrieve, critically and repentantly, the heritage of the Hebrew scriptures, apostolic writings and early tradition. This retrieval is also more urgent than ever if the churches are to become the kind of global and ecumenical community that the new age needs."[24]

Notes

Notes to Chapter 1

1. Ephraim Radner, *The End of the Church: A Pneumatology of Christian Division in the West* (Grand Rapids: Eerdmans, 1998). For two excellent essays that make this dense book quite accessible and also engage it in a most useful way, see Bruce D. Marshall, "The Divided Church and Its Theology," *Modern Theology* 16 (2000): 377-96, and Joseph L. Mangina's review essay in *Pro Ecclesia* 9 (2000): 490-96.

2. Cardinal Walter Kasper, "Present Day Problems in Ecumenical Theology," in *Reflections, Volume 6: The 2003 Public Lectures* (Princeton: Center of Theological Inquiry, 2003), pp. 56-88; 64-65.

3. Scripture quotations are from the New Revised Standard Version (NRSV).

4. Reinhard Hütter, *Suffering Divine Things: Theology as Church Practice* (Grand Rapids: Eerdmans, 2000), pp. 176ff.

5. For a review essay that represents the argument of my book more clearly and concisely than I ever could have done and that offers some pertinent criticism from which I have gladly learned, see Joseph L. Mangina, "After Dogma: Reinhard Hütter's Challenge to Contemporary Theology," *International Journal of Systematic Theology* 2 (2000): 330-46. For a critical engagement from a revisionist Baptist angle, see Jeff B. Pool, "Seizure by Divine Raptor: The Pathic Theology of Reinhard Hütter," *Perspectives in Religious Studies* 30 (2003): 55-69. After a thorough summary of the book, Pool adopts a combined revisionist (i.e., Chicago) and liberal, free will Baptist perspective, in light of which he identifies six weaknesses in my account — all programmatically determined by his theological venue. Unsurprisingly, the theologically substantive concerns pertain to "classical theism" and "human freedom," two topics eminently worthy of theological meditation and inquiry. And, indeed, I admit that I am taking my lead in these matters from Augustine, Aquinas, and Luther. Human freedom — being first of all created and therefore in a noncompetitive relationship to the Creator — lies fully within the order of divine providence that gives rise to the mystery of predestination. More specifically, the latter is entailed in the doctrines of original sin, election, and prevenient grace.

6. The "one and the same" is an attempt to render the "completum et simplex" as Thomas Aquinas puts it in *De potentia* 1.1: "Esse significat aliquid completum et simplex, sed non subsistens." *Esse* is the ultimate gift that erases itself *(sed non subsistens!)* in the giving. Yet it remains one and the same. I am indebted to Ferdinand Ulrich, *Homo Abyssus: Das Wagnis der Seinsfrage*, with an introduction by Martin Bieler, 2nd ed. (Freiburg: Johannes Verlag, 1998), who put it the following way: "Je ursprünglicher das Sein als mitgeteilte *Fülle* begriffen wird, desto intensiver erhellt es seine Nichtsubsistenz" ["The more radically being is conceived as communicated abundance, the more intensely becomes transparent its nonsubsistence"] (p. 28). Bieler's excellent introduction offers the best entry into Ulrich's demanding *opus magnum*.

7. For a remarkable constructive reception of Ephraim Radner's prophetic challenge, see R. R. Reno, *In the Ruins of the Church* (Grand Rapids: Brazos, 2002).

8. For two important recent reconstructions of Kantian autonomy, see J. B. Schneewind, *The Invention of Autonomy: A History of Modern Moral Philosophy* (Cambridge: Cambridge University Press, 1998), pp. 483-530, and Allen W. Wood, *Kant's Ethical Thought* (Cambridge: Cambridge University Press, 1999), pp. 156-90.

9. For a thoughtful application of this principle in contemporary American politics, see the report from the Council on Civil Society, *A Call to Civil Society: Why Democracy Needs Moral Truths* (New York: Institute for American Values, 1998). This document was signed by David Blankenhorn, Senator Dan Coats, Jean Bethke Elshtain, Francis Fukuyama, William A. Galston, Mary Ann Glendon, Sylvia Ann Hewlett, Senator Joseph Lieberman, Cornel West, James Q. Wilson, and Daniel Yankelovich.

10. Reducing freedom to license, of course, is much older than "postmodernity" (a term I am using in the philosophically unclarified and rhetorically charged sense that currently transposes all discourses in morals and metaphysics into power discourses). Rather, what is new with this postmodernity is the transposition of its despair about freedom — hence its not wanting to be a narratively coherent and therefore accountable self — into theory. For a compelling critique of this currently quite fashionable theoretical posture, see Alasdair MacIntyre, *Three Rival Versions of Moral Enquiry: Encyclopaedia, Genealogy, and Tradition* (Notre Dame: University of Notre Dame Press, 1990), pp. 196-215.

11. Quoted from Michael Allen Gillespie, *Nihilism before Nietzsche* (Chicago: University of Chicago Press, 1995), p. 135.

12. Jean Paul, *Siebenkäs* (1796), English: *Jean Paul: A Reader*, trans. and ed. Timothy J. and Erika Casey (Baltimore: Johns Hopkins University Press, 1992), pp. 179-83.

13. Friedrich Nietzsche, *The Gay Science, with a Prelude in Rhymes and an Appendix of Songs*, trans. with commentary by Walter Kaufmann (New York: Random House, 1974), pp. 181-82; #125.

14. C. S. Lewis, *God in the Dock: Essays on Theology and Ethics*, ed. Walter Hooper, 2nd ed. (Grand Rapids: Eerdmans, 1982), p. 244.

15. Jean-Paul Sartre, *L'Existentialisme est un Humanisme* (Paris: Les Editions Nagel, 1946), p. 37.

16. The best interpretation of this dynamic in Nietzsche's thought is still Karl Löwith, *Nietzsche's Philosophy of the Eternal Recurrence of the Same*, trans. J. Harvey Lomax (Berkeley: University of California Press, 1997).

17. A contingent conglomeration of cells cannot ask this question, nor can it receive

a liberating and transforming answer. Hasn't the human already turned into a "thing" about which we still habitually continue to talk in human terms? In the words of the German philosopher Robert Spaemann: "Der Mensch selbst wird zum Anthropomorphismus" ["The human being itself turns into an anthropomorphism"]. Spaemann, "Die christliche Religion und das Ende des modernen Bewußtseins," *Communio* 8 (1979): 251-70; 254. Spaemann's work is of utmost importance for this problematic; cf. especially his *Personen: Versuche über den Unterschied zwischen "etwas" und "jemand"* (Stuttgart: Klett-Cotta, 1996) and, most recently, his *Grenzen: Zur ethischen Dimension des Handelns* (Stuttgart: Klett-Cotta, 2001).

18. Aldous Huxley, *Brave New World and Brave New World Revisited* (San Francisco: HarperCollins, 1973). If Huxley's dystopic picture seems "unrealistic," cf. Jeremy Rifkin's farsighted account of the present biotechnological revolution: *The Biotech Century: Harnessing the Gene and Remaking the World* (New York: Jeremy P. Tarcher/Putnam, 1998).

19. The English version of the encyclical *Evangelium Vitae, The Gospel of Life*, can best be found in *Origins*, or even better on the Vatican Web page: www.vatican.va. For a Protestant engagement of this important encyclical, see Reinhard Hütter and Theodor Dieter, eds., *Ecumenical Ventures in Ethics: Protestants Engage Pope John Paul II's Moral Encyclicals* (Grand Rapids: Eerdmans, 1998).

20. According to the Reformation principle *fides ex auditu*, faith comes through hearing (Rom 10:17).

21. Cf. Oswald Bayer, *Schöpfung als Anrede: Zu einer Hermeneutik der Schöpfung*, 2nd ed. (Tübingen: Mohr, 1990).

22. See Hans W. Frei, *The Eclipse of Biblical Narrative: A Study in Eighteenth and Nineteenth Century Hermeneutics* (New Haven/London: Yale University Press, 1974), pp. 17-37.

23. Martin Luther, *Lectures on Genesis (Chapters 1–5)*, in *Luther's Works*, ed. Jaroslav Pelikan and Helmut T. Lehmann, American edition, 55 vols. (St. Louis: Concordia; Philadelphia: Fortress, 1955-86), 1:94, hereafter cited as LW; *D. Martin Luthers Werke: Kritische Gesamtausgabe*, ed. J. F. K. Knaake et al. (Weimar: Hermann Böhlaus Nachfolger, 1883ff.), 42:71, hereafter cited as WA. For the full picture of Luther's rather complex account of Adam and Eve's original righteousness in the primal creation, see William H. Lazareth, *Christians in Society: Luther, the Bible, and Social Ethics* (Minneapolis: Fortress, 2001), pp. 58-84.

24. Martin Luther, *On the Councils and the Church* (1539), LW 41:144, 166; cf. WA 50:625,25-39; 642,30–643,2; 643,20-26. In short, quite contrary to Radical Lutheranism, Luther *does* have a strong and explicit account of sanctification (albeit not conceptually distinguished from justification, but in a dynamic unity with it).

25. Antti Raunio, *Summe des christlichen Lebens: Die "Goldene Regel" als Gesetz der Liebe in der Theologie Martin Luthers von 1510 bis 1527*, Reports of the Department of Systematic Theology of Helsinki University 13 (Helsinki, 1993). For a shorter account, see Raunio, "Natural Law and Faith: The Forgotten Foundations of Ethics in Luther's Theology," in *Union with Christ: The New Finnish Interpretation of Luther*, ed. Carl E. Braaten and Robert W. Jenson (Grand Rapids: Eerdmans, 1998), pp. 96-124.

26. Martin Luther, *Sermons on Exodus* (1524/25), WA 16:285,9.

27. Martin Luther, *The Small Catechism* (1529), in *The Book of Concord: The Confes-*

sions of the Evangelical Lutheran Church, ed. Robert Kolb and Timothy J. Wengert (Minneapolis: Fortress, 2000), p. 354.

28. Augustine, *De doctrina Christiana* 3.8; *De spiritu et littera* 30.52; *De natura et gratia* 57.67.

29. Augustine also reminds us that restored by charity for true freedom, the image of God shows forth in human action, thus mirroring divine goodness (see, among numerous other instances, *De trinitate* 14.15.21–14.19.25). Cf. Robert W. Jenson, *Systematic Theology*, vol. 1, *The Triune God* (New York/Oxford: Oxford University Press, 1997) for a compelling contemporary way of thinking through the love of the Trinity as God's freedom: freedom is the way love unfolds. Freedom collapsed — into modernity — the very moment the heartbeat of *caritas* ceased. The conceptual resituating of the sovereign freedom in the human subject was only the official burial ceremony of a lifeless freedom devoid of charity.

30. Michel Foucault, *Fearless Speech*, ed. Joseph Pearson (Los Angeles: Semiotext(e), 2001), p. 12. I am indebted to Paul Griffiths for pointing me to this insightful set of lectures by Foucault. For the rich and varied use of *parrhēsia* and its cognates in the New Testament, see the informative article by Heinrich Schlier, "παρρησία, παρρησιάζομαι," *Theological Dictionary of the New Testament* [*TDNT*], ed. Gerhard Kittel and Gerhard Friedrich, trans. Geoffrey W. Bromiley, 10 vols. (Grand Rapids: Eerdmans, 1967-76), 5:871-86.

31. Foucault, *Fearless Speech*, p. 14.

32. Foucault, *Fearless Speech*, pp. 15-16.

33. Foucault, *Fearless Speech*, p. 16.

34. Foucault, *Fearless Speech*, p. 16. This applies especially to *parrhesia* as used in Acts. Cf. Schlier, "παρρησία, παρρησιάζομαι," *TDNT*, 5:882.

35. Cf. Wilhelm Stählin, "Parousia und Parrhēsia," in *Wahrheit und Verkündigung. Michael Schmaus zum 70. Geburtstag*, ed. Leo Scheffczyk et al. (Paderborn: Schöningh, 1967), pp. 229-35, esp. 233.

36. I am thinking here of his extremely critical assessment of Vatican II: *Kirche und Rechtfertigung: Eine kontroverstheologische Untersuchung, ausgehend von den Texten des Zweiten Vatikanischen Konzils* (Göttingen: Vandenhoeck & Ruprecht, 1969).

37. Eberhard Jüngel, *Justification. The Heart of the Christian Faith: A Theological Study with an Ecumenical Purpose*, trans. Jeffrey F. Cayzer (Edinburgh: T&T Clark, 2001).

38. Miroslav Volf, *After Our Likeness: The Church as the Image of the Trinity* (Grand Rapids: Eerdmans, 1998).

39. In the United States, this form of *parrhēsia* is being practiced — for some most notoriously, for others most admirably, but definitely most consistently — by the Center for Catholic and Evangelical Theology and its journal, *Pro Ecclesia*. In the German context I highlight only two names among many: the Lutheran Ulrich Kühn and the Roman Catholic Otto Hermann Pesch.

40. Signed by William Abraham, Mark Achtemeier, Brian Daley, John H. Erickson, Vigen Guroian, George Lindbeck, Lois Malcolm, Bruce McCormack, R. R. Reno, Michael Root, William G. Rusch, Geoffrey Wainwright, Susan K. Wood, Telford Work, J. Robert Wright, David Yeago (Grand Rapids: Eerdmans, 2003).

41. For the exemplary clarity and evenhandedness in his ecumenical *parrhēsia* I cite, representative of his whole ecumenical existence as Christian and theologian, Geoffrey

Wainwright's *Is the Reformation Over? Catholics and Protestants at the Turn of the Millennia*, Père Marquette Lecture in Theology, 2000 (Milwaukee: Marquette University Press, 2000). For an exercise in the practice of ecumenical *parrhēsia* together in one volume of constructive theology, see James J. Buckley and David S. Yeago, eds., *Knowing the Triune God: The Work of the Spirit in the Practices of the Church* (Grand Rapids: Eerdmans, 2001).

42. Kasper, "Present Day Problems in Ecumenical Theology," pp. 56-88; 63-64.

Notes to Chapter 2

1. In the phase of what currently is called "postmodernity," modernity is far from being overcome or left behind. Rather, modernity has entered an increasingly self-critical stage in which an intensified plurality has become its characteristic signature. It belongs to the ironies of modernity that exactly those who are the most modern increasingly claim postmodernity as modernity's most recent advance. See Wolfgang Welsch, *Unsere postmoderne Moderne* (Weinheim: Acta Humaniora, 1987) for an excellent discussion of the emergence of the term "postmodernism" and its various uses in art, literature, and philosophy.

2. This essay is concerned primarily with Protestantism. To what degree Eastern Orthodoxy and Roman Catholicism are in the same predicament is an interesting question, but one that cannot be pursued here.

3. For an interesting study of the creative, destructive — and inescapable — reality of modernity, see Marshall Berman's *All That Is Solid Melts into Air: The Experience of Modernity* (New York: Simon and Schuster, 1982): "Modern environments and experiences cut across all boundaries of geography and ethnicity, of class and nationality, of religion and ideology: in this sense, modernity can be said to unite all mankind. But it is a paradoxical unity, a unity of disunity: it pours us all into a maelstrom of perpetual disintegration and renewal, of struggle and contradiction, of ambiguity and anguish. To be modern is to be part of a universe in which, as Marx said, 'all that is solid melts into air'" (p. 15).

4. For a biographical and interpretative study of Erik Peterson's life and work that is as fascinating as it is detailed, see Barbara Nichtweiss, *Erik Peterson: Neue Sicht auf Leben und Werk* (Freiburg: Herder, 1992).

5. See Michael Hollerich's two significant contributions in *Pro Ecclesia:* his article "Retrieving a Neglected Critique of Church, Theology, and Secularization in Weimar Germany" and his translation of Erik Peterson's correspondence with Adolf von Harnack, *Pro Ecclesia* 2 (1993): 305-32, 333-44.

6. Michael Hollerich, "Erik Peterson's Correspondence with Adolf von Harnack and an Epilogue," *Pro Ecclesia* 2 (1993): 338. Of course I do not want to claim that Americans are less religious than at previous times. Quite the contrary. For a challenging account of these emerging neognostic trends, see Harold Bloom, *The American Religion: The Emergence of the Post-Christian Nation* (New York: Simon and Schuster, 1992).

7. Further down I will elaborate on the term "public." Suffice it to say for now that "public" refers to a human "space" that is constituted by binding teachings, principles, and norms, that makes possible a "coming together" for action and interaction, and that creates a common identity and mutual accountability.

8. For a detailed analysis and critique of these new realities from a distinctly theological perspective, especially on how "politics" and "economics" are to be understood as distinct projects of modernity, see John Milbank, *Theology and Social Theory: Beyond Secular Reason* (Oxford: Blackwell, 1990).

9. Two dynamics of modernity in particular threaten to suffocate public life: the ever increasing privatization of the "life-world" and the erosion of the political public by a "system" in which the market and bureaucracies play the essential roles. In a society increasingly dominated by the logic of commodity exchanges, religion itself increasingly becomes just another commodity regulated by market forces. For a highly sophisticated and sustained defense of the "life-world" on sociological grounds within the boundaries of the "project of modernity," see Jürgen Habermas, *Theory of Communicative Interaction*, 2 vols. (Boston: Beacon, 1984/1987). For an excellent analysis of the ideology of marketing "religion" in the church, see Philip D. Kenneson, *Selling Out the Church: The Dangers of Church Marketing* (Nashville: Abingdon, 1997).

10. Hollerich, "Erik Peterson's Correspondence," p. 338.

11. Hollerich, "Erik Peterson's Correspondence," p. 342.

12. Both of them share a history of dispute with Barth. There was first the open exchange between Adolf von Harnack and Karl Barth in 1923: "Wissenschaftliche Theologie oder Theologie der Offenbarung Gottes? Ein Briefwechsel zwischen Karl Barth und Adolf von Harnack," *Christliche Welt*, 37. Jg. 1923, 1/2, 5/6, 9/10, 16/17, 20/21, reprinted in Jürgen Moltmann, ed., *Anfänge der dialektischen Theologie. Teil 1: Karl Barth, Heinrich Barth, Emil Brunner,* Theologische Bücherei 17 (Munich: Kaiser, 1977), pp. 323-47. In 1925 Erik Peterson published the essay "What Is Theology?" as an attack upon early dialectical theology, especially directed at Karl Barth's essay "Das Wort Gottes als Aufgabe der Theologie," in *Das Wort Gottes und die Theologie: Gesammelte Vorträge* (Munich: Kaiser, 1925), pp. 156-78. Barth responded with the 1925 public lecture "Church and Theology" ("Kirche und Theologie"), given on October 7, 1925, in Göttingen and on October 23, 1925, in Elberfeld, *Zwischen den Zeiten* 4/1 (1926); reprinted in Karl Barth, *Die Theologie und die Kirche: Gesammelte Vorträge 2. Band* (Munich: Kaiser, 1928), pp. 302-28. Peterson did not respond directly again. Ironically, Barth holds in relation to Harnack and Peterson an ecclesial and ecclesiological middle ground that the one attacks from the "left," the other from the "right" — ecclesiastically speaking. In *Church Dogmatics* [*CD*] I/1 the two positions over against which Barth develops his understanding of what a "church dogmatics" should be about are "Neuprotestantismus," for which Harnack would be a paradigmatic example, and post–Vatican I Roman Catholicism, for which Peterson — after his conversion in 1930 — could function as ideal type. Despite the fact that there is only one explicit reference to Peterson in *CD* I/1, the first half of the volume can easily be read as an extensive rejoinder to Peterson's challenge in "What Is Theology?"

13. Over against this, Peterson claims two tangible "subject matters" — Scripture and dogma. But only one of these is relevant for theology and, because of its direct access to divine authoritative reality, makes theology a true science and lifts it high above all humanities into a sphere where a man [*sic*] can live (p. 150). In Peterson's view, the first objective reality is the Bible, which is — as inspired Scripture — the primary authority (p. 143). Yet, as such, the Bible belongs to the prophetic announcement of God's word in the cultus, the liturgy. The Bible is not that subject matter to which theology is directed, on which

theology draws, and to the authority of which theology submits. Rather, that reality is dogma. ("Die Bibel ist der Leib des prophetischen Wortes, der Leib des Logos Gottes aber ist nicht die Bibel, sondern die Kirche und das mit der Kirche gesetzte Dogma"; p. 147.) Dogma and sacrament are as much the continuation and prolongation of the incarnation and of the speaking of God's Logos as exegesis and preaching are continuations of prophecy (pp. 147-48). Thus, for Peterson, dogma is decidedly not the prolongation of the human act of faith — which is confession and has nothing to do with dogma. Rather, dogma is the prolongation of Christ's speaking about God: "Since as much as dogma exists only since the ascension — as well as the church only exists from then on — as much did theology only exist from this moment on. One cannot give an answer to the question 'What is theology?' if one forgets that the Word of God became flesh and has spoken about God. Yet one cannot give an answer to the question 'What is theology?' either, if one forgets the other point, namely that Christ ascended into heaven and that [on earth now] there exists dogma." ["Denn wie es Dogma erst seit der Himmelfahrt gibt und Kirche erst seitdem gibt, so gibt es auch Theologie erst von diesem Zeitpunkt an. Man kann keine Antwort auf die Frage: Was ist Theologie? geben, wenn man vergißt, daß das Wort Gottes Fleisch geworden ist and von Gott geredet hat. Man kann aber auch keine Antwort auf die Frage: Was ist Theologie? geben, wenn man das andere vergißt, daß Christus zum Himmel gefahren ist und daß es Dogma gibt"; p. 150.] For Peterson, it is exactly dogma that prevents all human dogmatizing in theology — a salient point to ponder!

14. See Nichtweiss, *Erik Peterson,* pp. 512-17, for a detailed description of the circumstances.

15. Eberhard Jüngel has traced this issue minutely in an excellent essay, "Von der Dialektik zur Analogie: Die Schule Kierkegaards und der Einspruch Petersons," in *Barth-Studien* (Zürich: Benzinger; Gütersloh: Gütersloher Verlagshaus, 1982), pp. 127-79.

16. All parenthetical references in the text in regard to Erik Peterson's "Was ist Theologie?" and Karl Barth's "Kirche und Theologie" refer to *Theologie als Wissenschaft: Aufsätze and Thesen herausgegeben und eingeleitet von Gerhard Sauter,* Theologische Bücherei 43 (Munich: Kaiser, 1971). References to the English translation of Barth's "Church and Theology" refer to Karl Barth, *Theology and Church: Shorter Writings, 1920-1928* (New York/Evanston: Harper & Row, 1962), pp. 286-306. In regard to Barth's essay, the first reference given refers to the German, the second to the English translation.

17. "Das Evangelium ist ja keine frohe Botschaft, die sich 'an alle' richtet — wie unterschiede sie sich da noch von dem kommunistischen Manifest? — sondern es ist ein positiver Rechtsanspruch Gottes, der aus dem Leibe Christi heraus einen jeden von uns konkret trifft, und zwar iure divino trifft" (p. 146).

18. In good Reformed fashion Barth sees this self-actualization occurring in and through the proclamation of the gospel in preaching. I think it to be an unfortunate reduction from Barth's side (and Protestantism's in general) to focus on preaching at the expense of the Lord's Supper as the key location of the gospel's proclamation. Might the two not indissolubly belong together? Heinrich Schlier in his essay "Die Verkündigung im Gottesdienst der Kirche," in *Die Zeit der Kirche,* 2nd ed., Exegetische Aufsätze und Vorträge 1 (Freiburg: Herder, 1958), pp. 244-64, maintains exegetically the threefold proclamation in the Pauline congregations: the Lord's Supper, the liturgy, and preaching. In other words, to emphasize the proclamation of the gospel as God's own activity does not imply a problem-

atic and unwarranted privileging of preaching as the only and sole instance where this proclamation occurs. While the *fides ex auditu* unquestionably comes through the proclamation of the gospel, the latter is not simply identical with preaching.

19. What Barth gives us here in a nutshell is what he develops in much stronger form in *Anselm: Fides Quaerens Intellectum* (1931; ET 1960) and in his *Church Dogmatics*. Cf. especially *CD* I/1, §17. Interestingly, all of this falls into the time after his own exchange with Peterson and after the Peterson-Harnack correspondence. The Anselm book was published in 1931; *CD* I/1, in 1932.

20. That this is the case we can see in the fact that Barth had to advance himself considerably from the 1924 lecture "The Word of God as Task of Theology" in order to meet Peterson's challenge. And I think his later development from the Anselm book into the *Church Dogmatics* represents a necessary continuation and strengthening of the initial points he made in "Church and Theology" in order to meet Peterson's challenge. Cf. Jüngel, *Barth-Studien*, pp. 135-36.

21. There is the strong suspicion that part of the reason for this problem might lie in a pneumatological deficiency inherent in Barth's trinitarian theology, namely, that the Spirit is only the relationship between the Father and the Son. (Cf. Robert W. Jenson, "You Wonder Where the Spirit Went," *Pro Ecclesia* 2 [1993]: 296-304.) One result would be that the *Spiritus Creator*'s work can never be fully spelled out in relation to the church.

22. See Karl-Adolf Bauer, "Kerygma und Kirche: Der Weg Heinrich Schliers als Anfrage an die evangelische Kirche und ihre Theologie," *Evangelische Theologie* 41 (1981): 401-23.

23. For a complete bibliography of his work and a curriculum vitae, see Heinrich Schlier, *Der Geist und die Kirche*, ed. Veronika Kubina and Karl Lehmann, Exegetische Aufsätze und Vorträge 4 (Freiburg: Herder, 1980), pp. 290-306.

24. ". . . in der evangelischen Kirche die Kirche wieder zu gewinnen" (Schlier, *Der Geist und die Kirche*, p. 273). In the following I draw upon his autobiographical account, "Kurze Rechenschaft," given after his conversion to Roman Catholicism in 1953 (Schlier, *Der Geist und die Kirche*, pp. 270-89). It is worth mentioning at this point that Schlier describes his "discovery of the church" that led to his eventual conversion to Roman Catholicism as a typically Protestant approach, namely, via the intensive study of Scripture: "But the decisive impulse came from another side. It came from the Holy Scripture of the New Testament, whose exegesis had become my profession. It was the New Testament that made me — slowly but surely — ask whether the Lutheran Confessions and especially the significantly deviating, more recent Protestant faith were congruous with its witness. And it was the New Testament which assured me more and more that the church it envisioned was the Roman Catholic Church. It was, if I may put it that way, a truly Protestant route that led me to the church — a route actually provided for in the Lutheran Confessions but by no means, of course, expected. I have to add one more point. What pointed me to the church was the New Testament as it presented itself to unconstrained historical exegesis" (pp. 274-75; my translation).

25. Dietrich Bonhoeffer, *Gesammelte Schriften*, ed. Eberhard Bethge, vol. 6 (Munich: Kaiser, 1974), pp. 485-86. The English translation is taken from Hollerich, "Erik Peterson's Correspondence," p. 305. I am indebted to him for pointing out this fascinating remark to me.

26. Hannah Arendt, *The Human Condition* (Chicago: University of Chicago Press, 1958), esp. pp. 194-99.

27. Arendt, *Human Condition*. See also Milbank, *Theology and Social Theory*, pp. 332-36.

28. See Heinrich Schlier, "ἐλεύθερος, ἐλευθερόω, ἐλευθερία, ἀπελεύθερος," in *Theological Dictionary of the New Testament*, ed. Gerhard Kittel and Gerhard Friedrich, trans. Geoffrey W. Bromiley, 10 vols. (Grand Rapids: Eerdmans, 1964-76), 2:487-502, esp. 487-92.

29. Cf. Frank Crüsemann, *Bewahrung der Freiheit: Das Thema des Dekalogs in sozialgeschichtlicher Perspektive* (Munich: Kaiser, 1983) and my way of relating his insights to an analogy between church and polis in *Evangelische Ethik als kirchliches Zeugnis* (Neukirchen-Vluyn: Neukirchener Verlag, 1993), pp. 259-65.

30. It has never been essential for Israel, as a public, to organize itself simultaneously as a state. Under certain circumstances it has seemed necessary; under others it has proved undesirable, untenable, or simply impossible. In other words, whether or not Israel is structured as a state, it is still a public in its own right as long as the Torah's normativity is acknowledged and implemented. However, the lack of such structure has constituted a fundamental crisis for Israel whenever it has been squeezed out as a public in its own right, whether through oppression and persecution (as in medieval and early modern Christendom), through the pressure of assimilation (as in the Enlightenment and post-Enlightenment periods), or — *horribile dictu* — through annihilation (as in the Holocaust). (By mentioning these three eclipses of Israel as a public in one single sequence, I by no means imply that the Holocaust might be an instance in any way comparable to the other two.) In response to these experiences, many have come to the conclusion that only by being organized as a modern nation-state can Israel be protected as a public in its own right.

31. Cf. the back of any U.S. one-dollar bill.

32. See Jürgen Roloff, *Die Kirche im Neuen Testament* (Göttingen: Vandenhoeck & Ruprecht, 1993), pp. 58-85.

33. Still very instructive in this regard is Heinrich Schlier's essay "Kerygma und Sophia: Zur neutestamentlichen Grundlegung des Dogmas," in *Die Zeit der Kirche*, pp. 206-32.

34. For a strong reminder that the triune God is none other than the God of Israel and that the identification of precisely this God is at stake in the liturgy, see Bruce Marshall, "Israel: Do Christians Worship the God of Israel?" in *Knowing the Triune God: The Work of the Spirit in the Practices of the Church*, ed. James J. Buckley and David S. Yeago (Grand Rapids: Eerdmans, 2001). For another strong reminder that the *ekklēsia* represents the strangers, the Gentiles, that were added on "against the very nature" of Israel and of the importance of this insight for church identity, see Eugene F. Rogers Jr., "The Stranger as Blessing," in *Knowing the Triune God*, ed. Buckley and Yeago, pp. 265-83.

35. For an interesting analysis of the theologico-political reality of the Pax Romana in contrast to Jesus and the early Christians, see Klaus Wengst, *Pax Romana and the Peace of Christ* (Philadelphia: Fortress, 1987).

36. For an excellent account of the complex interrelationship of early Judaism and the *ekklēsia*, see N. T. Wright, *The New Testament and the People of God* (Minneapolis: Fortress, 1992).

37. In this sense the Roman Empire saw the church precisely and rightly as a political challenge to its own normative theologico-political "public" of the Pax Romana.

38. I am drawing here on John Milbank's outstanding analysis in *Theology and Social Theory*, esp. pp. 9-50.

39. Especially his critical engagement with Carl Schmitt's "political theology" is still worth remembering. It is mainly to be found in Peterson's monograph *Der Monotheismus als politisches Problem*, reprinted in Peterson, *Theologische Traktate* (Munich: Kösel, 1951), pp. 45-147. For an excellent treatment of political theology in the 1930s in Germany, see John Stroup, "Political Theology and Secularization Theory in Germany, 1918-1939: Emmanuel Hirsch as a Phenomenon of His Time," *Harvard Theological Review* 80 (1987): 321-68.

40. The churches' current attempts to gain "relevance" through activism, mysticism, or rationalism only intensify the privatization of the Christian faith and the dividedness among the churches in that now Christians *increasingly* align themselves along political divisions of "progressive" versus "conservative," which are criteria of conflict in the secular public of political liberalism. Thus even the way Christians differ among themselves shows how they submit to the *dominant* criteriology of the secular public.

41. For an instructive exploration of the role of persuasion in Christian theology, see David S. Cunningham, *Faithful Persuasion: In Aid of a Rhetoric of Christian Theology* (Notre Dame: University of Notre Dame Press, 1991).

42. Lutheran orthodoxy has, therefore, insisted that the scriptural canon be *norma normans* and the confessions be *norma normata* in light of which and on the grounds of which the theological discourse takes place.

43. In *The Analogical Imagination* (New York: Crossroad, 1981), pp. 3-46, David Tracy has made a widely used distinction between the three publics of theology: society, academy, and church. Yet his description is a sociological one that is only implicitly political, namely, inasmuch as liberalism is the "politics" implied in the emerging discipline of sociology. In contrast to Professor Tracy, I understand "public" primarily politically. The sociological use of "public" is only one descriptive instantiation of the term inside that "public" that is constituted by those binding principles and practices according to which "sociology" is a meaningful enterprise. Yet this does not mean that theological discourse cannot and should not communicate with other publics besides the church and that there might not be a possible overlap of criteria. That is all granted. Yet a church theology that is operative also in the academic public and in the "wider" public, i.e., the *saeculum*, is different from a theology that is primarily *bound to* the secular public's civil religion, which then also operates in the church and in the academic public, determined by and accountable to the standards and criteria of the modern academy that also operates in the church and the secular public. All three — church, academy, and secular public — are different, and often competing, publics constituted by different, yet not necessarily mutually exclusive, sets of binding "doctrines."

44. "Es ist so sehr der adäquate Ausdruck für diesen Sachverhalt, daß jede Wendung gegen das Dogma, wie sie etwa der Ketzer unternimmt, sinnvollerweise auch eine am Leibe des Ketzers vorgenommene Bestrafung im Gefolge hat" (p. 146).

45. It is ironic that this argumentation is necessary in light of Peterson's perturbing formulation in "What Is Theology?" *before* his conversion to Roman Catholicism, while

my argument, as I sketched it out, could easily be made also on the grounds of Peterson's own writings *after* his conversion to Roman Catholicism! Cf. especially his essay "Zeuge der Wahrheit," in *Theologische Traktate*, pp. 167-224, where he understands the apostolic church as the suffering church, the church of the martyrs: "A church that does not suffer is not the apostolic church" (p. 173).

46. "Ἄρα οὖν οὐκέτι ἐστὲ ξένοι καὶ πάροικοι ἀλλὰ ἐστὲ συμπολῖται τῶν ἁγίων καὶ οἰκεῖοι τοῦ θεοῦ . . ." (Eph 2:19): Unless otherwise noted, Scripture quotations in English are from the New Revised Standard Version (NRSV).

47. Milbank, *Theology and Social Theory*, p. 364.

48. Aristotle, *Politics* 1253b ff. See also Jean Bethke Elshtain, *Public Man, Private Woman: Women in Social and Political Thought* (Princeton: Princeton University Press, 1981), pp. 40-54.

49. Letty Russell, *Church in the Round: Feminist Interpretation of the Church* (Louisville: Westminster/John Knox, 1993) consistently unfolds the ecclesiological concept of "household" in a feminist paradigm and thereby retrieves key elements of what should characterize the church as that unique public that is shaped by God's own *oikonomia*. Her emphasis on connecting with the margins rightly retrieves — under the conditions of modernity — a key practice of the New Testament and the early church. She points out creative new ways of continuing those practices that are faithful to God's *oikonomia* becoming "public" in the church. Yet her account remains disturbingly ambiguous since it is also deeply immersed in modernist assumptions. The normative horizon of her project does not seem to be God's *oikonomia* in Christ but rather modernity's metanarrative of total human emancipation and liberation, which is interpreted to be God's *oikonomia*. In other words, the fact that the project of human emancipation is done in a feminist paradigm (i.e., rightly exploding the middle- and upper-class self-definition of white men) does not catapult it out of the overarching modernist project. Therefore, the roundtable ecclesiology — reflecting key New Testament insights into some unique practices — stands in danger of becoming powerful and attractive precisely because it responds to our prior political self-understanding according to the project of modernity. This concern deepens when Russell employs *poiesis* language in regard to the church: the church being re-created by progressive and revolutionary human — not agency, but production. Here the church is in danger of being understood in analogy to other modern poietic projects, as, for example, the American project: humans go out and create new realities. While Russell unearths and prophetically remembers key New Testament practices of *koinōnia* and *diakonia* under the conditions of modernity, her overall critique and the difference she creates between her own account and the "tradition" is embedded in a normative metanarrative — namely, the project of modernity — that itself is the major source of the eclipse of the church as the public of God's *oikonomia*.

Insisting on the church as a public in its own right means insisting first of all on the irresolvable difference between God's *oikonomia*, God's project of salvation — a project inside of which justice and liberation have a definite and explicit place! — and other metanarratives, as, for example, that of the project of modernity, be it in its version of ever ongoing emancipation of the autonomous self or in its version of the endless advance of humanity through science and technology. The church can live in and with all of these changing conditions and contexts exactly as long as it remains free to witness, serve, critique, and engage these competing realities. In order to be able to do that it needs to be a public in its own right, namely, the public that is the "space" of God's own *oikonomia*.

50. Martin Luther, *On the Councils and the Church* (1539), in *Luther's Works*, ed. Jaroslav Pelikan and Helmut T. Lehmann, American edition, 55 vols. (St. Louis: Concordia; Philadelphia: Fortress, 1955-86), 41:143-78, hereafter cited as LW. For a fine example of how urgent it is to continuously explicate and engage these seven marks of the church, see the ecumenically important collection edited by Carl E. Braaten and Robert W. Jenson, *Marks of the Body of Christ* (Grand Rapids: Eerdmans, 1999). For a list of core practices that is fully reflective of the Mennonite theological tradition, see John Howard Yoder, *Body Politics: Five Practices of the Christian Community before the Watching World* (Nashville: Discipleship Resources, 1992). Yoder focuses on binding and loosing, baptism, Eucharist, multiplicity of gifts, and open meeting.

51. "Now, wherever you hear or see this word preached, believed, professed, and lived, do not doubt that the true *ecclesia sancta catholica*, 'a Christian holy people' must be there, even though their number is very small. . . . And even if there were no other sign than this alone, it would still suffice to prove that a Christian holy people must exist there, for God's word cannot be without God's people, and conversely, God's people cannot be without God's word." Luther, *On the Councils and the Church* (1539), LW 41:150. For a useful account of how worship informs our knowledge of the triune God, see Susan Wood, "Participatory Knowledge of God in the Liturgy," in *Knowing the Triune God*, ed. Buckley and Yeago, pp. 95-118.

52. "That too is a public sign and a precious, holy possession by which God's people are sanctified." Luther, *On the Councils and the Church* (1539), LW 41:151.

53. "Third, God's people, or Christian holy people, are recognized by the holy sacrament of the altar, wherever it is rightly administered, believed, and received, according to Christ's institution. This too is a public sign and a precious, holy possession left behind by Christ by which his people are sanctified so that they also exercise themselves in faith and openly confess that they are Christian, just as they do with the word and with baptism." Luther, *On the Councils and the Church* (1539), LW 41:152.

54. "Fourth, God's people or holy Christians are recognized by the office of the keys exercised publicly. . . . Now where you see sins forgiven or reproved in some persons, be it publicly or privately, you may know that God's people are there. If God's people are not there, the keys are not there either; and if the keys are not present for Christ, God's people are not present. Christ bequeathed them as a public sign and a holy possession, whereby the Holy Spirit again sanctifies the fallen sinners redeemed by Christ's death, and whereby the Christians confess that they are a holy people in this world under Christ. And those who refuse to be converted or sanctified again shall be cast out from this holy people, that is, bound and excluded by means of the keys, as happened to the unrepentant Antinomians." Luther, *On the Councils and the Church* (1539), LW 41:153. Regarding the contemporary eclipse of this mark of the church, see David Yeago's poignant essay "The Office of the Keys: On the Disappearance of Discipline in Protestant Modernity," in *Marks of the Body of Christ*, ed. Braaten and Jenson, pp. 95-122.

55. "Fifth, the church is recognized externally by the fact that it consecrates or calls ministers, or has offices that it is to administer. There must be bishops, pastors, or preachers, who publicly and privately give, administer, and use the aforementioned four things or

holy possessions in behalf of and in the name of the church. . . ." Luther, *On the Councils and the Church* (1539), LW 41:154. "Now wherever you find these offices and officers, you may be assured that the holy Christian people are there; for the church cannot be without these bishops, pastors, preachers, priests; and conversely, they cannot be without the church. Both must be together" (LW 41:164). The recognition of the importance, role, and authority of ordained ministry for the whole church — locally, regionally, universally — is an important current ecumenical implication of this mark. I address this question in chapter 10 in the form of an engagement of the encyclical *That They May Be One/Ut Unum Sint*.

56. "Sixth, the holy Christian people are externally recognized by prayer, public praise, and thanksgiving to God. Where you see and hear the Lord's Prayer prayed and taught; or psalms or other spiritual songs sung, in accordance with the word of God and the true faith; also the creed, the Ten Commandments, and the catechism used in public, you may rest assured that a holy Christian people of God are present." Luther, *On the Councils and the Church* (1539), LW 41:164. For detailed accounts of how prayer and catechesis have traditionally functioned as practices in which formation in knowing the triune God takes place, see A. N. Williams, "Knowledge of God in Augustine's *De Trinitate*" and L. Gregory Jones, "A Dramatic Journey into God's Dazzling Light: Baptismal Catechesis and the Shaping of Christian Practical Wisdom," in *Knowing the Triune God*, ed. Buckley and Yeago, pp. 121-46 and 147-77. Regarding the contemporary urgency of catechesis, see Robert W. Jenson, "Catechesis for Our Time," in *Marks of the Body of Christ*, ed. Braaten and Jenson, pp. 137-49.

57. "Seventh, the holy Christian people are externally recognized by the holy possessions of the sacred cross. They must endure every misfortune and persecution, all kinds of trials and evil from the devil, the world, and the flesh (as the Lord's Prayer indicates) by inward sadness, timidity, fear, outward poverty, contempt, illness, and weakness, in order to become like their head, Christ. And the only reason they must suffer is that they steadfastly adhere to Christ and God's word. . . ." Luther, *On the Councils and the Church* (1539), LW 41:165. For our modern sensitivities, this is in many ways the most offensive and difficult of the seven public marks that Luther enumerates. It is also the one most strongly geared to his own situation. Yet "steadfastly adhering to Christ and God's word" precisely means to be not only hearers but doers of the word (James 1:25), so that this last mark intends nothing other than discipleship. Hence, this mark is expandable in various ways. For example, Luther suggests in this context that through suffering on the way of the cross "we learn to believe in God, to trust him, to love him, and to place our hope in him, as Romans 5[:1-5] says, 'Suffering produces hope, etc.'" (LW 41:165). This is a point that is pressed in a challenging way by Jon Sobrino, *The True Church and the Poor* (New York: Orbis, 1984). In what way do the poor and their suffering "mark" the church as true church? — Or is it the practice of suffering with and for the poor for Christ's sake that "marks" the church?

58. If, therefore, charity, friendship, and justice do not appear in the outer circle, it is not because I regard them as superfluous — far to the contrary — but because they are fully implied in the very first mark of the inner circle. It is important to spell them out in detail, but that is not the point and intention of this chapter and, moreover, is done by other authors currently *in extenso*. Another practice I regard as crucial is the confessing of our sin to one another in order to forgive and become reconciled with one another. While

it is a crucial practice and one that is mandated, it is not a practice that constitutes the church as the "public" of God's *oikonomia*. Insofar as it is publicly relevant it is implied in the first, third, and fourth marks.

59. While it needs to be clearly maintained that it is God's *oikonomia* that sanctifies humans, so that all Christians can rightly be addressed as "saints," as the Apostle Paul did in his letters and as Luther rightly maintained, it is of vital importance for the church publicly to identify and acknowledge paradigmatic examples of the Christian life that can be an orientation, a motivation, and a consolation for all Christians. Remembering saints and acknowledging new ones in every generation means to render public those concrete moments where God's *oikonomia* has become transparent — in obvious or hidden ways.

60. For a more detailed argumentation in this direction, see my essay "Be Honest in Just War Thinking: Lutherans, the Just War Tradition, and Selective Conscientious Objection," in *The Wisdom of the Cross: Essays in Honor of John Howard Yoder*, ed. Stanley Hauerwas et al. (Grand Rapids: Eerdmans, 1999), pp. 69-83.

61. Cf. the suggestions in Gerhard Lohfink, *Wem gilt die Bergpredigt? Beiträge zu einer christlichen Ethik* (Freiburg: Herder, 1988), p. 157. For his overall approach, see his instructive study *Jesus and Community* (Philadelphia: Fortress, 1984).

62. Luther had the interesting plan of organizing church government around regular church visitations and thereby retrieving the bishop's function in the early church. This would be a crucial practice for regaining the congregations as small publics. Cf. the interesting essay by Hermann Diem, "Kirchenvisitation als Kirchenleitung," in *Sine vi — sed verbo: Aufsätze, Vorträge, Voten* (Munich: Kaiser, 1965), pp. 161-83.

63. For a significant impulse in this direction, see Karl Lehmann and Wolfhart Pannenberg, *The Condemnations of the Reformation Era: Do They Still Divide?* (Minneapolis: Fortress, 1990).

64. For an interesting account of the differences and commonalities between a Roman Catholic and a Protestant construal of this relationship, see Walter Kasper and Gerhard Sauter, *Kirche — Ort des Geistes* (Freiburg: Herder, 1976).

65. While I regard it as crucial to emphasize the Spirit's relationship to the church, this does not at all imply that the scope of the Spirit's work is confined to the church's scope and activity. Wolfhart Pannenberg rightly stresses the point that the Spirit's relationship to the church's proclamation and life is correctly understood only if the Spirit's relationship to all of creation and to the eschaton is equally taken into account; see his *Systematic Theology*, trans. Geoffrey W. Bromily, vol. 3 (Grand Rapids: Eerdmans, 1998), pp. 19-20. By referring to the Holy Spirit as the agent of God's *oikonomia* — God's salvific activity encompassing all of creation and culminating in the eschaton of a new heaven and a new earth — I attempt to do justice to this overarching scope of the Spirit's work.

66. From the perspective of this conclusion I can only fully agree with Bruce Marshall's claim that the church's binding decisions have to be understood as the Holy Spirit's creation: "If the mission of the Spirit creates a particular communal history which is on the way from Pentecost to the eschaton, and as such belongs to the gospel itself, this suggests that the specific historical decisions this community makes to structure its own life and secure its own identity are themselves the creation of the spirit and, indeed, part of the gospel." Bruce Marshall, "The Church in the Gospel," *Pro Ecclesia* 1 (1992): 27-41; 38.

67. For a creative and fresh approach to the complex and comprehensive reality and

activity of the Holy Spirit, see Michael Welker, *God the Spirit,* trans. John F. Hoffmeyer (Minneapolis: Fortress, 1994).

68. My translation. The Greek text reads "ἔδοξεν γὰρ τῷ πνεύματι τῷ ἁγίῳ καὶ ἡμῖν..."; the NRSV reads "For it has seemed good to the Holy Spirit and to us to impose on you no further burden than these essentials: that you abstain from what has been sacrificed to idols and from blood and from what is strangled and from fornication" (Acts 15:28-29). My translation follows the suggestion of Erik Peterson, "Die Kirche," in *Theologische Traktate,* pp. 420-22, who understands the opening formula as a copy of that formula by which the assembly of the polis (the *ekklēsia*) made and announced its binding decisions: ἔδοξη τῇ βουλῇ καὶ τῷ δήμῳ. Peterson also claims that the formula of Acts 15:28 was repeated in later times as an introductory formula for conciliar decisions (p. 428) — which exactly points to the role and function of "dogma."

69. For a forceful suggestion toward such an ecumenical *metanoia,* see Marshall, "The Church in the Gospel."

70. Cardinal Walter Kasper, "Present Day Problems in Ecumenical Theology," in *Reflections, Volume 6: The 2003 Public Lectures* (Princeton: Center of Theological Inquiry, 2003), pp. 56-88; 64.

71. Carl E. Braaten and Robert W. Jenson, eds., *In One Body through the Cross: The Princeton Proposal for Christian Unity* (Grand Rapids: Eerdmans, 2003), #71. The signatories of this probably most significant recent ecumenical initiative from a largely Protestant side — yet including Roman Catholic and Eastern Orthodox theologians — are William Abraham, Mark Achtemeier, Brian Daley, John H. Erickson, Vigen Guroian, George Lindbeck, Lois Malcolm, Bruce McCormack, R. R. Reno, Michael Root, William G. Rusch, Geoffrey Wainwright, Susan K. Wood, Telford Work, J. Robert Wright, and David Yeago.

72. This question obviously is highly complex and hotly contested among theologians, philosophers, and political theorists. For a dominant version that reflects the genealogical self-understanding of modernity, see Wolfhart Pannenberg, *Christianity in a Secularized World* (New York: Crossroad, 1989), esp. pp. 3-19, and Pannenberg, *Systematic Theology,* vol. 3, pp. 515-17. For a compelling argument that questions the standard account, see William T. Cavanaugh, *Theopolitical Imagination: Discovering the Liturgy as a Political Act in an Age of Global Consumerism* (London/New York: T&T Clark, 2002), pp. 9-52. Questioning the role of the religious wars in bringing about the modern state, he argues that in the case of France "[t]he rise of a centralized bureaucratic state *preceded* these wars and was based on the fifteenth-century assertion of civil dominance over the Church in France. At issue in these wars was not simply Catholic versus Protestant, transubstantiation versus spiritual presence" (p. 29). "What is at issue behind these wars is the creation of 'religion' as a set of beliefs which is defined as personal conviction and which can exist separately from one's public loyalty to the state. The creation of religion, and thus the privatization of the Church, is correlative to the rise of the state" (p. 31).

Notes to Chapter 3

1. Cf. Martin Luther, *D. Martin Luthers Werke: Kritische Gesamtausgabe,* ed. J. F. K. Knaake et al. (Weimar: Hermann Böhlaus Nachfolger, 1883ff.), 40/1:664,15-21.

2. For some different yet mutually supportive accounts of this complex intellectual development, see Michael Buckley, *At the Origins of Modern Atheism* (New Haven/London: Yale University Press, 1987), Michael Allen Gillespie, *Nihilism before Nietzsche* (Chicago/London: University of Chicago Press, 1995), J. B. Schneewind, *The Invention of Modernity: A History of Modern Moral Philosophy* (Cambridge: Cambridge University Press, 1998), and Jeffrey Stout, *The Flight from Authority: Religion, Morality, and the Quest for Autonomy* (New Haven/London: Yale University Press, 1981).

3. Immanuel Kant, *Critique of Pure Reason*, B611-71. For useful introductions to Kant's thought, see Arsenij Gulyga, *Immanuel Kant: His Life and Thought* (Boston: Birkauser, 1987) and Otfried Höffe, *Immanuel Kant* (Albany: SUNY, 1994).

4. Immanuel Kant, *Critique of Practical Reason*, A223-38. For a good overview and introduction, see Bernard M. G. Reardon, *Kant as Philosophical Theologian* (Totowa, N.J.: Barnes & Noble, 1988).

5. Immanuel Kant, *Religion within the Limits of Reason Alone*, B137-44. Cf. Reardon, *Kant as Philosophical Theologian*, pp. 125-28.

6. See Friedrich Schleiermacher, "Second Speech: On the Essence of Religion," in *On Religion: Speeches to Its Cultured Despisers*, trans. R. Crouter (Cambridge/New York: Cambridge University Press, 1988) and Schleiermacher, *The Christian Faith*, trans. H. R. Mackintosh and J. S. Stewart (Edinburgh: T&T Clark, 1948), §4.

7. See Schleiermacher, *The Christian Faith*, §§3, 93-94.

8. For an excellent analysis and critique of this dynamic, see Philip D. Kenneson and James L. Street, *Selling Out the Church: The Dangers of Church Marketing* (Nashville: Abingdon, 1997).

9. The latter approach by no means excludes the fact that philosophy (metaphysics), science, and humanities are significant conversation partners that convey relevant knowledge. Yet what they do not convey is that knowledge of God through which we are being drawn into God's own life.

10. This is fundamentally Schleiermacher's route taken in response to the epistemological problematic defined by Kant's critical philosophy. See Schleiermacher, *The Christian Faith*, §50.

11. One of the genuinely challenging and intriguing questions in interpreting Vatican I is how not to read the Dogmatic Constitution on the Catholic Faith, *Dei Filius*, in precisely the above sense, a reading indeed strongly encouraged by nineteenth-century neo-scholasticism that in its initial stages — that is, before the promulgation of the encyclical *Aeterni Patris* by Pope Leo XIII — was philosophically more indebted to Christian Wolff than to Thomas Aquinas. Cf. the following samples: "The same holy mother church holds and teaches that God, the source and end of all things, can be known with certainty from the considerations of created things, by the natural power of human reason"; and "If anyone says that the one, true God, our creator and lord, cannot be known with certainty from the things that have been made, by the natural light of human reason: let him be anathema." Norman P. Tanner, SJ, ed., *Decrees of the Ecumenical Councils*, vol. 2 (Washington, D.C.: Georgetown University Press, 1990), pp. 806, 810.

12. Cf. the penetrating criticism of this way of knowing "God" under the conditions of the world in Jean-Luc Marion, *God without Being: Hors-Texte*, trans. Thomas A. Carlson (Chicago/London: University of Chicago Press, 1991), pp. 53-107.

13. Georg Wilhelm Friedrich Hegel, "Absolute Knowledge," in *Phenomenology of Mind*, trans. J. B. Baillie, 6th ed. (New York: Humanities, 1966). Cf. Søren Kierkegaard's penetrating critique of Hegelianism, especially in his *Philosophical Fragments*, trans. D. F. Swenson, rev. Howard V. Hong (Princeton: Princeton University Press, 1962).

14. This is preeminently the case in Barth's *The Epistle to the Romans*, trans. E. C. Hoskyns (Oxford/New York: Oxford University Press, 1933). Cf. on the "knowledge of God" without Christ: "But what does 'apart from and without Christ' mean? *The wrath of God is revealed against all ungodliness and unrighteousness of men*. These are the characteristic features of our relation to God, as it takes shape on this side [of the] resurrection. Our relation to God is *ungodly*. We suppose that we know what we are saying when we say 'God.' We assign to Him the highest place in our world: and in so doing we place Him fundamentally on one line with ourselves and with things. We assume that He *needs something*: and so we assume that we are able to arrange our relation to Him as we arrange our other relationships. We press ourselves into proximity with Him: and so, all unthinking, we make Him nigh unto ourselves. . . . Secretly we are ourselves the masters of this relationship. We are not concerned with God, but with our own requirements, to which God must adjust Himself. . . . And so, when we set God upon the throne of the world, we mean by God ourselves. In 'believing' on Him, we justify, enjoy, and adore ourselves. Our devotion consists in a solemn affirmation of ourselves and of the world and in a pious setting aside of the contradiction. . . . Such is our relation to God apart from and without Christ, on this side [of the] resurrection, and before we are called to order. God Himself is not acknowledged as God and what is called 'God' is in fact Man. By living to ourselves, we serve the 'No-God'" (p. 44). Cf. on the dialectic of judgment and grace in God's self-communication in Christ: "We have seen Adam and Christ, the old and the new world, the dominion of sin and the dominion of righteousness, linked together in a strict dialectical relationship. We have seen them apparently pointing to one another, determining one another, and authorizing one another. We have been careful, however, to emphasize (v. 15-17) the dialectical character of this relation. The first is dissolved by the second; the reverse process is impossible" (p. 188). And: "The continuity of the relation between sin and grace, Saul and Paul, forms the actus purus of an invisible occurrence in God. The unity of the divine will is divided only that it may be revealed in overcoming the division" (p. 189). But cf. also Barth, *Church Dogmatics* [*CD*] I/1, §5.4. On the inner logic of this dynamic, cf. Bruce L. McCormack, *Karl Barth's Critically Realistic Dialectical Theology: Its Genesis and Development, 1909-1936* (Oxford: Clarendon, 1995), pp. 245-62.

15. "The Truth itself has proclaimed to us that Truth is Truth and that we originally participate in it: — *The Spirit himself beareth witness with our spirit, that we are children of God*." Barth, *Epistle to the Romans*, p. 298.

16. See Gulyga, *Immanuel Kant*.

17. See Gillespie, *Nihilism before Nietzsche*, pp. 64-100.

18. See Barth, *CD* IV/3.2, §71.2, and Barth, "The Gift of Freedom: Foundation of Evangelical Ethics," trans. Thomas Wieser, in *The Humanity of God* (Richmond: John Knox, 1960), pp. 69-96.

19. See *CD* I/1, §§1, 7.

20. See George Hunsinger, *How to Read Karl Barth: The Shape of His Theology* (New

York/Oxford: Oxford University Press, 1991), pp. 30ff., 43-49, and McCormack, *Karl Barth's Theology*, pp. 129ff.

21. See *in nuce* his essay "Church and Theology," in *Theology and Church: Shorter Writings, 1920-1928*, trans. L. P. Smith (New York: Harper & Row, 1962), pp. 286-306, and extensively, Barth, *CD* I/2, §§21-24.

22. See most clearly Barth, *CD* I/1, p. 450: "The creature needs the Creator to be able to live. It thus needs the relation to Him. But it cannot create this relation. God creates it by His own presence in the creature and therefore as a relation of Himself to Himself. The Spirit of God is God in His freedom to be present to the creature, and therefore to create this relation, and therefore to be the life of the creature." See also *CD* I/1, p. 470: "[The Holy Spirit] is the common element, or, better, the fellowship, the act of communion, of the Father and the Son." Karl Barth, *Church Dogmatics* I/1, trans. G. W. Bromiley, 2nd ed. (Edinburgh: T&T Clark, 1975).

23. See Robert W. Jenson, "You Wonder Where the Spirit Went," *Pro Ecclesia* 2 (1993): 296-304.

24. The emphasis on the Holy Spirit's own economy is especially strong in Eastern Orthodox theology. Yet it is also found in the Western tradition — arguably on the basis of Eastern Orthodox influences — e.g., among Lutheran theologians like Peter Brunner, Wolfhart Pannenberg, and Robert W. Jenson. (It is no accident that the latter two were students of Peter Brunner at the University of Heidelberg.)

25. Cf. the exchange between Erik Peterson and Karl Barth regarding the nature and task of theology in relation to doctrine in chapter 2.

26. Cf. Ernstpeter Maurer, *Sprachphilosophische Aspekte in Karl Barths "Prolegomena zur Kirchlichen Dogmatik"* (Frankfurt/New York: Peter Lang, 1989).

27. While I disagree with his constructive turn, I largely agree with the issues Erik Peterson raised critically over against Barth in his essay "Was ist Theologie?" in *Theologische Traktate* (Munich: Kösel, 1951), pp. 9-43. See also Oswald Bayer's critique along similar lines in the long and astute analysis of Barth in his *Theologie* (Gütersloh: Gütersloher Verlagshaus, 1994), pp. 310-88, esp. 310-18, and the discussion here in chapter 2.

28. For an extended version of the following, see my *Suffering Divine Things: Theology as Church Practice* (Grand Rapids: Eerdmans, 2000), pp. 115-45.

29. See, among many, John D. Zizioulas, *Being as Communion: Studies in Personhood and the Church* (Crestwood: St. Vladimir's Seminary Press, 1985); Zizioulas, "Die pneumatologische Dimension der Kirche," *Internationale katholische Zeitschrift Communio* 2 (1973): 133-47; Nikos A. Nissiotis, *Die Theologie der Ostkirche im ökumenischen Dialog: Kirche und Welt in orthodoxer Sicht* (Stuttgart: Evangelisches Verlagswerk, 1968); Nissiotis, "Der pneumatologische Ansatz und die liturgische Verwirklichung des neutestamentlichen νῦν," in *Oikonomia: Heilsgeschichte als Thema der Theologie*, ed. Felix Christ (Hamburg/Bergstedt: Berg, 1967), pp. 302-9; and Dimitru Staniloae, *Theology and the Church* (Crestwood: St. Vladimir's Seminary Press, 1976).

30. Martin Luther, *On the Councils and the Church* (1539), in *Luther's Works*, ed. Jaroslav Pelikan and Helmut T. Lehmann, American edition, 55 vols. (St. Louis: Concordia; Philadelphia: Fortress, 1955-86), 41:143-78.

31. For an account of this concept of doctrine, see my *Suffering Divine Things*, pp. 134-45.

32. For an account that forcefully shows how Scripture has functioned in this way in the tradition, see David S. Yeago, "The Spirit, the Church, and the Scriptures: Biblical Inspiration and Interpretation Revisited," in *Knowing the Triune God: The Work of the Spirit and the Practices of the Church*, ed. James J. Buckley and David S. Yeago (Grand Rapids: Eerdmans, 2001), pp. 49-93.

33. See the instructive essay on the rule of faith for theological statements by Bengt Hägglund, "Die Bedeutung der 'regula fidei' als Grundlage theologischer Aussagen," *Studia theologica* 12 (1958): 1-44.

34. For a more extensive discussion of the relationship between doctrine and the core practices, see my *Suffering Divine Things*, pp. 134-45, and especially Eeva Martikainen, *Doctrina: Studien zu Luthers Begriff der Lehre* (Helsinki: Luther-Agricola-Gesellschaft, 1992).

35. Here I draw upon the Luther research of the "Helsinki school" of Tuomo Mannermaa. For a fine introduction to this significant movement of a relecture of Luther's theology in light of the dialogue with Eastern Orthodox theology, see Carl E. Braaten and Robert W. Jenson, eds., *Union with Christ: The New Finnish Interpretation of Luther* (Grand Rapids: Eerdmans, 1998).

36. This move preserves the critical moment in Karl Barth precisely by offering a pneumatological account that is more concrete — according to Luther's rule implicit in the pneumatological ecclesiology of his *On the Councils and the Church:* The more pneumatological, the more concrete! This pneumatological rule constitutes the core of my critique of Karl Barth's ecclesiology in chapter 5.

37. This idea will be more fully developed in chapter 4. For a fine exercise in reinterpreting and recommunicating Christian doctrine via the works of theologians who were most formative in its development, and in retrieving its comprehensive soteriological telos, see Ellen Charry, *By the Renewing of Your Minds: The Pastoral Function of Christian Doctrine* (Oxford: Oxford University Press, 1997).

38. One of the most intricate problems facing and challenging this very account is, of course, the disunity and deep doctrinal disagreement between the churches. This fundamental problem is addressed by James J. Buckley in "The Wounded Body: The Spirit's Ecumenical Work on Divisions among Christians," in *Knowing the Triune God*, ed. Buckley and Yeago, pp. 205-30. See also Ephraim Radner, *The End of the Church: A Pneumatology of Christian Division in the West* (Grand Rapids: Eerdmans, 1998).

39. See in detail Susan K. Wood, "Participatory Knowledge of God in the Liturgy," in *Knowing the Triune God*, ed. Buckley and Yeago, pp. 95-118. For an instructive example of how to travel this two-way street as a Methodist systematic theologian, see Geoffrey Wainwright, *Doxology: The Praise of God in Worship, Doctrine, and Life. A Systematic Theology* (New York: Oxford University Press, 1980). An older — yet still important — Lutheran example is Peter Brunner, *Worship in the Name of Jesus*, trans. M. H. Bertram (St. Louis: Concordia, 1968).

40. This is the way Luther describes the Spirit's work in his exposition of the third article of the Apostles' Creed in the *Large Catechism*. See *The Book of Concord: The Confes-*

sions of the Evangelical Lutheran Church, ed. Robert Kolb and Timothy J. Wengert (Minneapolis: Fortress, 2000), pp. 438-39.

41. "For we know that if the earthly tent we live in is destroyed, we have a building from God, a house not made with hands, eternal in the heavens. For in this tent we groan, longing to be clothed with our heavenly dwelling — if indeed, when we have taken it off we will not be found naked. For while we are still in this tent, we groan under our burden, because we wish not to be unclothed but to be further clothed, so that what is mortal may be swallowed up by life. He who has prepared us for this very thing is God, who has given us the Spirit as a guarantee" (2 Cor 5:1-5).

Notes to Chapter 4

1. See Dorothy C. Bass, ed., *Practicing Our Faith: A Way of Life for a Searching People* (San Francisco: Jossey-Bass, 1997). Here I can only gesture toward the kind of theological taxonomy of practices that I presuppose in this book. Fundamental to this taxonomy is the distinction (*not* dichotomy) between God's economy of creation and God's economy of salvation. Those fundamental practices that we encounter as central to the sustenance and enhancement of human life across a variety of cultures and throughout time and that we therefore tend to call "universal" are theologically to be identified as belonging to God's economy of creation — in view of their very "point," the sustenance and enhancement of life. Practices that belong to God's economy of salvation are those through which God's salvific activity is both communicated and mediated, and those in which that communication and mediation is crucially embodied. As I will show in the case of some of the universal practices, the inherent interconnectedness of these practices is disclosed by the distinct beliefs of the Christian faith. To be precise: Particular practices are not legitimated by the Christian faith. Rather, the very fact that they cannot stand alone but depend decisively on other practices is made clear in light of the Christian faith. Especially interesting are those practices that may be considered both universal and distinctly Christian, as especially is the case with forgiveness. Regarding practices of this kind, I would like to suggest that what makes them possible in the first place, as well as what represents their final fulfillment, is revealed through their particular Christian equivalents as they communicate and reflect God's own practices. Such Christian or theological enactment is rooted in the core practices of the church. This theological taxonomy also makes sufficiently clear that the use of the term "practices" for the church's core practices is an ultimately analogical use, since the Holy Spirit is the subject who works his mission in and through these practices.

2. For a rigorous and highly compelling account of how this theological claim needs to be thought through in light of the most recent advances in analytic philosophy of language, see Bruce D. Marshall, *Trinity and Truth* (Cambridge: Cambridge University Press, 2000), esp. pp. 242-82. On the logic of the epistemic primacy of Christian beliefs that is presupposed in the following, see in Marshall's account pp. 44-49 and 115-26.

3. C. S. Lewis, *The Great Divorce* (New York: Macmillan, 1946). Page references from this edition are given parenthetically in the text.

4. The character Napoleon serves as the paradigmatic example. "The nearest of those old ones is Napoleon. We know that because two chaps made the journey to see

him. . . . He'd built himself a huge house all in the Empire style — rows of windows flaming with light, though it only shows as a pin prick from where I live. . . . They went up and looked through one of the windows. Napoleon was there all right. . . . Walking up and down — up and down all the time — left-right, left-right — never stopping for a moment. The two chaps watched him for about a year and he never rested. And muttering to himself all the time. 'It was Soult's fault. It was Ney's fault. It was Josephine's fault. It was the fault of the Russians. It was the fault of the English.' Like that all the time. Never stopped for a moment. A little, fat man and he looked kind of tired. But he didn't seem able to stop it" (pp. 10-11).

5. Lewis offers in these lines a wonderful Augustinian satire of the hopes and pretensions of modern philosophical discourse in the very form of their postmodern demise.

6. "'Do you mean then that Hell — all that infinite empty town — is down in some little crack like this?' 'Yes. All Hell is smaller than one pebble of your earthly world: but it is smaller than one atom of *this* world, the Real World. . . .' 'It seems big enough when you're in it, Sir.' 'And yet all loneliness, angers, hatreds, envies and itchings that it contains, if rolled into one single experience and put into the scale against the least moment of the joy that is felt by the least in Heaven, would have no weight that could be registered at all'" (pp. 126-27).

7. See the moving account of such a transformation on pp. 103-4.

8. I have found the nuanced and penetrating analysis of the Christian practice of forgiveness by L. Gregory Jones to be profoundly instructive: *Embodying Forgiveness: A Theological Analysis* (Grand Rapids: Eerdmans, 1995).

9. For more ways in which the practice of hospitality is distorted, see the fine account in Christine D. Pohl, *Making Room: Recovering Hospitality as a Christian Tradition* (Grand Rapids: Eerdmans, 1999), pp. 141ff. I am indebted to Pohl's account of hospitality for pointing out the inherent link between the practices of hospitality and honoring the truth disclosed by the Christian faith.

10. The life, self-interpretation, and self-justification of the Nazi-architect and organizer of Hitler's armament program, Albert Speer, offer a fascinating example of the power and intricacy of self-deception. See Stanley Hauerwas with David B. Burrell, "Self-Deception and Autobiography: Reflections on Albert Speer's *Inside the Third Reich*," in Hauerwas, *Truthfulness and Tragedy: Further Investigations in Christian Ethics* (Notre Dame/London: University of Notre Dame Press, 1977), pp. 82-98. Gitta Sereny has contributed a fascinating book-length account to the debate: *Albert Speer: His Battle with Truth* (New York: Knopf, 1995). See the perceptive review of the latter by L. Gregory Jones, "Becoming a Different Man: Inside Albert Speer," *Christian Century* 113 (1996): 516-19.

11. For a full account of the crucial relationship between embodiment and personhood, see John Paul II, *The Theology of the Body* (Boston: Pauline Books and Media, 1997).

12. The theologian and ethicist who first taught me the fundamental link between hospitality and truth is Stanley Hauerwas. See his *The Peaceable Kingdom: A Primer in Christian Ethics* (Notre Dame: University of Notre Dame Press, 1983), pp. 142-46.

13. See Dietrich Bonhoeffer, "What Is Meant by 'Telling the Truth,'" in *Ethics*, trans. N. H. Smith (1st English edition 1955; New York: Simon & Schuster, 1995), pp. 358-68.

Bonhoeffer shows how distinct relationships of responsibility and accountability are crucial for a genuine honoring of the truth.

14. To tell a Gestapo officer the "truth" when he asks me about the whereabouts of my dissident friend is not to honor the truth but to betray a friendship. Herein lies the fundamental difference between Kant's absolute prohibition of lying and Augustine's. While Kant sees it as the result of a purely formal moral law, the categorical imperative, Augustine rests it in the very identity of what it means to be a Christian, namely, living in the ongoing reception of the gift of God's truth. For Kant, see his *The Metaphysics of Morals,* trans. and ed. Mary Gregor (Cambridge: Cambridge University Press, 1996), pp. 182-84, and also his "Über ein vermeintliches Recht, aus Menschenliebe zu lügen," in *Werke in sechs Bänden,* vol. 4, *Schriften zur Ethik und Religionsphilosophie,* ed. Wilhelm Weischedel (Darmstadt: Wissenschaftliche Buchgesellschaft, 1968), pp. 637-43; for Augustine, see the excellent essay by Paul J. Griffiths, "The Gift and the Lie: Augustine on Lying," *Communio: International Catholic Review* 26 (1999): 3-30, and, most recently, the stunning interpretation of Augustine in his *Lying: An Augustininan Theology of Duplicity* (Grand Rapids: Brazos, 2004).

15. The following reading of the Emmaus story is not without influence from Jean-Luc Marion's account of it in his *God without Being: Hors-Texte,* trans. Thomas A. Carlson (Chicago: University of Chicago Press, 1991), pp. 146-52. After its completion came Marion's essay "They Recognized Him; and He Became Invisible," trans. Stephen E. Lewis, *Modern Theology* 18 (2002): 145-52 — a coincidence of thought and interpretation that I happily acknowledge.

16. Unless otherwise noted, Scripture quotations are from the New Revised Standard Version (NRSV).

17. For an intricate and highly sophisticated elaboration of this matter, see Hans W. Frei, *The Identity of Jesus Christ: The Hermeneutical Bases of Dogmatic Theology* (Philadelphia: Fortress, 1975).

18. Cf. Bruce Marshall, *Trinity and Truth:* "The resurrection narratives indicate this in a striking way: even though they see him and talk to him, the two disciples on the Emmaus road and Mary Magdalene at the empty tomb cannot recognize Jesus, and so have the belief that he is risen, until his own deliberate action — his eucharistic blessing in the one case (Lk. 24:30), his personal address in the other (Jn. 20:16) — enables them to do so. Their true belief that he is risen depends on his self-presentation to them, his utter self-giving. This goes *a fortiori* for those who have not seen the risen Jesus, and whose belief must come by way of the worship and witness of the Christian community" (p. 247).

19. What is at stake emerges in the difference between Augustine's and Kant's ways of honoring the truth. Both offer rigorist accounts of truth-telling, yet while Augustine's account rests on the notion of a truth received, Kant's account does not. The same is the case with the difference between Dorothy Day's concept and practice of hospitality and, let's say, John Rawls's liberal account of it. While Day's concept rests on a hospitality received, Rawls's account knows nothing of that. While Kant's and Rawls's might rightly foreshadow a fundamental truth, they are unable to accommodate those fundamental obstacles and distortions that simply make impotent what they presuppose. Augustine and Day have first received and are thereby continuously transformed by what they practice.

20. See Bruce Marshall, *Trinity and Truth,* pp. 24-49 and 242-82.

21. Robert W. Jenson, *Systematic Theology*, vol. 1, *The Triune God* (New York/Oxford: Oxford University Press, 1997), pp. 42-89.

22. For an extensive meditation on God's costly hospitality in Christ, see Hans Urs von Balthasar, *Mysterium Paschale: The Mystery of Easter*, trans. Aidan Nichols (Edinburgh: T&T Clark, 1999).

23. See Ferdinand Hahn, "Gottesdienst. III. Neues Testament," in *Theologische Realenzyklopädie* 14 (Berlin/New York: de Gruyter, 1985), pp. 28-39, esp. 33-35. Hahn counts the following among the elements of earliest Christian worship: reading of Scripture (Old Testament), proclamation of the gospel, prayer and praise, gifts of the Spirit, Lord's Supper, and baptism. According to Frank Senn, Justin Martyr, in his *First Apology* (c. 150), reports a unified morning service of word and meal, or *synaxis*, to Emperor Antonius Pius and the Senate of Rome. Senn points out that one can discern a "shape of the liturgy" in Justin's report that has remained virtually intact since that time: "It is: gathering, readings, preaching, intercessory prayers, kiss of peace, presentation of bread and wine, great thanksgiving, distribution and reception of eucharistic gifts, extended distribution to the absent." Frank Senn, *Christian Liturgy: Catholic and Evangelical* (Minneapolis: Fortress, 1997), p. 76.

24. See Ernst Käsemann, "Worship in Everyday Life: A Note on Romans 12," in *New Testament Questions of Today*, trans. W. J. Montague (London: SCM, 1969), pp. 188-95.

25. For a more detailed argument, see my *Suffering Divine Things: Theology as Church Practice* (Grand Rapids: Eerdmans, 2000), pp. 128-33 — as elaborated in chapter 2 of this volume.

26. My own understanding of these matters is drawn primarily from Martin Luther's account as developed especially in his treatise *On the Councils and the Church* (1539), in *Luther's Works*, ed. Jaroslav Pelikan and Helmut T. Lehmann, American edition, 55 vols., vol. 41 (St. Louis: Concordia; Philadelphia: Fortress, 1955-86).

27. For the practices that have emerged in the radical wing of the Reformation and their contemporary relevance and interpretation, see John H. Yoder, *Body Politics: Five Practices of the Christian Community before the Watching World* (Nashville: Discipleship Resources, 1992), and for a nuanced yet brief account of the seven sacraments in post-Tridentine Roman Catholicism, see *Catechism of the Catholic Church* (New York: Doubleday, 1994), ##1066-1658.

28. In 1 Peter 3:15 we find the following exhortation: "Always be ready to make your defense to anyone who demands from you an accounting for the hope that is in you." It is precisely — and only — in worship that, again and again, we become ready to offer this account of our hope, because it is in worship that, again and again, we tangibly receive the reason for hope. It is in worship that, again and again, we "have tasted that the Lord is good" (1 Pet 2:3). On this profound connection between worship — especially the Lord's Supper — and hope, see Peter Brunner, *Worship in the Name of Jesus* (St. Louis: Concordia, 1968), Geoffrey Wainwright, *Eucharist and Eschatology*, 2nd ed. (London: Epworth, 1978), and Gerhard Sauter, *What Dare We Hope? Reconsidering Eschatology* (Harrisburg, Pa.: Trinity Press International, 1999), esp. pp. 202-8.

29. While the relationship between Scripture and the practice of theology is unquestionably of fundamental importance, consideration of this complex subject matter would require a separate nuanced set of reflections. Suffice it to say at this point that while Scrip-

ture is being read in the church and while doctrine — and therefore also theology — remains accountable to Scripture, the latter obviously does not simply represent a "superdoctrine," nor can Scripture be ultimately read in a purely "pre-theological" or "non-theological" way, in an ongoing isolation from doctrine. See on this matter David S. Yeago, "The Spirit, the Church, and the Scriptures: Biblical Inspiration and Interpretation Revisited," in *Knowing the Triune God: The Work of the Spirit in the Practices of the Church*, ed. James J. Buckley and David S. Yeago (Grand Rapids: Eerdmans, 2001), pp. 49-94. See also my *Suffering Divine Things*, pp. 138-39, 253-54.

30. For detailed and nuanced explorations of this issue, see Kathryn Tanner, *Theories of Culture: A New Agenda for Theology* (Minneapolis: Fortress, 1997) and Miroslav Volf, *Exclusion and Embrace: A Theological Exploration of Identity, Otherness, and Reconciliation* (Nashville: Abingdon, 1996). See also my review of Tanner's book in *Modern Theology* 15 (1999): 499-501.

31. I owe this expression to Gerhard Sauter. For a fascinating introduction to dogmatics as the art of discerning and judging theologically, see his *Gateways to Dogmatics: Reasoning Theologically for the Life of the Church* (Grand Rapids: Eerdmans, 2003).

32. For approaching this task from the other side, i.e., by asking what must be disbelieved under all circumstances, see Christopher Morse, *Not Every Spirit: A Dogmatics of Christian Disbelief* (Valley Forge, Pa.: Trinity Press, 1994).

33. Every concrete judgment exercised as part of carrying out a particular practice needs a point of reference that transcends the particulars that are at stake — particulars that will differ from circumstance to circumstance — precisely in order to be able to judge in the first place. "Dogmatics" as "faith seeking doctrine" *(fides quaerens doctrinam)* continuously searches for that in light of which sound theological judgment becomes possible. For a nuanced and thought-provoking case study of the messiness of such discerning and judging theologically when we closely attend to one particular practice and its concrete enactment, see Kathryn Tanner, "Theological Reflection and Christian Practices," in *Practicing Theology: Beliefs and Practices in Christian Life*, ed. Miroslav Volf and Dorothy Bass (Grand Rapids: Eerdmans, 2002), pp. 228-42.

34. As Karl Barth rightly put it once and for all: "The theologian who has no joy in his work is not a theologian at all. Sulky faces, morose thoughts and boring ways of speaking are intolerable in this science" (*CD* II/1, p. 656), and "It is to be noted further that when it is conceived and executed correctly and resolutely, yet also freely and modestly, theology is a singularly beautiful and joyful science . . . , so that it is only willingly and cheerfully or not at all that we can be theologians" (*CD* IV/3.2, p. 881). Barth, *Church Dogmatics*, trans. G. T. Thompson et al. (Edinburgh: T&T Clark, 1949ff.).

35. This is why the confession of sin and the granting and receiving of forgiveness need to be inherent in the practice of theology for it to remain truthful.

36. For a substantive account of genuine friendship in contrast to the exchange of nicety, that is, patterns of pleasing others with acts of nicety in order to be liked in return (what Aristotle would call friendships of use and friendships of pleasure), see Paul J. Wadell, *Friendship and the Moral Life* (Notre Dame: University of Notre Dame Press, 1989) and, more recently, his *Becoming Friends: Worship, Justice, and the Practice of Christian Friendship* (Grand Rapids: Brazos, 2002). While exchanges of nicety might have their

place, they become detrimental when they start to dominate basic interactions in the Christian way of life and, especially, in the practice of theology.

37. This is why the claims of theology will never be *definitive* (in contrast to doctrine) but are nevertheless *definite* (and thereby faithful to doctrine).

38. This is a translation into English from the German translation of the Pontifical mass that I found on the Web page of the Conference of German Catholic Bishops *(Deutsche Bischofskonferenz):* http://www.dbk.de./presse/fs_presse.html on March 27, 2000 ("Pontifikalgottesdienst von Papst Johannes Paul II. am 12.03.2000 in St. Peter in Rom").

Notes to Chapter 5

1. Karl Barth, "Der römische Katholizismus als Frage an die protestantische Kirche" (1928), in Barth, *Vorträge und kleinere Arbeiten 1925-1930,* ed. Hermann Schmidt (Zürich: TVZ, 1994), p. 313; my translation. Cf. Karl Barth, "Roman Catholicism: A Question to the Protestant Church," in Barth, *Theology and Church: Shorter Writings, 1920-1928,* trans. L. P. Smith (London: SCM, 1962), p. 310.

2. Grover Foley is one of the very few who have explicitly addressed this crucial element of Barth's theology. See his contribution, "Das Verhältnis Karl Barths zum Römischen Katholizismus," in *Parrhesia: Festschrift für Karl Barth zum achtzigsten Geburtstag am 10. Mai 1966,* ed. Eberhard Busch et al. (Zürich: TVZ, 1966), pp. 598-616, esp. 598-604. On the very interesting historical question of Barth's change from a more critical engagement of Roman Catholicism in the 1920s and 1930s to a more appreciative engagement in the 1960s, see Eberhard Busch's informative account "Der Papst ist nicht der Antichrist! I. Karl Barth und die römische Katholizismus," *Kirchenblatt für die reformierte Schweiz* 131/20 (9 October 1975): 306-10, and "Der Papst ist nicht der Antichrist! II. Barths ökumenische Sicht des Katholizismus in der Zeit von 1962-1968," *Kirchenblatt für die reformierte Schweiz* 131/21 (23 October 1975): 321-25.

3. Karl Barth, *Ad Limina Apostolorum: An Appraisal of Vatican II,* trans. Keith R. Crim (Richmond: John Knox, 1968), pp. 17-18.

4. Barth, *Ad Limina Apostolorum,* p. 18. See also Eberhard Busch, *Karl Barth: His Life from Letters and Autobiographical Texts,* trans. John Bowden (Philadelphia: Fortress, 1976), pp. 482-85.

5. So Barth in the preface to the fourth edition of *The Epistle to the Romans,* trans. Edwyn C. Hoskyns (Oxford: Oxford University Press, 1933), p. 21. I owe thanks to Jim Buckley for reminding me of this passage.

6. "In the 'Holy Office,' where not many 'separated brethren' come and go, I was instructed by Cardinal Ottaviani and Archbishop Parente concerning the more conservative direction and orientation of the Council." Barth, *Ad Limina Apostolorum,* p. 13.

7. When we study the Göttingen Dogmatics closely, it becomes clear that there was an inner, theological urgency to engage Roman Catholicism, an urgency that is precisely implicit in any serious encounter with and retrieval of Reformation theology, which simply is not intelligible without a parallel engagement of the common Catholic tradition and the Roman Catholic countercritique of the Reformation tradition. Genetically, the fundamental methodological principle of dialectical catholicity clearly emerges for the first time

in the so-called Göttingen Dogmatics, that is, Barth's lectures "Unterricht in der christlichen Religion," delivered in Göttingen from the summer term 1924 through the summer term 1925 and continued the following winter term 1925 in Münster. Crucial passages can be found in Karl Barth, *Unterricht in der christlichen Religion*, vol. 1, *Prolegomena* (1924), ed. Hannelotte Reiffen (Zürich: TVZ, 1985), pp. 38-39, 277, 305, 306, 307-8, and Barth, *Unterricht in der christlichen Religion*, vol. 2, *Die Lehre von Gott/Die Lehre vom Menschen* (1924/25), ed. Hinrich Stoevesandt (Zürich: TVZ, 1990), pp. 26-30, 36-38, 366-69, 427-35.

These engagements of Roman Catholicism in his first dogmatics lectures were predated by his intensive study of Roman Catholic texts in 1923 with Erik Peterson, who was at that time *Privatdozent* in Göttingen. These studies led to Barth's listening to Peterson's lecture course on Thomas Aquinas. For Christmas 1923 he received from his brother Heinrich a gift of Thomas Aquinas's *Summa theologiae* in order that he might intensify his studies. (See *Karl Barth–Eduard Thurneysen Briefwechsel*, vol. 2, *1921-1930*, ed. Eduard Thurneysen [Zürich: Theologischer Verlag, 1974], pp. 211, 217. Cf. for this period Barbara Nichtweiss, *Erik Peterson: Neue Sicht auf Leben und Werk* [Freiburg: Herder, 1992], pp. 505-12.) While his intensive study of Roman Catholic theology might have only begun in 1923, we find a quite extraordinary remark that anticipates later insights in his lectures on Calvin from 1922: "The situation is the same with Scholasticism as with the Roman Catholic church in general. Those who do not admire them, those who are not in danger of becoming scholastics themselves, simply have no inner right to pass judgment on them. We cannot dismiss historical entities of this power by simply tossing around catchwords." Karl Barth, *The Theology of John Calvin*, trans. Geoffrey W. Bromiley (Grand Rapids: Eerdmans, 1995), p. 26.

8. See Busch, *Karl Barth*, pp. 164-98.

9. The one exception is Tübingen, where Barth studied for only a very short time and in a relatively unengaged way. See Busch, *Karl Barth*, pp. 33-52.

10. The University of Münster, which originally included a Roman Catholic theological faculty, was founded in 1773. Only in 1914 was the Protestant theological faculty added. See Wolf-Dieter Hauschild, "Münster, Universität," in *Theologische Realenzyklopädie* (Berlin: de Gruyter, 1994), 23:409-14.

11. See Busch, *Karl Barth*, pp. 168-69 and esp. 177-89. See also Barth's correspondence with his friend Eduard Thurneysen, *Barth–Thurneysen Briefwechsel*, ed. Thurneysen, pp. 397-98, 460, 637-38, 651-55. Barth even became a regular participant in a theological group of largely lay Catholics. For a detailed description of this circle and of Barth's encounter with Roman Catholicism in general during his years in Münster, see Wilhelm Neuser, *Karl Barth in Münster, 1925-1930* (Zürich: TVZ, 1985), pp. 37-46. For a fine and accurate description of Roman Catholicism as a new and challenging conversation partner and for an accurate summary and interpretation of Barth's work during this time, see Bruce L. McCormack, *Karl Barth's Critically Realistic Dialectical Theology: Its Genesis and Development, 1909-1936* (Oxford: Clarendon, 1995), pp. 376-91. McCormack rightly characterizes Barth's appreciation of Roman Catholicism as the core of his encounter: "It is of the utmost importance for assessing Barth's attitude towards Catholicism to see that polemic was not, for him, a sign of contempt; just the opposite is the case. It is a sign of the deepest respect" (p. 380). Yet what McCormack does not make sufficiently explicit in his interpre-

tation is, *first*, that Roman Catholicism was — at least abstractly — already a conversation partner in the Göttingen Dogmatics, precisely because of the Reformers' own catholicity and, *second*, that the engagement of Roman Catholicism (as counterpoint to his critique of neo-Protestantism) emerged as an integral and fundamental methodological principle of his theology. In other words, it is precisely Barth's dialectical catholicity that we do not find in McCormack's interpretation of Barth. McCormack regards only (1) the retrieval of classical Reformed theology, (2) the critical conversation with neo-Protestantism, and (3) the ongoing challenge of Kant's epistemology as the constitutive points of reference in Barth's theology. One reason for this omission might be that McCormack fails to understand the importance of Peterson's attack on Barth as well as the importance of Barth's response to Peterson in this regard. What was primarily at stake between Peterson and Barth was not the nature of "dialectic" in theology, as McCormack assumes. Rather, it was the nature of "dogma" and "doctrine" in relation to theology. And in this regard Barth was forced to specify publicly his understanding of the nature of doctrine in relation to theology to a degree that he had not done before. This is the central issue at stake in his essay "Church and Theology" (1925). Two years later, when Barth published his *Die christliche Dogmatik im Entwurf* (ed. Gerhard Sauter [Zürich: TVZ, 1982]), the book contained a section "Das Dogma, die Dogmen und die Dogmatik" (pp. 159-64). While McCormack is right in claiming that the "Göttingen Prolegomena" already contain in broad strokes Barth's dogmatic method, he acknowledges that from the 1927 *Die christliche Dogmatik im Entwurf* on, "it is the dogmas which will become the starting point (or raw material) and goal of dogmatics" (p. 343). Arguably, it was Peterson's question and the problematic he pressed that forced Barth to further concretize his dogmatic method in a way that clarified his position and that made him increasingly appreciative of the challenge that Roman Catholic theology represents precisely in its dogmatic substance. Eberhard Jüngel's assessment of the importance of Peterson's attack for Barth's theology seems to me to be closer to the mark than McCormack's account of it. Cf. Eberhard Jüngel, "Von der Dialektik zur Analogie: Die Schule Kierkegaards und der Einspruch Petersons," in Jüngel, *Barth-Studien* (Zürich/Cologne: Benziger Verlag and Gütersloher Verlagshaus, 1982), pp. 127-79.

12. As a transition from the formal structure of his dialectical catholicity (engaging Roman Catholicism as a necessary element of the retrieval of Reformation theology) to a more substantive version, in which Roman Catholicism is the explicit conversation partner, see his 1925 essay "Church and Theology" and his 1927 lecture "The Concept of the Church." The latter was delivered to a Roman Catholic audience in Münster, and it has to be seen as precisely the "other side" of his 1928 lecture to a Protestant audience! The 1927 lecture has two parts. In the first part, Barth draws upon central texts from the confessional traditions in order to show how both Catholics and Protestants mean the same reality when they talk about the church. In the second part, he takes the passage "fide solum intelligimus" from the Catechismus Romanus and unfolds under the attributes "one," "holy," "catholic," and "apostolic" how this passage needs to be understood in the tradition of the church of the Reformation. In other words, he confronts his Roman Catholic audience with the ecclesial and ecclesiological self-understanding of the Reformation. It is interesting that he does not venture into an explicit critical engagement of Roman Catholic ecclesiology! This aspect remains purely implicit to the logical "other" of Reformation ecclesiology. Already here, Barth's "genuine Protestantism," which critically reflects on the

one fundamental principle on which everything hangs, emerges: "If a Protestant understands these three words [*fide solum intelligimus*] like a Catholic (here in their context) then he is basically a Catholic — even if he were a Professor of Protestant theology. And if a Catholic understands the same three words in the Protestant way, then he has in his heart become a Protestant, however he may stand outwardly. But a true Catholic and a true Protestant cannot unite on the meaning of these three words and therefore there can be no basic talk between them on the other points — or at most they can only discuss why they cannot discuss" (pp. 279-80). Yet Barth sees the difference at this time more starkly than he does one year later. In 1928 and before a Protestant audience, he describes Roman Catholicism as being closer to the church of the Reformers than contemporary Protestantism! This is a claim we would not expect if we read only "The Concept of the Church." Yet precisely both aspects together constitute the dialectical catholicity of Barth's "genuine Protestantism" as the critical retrieval of Reformation theology and ecclesiology. (Both "The Concept of the Church" [1927] and "Church and Theology" [1925] are found in Barth, *Theology and Church* [London: SCM, 1962], pp. 272-85 and 286-306.)

13. See Busch, *Karl Barth*, pp. 179-80. "Barth gave the lecture in Bremen in the middle of March, and found promising conversation partners here in the philosopher Hinrich Knittermeyer and the pastor Karl Refer, who was interested in the Old Testament. He then gave it again in Osnabrück. . . . Finally, he repeated it in the middle of April in the Lower Rhine Preachers' Conference in Düsseldorf" (p. 179).

14. Barth, "Roman Catholicism: A Question to the Protestant Church," p. 310.

15. Barth, "Roman Catholicism: A Question to the Protestant Church," p. 310.

16. Barth, "Roman Catholicism: A Question to the Protestant Church," p. 311.

17. Barth, "Roman Catholicism: A Question to the Protestant Church," p. 312.

18. The English translation renders "Neuprotestantismus" with "new Protestantism." Since the English translation of the *Church Dogmatics* consistently renders it with "Neo-Protestantism," I have changed it for clarity's sake in the translations of the earlier essays.

19. Barth, "Roman Catholicism: A Question to the Protestant Church," p. 314.

20. Barth, "Roman Catholicism: A Question to the Protestant Church," p. 314. This is not the first time Barth suggests this provocative step. We find it in the concluding remarks of his lecture course "The Theology of Schleiermacher," delivered in Göttingen during the winter term 1923/24: "Or should we in fact say that this was and is the normal and legitimate continuation of the Reformation, the completion of the work of Luther and Calvin: this doctrine of the feeling of absolute dependence or of the universum and all that is connected with it? If it were, for me the right thing to do would be to become a Roman Catholic again." Barth, *The Theology of Schleiermacher: Lectures at Göttingen Winter Semester 1923/24*, ed. Dietrich Ritschl, trans. Geoffrey W. Bromiley (Grand Rapids: Eerdmans, 1982), p. 259. See also the serious and quite telling comment in Barth's review of Emil Brunner's book on Schleiermacher in Barth, *Vorträge und kleinere Arbeiten 1922-1925*, ed. H. Finze (Zürich: TVZ, 1990), p. 423.

21. Barth, "Roman Catholicism: A Question to the Protestant Church," p. 322.

22. Barth, "Roman Catholicism: A Question to the Protestant Church," pp. 324-25.

23. Karl Barth, *Church Dogmatics* [*CD*] I/1, trans. G. W. Bromiley, 2nd ed. (Edin-

burgh: T&T Clark, 1975). See especially *CD* I/1, pp. 36-38 (*KD* I/1, pp. 33-35); *CD* I/1, pp. 40-47 (*KD* I/1, pp. 37-43); *CD* I/1, pp. 68-79 (*KD* I/1, pp. 62-73).

24. Barth, *CD* II/2, p. 529. *Church Dogmatics,* trans. G. T. Thompson et al. (Edinburgh: T&T Clark, 1949ff.).

25. Barth, *CD* II/2, p. 529.

26. Indeed, without this encounter and engagement the theology of the church of the Reformation will fall prey to nothing other than the open or secret continuation of the neo-Protestant paradigm. And if we wonder why in the world all this urgency: neo-Protestantism is, after all, the very heart of mainline Christianity in America! Nobody less than Dietrich Bonhoeffer has reminded us of this fact in a text that should still be required reading: "Protestantism without Reformation," in Bonhoeffer, *No Rusty Swords: Letters, Lectures, and Notes, 1928-1936,* Collected Works of Dietrich Bonhoeffer, vol. 1, ed. Edwin H. Robertson, trans. Edwin H. Robertson and John Bowden (New York: Harper & Row, 1965), pp. 92-118.

27. See especially his *The Future of Roman Catholic Theology: Vatican II — Catalyst for Change* (Philadelphia: Fortress, 1970) and *The Nature of Doctrine: Religion and Theology in a Postliberal Age* (Philadelphia: Westminster, 1984). Two Lutheran students of Lindbeck, Bruce Marshall and David Yeago, have continued in their own work this dialogue with and engagement of Roman Catholic theology in more recent years.

28. See especially his *Unbaptized God* (Minneapolis: Fortress, 1992) and his *Systematic Theology,* vol. 1, *The Triune God* (New York/Oxford: Oxford University Press, 1997).

29. Among many of his texts, see especially his *In Good Company: The Church as Polis* (Notre Dame: University of Notre Dame Press, 1995).

30. Dietrich Korsch, *Die dialektische Theologie nach Karl Barth* (Tübingen: Mohr Siebeck, 1996), p. vii. Next to the work of Korsch and a number of other German interpreters linked to Göttingen, this tendency to read Barth's theology primarily if not exclusively in relation to the Reformers, the Enlightenment problematic, and Protestant liberalism can be found in the otherwise very important work of Bruce McCormack. See note 11, above, and my review essay "Barth between McCormack and von Balthasar: A Dialectic," *Pro Ecclesia* 8 (1999): 105-9.

31. See Erik Peterson's critique of Karl Barth, as discussed in chapter 2.

32. Barth, "Roman Catholicism: A Question to the Protestant Church," p. 311.

33. Barth, *CD* II/2, p. 149.

34. See my detailed account of this relationship in *Evangelische Ethik als kirchliches Zeugnis: Interpretationen zu Schlüsselfragen evangelischer Ethik* (Neukirchen-Vluyn: Neukirchener Verlag, 1993), pp. 29-44.

35. Hans Urs von Balthasar, *The Theology of Karl Barth: Exposition and Interpretation,* trans. Edward T. Oakes, SJ (San Francisco: Ignatius, 1992), pp. 174-88.

36. See Hütter, *Evangelische Ethik,* pp. 36-39.

37. "To this unity and twofold form of Jesus Christ Himself there corresponds that of the community of God and its election. It exists according to God's eternal decree as the people of Israel (in the whole range of its history in past and future, *ante* and *post Christum natum*), and at the same time as the Church of Jews and Gentiles (from its revelation at Pentecost to its fulfilment by the second coming of Christ). . . . The community, too, is as Israel and as the Church indissolubly one. It, too, as the one is ineffaceably these

two, Israel and the Church. It is as the Church indeed that it is Israel and as Israel indeed that it is the Church. This is the ecclesiological form of what we have previously described in christological terms." Barth, *CD* II/2, p. 198.

38. "Israel is the people of the Jews which resists its election; the Church is the gathering of Jews and Gentiles called on the ground of its election. This is the formulation which we have adopted and this or a similar formulation is necessary if the unity of the election of the community (grounded in the election of the one Jesus Christ) is to remain visible. We cannot, therefore, call the Jews the 'rejected' and the Church the 'elected' community. The object of election is neither Israel for itself nor the Church for itself, but both together in their unity. (In speaking of elected Israel or of the elected Church, we must be clear that we are speaking 'synecdochically.') What is elected in Jesus Christ (His 'body') is the community which has the twofold form of Israel and the Church." Barth, *CD* II/2, p. 199. After the Holocaust, the dangers of misunderstanding Barth's doctrine of the election of Israel are almost inescapable. For two nuanced critiques see Berthold Klappert, *Israel und Kirche: Erwägungen zu Karl Barths Israellehre* (Munich: Kaiser Verlag, 1980), pp. 38-65, and Katherine Sonderegger, *That Jesus Christ Was Born a Jew: Karl Barth's "Doctrine of Israel"* (University Park, Pa.: Pennsylvania State University Press, 1992). See also the challenging yet, in my opinion, highly accurate critique put forward by R. Kendall Soulen, "Karl Barth and the Future of the God of Israel," *Pro Ecclesia* 6 (1997): 413-28.

39. See Hütter, *Evangelische Ethik,* pp. 39-41.

40. Barth, *CD* II/2, p. 149.

41. While "identity" and "difference" are inherently related concepts to the point that one cannot be conceived without the other, it remains crucial how the dialectic of their relationship is to be understood. And here we have to strictly differentiate between a methodological and a substantive dialectic in Barth's thought. While his methodological dialectic is much closer to Hegel, Barth's substantive dialectic is clearly Kierkegaardian. The infinite qualitative difference between the church's identity, which rests in God's constitutive act, and the church's response to God's act is not to be sublated but to be constantly kept in critical awareness. And the latter is precisely the point of "genuine Protestantism's" self-reflexivity! (For a fine analysis of the parallels between Hegel's and Barth's methods, see Michael Welker, "Barth und Hegel: Zur Erkenntnis eines methodischen Verfahrens bei Barth," *Evangelische Theologie* 43 [1983]: 307-28. Welker's analysis supports the radical difference regarding the nature of a substantive dialectic between Hegel and Barth; see pp. 325ff.) Might it not be the case that Hans Urs von Balthasar in his engagement of Barth was correct to wonder whether Barth was more committed to German Idealism (including Kierkegaard's opposition to it!) regarding the form of his thought than he was ready to admit? (See von Balthasar, *Theology of Karl Barth,* pp. 199-247.)

42. Barth's way of addressing the deep problem of the division between the churches is, of course, a consequent application of his "genuine Protestantism," his "*fides ex auditu* ecclesiology." The very truth of the confession of Christ and dissension about this confession, a dissension impossible to transcend on another level, necessitates divisions. The difference between "ecclesial division" and "ecclesial difference" is that in the case of the former the church's identity in Christ is itself at stake, while in the case of the latter the identity is unquestioned. See Karl Barth, *Die Kirche und die Kirchen,* Theologische Existenz heute 27 (Munich: Kaiser, 1935). Yet even here Barth's dialectical catholicity wins the day.

Difference finally outweighs division. This can easily be seen in the fact that the term "church" is used for communions, and even more clearly in the way that Barth locates again the church's identity and therefore unity solely in Christ: "Wollen wir Christus hören als den, der selber die Einheit der Kirche ist und in dem auch ihre Einigung schon vollzogen ist, dann müssen wir uns vor allem, bescheiden aber in gediegener Sachlichkeit, zu unserer *besonderen* kirchlichen Existenz bekennen" ["If we want to belong to Christ as the one who is himself the unity of the church and in whom its unification is already accomplished, we must — unpretentiously, albeit in genuine objectivity — declare our allegiance to our *specific* churchly existence"] (p. 21).

43. Barth, "Roman Catholicism: A Question to the Protestant Church," pp. 324-25.

44. For a fascinating treatment of this problematic, see Scott C. Bader-Saye, *Church and Israel after Christendom: The Politics of Election* (Boulder, Colo.: Westview, 1999). For his critique of Barth's concept of election, see pp. 73-77. Bader-Saye also offers an instructive account of how the concept of election functioned as a strategy of legitimation in Western Christendom, early secular modernity, and the emerging nationalisms of the nineteenth century. Most important, in his last chapter, Bader-Saye sketches a "politics of election" that transcends the dangers of supersessionist politics.

45. Nicholas M. Healy, "The Logic of Karl Barth's Ecclesiology: Analysis, Assessment, and Proposed Modifications," *Modern Theology* 10 (1994): 253-70; 264.

46. One of the places where Barth actually comes very close to such a concrete ecclesiology is his *Dogmatics in Outline*, trans. G. T. Thomson (New York: Harper & Row, 1959), pp. 164-72. The reason, it seems to me, is that he focuses here on the congregation as the concrete work of the Holy Spirit. ("Those called together by the work of the Holy Spirit assemble at the summons of their King.... By men assembling here and there in the Holy Spirit there arises here and there a visible Christian congregation" [p. 142].) The constitutive question (i.e., how the church is a "together" of both God's originating and humanity's responding and witnessing activity), which gets the dialectic between divine and human agency going, recedes into the background. We might wonder whether Barth in his shorter works, especially his expositions of the Apostolic Creed, is actually in closer proximity to Calvin's ecclesiology than in the doctrine of reconciliation of the *Church Dogmatics*, where ecclesiology is unfolded as an inherent element of God's reconciling activity in Christ.

47. See Healy, "Logic of Barth's Ecclesiology," pp. 258-63, and also the fine analysis and critique offered by Joseph L. Mangina, "Bearing the Marks of Jesus: The Church in the Economy of Salvation in Barth and Hauerwas," *Scottish Journal of Theology* 52 (1999): 269-305.

48. See David S. Yeago, "'A Christian, Holy People': Martin Luther on Salvation and the Church," *Modern Theology* 13 (1997): 101-20, and Yeago, "Messiah's People: The Culture of the Church in the Midst of the Nations," *Pro Ecclesia* 6 (1997): 146-71.

49. Martin Luther, *On the Councils and the Church* (1539), in *Luther's Works*, ed. Jaroslav Pelikan and Helmut T. Lehmann, American edition, 55 vols. (St. Louis: Concordia; Philadelphia: Fortress, 1955-86), 41:3-178, hereafter cited as LW. See esp. pp. 150-65 — as elaborated in chapter 2 of this volume.

50. David S. Yeago, "Theological Renewal in Communion: What Anglicans and Lutherans Can Learn from One Another," in *Inhabiting Unity: Theological Perspectives on the*

Proposed Lutheran-Episcopal Concordat, ed. Ephraim Radner and R. R. Reno (Grand Rapids: Eerdmans, 1995), pp. 206-23, and Mangina, "Bearing the Marks of Jesus."

51. Barth, *CD* IV/3.2, p. 826.

52. Healy, "Logic of Barth's Ecclesiology," p. 265.

53. My understanding of the Reformation and Luther's theology has been influenced by, among others, Peter Brunner, Albrecht Peters, Wilhelm Maurer, Hans Asmussen, and, most recently, the "Helsinki school" of Tuomo Mannermaa. This is probably one of the reasons I find the perspective of the Lutheran ecumenist and historical theologian George Lindbeck and of his student David Yeago so convincing. For Lindbeck, see especially his "Martin Luther and the Rabbinic Mind," in *Understanding the Rabbinic Mind: Essays on the Hermeneutic of Max Kadushin,* ed. Peter Ochs (Atlanta: Scholars Press, 1990), pp. 141-64. For Yeago, see especially "The Catholic Luther," in *The Catholicity of the Reformation,* ed. Carl E. Braaten and Robert W. Jenson (Grand Rapids: Eerdmans, 1996), pp. 13-34. See also Jenson, *Unbaptized God.*

54. Barth, *CD* II/1, p. 602.

55. See Healy, "Logic of Barth's Ecclesiology," pp. 263-64.

56. Therefore his "concrete catholicity" implies an ongoing direct engagement of the church of Rome regarding particular beliefs and practices. See Luther, *On the Councils and the Church* (1539), LW 41:143-78. It is a conflict that concerns concrete and particular matters, not a formal principle.

57. For a penetrating *theological* account of the divisions between the churches see Ephraim Radner, *The End of the Church: A Pneumatology of Christian Division in the West* (Grand Rapids: Eerdmans, 1998).

Notes to Chapter 6

1. This task has been accomplished recently in a most convincing way by Denys Turner, *The Darkness of God: Negativity in Christian Mysticism* (Cambridge: Cambridge University Press, 1995), to whose account of negative theology I am greatly indebted. See also the very useful volume he edited together with Oliver Davies, *Silence and the Word: Negative Theology and Incarnation* (Cambridge: Cambridge University Press, 2002). As the following will make plain, I fully agree with Turner's interpretation of the moment of negativity in Aquinas's theological speech in his contribution "Apophaticism, Idolatry and the Claims of Reason," in *Silence and the Word,* pp. 11-35, esp. 33-35.

2. Perhaps most prominently in the twentieth century to be found in the thought of Franz Rosenzweig and Emmanuel Levinas.

3. See John D. Caputo, *The Prayers and Tears of Jacques Derrida: Religion without Religion* (Bloomington, Ind.: Indiana University Press, 1997) and Harold Coward and Toby Foshay, eds., *Derrida and Negative Theology,* with a conclusion by Jacques Derrida (New York: State University of New York Press, 1992).

4. For the problematic transition from a negative theology (as a form of critiquing religious or mystical experience) to a mysticism that precisely focuses on such kinds of experience, see Turner, *Darkness of God,* esp. pp. 252-73, and for a trenchant, paradigmatically Protestant critique of apophaticism, see Eberhard Jüngel, *God as the Mystery of the World:*

On the Foundation of the Theology of the Crucified One between Theism and Atheism, trans. Darrell L. Guder (Grand Rapids: Eerdmans, 1983), esp. pp. 231-45 and 255-61.

5. For the phenomenon of the conceptual idol, I rely on Jean-Luc Marion, *God without Being: Hors-Texte,* trans. Thomas A. Carlson (Chicago/London: University of Chicago Press, 1991), pp. 25-52.

6. St. Maximus the Confessor, *Centuries on Theology and the Incarnate Dispensation of the Son of God* 2.39. The quote is taken from Andrew Louth, *Maximus the Confessor* (London/New York: Routledge, 1996), p. 53.

7. Vladimir Lossky, "Apophasis and Trinitarian Theology," in *In the Image and Likeness of God* (Crestwood, N.Y.: St. Vladimir's Seminary Press, 1974), p. 15.

8. It is, of course, only in the *ordo cognoscendi* that we can talk about the economy's antecedence. In the *ordo essendi* the reverse obtains.

9. The proper *modus recipiendi* for the economy's *est* is first and foremost faith in the togetherness of the existential act of the *fides qua creditur* and the discursive content of the *fides quae creditur.*

10. Baptism and the rite of confession and reconciliation need also to be mentioned in this context. See chapter 3 and, in more detail, my *Suffering Divine Things: Theology as Church Practice* (Grand Rapids: Eerdmans, 2000), esp. pp. 128-45.

11. Heinrich Bullinger, *Confessio Helvetica Posterior* (1566), ch. 1.

12. Being the normative apostolic *paradosis,* kerygma antecedes both chronologically and substantively the proclamation of the gospel. The specific nature of the apostolic *paradosis* makes possible as well as necessitates dogma and ecclesial doctrine. Cf. Heinrich Schlier, "Kerygma und Sophia: Zur neutestamentlichen Grundlegung des Dogmas," in *Die Zeit der Kirche,* 2nd ed., Exegetische Aufsätze und Vorträge 1 (Freiburg: Herder, 1958), pp. 206-32.

13. "Denn wie Christus nicht nur der Fleischgewordene ist, sondern auch der, der als Fleischgewordener von Gott geredet hat, so setzt sich die Fleischwerdung des Logos nicht nur in den Sakramenten fort, sondern auch die Rede des Logos im Dogma.... Das Dogma liegt also gar nicht in der Verlängerung des menschlichen Glaubensaktes...; sondern das Dogma liegt in der Verlängerung des Redens Christi von Gott" ["For as Christ is not only the Incarnate one, but also the one who as the Incarnate has spoken of God, the Incarnation of the Logos not only extends itself into the sacraments, but also extends the speech of the Logos into dogma.... Hence dogma is not an extension of the human act of faith but of Christ's speaking about God"]. Erik Peterson, *Theologische Traktakte* (Munich: Kösel, 1951), p. 30. Regarding Peterson's significance, see the excellent study by Barbara Nichtweiss, *Erik Peterson: Neue Sicht auf Leben und Werk* (Freiburg: Herder, 1992).

14. Nor should we be thinking of an exhaustive kenosis as Gianni Vattimo playfully suggests in his *Belief,* trans. Luca D'Isanto and David Webb (Stanford: Stanford University Press, 1999), esp. pp. 54-62.

15. This insight was most relentlessly pursued in the twentieth century by Karl Barth, first in the second edition of his *Der Römerbrief* (1922), and eventually in his magnum opus, *Die Kirchliche Dogmatik* (1932ff.). For the best recent interpretation of this most central motif of Barth's theology, see Bruce L. McCormack, *Karl Barth's Critically Realistic Dialectical Theology: Its Genesis and Development, 1909-1936* (Oxford: Clarendon, 1995).

16. Karl Barth, *Church Dogmatics* I/1, trans. G. W. Bromiley, 2nd ed. (Edinburgh: T&T Clark, 1975), pp. 315-33; on Exod 3:13-14, see esp. 322ff.

17. In the twentieth century this narrative structure of affirmative theology as the conceptual recollection of the divine economy was most prominently represented in Karl Barth's *Church Dogmatics* and Hans Urs von Balthasar's *Theo-Drama*. But see also, most recently, Robert W. Jenson, *Systematic Theology*, 2 vols. (Oxford/New York: Oxford University Press, 1997-99).

18. It might be appropriate at this point to recall that Heidegger once called Hegel the last Scotist.

19. See the explicit and implicit critique of Hegel's project in Gustav Siewerth, *Das Schicksal der Metaphysik von Thomas zu Heidegger* (Einsiedeln: Johannes Verlag, 1959) and Ferdinand Ulrich, *Homo Abyssus: Das Wagnis der Seinsfrage*, 2nd ed. (Einsiedeln: Johannes Verlag, 1998). On Siewerth's reading of the fate of metaphysics, see Andrzej Wiercinski, *Inspired Metaphysics? Gustav Siewerth's Hermeneutic Reading of the Onto-theological Tradition* (Toronto: Hermeneutic, 2003) and the very useful introduction to Siewerth's thought by Michael Schulz, *Überlegungen zur ontologischen Grundfrage in Gustav Siewerths Werk "Das Schicksal der Metaphysik von Thomas zu Heidegger"* (Einsiedeln: Johannes Verlag, 2003).

20. For the origin of the Christian doctrine of *creatio ex nihilo*, see Gerhard May, *Creatio ex Nihilo: The Doctrine of "Creation out of Nothing" in Early Christian Thought*, trans. A. S. Worrall (Edinburgh: T&T Clark, 1994).

21. Gustav Siewerth, *Das Schicksal der Metaphysik*, pp. 119-95.

22. In the transcendental dialectic, but especially in B595-733, "The Ideal of Pure Reason."

23. Martin Heidegger, "The Word of Nietzsche, 'God Is Dead'" (1943), in Heidegger, *The Question concerning Technology and Other Essays*, trans. William Lovitt (New York: Harper & Row, 1977), pp. 53-112, and Heidegger, *Nietzsche*, trans. David Farrell Krell (New York: Harper & Row, 1979-84); *Nietzsche* II, in *The End of Philosophy*, trans. Joan Stambaugh (New York: Harper & Row, 1973).

24. See especially his *Of Grammatology*, corr. ed. (Baltimore: Johns Hopkins University Press, 1997), *Writing and Difference* (Chicago: University of Chicago Press, 1978), *Positions* (Chicago: University of Chicago Press, 1981), and *Margins of Philosophy* (Chicago: University of Chicago Press, 1982).

25. On the concept of *einfache Gottesrede*, "direct God-talk," see Friedrich Mildenberger, *Biblische Dogmatik: Eine Biblische Theologie in dogmatischer Perspektive*, vol. 1 (Stuttgart: Kohlhammer, 1991), pp. 11-30.

26. Cf. Bengt Hägglund, "Die Bedeutung der 'regula fidei' als Grundlage theologischer Aussagen," *Studia theologica* 12 (1958): 1-44.

27. Oswald Bayer, *Theologie* (Gütersloh: Gütersloher Verlagshaus, 1994), pp. 310-75, esp. 332ff. and 371ff. See also my *Suffering Divine Things*, pp. 103-15.

28. For a detailed discussion, see chapter 5.

29. This, it seems to me, is the crucial constructive insight in Hans Urs von Balthasar's classic study *The Theology of Karl Barth: Exposition and Interpretation*, trans. Edward T. Oakes, SJ (San Francisco: Ignatius, 1992).

30. To be precise: The *analogia entis* would need to be reconsidered as an analogy of

participation similar to the way Aquinas seems to have construed his practice of analogizing on the basis of his metaphysics of creation. See the important recent research by Rudi A. Te Velde, *Participation and Substantiality in Thomas Aquinas* (New York: Brill, 1995).

31. See Nicolai de Cusa, *De Docta Ignorantia, Liber Primus,* 4th ed. (Hamburg: Meiner, 1994).

32. Probably the most penetrating analysis of this fundamental incurvature is Søren Kierkegaard's pseudonymous *The Sickness unto Death* (1849). See the instructive commentary by Joachim Ringleben, *Die Krankheit zum Tode von Sören Kierkegaard: Erklärung und Kommentar* (Göttingen: Vandenhoeck & Ruprecht, 1995), esp. pp. 209-62.

33. Calvin, *Institutio Christianae Religionis* (1559) 1.11.8: "Unde colligere licet, hominis ingenium perpetuam, ut ita loquar, esse idolorum fabrica."

34. Martin Luther, *Disputatio Heidelbergae habita* (1518): "XIX. Non ille digne Theologus dicitur, qui invisibilia Dei, per ea, quae facta sunt, intellecta conspicit. XX. Sed qui visibilia (et) posteria Dei, per passionibus (et) crucem conspecta intelligit." *D. Martin Luthers Werke: Kritische Gesamtausgabe,* ed. J. F. K. Knaake et al. (Weimar: Hermann Böhlaus Nachfolger, 1883ff.), 1:361-62. Cf. Walter von Loewenich, *Luthers Theologia crucis,* 5th ed. (Witten: Luther-Verlag, 1967), esp. pp. 26-52.

35. Owing to the strictly imputative logic of the *simul iustus et peccator,* radical theologians of the cross would deny the very possibility of a human discourse ever ceasing to be a discourse *sub conditione peccati*. If this were indeed to obtain, a theology of the cross would be the only appropriate theological discourse. For such a position, see Gerhard Forde, *On Being a Theologian of the Cross: Reflections on Luther's Heidelberg Disputation, 1518* (Grand Rapids: Eerdmans, 1997).

36. Turner, *Darkness of God,* pp. 34-35.

37. Turner, *Darkness of God,* p. 35.

38. The apophatic, on the other hand, is for Maximus strictly negative, in contrast to Denys, for whom the ascending movement of negation leads to a gradual transcendence that culminates in a super-affirmation that reflects in a way what God is. As Lars Thunberg put it, in contrast to Maximus, it is the case in Denys that "[t]he way of negation is the way of supreme affirmation." Lars Thunberg, *Microcosm and Mediator: The Theological Anthropology of Maximus the Confessor* (Lund: Gleerup, 1965), p. 435.

39. "Although Maximus follows Denys not simply in the language of 'apophatic' and 'cataphatic,' but also in some of his ways of explaining what he means by these terms, the way he focuses these two ways of theology on the Incarnate Word supports the contention of Ysabel de Andia that Maximus regards the distinction between apophatic and cataphatic theology as mirroring the patristic distinction between 'theology' and 'economy' — that is, the distinction between the doctrine of God as He is in Himself (in other words, the doctrine of the Trinity) and the doctrine of God's dealings with the world, especially the Incarnation." Louth, *Maximus the Confessor,* p. 54. See, in detail, Ysabel de Andia, "Transfiguration et Théologie négative," in *Denys l'Aréopagite et sa Postérité en Orient et en Occident: Actes du Colloque International, Paris, 21-24 septembre 1994,* ed. Ysabel de Andia (Paris: Institut d'Études Augustiniennes, 1997), pp. 293-328.

40. Insofar as Jüngel's critique of apophaticism aims at this problematic outcome, it is a correct and important reservation. See his *God as the Mystery of the World,* pp. 255-61.

For a Protestant critique of the limitations of Jüngel's engagement as well as a critique of negative theology, see most recently Ralf Stolina, *Niemand hat Gott je gesehen: Traktat über negative Theologie* (Berlin/New York: de Gruyter, 2000), pp. 67-77. On how to conceive the appropriate relationship between word and silence analogically, see Bruno Forte, "'Verbum e Silentio.' L'analogia della Parola e del Silenzio," in *Théologie négative,* ed. Marco M. Olivetti, Biblioteca dell' 'Archivio di Filosofia' 59 (Padua: CEDAM, 2002), pp. 171-84. For a very different but equally instructive account, which draws more on Hebrew sources and on Derrida, see Oliver Davies, "Towards a Theological Poetics of Silence," in *Silence and the Word,* ed. Davies and Turner, pp. 201-22.

41. For this most rigorous apophaticism, see *Meister Eckhart: Deutsche Predigten und Traktate,* ed. and trans. J. Quint (München: Hanser, 1977), on this particular point esp. pp. 229-30. For a helpfully nuanced interpretation of the complexities in Eckhart's thought, see Turner, *Darkness of God,* pp. 137-85, and on Eckhart's apophatic anthropology, see Jan Andrzej Kloczowski, OP, "Anthropologie négative," in *Théologie négative,* ed. Olivetti, pp. 477-88.

42. Johann Gottlieb Fichte, *Die Wissenschaftslehre: Zweiter Vortrag im Jahre 1804,* 2nd ed. (Hamburg: Meiner, 1986), pp. 260ff. For Fichte, see Wolfgang Janke, *Fichte: Sein und Reflexion: Grundlagen der kritischen Vernunft* (Berlin: de Gruyter, 1970), pp. 302-3, and for Derrida, see Hent de Vries, "The Theology of the Sign and the Sign of Theology: The Apophasis of Deconstruction," in *Flight of the Gods: Philosophical Perspectives on Negative Theology,* ed. Ilse N. Bulhof and Laurens ten Kate (New York: Fordham University Press, 2000), pp. 166-94. On the problem of the destruction of the affirmative, see Walter Jaeschke, "Negative Theologie und philosophische Theologie," in *Théologie négative,* ed. Olivetti, pp. 303-14.

43. Vladimir Lossky, "Apophasis and Trinitarian Theology," pp. 13-14.

44. See Leonid Ouspensky, *Theology of the Icon,* trans. Anthony Gythiel, 2 vols. (Crestwood, N.Y.: St. Vladimir's Seminary Press, 1992). Arguably, Maximus the Confessor's Christology and his respective theology are exemplary in this regard. See especially his *Ambigua* 41 (*PG* 91:1304-16) and Christoph Schönborn, *Christ's Human Face: The Christ Icon,* trans. Lothar Krauth (San Francisco: Ignatius, 1994), pp. 102-33.

45. See Ouspensky, *Theology of the Icon,* vol. 2, pp. 492ff., and Marion, *God without Being,* pp. 22ff. It would be fascinating to reflect upon the difference between the specific negativity involved in the logic of the icon and the kind of radical negativity entailed in Franz Rosenzweig's image of the variously possible paintings on the otherwise empty wall in his *The Star of Redemption,* trans. William W. Hallo (Notre Dame: University of Notre Dame Press, 1985), pp. 13-14.

46. Systematically expanding the insights of Te Velde's *Participation and Substantiality in Thomas Aquinas* and thereby bringing the dynamic character of the analogy of participation to the fore is a helpful feature in the recent interpretation of Thomas Aquinas by John Milbank and Catherine Pickstock, *Truth in Aquinas* (London: Routledge, 2001), esp. pp. 46-51.

Notes to Chapter 7

1. For the best sympathetic commentary that also sheds light on the encyclical's history, see Servais Pinckaers, OP, "An Encyclical for the Future: *Veritatis Splendor*," in *Veritatis Splendor and the Renewal of Moral Theology*, ed. J. A. DiNoia, OP, and Romanus Cessario, OP (Princeton: Scepter, 1999), pp. 11-71.

2. Jean-Luc Nancy, *The Experience of Freedom*, trans. Bridget McDonald, with a foreword by Peter Fenves (Stanford: Stanford University Press, 1993), p. 1.

3. John Henry Newman, "Letter to the Duke of Norfolk," V, in *Certain Difficulties Felt by Anglicans in Catholic Teaching*, vol. 2 (London: Longmans, Green, 1885), p. 248.

4. Isaiah Berlin, *Four Essays on Liberty* (Oxford/New York: Oxford University Press, 1969), pp. 122-23. With reference to John Stuart Mill's essay *On Liberty*, Berlin states concisely: "The defense of liberty consists in the 'negative' goal of warding off interference" (p. 127).

5. For the most recent discussion of this question, see Gary Watson, ed., *Free Will*, Oxford Readings in Philosophy (Oxford: Oxford University Press, 1982) and Daniel C. Dennet, *Elbow Room: The Varieties of Free Will Worth Wanting* (Cambridge, Mass.: MIT Press, 1984).

6. Berlin, *Four Essays on Liberty*, pp. 131ff.

7. On the political dangers of the concept of freedom as self-mastery in the continental tradition of Rousseau, Kant, Fichte, and Hegel, see Berlin, *Four Essays on Liberty*, pp. 132ff., 145-54.

8. See Georg Wilhelm Friedrich Hegel, *Hegel's Philosophy of Right*, trans. with notes by T. M. Knox (London: Oxford University Press, 1967), introduction, esp. §4.

9. For the doctrine of God, see the comprehensive treatment of God's freedom in Karl Barth, *Church Dogmatics* II/1, trans. G. T. Thompson et al. (Edinburgh: T&T Clark, 1957), pp. 440-677. Yet the topic also was and still is most central to theological anthropology. While somewhat opaque, the most forceful argument to be put forth is Luther's 1526 response to Erasmus, *The Bondage of the Will*, in *Luther's Works*, ed. Jaroslav Pelikan and Helmut T. Lehmann, American edition, 55 vols., vol. 33 (St. Louis: Concordia; Philadelphia: Fortress, 1955-86), hereafter cited as LW. For a concise interpretation of what is probably Luther's most demanding text, see Robert W. Jenson, *Systematic Theology*, vol. 2, *The Works of God* (New York/Oxford: Oxford University Press, 1999), pp. 105-8, and for the best Roman Catholic interpretation and engagement, see Harry J. McSorley, CSP, *Luther: Right or Wrong? An Ecumenical-Theological Study of Luther's Major Work "The Bondage of the Will"* (New York: Newman; Minneapolis: Augsburg, 1969).

10. For a most rigorous theological interpretation of divine freedom as triune event, see Robert W. Jenson, *Systematic Theology*, vol. 1, *The Triune God* (New York/Oxford: Oxford University Press, 1997).

11. One way to overcome this problem is to irreversibly secure both terms for the human by usurping the notion of uncreated freedom as the unoriginate origin for human freedom. And part of the modern discourse of freedom must be read as the attempt to think freedom in precisely this way. It is interesting to note that Martin Heidegger attempted this line of reasoning in his 1930 lecture class at the University of Freiburg (*The Essence of Human Freedom: An Introduction to Philosophy*, trans. Ted Sadler [London/New

York: Continuum, 2002]) but abandoned it shortly thereafter by unequivocally prioritizing "being" over "freedom." Most recently, Jean-Luc Nancy, in his *Experience of Freedom*, returns to Heidegger's aborted attempt and claims the thinking of freedom as unoriginate origin of the task of philosophical reflection per se.

12. Here I happily acknowledge my indebtedness to a significant piece of work unjustly ignored in most Protestant circles: Martin Bieler, *Freiheit als Gabe: Ein schöpfungstheologischer Entwurf* (Freiburg: Herder, 1991).

13. For an excellent, concise interpretation of the "ethics of autonomy" as the principle of the ethics of Kant and German Idealism, see Dieter Henrich, "Ethik der Autonomie," in *Selbstverhältnisse: Gedanken und Auslegungen zu den Grundlagen der klassischen deutschen Philosophie* (Stuttgart: Reclam, 1993), pp. 6-56.

14. In different but mutually supportive ways this has been argued by Alasdair MacIntyre in his *After Virtue: A Study in Moral Theory*, 2nd ed. (Notre Dame: University of Notre Dame Press, 1984), as well as his *Three Rival Versions of Moral Enquiry: Encyclopaedia, Genealogy, and Tradition* (Notre Dame: University of Notre Dame Press, 1990), and by Robert Spaemann in his *Happiness and Benevolence*, trans. Jeremiah Alberg (Notre Dame: University of Notre Dame Press, 2000). Despite his much more positive view of the project of modernity, a similar argument can be found in Charles Taylor, *Sources of the Self: The Making of the Modern Identity* (Cambridge, Mass.: Harvard University Press, 1989).

15. Servais Pinckaers puts the matter and the reasons for my own interest succinctly: "In discussing the connection between truth and freedom, the encyclical strikes at the root of the present moral problem. It has the merit of revealing the two fundamental questions underlying the current debate: what is the nature of freedom and how does it relate to the moral law?" Pinckaers, "Encyclical for the Future," p. 40.

16. For a short but precise account, see Steffen Kjeldgaard-Petersen, "Antinomian Controversies," in *The Encyclopedia of Christianity* (Grand Rapids: Eerdmans; London: Brill, 1999-), 1:80-81.

17. The degree to which the antinomian displacement of the law needs to be seen as a key element of the distinctly Protestant version of Christian supersessionism requires a separate argument. It strikes me that at precisely the moment when the turn to the subject is completed and systematically spelled out in regard to religion — in Kant, Schleiermacher, and Hegel — the theological significance of the revealed law disappears together with even the faintest recollection of the theological significance of the Jewish people. (For a good beginning to consider these matters, see the chapter "Christian Divinity without Jewish Flesh: Kant and Schleiermacher," in R. Kendall Soulen, *The God of Israel and Christian Theology* [Minneapolis: Fortress, 1996], pp. 57-80.) Only such a theological "outsider" and critic of the Enlightenment as A. C. F. Vilmar had the chutzpah to return in his *Theologische Moral* (1871) to an interpretation of the revealed law.

18. For my own critical engagement of *Veritatis Splendor*'s way of relating law and gospel, see "Christliche Freiheit und die Wahrheit des Gesetzes: Das Anliegen der römisch-katholischen Enzyklika *Veritatis splendor* in der Perspektive reformatorischer Theologie," *Kerygma und Dogma* 42 (1996): 246-71.

19. "Die Weltgeschichte ist der Fortschritt im Bewußtsein der Freiheit, — ein Fortschritt, den wir in seiner Notwendigkeit zu erkennen haben." Georg Wilhelm Friedrich

Hegel, *Vorlesungen über die Philosophie der Weltgeschichte*, vol. 1, *Die Vernunft in der Geschichte*, ed. Johannes Hoffmeister, 6th ed. (Hamburg: Meiner, 1994), p. 63.

20. In many ways Robert Musil's unfinished epochal novel, *The Man without Qualities*, trans. Sophie Wilkins, 2 vols. (New York: Knopf, 1995), could be read in this way. In the genre of the philosophical narrative, Michael Allen Gillespie's *Nihilism before Nietzsche* (Chicago/London: University of Chicago Press, 1995) offers an implicit account of modernity's protagonist and its tragic fate told as the emergence of nihilism — which is nothing other than freedom unhinged from reason.

21. Adorno and Horkheimer *(Dialectic of Enlightenment)*, Blumenberg *(The Legitimacy of Modernity)*, Dupré *(Passage to Modernity)*, Gillespie *(Nihilism before Nietzsche)*, Habermas *(Philosophical Discourse of Modernity)*, Löwith *(The Meaning of History)*, Lukacs *(The Destruction of Reason)*, MacIntyre *(After Virtue)*, Milbank *(Theology and Social Theory)*, Schneewind *(The Invention of Autonomy)*, Schulz *(Philosophie in einer veränderten Welt)*, Stout *(Flight from Authority)*, Taylor *(Sources of the Self)*, Toulmin *(Cosmopolis: The Hidden Agenda of Modernity)*, et al. offer different and often contradictory genealogical accounts and narrative displays of the phenomenon called "modernity," or "Neuzeit." Each narration has to render an account of how the two main protagonists of modernity, freedom and reason, relate. Yet the very production of these competing post-Hegelian narratives of modernity's origin, meaning, and fate betrays the fundamental urge to narrate a deeply ambiguous *Geschehen* apologetically or critically. Thus the production itself inadvertently admits the very loss of its two protagonists' inherent plausibility and self-legitimation.

22. Quoted from Michael Gillespie, *Nihilism before Nietzsche*, p. 135. I am using this image in commemoration of Hans Urs von Balthasar's unjustly neglected — and by now largely forgotten — first major work, his three-volume *Apokalypse der deutschen Seele: Studien zu einer Lehre von den letzten Haltungen* (1937-39; reprint, Freiburg: Johannes Verlag, 1998). In 1947 von Balthasar republished the first of the three volumes, a consideration of German Idealism, under the title "Prometheus." In a fascinating chapter with the heading "The Prometheus Principle," von Balthasar argues that the root of modernity's moral sovereignty and self-sufficiency — i.e., the root of modernity's sense of freedom — lies in its claim of "poiesis," of creativity. Von Balthasar also quotes the last stanza of Goethe's poem to illustrate this fundamental claim: "Ich habe sie geformt nach meinem Bilde, / Ein Geschlecht, das mir gleich sei, / Zu leiden, weinen, zu genießen und zu freuen sich / Und dein nicht zu achten, / Wie ich!" Von Balthasar, *Apokalypse der deutschen Seele*, vol. 1, p. 148.

23. For the myth of Prometheus and the myth of Daedalus and his son Icarus, see Simon Hornblower and Anthony Spawforth, eds., *The Oxford Classical Dictionary*, 3rd ed. (Oxford/New York: Oxford University Press, 1996), pp. 1253-54 and 425-26.

24. Both Isaiah Berlin *(Four Essays on Liberty*, pp. 118-19) and Pope John Paul II distinguish themselves by their acute awareness of the potentially and actually fatal consequences of false ideas for the health of cultures and societies. It may not be an accidental circumstance that both experienced the fatal effects of Communism at first hand.

25. Some might wonder why I draw upon this "Continental" — or, to be precise, German — instead of Anglo-Saxon or, especially, American lineage. Could I have made the same point with Locke, Mill, Jefferson, Dewey, and Rorty? Indeed, I think it would have

been possible to develop a similar point, although it would have had to be worked out in a somewhat different way. Yet instead of getting entangled in an "Americanist" argument, I prefer to exercise the kind of self-distancing that ultimately allows a better self-understanding. In addition, we should not underestimate the impact that this Continental trajectory (including, most lately, Nietzsche) has had on the American mind — if we want to give any credence to Allan Bloom's almost apocalyptic warning in *The Closing of the American Mind: How Higher Education Has Failed Democracy and Impoverished the Souls of Today's Students* (New York: Simon & Schuster, 1987).

26. Sartrean existentialism needs to be read as a renewal of the dream in its desperate form based on *Geworfensein* and the radicalization of the poietic. This renewal did not last for long.

27. For a strong contestation of this reading, see especially Jürgen Habermas's sustained defense of the "project of modernity" in his own narrative account of the modern philosophical discourse, *The Philosophical Discourse of Modernity*, trans. Frederick Lawrence (Cambridge, Mass.: MIT Press, 1987).

28. See Gillespie, *Nihilism before Nietzsche*, pp. 33-63, and Jean-Luc Marion, *On Descartes' Metaphysical Prism: The Constitution and the Limits of Onto-theo-logy in Cartesian Thought*, trans. Jeffrey L. Kosky (Chicago: University of Chicago Press, 1999).

29. See Georg Picht, *Kants Religionsphilosophie*, 2nd ed. (Stuttgart: Klett-Cotta, 1990), pp. 487-541.

30. Immanuel Kant, *Critique of Pure Reason*, B560-86. Cf. Henry E. Allison, *Kant's Theory of Freedom* (Cambridge: Cambridge University Press, 1990), pp. 11-53.

31. Immanuel Kant, *Critique of Practical Reason*, remark on §7, "Fundamental Law of Pure Practical Reason" (A55-57; *Akademie-Ausgabe*, 5:31-33).

32. It is by no means accidental that this sounds like a divine attribute. See Gordon E. Michalson Jr., *Kant and the Problem of God* (Oxford/Malden, Mass.: Blackwell, 1999), pp. 41-56, on the subtle transfer of divine attributes to the human agent in Kant's work.

33. Allison, *Kant's Theory of Freedom*, pp. 129-45, and the still important introductory essay "The Ethical Significance of Kant's *Religion*," by John R. Silber, in Immanuel Kant, *Religion within the Limits of Reason Alone*, trans. with introduction and notes by Theodore M. Greene and Hoyt H. Hudson (New York: Harper & Row, 1960), pp. lxxix-cxxxiv.

34. Kant, *Critique of Pure Reason*, B429-32.

35. Hartmut and Gernot Böhme, *Das Andere der Vernunft: Zur Entwicklung von Rationalitätsstrukturen am Beispiel Kants* (Frankfurt: Suhrkamp, 1983).

36. On the latter, see Michalson's fine rendition of Kant's secular eschatology in the chapter "Heaven Comes to Earth: The Ethical Commonwealth," in *Kant and the Problem of God*, pp. 100-122.

37. The most fundamental — and also the most controversial — of Kant's "checks and balances" is his concept of the "thing-in-itself" or, more precisely, "thing viewed in itself" *(ens per se)*. Kant calls it "merely a limiting concept" (*Critique of Pure Reason*, B311; *Prolegomena to Any Future Metaphysic*, §57), pointing to the completely indeterminate cause of sensation. Kant wants to assure that in knowledge there is a participant that is different from the a priori and the empirical subjectivity. Ironically, it is precisely this concept

that becomes the stumbling block and starting point for absolute idealism. If the "thing-in-itself" is ultimately a *concept,* then being is object construed by reason, and, as Fichte puts the consequence, "reason is absolutely autonomous, only for itself." *Johann Gottlieb Fichte's sämmtliche Werke,* ed. Immanuel Hermann Fichte, 8 vols. (Berlin: Veit, 1845), 1:474, hereafter cited as F. For a reading of Kant that demonstrates Kant's vulnerability to this development of his thought and for a reading of Fichte's work as a consequent deepening of Kant's project, see Richard Kroner, *Von Kant bis Hegel,* vol. 1 (Tübingen: Mohr, 1921), pp. 95-119, 387-92.

38. Gillespie, *Nihilism before Nietzsche,* pp. 84-85.

39. Gillespie, *Nihilism before Nietzsche,* p. 76.

40. Henrich, *Selbstverhältnisse,* pp. 57-82. It is the distinct achievement of Henrich's interpretation to show convincingly that Fichte continued to develop his theory of subjectivity in an internally coherent way that overcame its early, more problematic stage. Yet, as Gillespie argues, it was the Fichte of the Jena years who had a deep influence on early Romanticism and its fantasies of the supremacy of the human will. See Gillespie, *Nihilism before Nietzsche,* pp. 104-34. It is early Fichte's reception and impact with which I am primarily concerned here, and less so a comprehensive interpretation of his complete opus. (At some future point, the history of a particular living room in Göttingen in the 1950s and 1960s needs to be written, a room in which an equally ingenious as problematic Protestant theologian — forced into early retirement because of his membership in the National-Socialist party and his active support of the Nazi regime — passed on his own reception and interpretation of Fichte to a group of students that eventually shaped the return of liberal Protestantism in Germany from the 1960s through the 1990s. For an introduction to this theologian, see John Stroup, "Political Theology and Secularization Theory in Germany, 1918-1939: Emmanuel Hirsch as a Phenomenon of His Time," *Harvard Theological Review* 80 [1987]: 321-68, and Jack Forstman, *Christian Faith in Dark Times: Theological Conflicts in the Shadow of Hitler* [Louisville: Westminster/John Knox, 1992], pp. 210-21.) For the catalytic role that Hirsch played in Karl Barth's dismissal from his chair at the University of Bonn in 1934, see the detailed historical account of Heinrich Assel, "'Barth ist entlassen . . .' Emanuel Hirschs Rolle im Fall Barth und seine Briefe an Wilhelm Stapel," *Zeitschrift für Theologie und Kirche* 91 (1994): 445-75.

41. As felicitously put by Gillespie, *Nihilism before Nietzsche,* p. 85.

42. Gillespie, *Nihilism before Nietzsche,* pp. 99-100.

43. Johann Gottlieb Fichte, *Grundlage der gesamten Wissenschaftslehre als Handschrift für seine Zuhörer* (1794), *J. G. Fichte — Gesamtausgabe der Bayerischen Akademie der Wissenschaften,* ed. Reinhard Lauth and Hans Jacob (Stuttgart-Bad Cannstatt: Frommann, 1964ff.), I/2:300, hereafter cited as GA (F 1:143).

44. Fichte, GA I/2:301 (F 1:144); my translation.

45. Johann Gottlieb Fichte, *System der Sittenlehre nach den Prinzipien der Wissenschaftslehre* (1798), GA I/5:208 (F 4:229); my translation. I am indebted to Friedrich Mildenberger's essay "Freiheitsverständnisse und ihre Folgen," *Zeitschrift für Theologie und Kirche* 91 (1994): 329-45, for pointing me to this particularly instructive quote from Fichte's works. In the context of his noteworthy theological anthropology, Mildenberger offers a more extensive discussion and critique of Fichte's thought along theological lines, with which I am in fundamental agreement. See Friedrich Mildenberger, *Biblische*

Dogmatik: Eine Biblische Theologie in dogmatischer Perspektive, vol. 3, *Theologie als Ökonomie* (Stuttgart: Kohlhammer, 1993), pp. 60-74.

46. "Die formale Bedingung der Moralität unserer Handlungen, oder ihre vorzugsweise sogenannte Moralität besteht darin, daß man sich schlechthin um des Gewissens willen zu dem, was dasselbe fordert, entschließe. Das Gewissen aber ist *das unmittelbare Bewußtsein unserer bestimmten Pflicht.*" Fichte, GA I/5:160-61 (F 4:173). A. E. Kroeger translates this the following way: "The formal condition of the morality of our acts, or their preeminently so-called morality, consists in this, that we resolve to do that which conscience requires, solely for the sake of conscience. But conscience is *the immediate consciousness of our determined duty.*" Johann Gottlieb Fichte, *The Science of Ethics as Based on the Science of Knowledge,* trans. A. E. Kroeger, ed. W. T. Harris (London: Kegan Paul, Trench, Trübner & Co., 1897), pp. 182-83.

47. Mildenberger, "Freiheitsverständnisse und ihre Folgen," p. 335.

48. It is worthwhile to quote the remark in full, since the two notions of freedom that Fichte employs here precisely reflect the two "I's" discussed in the quote above: "The moral impulse demands *freedom* for the sake of freedom. Who does not perceive that the word freedom is used here in two different meanings? In the latter instance it is used to designate an objective condition to be produced, or the final absolute end, namely, complete independence from all externality; whereas, in the first instance, it signifies, in short, something purely subjective. I am to *act free* in order to *become free.*" Fichte, *Science of Ethics,* p. 161 (F 4:153).

49. Gillespie, *Nihilism before Nietzsche,* p. 92.

50. I am thinking here of Schelling's *Philosophical Investigations into the Essence of Human Freedom and Related Matters,* of Fichte's late philosophy of religion, and of Hegel's complete system. For the first, see the introduction and bibliography in Friedrich Wilhelm Joseph Schelling, *Philosophische Untersuchungen über das Wesen der menschlichen Freiheit und die damit zusammenhängenden Gegenstände,* ed. Thomas Buchheim (Darmstadt: Wissenschaftliche Buchgesellschaft, 1997), pp. ix-lxix; for the second, see Dirk Schmid, *Religion und Christentum in Fichtes Spätphilosophie 1810-1813* (Berlin: de Gruyter, 1995); and for the third, see Vittorio Hösle, *Hegels System,* 2nd ed. (Hamburg: Meiner, 1998).

51. Karl Marx, "Nationalökonomie und Philosophie" (1844), in Marx, *Die Frühschriften,* ed. Siegfried Landshut, 6th ed. (Stuttgart: Kröner, 1971), p. 246; my translation.

52. On Schopenhauer's hidden indebtedness to speculative idealism in general and to Fichte in particular, see Gillespie, *Nihilism before Nietzsche,* pp. 68, 193-97.

53. Friedrich Nietzsche, *Werke: Kritische Gesamtausgabe,* ed. Giorgio Colli and Mazzino Montinari, vol. 4, pt. 2 (Berlin: de Gruyter, 1967ff.), p. 121; my translation.

54. "Es giebt kein 'Sein' hinter dem Thun, Wirken, Werden; 'der Täter' ist zum Thun bloss hinzugedichtet, — das Thun ist alles." Friedrich Nietzsche, *Werke: Kritische Studienausgabe,* ed. Giorgio Colli and Mazzino Montinari, vol. 5 (Berlin: de Gruyter, 1980), p. 279; my translation.

55. See Michael Haar, *Nietzsche and Metaphysics,* trans. and ed. Michael Gendre (New York: SUNY, 1993), chs. 1, 3.

56. Karl Löwith rightly interprets this teaching as the anti-Christian repetition of antiquity on the very acme of modernity. See Löwith, *Nietzsche's Philosophy of the Eternal*

Recurrence of the Same, trans. J. Harvey Lomax, with a foreword by Bernd Magnus (Berkeley: University of California Press, 1997). Löwith argues in this book — *pace* Heidegger — that the will to power and the eternal recurrence of the same are finally irreconcilable in Nietzsche's thought. While Löwith ultimately rejects Nietzsche's account of the eternal return as fundamentally self-contradictory, cf. Gilles Deleuze, *Nietzsche and Philosophy,* trans. Hugh Tomlinson (New York: Columbia University Press, 1983) for a nuanced defense of Nietzsche's doctrine.

57. For the latter, see, among many, Nancy, *Experience of Freedom,* Slavoj Žižek/ F. W. J. von Schelling, *The Abyss of Freedom/Ages of the World,* trans. Judith Norman (Ann Arbor: University of Michigan Press, 1997), and Slavoj Žižek, *The Ticklish Subject: The Absent Center of Political Ontology* (London/New York: Verso, 1999). What is celebrated as the deconstruction of logocentrism opens up to nothing other than the return of the will as sovereign.

58. I am indebted for this term to Andrzej Szostek, "Der Mensch als Autokreator: Die anthropologischen Grundlagen der Ablehnung der Enzyklika 'Humanae vitae,'" *Forum katholische Theologie* 9 (1993): 260-74. See also his more extensive treatment of these issues in Szostek, *Natur — Vernuft — Freiheit: Philosophische Analyse der Konzeption 'schöpferischer Vernunft' in der zeitgenössischen Moraltheologie* (Frankfurt am Main/New York: Peter Lang, 1992).

59. *Pace* Habermas's critique *(Philosophical Discourse in Modernity),* Horkheimer and Adorno have described key elements of this turning *(Umschlagen)* from one into the other in their *Dialectic of Enlightenment,* trans. John Cumming (New York: Herder & Herder, 1972).

60. In the second section I am drawing on my essay "'God's Law' in *Veritatis Splendor:* Sic et Non," in *Ecumenical Ventures in Ethics: Protestants Engage Pope John Paul II's Moral Encyclicals,* ed. Reinhard Hütter and Theodor Dieter (Grand Rapids: Eerdmans, 1998), pp. 84-114.

61. For a nuanced account of Pope John Paul II's personalist integration of freedom and law, see Lois Malcolm, "Freedom and Truth in *Veritatis Splendor* and the Meaning of Theonomy," in *Ecumenical Ventures in Ethics,* ed. Hütter and Dieter, pp. 159-84.

62. John Paul II, *Veritatis Splendor/The Splendor of Truth* [*VS*]. Quotations are from the English edition *The Splendor of Truth — Veritatis Splendor: Encyclical Letter, August 6, 1993,* Publication No. 679-4 (Washington, D.C.: United States Catholic Conference, 1993).

63. Since the encyclical uses the term "law" analogically — albeit not adequately when it comes to the "new law" — there is no need to differentiate strictly between "law" and "commandment." This becomes necessary only when "law" is used in a univocal sense, as among those Lutheran theologians who strictly insist on two "uses" of the law (as did most prominently in the twentieth century the German Lutheran theologian Werner Elert).

64. "Nevertheless, *the autonomy of reason cannot mean* that reason itself *creates values and moral norms.* Were this autonomy to imply a denial of the participation of the practical reason in the wisdom of the divine Creator and Lawgiver, or were it to suggest a freedom which creates moral norms, on the basis of historical contingencies or the diversity of societies and cultures, this sort of alleged autonomy would contradict the Church's teaching on the truth about man" (*VS* 40). "Law must therefore be considered an expres-

sion of divine wisdom: by submitting to the law, freedom submits to the truth of creation" (*VS* 41). "Patterned on God's freedom, man's freedom is not negated by his obedience to the divine law; indeed, only through this obedience does it abide in the truth and conform to human dignity" (*VS* 42).

65. This is the very principle of "autonomy" in Kant: Everyone is subject to his or her own legislation, which nevertheless — because of the universality of reason — is a universal legislation. Immanuel Kant, *Groundwork of the Metaphysic of Morals*, B/A73. Everyone is subject to those laws and only those laws that his or her own reason legislates itself (or could have legislated). Only as "self-legislating" is the will subject to the moral law. Kant, *Groundwork*, B71/A72.

66. It is important to notice here that this inner law of practical reason is called *natural* law, because it is the measure that corresponds to the human's nature as moral being, in which the eternal law (God the Creator's own reason) finds expression.

67. Here we see how a fundamental distinction drawn by Augustine bears itself out constructively. Augustine differentiates clearly between free choice, or free will *(liberum arbitrium)*, and freedom *(libertas)*. As aptly put by Richard McKeon: "Free choice leaves open the possibility to do evil, whereas freedom is the good use of free choice. The will is always free in the sense of possessing free choice, but is not always good, and therefore is not always free in the sense of possessing freedom." Richard McKeon, *Freedom and History and Other Essays*, ed. Zahava K. McKeon (Chicago/London: University of Chicago Press, 1990), p. 199. The later Augustine sharpens this distinction, which Luther inherits and continues in his *De servo arbitrio*. The *liberum arbitrium* has lost the capacity for *libertas*, which can be regained only by its reception in communion with the triune God, who is the only Good and therefore also the only *libertas*.

68. Here the encyclical follows Aquinas's teaching very closely by using the "new law" as a hermeneutical key for the interpretation of the "old law." This move allows Aquinas to productively differentiate in the "old law" between judicial law, cultic law, and natural law and to emphasize in light of salvation history the unity of this law as God's gift to Israel. This, in turn, makes it possible for him to claim the revelatory character of the whole "old law" without having to claim at the same time the binding character of the whole Torah for Christians. For a good discussion of some of these matters, see Pamela Hall, *Narrative and the Natural Law: An Interpretation of Thomistic Ethics* (Notre Dame: University of Notre Dame Press, 1994), pp. 45-64.

69. "Saint Thomas writes that this law 'can be called law in two ways. First, the law of the spirit is the Holy Spirit . . . who, dwelling in the soul, not only teaches what it is necessary to do by enlightening the intellect on the things to be done, but also inclines the affections to act with uprightness. . . . Second, the law of the spirit can be called the proper effect of the Holy Spirit, and thus faith working through love (cf. *Gal* 5:6), which teaches inwardly about the things to be done . . . and inclines the affections to act'" (*VS* 45). The encyclical quotes from Thomas Aquinas's commentary *In Epistulam ad Romanos*, c. 8, lect. 1. See also *ST* I-II.106.1 ad 2: "Lex nova est indita homini, non solum indicare quid sit faciendum, sed etiam adiuvans ad implendum" ["In this way the New Law is instilled into man, not only by indicating to him what he should do, but also by helping him to accomplish it"]. Cf. Pinckaers, "Encyclical for the Future," pp. 29, 36-37.

70. "Alio modo potest etiam intellegi inquantum hominis opera qui Spiritu Sancto

agitur, magis dicuntur esse opera Spiritus Sancti quam ipsius hominis. Unde cum Spiritus Sanctus non sit sub lege, sicut nec filius, ut supra (a.4 ad 2) dictum est; sequitur quod huiusmodi opera, inquantum sunt Spiritus Sancti, non sint sub lege." ["Secondly, it can be understood as meaning that the works of a man, who is led by the Holy Ghost, are the works of the Holy Ghost rather than his own. Therefore, since the Holy Ghost is not under the law, as neither is the Son, as stated above (a.4 ad 2); it follows that such works, in so far as they are of the Holy Ghost, are not under the law."] *ST* I-II.93.6 ad 1. All English quotations from the *Summa theologiae* are taken from the translation of the Fathers of the English Dominican Province (1911; rev. 1920). See also Hall, *Narrative and Natural Law*, p. 69.

71. Ulrich Kühn, *Via caritatis: Theologie des Gesetzes bei Thomas von Aquin* (Berlin: Evangelische Verlagsanstalt, 1964), pp. 192-93; my translation. See also Kühn's critical remarks about Thomas's use of the term "new law" for his interpretation of the gospel in Kühn, "Evangelische Anmerkungen zum Problem der Begründung der moralischen Autonomie des Menschen im Neuen Gesetz nach Thomas," in *Freiheit im Leben mit Gott: Texte zur Tradition evangelischer Ethik*, ed. with an introduction by Hans G. Ulrich (Gütersloh: Gütersloher Verlagshaus, 1993), pp. 78-88.

72. Aquinas, *ST* I-II.93.6 ad 1, quoting 2 Cor 3:17.

73. Martin Luther, *The Large Catechism*, in *The Book of Concord: The Confessions of the Evangelical Lutheran Church*, ed. Robert Kolb and Timothy J. Wengert (Minneapolis: Fortress, 2000), p. 392.

74. On grounds of Matt 19:17, the encyclical understands God's commandments as intrinsically linked with God's promise: in the old covenant with the promise of the land, in the new covenant with the promise of eternal life (cf. *VS* 12). With this move the encyclical avoids the danger of isolating God's commandments from the economy of salvation. While *Veritatis Splendor* is thus able to interpret the commandments as an integral element of God's salvific activity in the overall framework of a soteriological teleology, Luther's reminder that the fulfillment of the commandments hangs on the first (which is fulfilled through faith) is crucial lest the commandments' fulfillment subtly shift into a conditional relationship vis-à-vis God's saving activity in Christ.

75. See also Alasdair MacIntyre: "What God commands of us in commanding these precepts is therefore what we already knew or could have known for ourselves as required for our good. What God asks of us, both in the Old Law and in its reaffirmation by Jesus Christ, is what, if we were adequately rational, we would ask of ourselves. God's commands are to be and do what will restore us to our freedom, and the Church's teaching concerning the divine commands has the same aim and content. 'Hence obedience to God is not, as some would believe, a heteronomy' (VS 41.1). We are not to have divided wills, divided minds, or divided hearts." Alasdair MacIntyre, "How Can We Learn What *Veritatis Splendor* Has to Teach?" in *Veritatis Splendor and the Renewal of Moral Theology*, ed. DiNoia and Cessario, pp. 73-94; 78-79. The one important reservation I have in regard to MacIntyre's way of putting the matter is the Augustinian/Lutheran concern that — *sub conditione peccati* — being "adequately rational" (with the emphasis on *adequately*) is simply not an option at our disposal. And precisely for this reason the Decalogue will strike us as heteronomy — unless, to put it in the encyclical's terminology, the Holy Spirit resides in the soul.

76. The quote is from Augustine's *In Iohannis Evangelium tractatus* 41.10 (CCSL 36:363).

77. It is therefore not at all surprising that the encyclical emphasizes Christ's universal relevance as *teacher* of morality: "*People today need to turn to Christ once again in order to receive from him the answer to their questions about what is good and what is evil*. Christ is the Teacher, the Risen One who has life in himself and who is always present in his Church and in the world. It is he who opens up to the faithful the book of the Scriptures and, by fully revealing the Father's will, teaches the truth about moral action. At the source and summit of the economy of salvation . . . Christ sheds light on man's condition and his integral vocation" (*VS* 8).

78. It is not possible here to sustain this claim. But it seems necessary to me to read the pneumatological passages in *Veritatis Splendor* in light of and continuity with John Paul II's earlier encyclical devoted exclusively to the Holy Spirit, *Dominum et Vivificantem* (*Origins* 16/4 [1986]: 77-102), esp. articles 58-60. One wonders why this strong pneumatological emphasis did not sufficiently open up the rather univocal use of the term "law" in the middle part of the encyclical to a fully analogical use in Aquinas's sense.

79. Livio Melina, "Desire for Happiness and the Commandments in the First Chapter of *Veritatis Splendor*," in *Veritatis Splendor and the Renewal of Moral Theology*, ed. DiNoia and Cessario, pp. 143-60; 155.

80. The crucial link is the concept of *Geist* as continuously enacted in the *cogito*. The I is pure subjectivity and God reappears as the "ground" of pure subjectivity, namely, as the unthinkable subject — absolute spirit — that thinks us. This move is initiated by the later Fichte and completed by Hegel.

81. Livio Melina rightly emphasizes this important aspect: "In the ethics of classical inspiration, and particularly in Thomistic ethics, the concept of *lex* is secondary and subordinate to that of *virtus*. The law, which maintains an irreducible character of exteriority, but which at the same time is recognized in its intrinsic rationality, has as its aim the guidance of men toward virtue. . . . Therefore the Commandments exist in function of an education of desire." Melina, "Desire for Happiness and the Commandments," p. 148. Stanley Hauerwas's emphasis on the virtues and, more recently, his appreciation of the commandments must be read in this light. For Hauerwas, Christian theology and especially Christian ethics should do nothing other than lead to an education or, even stronger, a transformation of desire. See, most recently, his *Christians among the Virtues: Theological Conversations with Ancient and Modern Ethics*, together with Charles Pinches (Notre Dame: University of Notre Dame Press, 1997), *Sanctify Them in the Truth: Holiness Exemplified* (Edinburgh: T&T Clark, 1998), and *The Truth about God: The Ten Commandments in Christian Life*, together with William H. Willimon (Nashville: Abingdon, 1999).

82. MacIntyre, "How Can We Learn," p. 78.

83. All this occurs in and through the Spirit, not as *facere quod in se est* — not as the self-actualization of humanity's "natural" capacity to act freely in the Ockhamist sense. For Luther *(Treatise on Good Works)*, the Decalogue serves as the instruction for good works in faith, for "intrinsically good works." For an interesting proximity in this regard, cf. *VS* 15.2 and Melina, "Desire for Happiness and the Commandments," p. 157.

84. Yet with reference to Aquinas's *Super epistolam ad Romanos* (c. 12, lect. 1), Livio Melina raises the important caveat that "[n]onetheless, even under the regime of the New

Law the Commandments remain necessary reference points, since we possess only the first fruits of the Spirit." Melina, "Desire for Happiness and the Commandments," p. 158. In his *Lectures on Galatians* (1535), Luther makes a very similar point when he emphasizes the disciplinary role of the law in the struggle between flesh and Spirit as it characterizes the Christian life this side of the eschaton (LW 26:350).

85. In his essay "Salvadoran Martyrs: A Love That Does Justice," *Horizons* 28 (2001): 7-29, Thomas L. Schubeck, SJ, lays out an informative sketch of the origins and the development of martyrdom and convincingly argues for the fundamental link between truth and love in the martyr's witness, a link that can justifiably — and possibly, must necessarily — be extended to the witness against grave injustices.

86. See Avery Dulles, SJ, "The Truth about Freedom: A Theme from John Paul II," in *Veritatis Splendor and the Renewal of Moral Theology*, ed. DiNoia and Cessario, pp. 129-42; 133-34.

87. In other words, martyrdom presupposes the law's objectivity and concreteness. Without the latter, martyrdom as supreme witness to the holiness of God's law would be impossible. In this way, the martyr's very witness unmasks the falsity and self-deception that arise whenever the freedom of conscience is misinterpreted in a licentious way. And that happens whenever we maintain that the form of the law that is concretely binding on us can never be specified, that therefore everything remains fundamentally ambiguous and consequently a matter of "free," i.e., indifferent choice. The quote from John Henry Newman cited at the beginning of the chapter identifies this very issue.

88. For diverging historical assessments of the teaching on intrinsically evil acts, see the critical account by John Mahoney, *The Making of Moral Theology: A Study of the Roman Catholic Tradition* (New York: Oxford University Press, 1987) and the positive account by Servais Pinckaers, OP, *Ce qu'on ne peut jamais faire: La question des actes intrinsèquement mauvais. Histoire et discussion*, Studien zur theologischen Ethik 19 (Fribourg: Éditions Universitaires, 1986). See also Jean Porter's nuanced account of the conceptual problems involved in this teaching in her *Moral Action and Christian Ethics* (Cambridge: Cambridge University Press, 1995). The present debate is best documented in the exchange between Richard McCormick, "Some Early Reactions to *Veritatis Splendor*," *Theological Studies* 55 (1994): 481-506, and Martin Rhonheimer, "Intrinsically Evil Acts and the Moral Viewpoint: Clarifying a Central Teaching of *Veritatis Splendor*" and "Intentional Actions and the Meaning of Object: A Reply to Richard McCormick," in *Veritatis Splendor and the Renewal of Moral Theology*, ed. DiNoia and Cessario, pp. 161-93 and 241-68. For a constructive Lutheran engagement of this teaching, see Bernd Wannenwetsch, "'Intrinsically Evil Acts'; or, Why Abortion and Euthanasia Cannot Be Justified," in *Ecumenical Ventures in Ethics*, ed. Hütter and Dieter, pp. 185-215.

89. It thus undercuts what Alasdair MacIntyre has aptly called the "sovereign independence" of conscience: "Another expression of this distorted view of the self is the conferring upon the individual conscience of a sovereign independence of any standards external to its own justification." MacIntyre, "How Can We Learn," p. 90.

90. By referring to the hearings on the nomination of Clarence Thomas to the U.S. Supreme Court, MacIntyre points out the widespread nature of this assumption: "There is in the dominant moral culture of our particular time and place a widespread and influential conception of human beings as individuals who initially confront a range of possible

objects of rational desire, a range of goods, among which each of them has to make his or her own choices, and which each individual has to order for himself or herself, in accordance with his or her set of preferences. . . . Hence it is on the basis of individual preferences and choices that values and norms, including those of morality, come into being and from those preferences and choices that they derive their authority. . . . Their choices and preferences are to be treated as sovereign, and their liberty consists in the exercise of this sovereignty. . . . During the hearings on the nomination of Clarence Thomas to the U.S. Supreme Court, Senator Joseph Biden expressed a fear 'that natural law dictates morality to us, instead of leaving matters to individual choice' (*The Washington Post*, September 8, 1991). But this conception of moral freedom as a power in each of us to make our own fundamental premoral choice of moral norms and values is illusory and deceptive." MacIntyre, "How Can We Learn," pp. 82-83.

91. Dulles, "The Truth about Freedom," p. 137.

92. Cf. MacIntyre, "How Can We Learn," pp. 89-90.

93. MacIntyre puts this relationship in positive terms, namely, the enabling function of exceptionless negative precepts for the emergence of genuine freedom: "The virtue which we need if we are to become capable of right choice is the Aristotelian virtue of *phronesis, prudentia*. The acquisition of that virtue is impossible without a recognition of the rational authority of the precepts of the natural law, most of all perhaps of the negative exceptionless precepts. Thereby we become able to choose in a way that is not self-frustrating, but liberates our capacities for judgment and action directed toward our good. This is why the negative precepts are what I called them earlier, enabling, and why acknowledgement of their rational authority is a constitutive element of human autonomy." MacIntyre, "How Can We Learn," p. 84.

94. Calvin O. Schrag, *The Self after Postmodernity* (New Haven: Yale University Press, 1997).

95. The dissolving of the notion of a moral self and a moral law coherent across time and in a variety of circumstances results in the tacit or open circumstantiality and provisionality of moral judgments, a point well made by MacIntyre, "How Can We Learn," p. 81. (For a fuller account of this point, see his *Three Rival Versions of Moral Enquiry*, pp. 196-215.) MacIntyre condenses this late modern phenomenon in the notion of "temporariness": "Temporariness becomes a crucial feature of the moral life and the virtue of integrity — of a willingness and an ability to stand by one's central commitments whatever the consequences — becomes thought of not as a virtue, but as a piece of moral irrationality. So a consistent consequentialism in everyday life would entail the loss of what is from the standpoint of the natural law a constitutive virtue of the mature self" (p. 91).

96. Cf. Hauerwas, *Sanctify Them in the Truth*, pp. 111-16. For another nuanced account from a Protestant perspective, see Bernd Wannenwetsch, "Intrinsically Evil Acts," pp. 190-210.

97. It is worth remembering that in his *Smalcald Articles*, Martin Luther indeed expected this: "Therefore it is necessary to know and teach that when holy people — aside from the fact that they still have and feel original sin and also daily repent of it and struggle against it — somehow fall into a public sin (such as David, who fell into adultery, murder, and blasphemy against God), at that point faith and the Spirit have departed. The Holy

Spirit does not allow sin to rule and gain the upper hand so that it is brought out to completion, but the Spirit controls and resists so that sin is not able to do whatever it wants. However, when sin does whatever it wants, then the Holy Spirit and faith are not there." *Book of Concord*, p. 319, §§43-45.

98. Most famously we can find this view in Hegel's interpretation of the Reformation: "The principle of the Reformation then was the moment of spirit's being-with-itself, of its being free, its coming to itself. That is just what freedom means: to relate oneself to oneself, in the determinate content." Georg Wilhelm Friedrich Hegel, *Lectures on the History of Philosophy: The Lectures of 1825-1826*, ed. Robert F. Brown, vol. 3 (Berkeley: University of California Press, 1990), p. 102. It has been the hallmark of a significant strand of European and North American Protestant theology of the nineteenth and twentieth centuries to interpret the "project of modernity" as the Reformation's child (legitimate for some, illegitimate for others, but unquestionably brought about by the Reformation's legitimate aspirations) and therefore as the object of Protestantism's genuine responsibility as well as the major reason for Protestantism's authoritative claim on the project of modernity.

99. See David S. Yeago, "Gnosticism, Antinomianism and Reformation Theology: Reflections on the Cost of a Construal," *Pro Ecclesia* 2 (1993): 37-49.

100. Oswald Bayer, *Leibliches Wort: Reformation und Neuzeit im Konflikt* (Tübingen: Mohr, 1992) and Bayer, *Freiheit als Antwort: Zur theologischen Ethik* (Tübingen: Mohr, 1995). Yet it can already be found in Ebeling's interpretation of Luther.

101. Robert W. Jenson, "An Ontology of Freedom in the *De Servo Arbitrio* of Luther," *Modern Theology* 10 (1994): 247-52, and Jenson, *Systematic Theology*, vol. 2, *The Works of God*, pp. 105-8.

102. George Lindbeck, "Martin Luther and the Rabbinic Mind," in *Understanding the Rabbinic Mind: Essays on the Hermeneutic of Max Kadushin*, ed. Peter Ochs (Atlanta: Scholars Press, 1990), pp. 141-64.

103. See my *Suffering Divine Things: Theology as Church Practice* (Grand Rapids: Eerdmans, 2000), pp. 128-45.

104. Martin Luther, *On the Councils and the Church* (1539), LW 41:9-178, esp. 143-78.

105. See my essays "Christliche Freiheit und die Wahrheit des Gesetzes," pp. 246-71, and "'God's Law' in *Veritatis Splendor*," pp. 84-114.

106. I critically engage the encyclical on this issue by raising the question whether it sufficiently follows Aquinas, whose discussion of the law is anteceded in the theological *summa* by a discussion of virtue — a concept glaringly absent from the encyclical. I raise these issues under the heading "Whose Aquinas? Which Law?" in "'God's Law' in *Veritatis Splendor*," pp. 89-92, and under the heading "Secundum Thomam?" in "Christliche Freiheit und die Wahrheit des Gesetzes," pp. 262-63.

107. Martin Luther, *Theses against the Antinomians* (1537), in *D. Martin Luthers Werke: Kritische Gesamtausgabe*, ed. J. F. K. Knaake et al. (Weimar: Hermann Böhlaus Nachfolger, 1883ff.), 39/1:334-58, hereafter cited as WA. What *is* available in English is the treatise *Against the Antinomians* from 1539, found in LW 47:107-19. For one of the very few theological interpretations of these theses, see Rudolf Hermann, *Zum Streit um die Überwindung des Gesetzes: Erörterungen zu Luthers Antinomerthesen* (Weimar: Hermann Böhlaus Nachfolger, 1958).

108. Notable exceptions are Asendorf, Bayer, Hof, and Yeago.

109. Luther, *Theses against the Antinomians* (1537), WA 39/1:344-45. "1. Lex non est digna, ut vocetur verbum Dei. 2. *Bistu ein hure, bube, ehebrecher, oder sonst ein sunder, gleubstu, so bistu im wege der seligkeit.* 3. *Wenn du mitten jnn der sunden stickest auffs hohest, vnd bist, Gleubstu, so bistu mitten jnn der seligkeit.* 1. *Decalogus gehort auff das Ratthaus, nicht auff den Predigtstuel.* 2. *Alle die mit Mose vmbgehen, mussen zum Teufel faren, an galgen mit Mose.* 3. *Wir sollen nicht die Menschen bereiten zum Euangelio, durch die predigt des Gesetzs, Gott mus es thun, des werck sey es.* 4. In Evangelio non debet agi de violatione legis, sed de violatione filii. 5. Audire verbum et ita vivere, est consequentia legis. 6. Audire verbum et sentire in corde, est proprium Evangelii methodo. 7. *Petrus hat Christliche freiheit nicht gewust, sein spruch:* Certam facientes vocationem vestram per bona opera, non valet. 8. *Als balde du gedenckest, So vnd so solt es jnn der Christenheit zugehen, es solten feine, erbare, zuchtige, heilige, keusche leute sein, So hastu des Euangelium schon gefeilet, cap 6. Luce.*"

110. For the historical background see James Mackinnon, *Luther and the Reformation*, vol. 4 (London/New York: Longmans, Green, 1925-30), pp. 161-79, Wilfried Joest, *Gesetz und Freiheit: Das Problem des Tertius Usus Legis bei Luther und die neutestamentliche Parainese*, 2nd ed. (Göttingen: Vandenhoeck & Ruprecht, 1956), pp. 45-55, and Martin Brecht, *Martin Luther*, vol. 3, *Die Erhaltung der Kirche 1532-1546* (Stuttgart: Calwer Verlag, 1987), pp. 158-73.

111. Luther, LW 47:104-5 (WA 39/1:571ff.).

112. "Quare lex numquam in aeternum tollitur, sed manebit vel implenda in damnatis, vel impletur in beatis." Luther, *Theses against the Antinomians* (1537), WA 39/1:350,3-4.

113. "1. Ista consequentia s. Pauli: Ubi non est lex, ibi nec praevaricatio, non solum theologice, sed etiam politice et naturaliter bona est. 2. Similiter et illa: Ubi non est peccatum, ibi nec poena nec remissio. 3. Similiter et illa: Ubi non est poena nec remissio, ibi nec ira nec gratia. 4. Similiter et illa: Ubi non est ira nec gratia, ibi nec divina nec humana gubernatio. 5. Similiter et illa: Ubi non est divina nec humana gubernatio, ibi nec Deus nec homo. 6. Similiter et illa: Ubi non est Deus nec homo, ibi nihil nisi forte diabolus."

114. Luther, *Against the Antinomians* (1539), LW 47:119.

115. Jenson, "Ontology of Freedom."

116. Joest, *Gesetz und Freiheit*, p. 203 n. 62.

117. It is one thing to assume an analogical relationship between eternal law and natural law, as Aquinas did, but quite a different and distinctly modern move to assume a moral community that includes both God and humans and is based on a strictly univocal concept of reason and law: "To be good is . . . to be willed by a will governed by the moral law. Our will is such a will, and so is God's. Kant transposes onto human practical reason the relation he tried to work out earlier between God and the goodness of the outcomes of his choices. His astonishing claim is that God and we can share membership in a single moral community only if we all equally legislate the law we are to obey. The mature Kant does not hesitate to make an explicit comparison between human agents and God." J. B. Schneewind, *The Invention of Autonomy: A History of Modern Moral Philosophy* (Cambridge: Cambridge University Press, 1988), p. 512.

118. Martin Luther, *Lectures on Genesis (Chapters 1–5)*, LW 1:94 (WA 42:71).

119. David S. Yeago, "Martin Luther on Grace, Law, and Moral Life: Prolegomena to an Ecumenical Discussion of *Veritatis Splendor,*" *The Thomist* 62 (1998): 177.

120. Already in Luther's treatise *The Freedom of a Christian* (1520) the link to paradise can be found. Quite well-known is Luther's argument that genuine freedom is found in faith by receiving Christ's righteousness in the "happy exchange," a righteousness in and through which we participate in God's own *libertas*. Yet it is less well-known that Luther does not regard this freedom as the pure and formless spontaneity that quite a number of Protestant theologians make it to be. Rather, justifying and liberating faith restores the believer to the freedom of the original paradisial state, a state characterized and thus formed by the works done in original communion with God. "We should think of the works of a Christian who is justified and saved by faith because of the pure and free mercy of God, just as we would think of the works which Adam and Eve did in Paradise, and all their children would have done if they had not sinned." Martin Luther, *The Freedom of a Christian* (1520), LW 31:360. For a fuller discussion of this treatise, see the section "Luther's Theology of Christian Freedom" in chapter 8 of this volume. For the "happy exchange," see especially note 30 in chapter 8.

121. "So then, this tree of the knowledge of good and evil, or the place where trees of this kind were planted in large number, would have been the church at which Adam, together with his descendants, would have gathered on the Sabbath day. And after refreshing themselves from the tree of life he would have praised God and lauded Him for the dominion over all the creatures on earth which had been given to mankind. . . . Adam would have extolled the greatest gift, namely, that he, together with his descendants, was created according to the likeness of God. He would have admonished his descendants to live a holy and sinless life, to work faithfully in the garden, to watch it carefully, and to beware with the greatest care of the tree of good and evil." Luther, *Lectures on Genesis (Chapters 1–5)*, LW 1:105-6.

122. What often causes unnecessary confusion is our losing sight of the fact that Luther regards the life of faith as a dramatic affair, an ongoing struggle between the newly restored communion with God and the ongoing life of usurped sovereignty. The Spirit who has been received in faith struggles against the flesh, against the ongoing onslaught of a world that urges conformation to its schemes. For this very reason, the law continues to play an essential role in the preaching and teaching of the church, as Luther urges in his *Theses against the Antinomians*. The law is necessary for a daily discipline that keeps us accountable and prevents self-deception in the middle of the struggle of faith: "Thus the conscience takes hold of Christ more perfectly day by day; and day by day the law of flesh and sin, the fear of death, and whatever other evils the Law brings with it are diminished. For as long as we live in a flesh that is not free from sin, so long the Law keeps coming back and performing its function, more in one person and less in another, not to harm but to save. The discipline of the law is the daily mortification of the flesh, the reason, and our powers, and the renewal of our mind (2 Cor. 4:16)." Luther, *Lectures on Galatians* (1535), LW 26:350. Thus in its ongoing unmasking function, God's law keeps the believer focused on Christ as gift and the need to continuously receive this gift of God's self-giving, which constitutes genuine freedom.

123. Antti Raunio, *Summe des christlichen Lebens: Die "Goldene Regel" als Gesetz der*

Liebe in der Theologie Martin Luthers von 1510 bis 1527, Reports of the Department of Systematic Theology of Helsinki University 13 (Helsinki, 1993). For a shorter account, see Raunio, "Natural Law and Faith: The Forgotten Foundations of Ethics in Luther's Theology," in *Union with Christ: The New Finnish Interpretation of Luther*, ed. Carl E. Braaten and Robert W. Jenson (Grand Rapids: Eerdmans, 1998), pp. 96-124.

124. "Quando haec dilectio, facit, quod deus iubet. Tum lex non facit malam conscientiam, sed gaudium, quia iam alius homo factus." Martin Luther, *Sermons on Exodus* (1524/25), WA 16:285,9. See the important study by Andreas Wöhle, *Luthers Freude an Gottes Gesetz: Eine historische Quellenstudie zur Oszillation des Gesetzesbegriffes Martin Luthers im Licht seiner alttestamentlichen Predigten* (Frankfurt/M: Haag & Herchen, 1998). Wöhle convincingly shows that Luther's use of the concept of "law" is ultimately analogical, because he can use it both for what terrorizes the sinner's conscience — what reflects God's wrath, what constrains and convicts (and often Lutherans, myself included, have tended to strictly limit the term "law" to this negative sense, using "precept" and "commandment" for the positive, and thereby to reject the terminology of a "third" use of the law, while respecting its intention) — and for God's law of love, which finds its response in the believer's *dilectio legis*, delight in the law. To put it in the form of a question: In light of these insights, could there be a far greater proximity than conventionally assumed between Luther's complex and, at least on its margins, implicitly analogical use of the term "law" and Aquinas's explicitly analogical use in the *Summa theologiae*?

125. For a short and accurate summary of Luther's theology of law and gospel, see Bernhard Lohse, *Martin Luther's Theology: Its Historical and Systematic Development*, trans. and ed. Roy A. Harrisville (Minneapolis: Fortress, 1999), pp. 178-84, 267-76. See also the nuanced account offered by Ulrich Asendorf, "Die Unterscheidung von Gesetz und Evangelium aufgrund der Predigten Luthers," in *Die Kunst des Unterscheidens*, ed. Joachim Heubach (Erlangen: Martin Luther Verlag, 1990), pp. 73-89. Both authors point out (implicitly contradicting the whole "Elertian" way of rendering Luther) that the law for Luther transcends the law-gospel dialectic. It is present and relevant for the believer, but now in a way different from the first and second uses and therefore no longer "law" in the enforcing and convicting sense. If the term "law" is used univocally, it is of eminent value to strictly distinguish between "law" and "commandment," reserving "law" *(Gesetz)* for the first and second uses (enforcing and convicting) and "commandment" *(Gebot)* for that which gives direction to genuine freedom. Paul Althaus and, more recently, William H. Lazareth, *Christians in Society: Luther, the Bible, and Social Ethics* (Minneapolis: Fortress, 2001) have taken this approach. While I am basically sympathetic to it (see the fuller discussion in chapter 8, esp. notes 9 and 34), I increasingly wonder about the merits of using the term "law" in an analogical sense, which obviously brings me into the vicinity not only of Aquinas but also of the much and wrongly disparaged Melanchthon.

126. Robert W. Jenson, *Systematic Theology*, vol. 1, *The Triune God* (New York: Oxford University Press, 1997), p. 63.

127. See Frank Crüsemann's work on the interpretation of the Decalogue and later of the whole Torah in this light: *Bewahrung der Freiheit: Das Thema des Dekalogs in sozialgeschichtlicher Perspektive* (Munich: Kaiser, 1983) and *Torah: Theology and Social History of Old Testament Law*, trans. Allan W. Mahnke (Minneapolis: Fortress, 1996). The Reformed theologian Jan Milič Lochman developed a similar link between freedom and

commandment in his interpretation of the Decalogue, *Signposts to Freedom: The Ten Commandments and Christian Ethics,* trans. David Lewis (Minneapolis: Augsburg, 1982).

128. I owe this expression to Hans G. Ulrich, who uses it as the title of what is probably the best collection of essays on "genuine freedom," *Freiheit im Leben mit Gott,* ed. Ulrich.

129. Jeremiah 31:31-34 can be read as a text in which this problematic intensifies in a dramatic yet ultimately promising way.

130. Cf. Luther's *Fifth Disputation against the Antinomians* (1538), WA 39/1, theses 61 and 62, where he states that God's law — which we do not fulfill — reflects God's own goodness, and precisely because God's law is good and perfect, it condemns us.

131. I owe this expression to R. Kendall Soulen. See his important and thought-provoking reflections in Soulen, *God of Israel and Christian Theology,* pp. 156-77.

132. In his exposition of the Decalogue in the *Large Catechism,* Luther does not use any "law" language, precisely because it remains open how the Decalogue is received — whether in faith as freedom's form (and therefore not as *alia lex* but as freedom received in obedience to and communion with God) or without faith (as *alia lex* for the sake of human life under the condition of sin). George Lindbeck put it exactly right when he observed regarding the logic of the Decalogue in the *Large Catechism:* "As Luther perceived it, Christian tradition has confused two fundamentally different senses of the concepts of 'precept' (his usual word for 'commandment') and therefore also of 'obedience.' . . . His innovative method of unmasking the confusions was to call precepts 'doctrine' or instruction and confine the term 'law' exclusively to the sphere of legally enacted norms enforced by punishments and rewards. Luther described God's precepts as instructions in the performance of practices, which, when well learned, are intrinsically satisfying. As fallen creatures, to be sure, we do not spontaneously experience the practices in which the commandments instruct us as intrinsically good, but God's goodness gives us the confidence that that is what they are. We thus need not hesitate to train ourselves in them, even without faith or desire. . . . The practices God commands can to some degree be satisfying in themselves, quite apart from rewards and punishments, even when performance is as inadequate as it always is for human beings, and even when true faith and love of God and neighbor is lacking." Lindbeck, "Martin Luther and the Rabbinic Mind," pp. 156-57.

133. Joest, *Gesetz und Freiheit,* p. 203 n. 62.

134. Kant saw this in a limited sense. According to Kant, we encounter the law and interpret it as both co-constituted and received.

135. Here occurs the "either/or" between Aquinas and Scotus, that is, between intellectualism and voluntarism in the conception of the law. For an account that uses this "either/or" to map the inner tension in the way modern natural law emerged in Europe during and after the wars of religion, see Schneewind, *Invention of Autonomy.*

136. This is the case for Gentile Christians. For members of Israel who join "the way," Acts 15 reflects the seriousness of the question of continuing life according to the Torah in the very early Christian communities. This burning ecclesiological (!) question unfortunately disappeared with the disappearance of Jewish Christians in the following centuries and the increasing antagonism between church and synagogue. Only in light of the Holocaust and a renewed Jewish-Christian dialogue has this question resurfaced. For an excellent discussion, see the "Symposium on 'Jewish-Christians and the Torah,'" *Modern*

Theology 11 (1995): 163-241. For an engagement with a significant contemporary effort to address this question — the Pontifical Biblical Commission's *The Jewish People and Their Sacred Scriptures in the Christian Bible* — see chapter 12.

137. For a fascinating new exegetical initiative in this area, see Markus Bockmuehl, *Jewish Law in Gentile Churches: Halakha and the Beginning of Christian Public Ethics* (Edinburgh: T&T Clark, 2000).

138. Stanley Hauerwas has pressed this insight in his recent work. See especially "The Truth about God: The Decalogue as Condition for Truthful Speech," in *Sanctify Them in the Truth*, pp. 37-59, and *The Truth about God: The Ten Commandments in Christian Life*, with William H. Willimon (Nashville: Abingdon, 1999).

139. I am indebted to Judge Laurie Ackermann for this insight. A member of the new South African supreme court, he was part of the juridical committee that approved the new constitution of South Africa.

140. It is by no means accidental that political liberalism continues to be haunted by the specter of Carl Schmitt. For intense engagements of this problematic, see Chantal Mouffe, ed., *The Challenge of Carl Schmitt* (London/New York: Verso, 1999) and Gopal Balakrishnan, *The Enemy: An Intellectual Portrait of Carl Schmitt* (London/New York: Verso, 2000). If negative freedom is not continuously protected by the ongoing reception of genuine freedom, it becomes vulnerable to the kind of deconstruction that Carl Schmitt's work represents — *pace* Isaiah Berlin. In other words, Pope John Paul II's international defense of human rights (and thereby of negative freedom) rests on resources that political liberalism, cut off from its theological and metaphysical roots, has long lost.

Notes to Chapter 8

1. To be perfectly clear, I understand "freedom" in this context as an original gift of the Creator to the human being, a gift that is substantively damaged under the condition of sin and only restored through grace in the life of faith. Consequently, there is no de facto path whatsoever from the human, under the condition of sin, back to the Creator. God, as the ultimate good, and created goods do not of course fall under a common genus called "good." Hence, "good" must be understood analogically.

2. For my own ecclesiological presuppositions concerning "Lutheranism" as a confessing movement in the church catholic, see "The Church's Public Ministry in Her Babylonian Captivity," *Pro Ecclesia* 2 (1993): 18-20. The following engagement with both "classical" Protestant ethics (since the Enlightenment) and the Roman Catholic tradition arises from this understanding of Lutheranism's evangelical catholic vocation in the church universal.

3. See Walter von Loewenich's poignant formulation: "Das sola fide ist für Luther der articulus stantis et cadentis ecclesiae; das bedeutet aber für ihn nicht die Versklavung der Wirklichkeit des christlichen Lebens unter ein systematisches Prinzip" ["For Luther, the *sola fide* is the article by which the church stands and falls. Yet this does not mean for him the enslavement of the reality of the Christian life under a systematic principle"]. Walter von Loewenich, *Duplex Iustitia: Luthers Stellung zu einer Unionsformel des 16. Jahrhunderts* (Wiesbaden: Steiner, 1972), p. 72. For an interpretation of the doctrine of jus-

tification as precisely a systematic principle that is as brilliant in its inner consequence as it is, for the very same reason, problematic, see Eberhard Jüngel, *Justification: The Heart of the Christian Faith: A Theological Study with an Ecumenical Purpose*, trans. Jeffrey F. Cayzer (Edinburgh/New York: T&T Clark, 2001), where the systematic principle takes the form of the principal and ruling hermeneutical category for all of Christian theology.

4. Gerhard Forde's chapter "Christian Life" in *Christian Dogmatics*, ed. Carl E. Braaten and Robert W. Jenson, vol. 2 (Philadelphia: Fortress, 1984), pp. 395-469, is a case where this problematic concentration on — and overstretching of — the doctrine of justification becomes quite visible. While I am in deep agreement with most of what Forde lays out under the doctrine of justification, his account ultimately swallows up everything else pertinent to the Christian life. This rendition neither captures the richness and complexity of Luther's account of the Christian life nor accommodates the development of Melanchthon's trajectory. Rather, it is reflective of the so-called existential Luther interpretation, a tradition tacitly but deeply indebted to the antimetaphysical bent of Kant's philosophy. While Forde clearly sees the trap of antinomianism and affirms the law's truth, he nevertheless does not spell out the latter in a way that successfully diverts the danger of the former. Indeed, this seems to be impossible for him precisely because of his exclusive focus on the doctrine of justification by faith as the sole descriptor of the Christian life.

5. The point that through faith we not only are declared righteous on the grounds of Christ's righteousness but, by receiving Christ himself in faith, are actually beginning to become righteous was expressed by Luther early in his *Sermo de duplex iustitia* (1519). While he later modified his thinking, he still maintained a clear emphasis on Christ as the very "form" of faith, as thereby himself present in faith, in his *Lectures on Galatians* and in the notion of a *iustitia incepta* in his late disputations. See von Loewenich, *Duplex Iustitia*; Paul Althaus, *Die Theologie Martin Luthers* (Gütersloh: Gütersloher Verlagshaus, 1962), pp. 207-8; and especially Tuomo Mannermaa, *Der im Glauben gegenwärtige Christus: Rechtfertigung und Vergottung: Zum ökumenischen Dialog* (Hannover: Lutherisches Verlagshaus, 1989). See also David S. Yeago, "The Bread of Life: Patristic Christology and Evangelical Soteriology in Martin Luther's Sermons on John 6," *St. Vladimir's Theological Quarterly* 39 (1995): 257-79, esp. 271ff.

6. What I am attempting to address here is a complex phenomenon that is observable across the board in Protestant theological "camps." It can be seen, for example, in an Elert and a Bultmann, in a Forde and a Tillich. The whole problematic has to do with the particular core assumptions of Kantian philosophy as they found their way through the line of Kant-Lotze-Ritschl-Herrmann into the central construals of the Luther renaissance in the 1920s. For an analysis of this phenomenon, see Risto Saarinen, *Gottes Wirken auf uns: die transzendentale Deutung des Gegenwart-Christi-Motivs in der Lutherforschung* (Stuttgart: Steiner, 1990) and, more accessibly, David S. Yeago, "Gnosticism, Antinomianism, and Reformation Theology: Reflections on the Costs of a Construal," *Pro Ecclesia* 2 (1993): 37-49.

7. See Yeago, "Gnosticism, Antinomianism, and Reformation Theology," pp. 40-41: "Since the law/gospel distinction is placed in no wider context, but is itself the context into which everything else in theology must be integrated, the grounds for the oppressiveness of the law must be sought in the law itself.... If it is true that the law oppresses simply because of its formal character as ordered demand, then the converse would seem also to

hold: anything with the formal character of ordered demand oppresses. That is to say, anything which proposes some particular ordering of our existence or calls for a determinate response from us will be perceived as being, simply put, the oppressive law from which the gospel delivers us. And since the gospel's liberating character is defined in terms of its antithesis to the law, it will not be our sinful abuse of the law and hostility to the commandment, and God's wrath against us on that account, from which the gospel liberates us. Rather, the gospel will liberate us from the situation of having to hear commandment at all, from having to reckon with any word whatsoever which has the formal character of ordered demand." For Luther — in contrast to neo-Protestantism — this meant two things: first, the insistence that the law continues to be present in the church for Christ's sake (its second use); and second, the insistence that the Decalogue, as remembrance of the law that is written in our hearts, is the way of life for humanity intended by God. As such, it is to be taught to all humans, whether believers or unbelievers. Regarding the first point, see Thesis 2 at the end of chapter 7. Regarding the second point, see George Lindbeck, "Martin Luther and the Rabbinic Mind," in *Understanding the Rabbinic Mind: Essays on the Hermeneutic of Max Kadushin,* ed. Peter Ochs (Atlanta: Scholars Press, 1990), pp. 141-64, esp. 149-55. See also Luther's *Second Disputation against the Antinomians* (1538), in *D. Martin Luthers Werke: Kritische Gesamtausgabe,* ed. J. F. K. Knaake et al. (Weimar: Hermann Böhlaus Nachfolger, 1883ff.), 39/1:454,4-16, hereafter cited as WA. Here Luther claims that the Decalogue, the renovation of that one law written in the hearts of all humans but increasingly forgotten under the condition of sin, has to serve as a visible remembrance of what humans were before Adam's fall and what they yet will be in Christ!

8. For the crucial distinction between "libertas" and "libentia" in Luther's understanding of "freedom," see Robert W. Jenson, "An Ontology of Freedom in the *De Servo Arbitrio* of Luther," *Modern Theology* 10 (1994): 247-52.

9. A short note on the "third," or pedagogical, use of the law might be in order. While I am in agreement with the intention of the third use of the law in its analogical sense, in a univocal framework it is crucial to distinguish between "law" on the one hand and "commandment," "mandate," "torah" on the other. Under the condition of sin, "law" has in its first and second uses an enforcing, restraining, and convicting character — which is not inherent in God's law but is the result of the radical human estrangement from God and God's ways. But as the gestalt of the very way of life with God, which is the embodiment of genuine human freedom, its enforcing, restraining, and convicting character is lost. The "commandment," in distinction from "law" (as Paul Althaus has suggested), embodies the goods constitutive of life in communion with God; it is the *usus practicus evangelii* (in Wilfried Joest's terminology), or the "second use of the gospel" (in William Lazareth's words). To be clearly understood: In this life the struggle between flesh and spirit is not yet over; the estrangement from God is broken "in faith" but not yet fully overcome. Therefore, the *substantive dialectic* between law and gospel still applies to Christians. In our ongoing estrangement from God, God's law restrains and convicts, yet in our reconciliation through Christ in faith God's commandment liberates and informs. Christian freedom receives its distinct gestalt through a way of life according to the commandments: the Decalogue, the Sermon on the Mount, and the double love commandment. With all of this I am basically drawing upon article VI of the *Solid Declaration, Formula of Concord.* For the substantive dialectic between law and gospel that arises from the not yet

complete renewal of the Christian, see p. 588, §§5-8; for the struggle between flesh and spirit, see pp. 588-90, §§8-9, 18; and for God's commandments as the embodiment of Christian freedom, see p. 589, §§10-14. *The Book of Concord: The Confessions of the Evangelical Lutheran Church,* ed. Robert Kolb and Timothy J. Wengert (Minneapolis: Fortress, 2000).

10. In many ways still the clearest and most "successful" account is Joseph Fletcher, *Situation Ethics: The New Morality* (Philadelphia: Westminster, 1974).

11. For a fascinating analysis of these complex problems, see the chapters "Emotivism: Social Content and Social Context," "'Fact,' Explanation and Expertise," and "The Character of Generalizations in Social Science and Their Lack of Predictive Power" in Alasdair MacIntyre, *After Virtue: A Study in Moral Theory,* 2nd ed. (Notre Dame: University of Notre Dame Press, 1984), pp. 23-35, 79-87, 88-108.

12. For three fine accounts of various aspects of its history, see John Mahoney, *The Making of Moral Theology: A Study of the Roman Catholic Tradition* (Oxford: Clarendon, 1987), Servais Pinckaers, OP, *The Sources of Christian Ethics* (Washington, D.C.: Catholic University of America Press, 1995), pp. 191-323, and Donal Dorr, *Option for the Poor: A Hundred Years of Catholic Social Teaching* (Maryknoll: Orbis, 1983; exp. 1992).

13. Immanuel Kant put it the following way: "Autonomy of the will is that property of it by which it is a law to itself independently of any property of objects of volition. Hence the principle of autonomy is: Never choose except in such a way that the maxims of the choice are comprehended in the same volition as a universal law." Immanuel Kant, *Foundations of the Metaphysics of Morals,* trans. with an introduction by L. W. Beck (New York: Liberal Arts, 1959), p. 59.

14. For a fascinating attempt to recover this insight "after modernity," see Karl Barth, *The Holy Spirit and the Christian Life: The Theological Basis of Ethics,* trans. Birch Hoyle (Louisville: Westminster/John Knox, 1993; orig. German 1929; orig. English 1938).

15. Gerhard Forde captures this modern self's self-assertion as "will to power" very well when he writes: "But what is false is that it is always the law that is negated, not the old Adam. The old Adam escapes unscathed and appears on the stage of history as the one who embodies, understands, and eventually carries out the negation. Unnegated themselves, old beings appear now in the role of arch-negators, revolutionaries, the arbiters over the lives and deaths of other beings. The truth, the law, is relative to their vision. Human beings are expendable." Forde, "Christian Life," p. 468.

16. See Immanuel Kant, *Critique of Practical Reason and Other Writings in Moral Philosophy,* trans. and ed. L. W. Beck (Chicago: University of Chicago Press, 1949), pp. 227-34. It is necessary to emphasize Nietzsche's work as a radical critique of the "Kantian Christianity" of the nineteenth century and its way of "saving" God as a transcendental idea of practical reason. For Nietzsche, the rationally justified moral agent of the eighteenth century is also a fiction. See on that especially *The Joyful Wisdom* (1882), §335, close to the end of which Nietzsche writes: "Let us *confine* ourselves, therefore, to the purification of our opinions and appreciations, and to the *construction of new tables of value of our own:* — we will, however, brood no longer over the 'moral worth of our actions'! Yes, my friends! As regards the whole moral twaddle of people about one another, it is time to be disgusted with it! To sit in judgment morally ought to be opposed to our taste! Let us leave this nonsense and this bad taste to those who have nothing else to do, save to drag the past

a little distance further through time, and who are never themselves the present, — consequently to the many, to the majority! We, however, *would seek to become what we are*, — the new, the unique, the incomparable, making laws for ourselves and creating ourselves! And for this purpose we must become the best students and discoverers of all the laws and necessities of the world. We must be *physicists* in order to be *creators* in that sense." Friedrich Nietzsche, *Joyful Wisdom*, trans. Thomas Common (New York: Frederick Ungar, 1960), pp. 262-63.

17. The two main representatives of this school are Jürgen Habermas and Karl-Otto Apel. See among Habermas's numerous works especially *The Philosophical Discourse of Modernity: Twelve Lectures* (Cambridge: MIT Press, 1987) and *Moral Consciousness and Communicative Action* (Cambridge: MIT Press, 1990). The relationship between Habermas's and Apel's "discourse ethics" and theology is quite complex. For fine engagements, criticisms, and constructive ways to draw upon Habermas's and Apel's work, see Don S. Browning and Francis Schüssler Fiorenza, eds., *Habermas, Modernity, and Public Theology* (New York: Crossroad, 1992), especially the essays by Helmut Peukert ("Enlightenment and Theology as Unfinished Projects"), Matthew Lamb ("Communicative Praxis and Theology: Beyond Modern Nihilism and Dogmatism"), and Gary M. Simpson ("Theologia Crucis and the Forensically Fraught World: Engaging Helmut Peukert and Jürgen Habermas").

18. But see Franklin I. Gamwell, *The Divine Good: Modern Moral Theory and the Necessity of God* (New York: HarperCollins, 1990), Glenn Tinder, *The Political Meaning of Christianity: The Prophetic Stance* (New York: HarperCollins, 1991), David Walsh, *After Ideology: Recovering the Spiritual Foundations of Freedom* (New York: HarperCollins, 1990), Václav Havel, *Living in Truth*, ed. Jan Vladislav (London: Faber & Faber, 1987).

19. Karl Barth, *Die Kirchliche Dogmatik* II/2 (Zürich: TVZ, 1942), p. 574. See also Barth, *Epistle to the Romans* (London/New York: Oxford University Press, 1933), pp. 425-526, and "Das Problem der Ethik in der Gegenwart," in Barth, *Das Wort Gottes und die Theologie* (Munich: Kaiser, 1925), pp. 125-55.

20. For Barth's late ethics and its impact on the reading of the whole *Church Dogmatics*, see the excellent study by John Webster, *Barth's Ethics of Reconciliation* (Cambridge: Cambridge University Press, 1995). For Bonhoeffer, see his *Ethics* (New York: Simon & Schuster, 1995), and for a fine exposition of the implications of Bonhoeffer's theology and personal witness for today, see Larry L. Rasmussen (with Renate Bethge), *Dietrich Bonhoeffer — His Significance for North Americans* (Minneapolis: Fortress, 1990), esp. pp. 144-73.

21. See George F. Thomas, *Christian Ethics and Moral Philosophy* (New York: Scribner, 1955), pp. 485-522; Paul Ramsey, *Basic Christian Ethics* (reprinted in the series Library in Theological Ethics, Louisville: Westminster/John Knox, 1993), pp. 191-223, and, most notably, Stanley Hauerwas. Among his numerous books on these topics, see especially *Character and the Christian Life: A Study in Theological Ethics* (San Antonio: Trinity University Press, third printing with new introduction, 1985) and (with Charles Pinches) *Christians among the Virtues: Theological Conversations with Ancient and Modern Ethics* (Notre Dame: University of Notre Dame Press, 1997). From a Lutheran perspective, see Gilbert Meilaender, *The Theory and Practice of Virtue* (Notre Dame: University of Notre Dame Press, 1984). For a good summary and analysis of the "comeback" of the virtues in

philosophical ethics, see Wybo J. Dondorp, *The Rehabilitation of Virtue* (Amsterdam: VU University Press, 1994).

22. I borrow this expression from Charles Taylor, *The Sources of the Self* (Cambridge, Mass.: Harvard University Press, 1989), p. 159. He uses it as a heading for his discussion of John Locke, who is arguably of much greater importance than Kant for the success of individualism and its related concept of freedom in the Anglo-Saxon world.

23. See, among many, Enrique Dussel, *Ethics and the Theology of Liberation* (Maryknoll: Orbis, 1978) and *Ethics and Community* (Maryknoll: Orbis, 1988) and, from a Lutheran perspective, Walter Altmann, *Luther and Liberation: A Latin American Perspective* (Minneapolis: Fortress, 1992).

24. Among many, see Mary McClintock Fulkerson, *Changing the Subject: Women's Discourses and Feminist Theology* (Minneapolis: Fortress, 1994) and, from the angle of political theory and practice, Jean Bethke Elshtain, *Public Man — Private Woman: Women in Social and Political Thought* (Princeton: Princeton University Press, 1981) and *Women and War* (with a new epilogue; Chicago: University of Chicago Press, 1995).

25. For explicitly Lutheran approaches to this recontextualization of the human in creation, see Viggo Mortensen, ed., *Concern for Creation: Voices on the Theology of Creation* (Uppsala: Tro & Tanke/Svenska kyrkan, 1995). Among many others, see Larry L. Rasmussen, *Earth Community, Earth Ethics* (Maryknoll: Orbis, 1996) and Charles Pinches and Jay B. McDaniel, eds., *Good News for Animals? Christian Approaches to Animal Well-Being* (Maryknoll: Orbis, 1993). For doing this recontextualization in an explicitly trinitarian framework, see Jürgen Moltmann, *God in Creation: A New Theology of Creation and the Spirit of God* (Minneapolis: Fortress, 1993).

26. Early indications of this move can be found in the ecclesiology and ethics of Karl Barth, *Church Dogmatics* [*CD*] III/4, §§53, 55.3, and the fragment *The Christian Life*, in *CD* IV/4; Dietrich Bonhoeffer, *Ethics* (New York: Simon & Schuster, 1995), pp. 199ff., 294ff.; and Paul Lehmann, *Ethics in a Christian Context* (New York: Harper & Row, 1967), pp. 45-73. On Paul Lehmann's work, see the recent study by Nancy Duff, *Humanization and the Politics of God: The Koinonia Ethics of Paul Lehmann* (Grand Rapids: Eerdmans, 1992). This approach was developed more strongly in John H. Yoder, *The Politics of Jesus: Vicit Agnus Noster* (Grand Rapids: Eerdmans, 1972), *The Priestly Kingdom: Social Ethics as Gospel* (Notre Dame: University of Notre Dame Press, 1984), and *The Royal Priesthood: Essays Ecclesiological and Ecumenical*, ed. Michael G. Cartwright (Grand Rapids: Eerdmans, 1994); and Stanley Hauerwas, *A Community of Character: Toward a Constructive Social Ethic* (Notre Dame: University of Notre Dame Press, 1981), *The Peaceable Kingdom: A Primer in Christian Ethics* (Notre Dame: University of Notre Dame Press, 1983), *Christian Existence Today: Essays on Church, World, and Living In Between* (Durham: Labyrinth, 1988), and *In Good Company: The Church as Polis* (Notre Dame: University of Notre Dame Press, 1995). For detailed discussions of this new approach to Protestant ethics, see Reinhard Hütter, *Evangelische Ethik als kirchliches Zeugnis* (Neukirchen-Vluyn: Neukirchener Verlag, 1993), Arne Rasmusson, *The Church as Polis* (Notre Dame: University of Notre Dame Press, 1995), and Martin Walton, *Marginal Communities: The Ethical Enterprise of the Followers of Jesus* (Kampen: Kok Pharos, 1994). But see also Timothy F. Sedgwick, *Sacramental Ethics: Paschal Identity and the Christian Life* (Philadelphia: Fortress, 1987), Vigen Guroian, *Ethics after Christendom: Toward an Ecclesial Christian Ethic* (Grand

Rapids: Eerdmans, 1994), Sally Purvis, *The Power of the Cross: Foundations for Christian Feminist Ethic of Community* (Nashville: Abingdon, 1993), and Larry L. Rasmussen, *Moral Fragments and Moral Community: A Proposal for Church in Society* (Minneapolis: Fortress, 1993).

27. Cf. Oswald Bayer, *Freiheit als Antwort: Zur theologischen Ethik* (Tübingen: Mohr, 1995) and Hans G. Ulrich, ed., *Freiheit im Leben mit Gott: Texte zur Tradition evangelischer Ethik* (Gütersloh: Gütersloher Verlagshaus, 1993).

28. Martin Luther, *The Freedom of a Christian* (1520), in *Luther's Works*, ed. Jaroslav Pelikan and Helmut T. Lehmann, American edition, 55 vols. (St. Louis: Concordia; Philadelphia: Fortress, 1955-86), 31:344, hereafter cited as LW; WA 7:21 and 7:49.

29. For a sustained critique of this pervasive but deeply distorted reading of Luther's "two kingdoms doctrine," see Ulrich Duchrow, *Christenheit und Weltverantwortung: Traditionsgeschichte und systematische Struktur der Zweireichelehre* (Stuttgart: Klett Cotta, 1983). For more accessible studies and source collections, see Ulrich Duchrow, ed., *Lutheran Churches — Salt or Mirror of Society? Case Studies on the Theory and Practice of the Two Kingdoms Doctrine* (Geneva: LWF Department of Studies, 1977) and Karl H. Hertz, *Two Kingdoms and One World* (Minneapolis: Augsburg, 1976).

30. Since for Luther this "happy exchange" (Christ's receiving our sin, and our receiving Christ's holiness, righteousness, truthfulness, peacefulness, and freedom) has its root in baptism, the preached word of the gospel received in faith, and the reception of the Lord's Supper, and since for Luther this "happy exchange" constitutes the very root of Christian freedom, we have to conclude that for Luther, Christian freedom is rooted in the very practices of Christian worship. In other words, it is a freedom that is received in and through word and sacrament. This insight has been convincingly developed by Bernd Wannenwetsch, *Gottesdienst als Lebensform: Ethik für Christenbürger* (Stuttgart: Kohlhammer, 1997), pp. 189-90. See also his more accessible essay "The Political Worship of the Church: A Critical and Empowering Practice," *Modern Theology* 12 (1996): 269-99.

31. Luther, *Freedom of a Christian* (1520), LW 31:365-67 (WA 7:64-65).

32. As David Yeago has rightly pointed out to me, the christological pole of Luther's account of Christian freedom is obviously much more protected from the thinness of "Protestantism lite" than I seem to allow in my brief discussion of *The Freedom of a Christian* (1520). For another place where the substantive christological pole in Luther's thought comes to the fore, we might turn to the distinction and relation between Christ as gift and Christ as example in the *Brief Instruction on What to Look For and Expect in the Gospels* (1522). First, the gospel proclamation brings the Christ of the gospels to us as gift: Christ's life is not his own but "for us." But just so, this evangelical *pro me* establishes the reception of the Christ of the gospels as example: here is depicted the very life that has become my own, as an example and paradigm for me. Christian freedom is not tied simply to a general notion of self-giving love but to a concrete and detailed narrative paradigm. In a sense, there is a movement within the christological pole, between gift and example, that parallels the movement I describe between Christian freedom and the remembrance of the commandments. Inherently connected with this, of course, is meditation on the life of Christ. For a detailed account, see Martin Nicol, *Meditation bei Luther* (Göttingen: Vandenhoeck & Ruprecht, 1984).

33. Luther, *Freedom of a Christian* (1520), LW 31:360. The section continues: "Since,

however, we are not wholly recreated, and our faith and love are not yet perfect, these are to be increased, not by external works, however, but of themselves." Cf. WA 7:61.

34. At this point, a short note on my use of "law" and "commandment" might be useful. In a univocal framework, I tend to use the term "commandment" for the form of creaturely freedom both in the state of original grace and "in faith." This form is not static but has an eschatological dynamic in that it stretches between the Decalogue, its beginning, and the Sermon on the Mount, its fulfillment. I reserve the term "law," in its first and second uses (see note 9), for the human encounter with God's will under the condition of sin. In this specific sense "law" has an inherently heteronomous character, because it is resented by humans in their estrangement from God. Since Christians are still involved in the eschatological struggle between flesh and Spirit (Gal 5:17), both "law" and "commandment" apply to their existence, although in different ways. In other words, there is no substantive difference between God's "law" and God's "commandments." The difference is one of reception: *either* under the condition of sin, as encounter with God's will, *or* in communion with God, as the form of freedom. For Luther, a decisive outcome of the eschatological fulfillment of faith in Christ is the *dilectio legis*, the delight in the law, "where the law is not anymore law" (WA 50:565,18-19). It is precisely for this reason that Psalm 119, with its rich and mixed use of "law," "commandment," "mandate," and "torah," stands for Luther at the very center of the Psalter. For an instructive study on the complexity of the usage of "law" in Luther's theology, see Andreas Wöhle, *Luthers Freude an Gottes Gesetz: Eine historische Quellenstudie zur Oszillation des Gesetzesbegriffes Martin Luthers im Licht seiner alttestamentlichen Predigten* (Frankfurt/M: Haag & Herchen, 1998).

35. David S. Yeago, "Martin Luther on Grace, Law, and Moral Life: Prolegomena to an Ecumenical Discussion of *Veritatis Splendor*," *The Thomist* 62 (1998): 180.

36. Martin Luther, *De abroganda missa privata Martini Lutheri sententia* (1521), WA 8:458; Yeago's translation from "Martin Luther on Grace, Law, and Moral Life," p. 189. For a discussion of the third use of the law, see note 9. Luther's way of relating Christ and the law is paralleled in the way the Spirit and the law are related in article VI of the *Solid Declaration, Formula of Concord*. See *Book of Concord*, pp. 589ff.

37. Regarding the interpretation of the Decalogue in Luther as a form of halakah, I am indebted to George Lindbeck's essay, "Martin Luther and the Rabbinic Mind," in *Understanding the Rabbinic Mind*, ed. Ochs.

38. *Book of Concord*, p. 388.

39. Hauerwas, *Peaceable Kingdom*, pp. 30-34.

40. This passage is found in Luther's exposition of the second article of the Creed in his *Large Catechism, Book of Concord*, p. 434.

41. While I do not make explicit reference to them, I assume that analyses of the political, social, and economic life are to a greater or lesser degree always included in any form of ethical reflection and concrete moral deliberation. Yet I do not want to make them an abstractly required element of an ecclesial hermeneutics, because, as we know, these analyses are far from unambiguous. Some are very obvious, some less so, and others are debatable or downright questionable.

42. Here I have in mind Dietrich Bonhoeffer's stressing of the importance of learning to read Scripture *over against* ourselves, instead of *for* ourselves. See Dietrich Bonhoeffer, "The Presentation of New Testament Texts," in Bonhoeffer, *No Rusty Swords:*

Letters, Lectures, and Notes, 1928-1936, ed. with an introduction by Edwin H. Robertson, trans. Robertson and John Bowden (London: Collins, 1970), pp. 302-20. Especially an ongoing ecclesial hermeneutics of the Decalogue and of the Sermon on the Mount will require this self-decentering exercise of reading Scripture over against ourselves. For a broader discussion of these issues, see the suggestive approach in Stephen E. Fowl and L. Gregory Jones, *Reading in Communion: Scripture and Ethics in Christian Life* (Grand Rapids: Eerdmans, 1991).

43. *Book of Concord*, p. 390.

44. Frequently the argument is put forth that the Decalogue does not explicitly articulate the moral obligation to love and serve nonhuman creation. I would answer that an ongoing exegesis and examination of God's commandments very much implies unambiguous directives toward the right stewardship of creation. I am, however, deeply hesitant to entertain the notion of a "moral obligation" toward the nonhuman creation. "Morality" is a constitutive element of the inherently inter-human reality; it is constitutive neither of our *primary* relationship to God nor of our relationship to nonhuman creatures, except insofar as nonhuman creation is again related to other humans, for example, to future generations of human beings. (Concerning our relationship to God, I distinguish between a *constitutive, primary relationship*, God's relationship to us as Creator, which is one of pure passivity from the human side, and a *secondary relationship*, our human vocation as stewards, which is one of responsibility and accountability.) Now, to assume that the absence of a strictly moral obligation implies license is to see the world not as "creation" but as a bunch of "things" for free perusal and disposal, which is the very mode of existence *etsi Deus non daretur*. The Decalogue precisely prohibits this mode of existence: the first commandment identifies all of us as creatures (think of Luther's wonderful exposition of the first commandment in his *Small Catechism*); the third commandment commands the honoring of the Sabbath, which should include all creatures in the resting of creation (see Moltmann, *God in Creation*, pp. 276-96, and especially the interesting reflections of Bernd Wannenwetsch, *Gottesdienst als Lebensform*, pp. 328-38, on the relationship between the scope and limit of human responsibility and the third commandment); the commandment not to steal relates to all future generations; and the last commandment is directed to our coveting, our unchecked desires. The first commandment, I think, also implies a fundamental and radical relationship of accountability to God for all that is dependent upon us, on our care and attention. This is the whole point of being both steward and co-creature. The more that is dependent upon us, the more accountable and responsible we are. Therefore, *in relation to God*, humans, as co-created stewards, are increasingly accountable and responsible for caring for creation: *in relation to our forebears*, we have the obligation not to squander what we have received, and *in relation to future generations*, we have the obligation to pass on what we have received. While humans, as stewards, are undoubtedly responsible *to* God also *for* nonhuman creation, we do not have *a direct moral obligation* to the atmosphere and rivers, the forests and wildlife. Nevertheless, our scope of responsibility *for* them widens with their ever increasing dependence on the rightness or wrongness of our activity. For the ethical implications of this widening of human responsibility, see especially Hans Jonas, *The Imperative of Responsibility: In Search of an Ethics for the Technological Age*, trans. Hans Jonas with coll. of David Herr (Chicago/London: Uni-

versity of Chicago Press, 1984) and William Schweiker, *Responsibility and Christian Ethics* (Cambridge: Cambridge University Press, 1995).

45. The one who most successfully introduced the importance of "vision" for Christian ethics is Stanley Hauerwas. See especially his "The Significance of Vision: Toward an Aesthetic Ethic," in *Vision and Virtue: Essays in Christian Ethical Reflection* (Notre Dame: University of Notre Dame Press, 1981), pp. 30-47.

46. *Book of Concord*, p. 398.

47. For an excellent analysis and theological critique of this captivity of desire and its liberation, see Daniel M. Bell, *Liberation Theology after the End of History: The Refusal to Cease Suffering* (London/New York: Routledge, 2001), esp. pp. 9-35.

48. St. Augustine, *The Confessions*, intr., trans., and notes by Maria Boulding, OSB (Hyde Park, N.Y.: New City, 1997), p. 39. I have deep reservations about the currently fashionable but, I think, essentially misconceived reading of Augustine as, first, denigrating the body and, second, regarding sexuality as a post-fall phenomenon. Concerning the first issue, see the differentiated and nuanced account given by Margaret Miles in her books *Augustine on the Body* (Missoula: Scholars Press, 1979) and *Fullness of Life: Historical Foundations for a New Asceticism* (Philadelphia: Westminster, 1981), pp. 62-78, and by Jean Bethke Elshtain, *Augustine and the Limits of Politics* (Notre Dame: University of Notre Dame Press, 1995). Augustine actually liked to unmask the hypocrisy behind the claim, common in late antiquity, that the body was to be despised: "Neither does anyone hate his own body. For the apostle truly said, 'No one ever hated his own flesh.' And when some say that they would rather be without a body altogether, they entirely deceive themselves. For it is not their body but its heaviness and corruption which they hate. And so it is not no body, but an uncorrupted and very light body that they want." Augustine, *De doctrina christiana* 1.24.24. Concerning the second issue, Augustine assumed that sexual intercourse inherently belonged to human life in paradise (*City of God* 14.26) but that after the fall sexuality became disjunctive and incongruent with reason. For a differentiated discussion of Augustine's views, including his increasingly harsher views regarding "fallen sexuality" close to the end of his life, see Miles, *Augustine on the Body*, pp. 70-77.

49. See the interesting gestures toward a "new asceticism" in Miles, *Fullness of Life*.

50. For how seriously Luther took covetousness and how much it mattered in his anthropology and economic ethics, see the study of Ricardo Rieth, *"Habsucht" bei Martin Luther: Ökonomisches und theologisches Denken, Tradition und soziale Wirklichkeit im Zeitalter der Reformation* (Weimar: Verlag Hermann Böhlaus Nachfolger, 1996), especially the discussion of covetousness in the catechisms, pp. 98-101.

51. Yet the first commandment's fulfillment in faith has its own distinct practice, which is thematized in the third commandment — the Sabbath sanctification! See Wannenwetsch, *Gottesdienst als Lebensform*, pp. 328ff.

52. Scripture quotations are from the New Revised Standard Version (NRSV).

53. Dietrich Bonhoeffer begins the first fragment of his *Ethics* (ed. Eberhard Bethge, trans. Neville Horton Smith [New York: Simon & Schuster, 1995], pp. 21-22) with this startling insight into the radical nature of Christian ethics, which precisely presupposes Luther's "back in paradise" of Christian freedom: "The knowledge of good and evil seems to be the aim of all ethical reflection. The first task of Christian ethics is to invalidate this knowledge.... Already in the possibility of the knowledge of good and evil Christian eth-

ics discerns a falling away from the origin. Man at his origin knows only one thing: God. It is only in the unity of this knowledge of God that he knows of other men, of things, and of himself. He knows all things only in God, and God in all things. The knowledge of good and evil shows that he is no longer at one with this origin. In the knowledge of good and evil man does not understand himself in the reality of the destiny appointed in his origin, but rather in his own possibilities, his possibility of being good or evil. . . . The knowledge of good and evil is therefore separation from God. Only against God can man know good and evil."

54. The idea that the natural law is something "at hand" to be read from the structure of our rationality or the structure of our human nature is a modern phenomenon. For that reason "natural law" has been taken in modern times as an account of how to reach moral agreement that is neutral with respect to different worldviews and basic beliefs; it has been seen as an ethical methodology that transcends particularities. Yet for theologians such as Augustine, Aquinas, and Luther, albeit to different degrees, it is precisely *sub conditione peccati* that the natural law is decisively weakened. Russell Hittinger points to Aquinas's affirmation in a series of Lenten conferences in 1273: "Now although God in creating man gave him this law of nature, the devil oversowed another law in man, namely, the law of concupiscence. . . . Since the law of nature was destroyed by concupiscence, man needed to be brought back to works of virtue, and to be drawn away from vice: for which purpose he needed the written law." Russell Hittinger, *The First Grace: Rediscovering the Natural Law in a Post-Christian World* (Wilmington, Del.: ISI Books, 2003), p. 11. Thus for Aquinas, the point of the "old law" is to provide a *training* in the natural law, which is precisely not simply available to human reason. Pamela Hall puts Aquinas's view succinctly: "We must learn (or relearn) the natural law because sin obscures our understanding of it and of our end; at the same time, we discover that we cannot do what we know to be good. The work of the Old Law is to teach us the natural law." Pamela Hall, *Narrative and the Natural Law: An Interpretation of Thomistic Ethics* (Notre Dame: University of Notre Dame Press, 1994), p. 48. These key elements of a *theology of natural law* are the ones that have been eclipsed in the modern era. "Natural law" is no longer something essentially lost, something to be remembered under the guidance and tutorship of God's commandments; rather, it has come to be thought of as simply "at hand," as the self-evident principles of practical reason, inherently accessible to every human agent per se. This is why the project of modernity entertained the hope of reaching a societal consensus on moral matters irrespective of particular religious convictions. Yet neither Aquinas's nor — as we will see a bit further down — Luther's *theological* doctrine of natural law as such was intended to tell us much about "how" to reach moral agreement with non-Christians. For both, such agreement is not reached a priori, at the universal level, but in and through all kinds of ad hoc discussions of particular issues in positive law.

55. For a good introduction, see *Catechism of the Catholic Church*, ##1776-1802.

56. To be sure, the traditional Roman Catholic concept of conscience is also fundamentally an address by God. But when we listen to *Gaudium et Spes* (article 16), we get the impression that God's voice is somewhat unclear and distant — yet somehow genuinely "at hand": "His conscience is man's most secret core and his sanctuary. There he is alone with God whose voice echoes in his depths." Not so for Luther. Our estrangement from God has turned our conscience into a deeply ambiguous reality. It tends to frighten us, to

make the world close in on us, because, as Gerhard Forde aptly says, "It does not represent God's presence within us, it represents his absence, that we are left to ourselves." Forde, "Christian Life," p. 417.

57. Forde, "Christian Life," p. 417.

58. Precisely because of our essentially frightened conscience, the world tends to close in on us, to become "too small," as Luther described it, drawing upon the "rustling leaf" of Lev 26:36: "There is nothing smaller and more ignored than a dry leaf lying on the ground crawled on by worms and unable to protect itself from the dust. . . . But when the moment comes, horse, rider, lance, armor, king, princes, all the strength of the army and all power is frightened by its rustling. Are we not fine people? We have no fear of God's wrath and stand proudly, but yet are terrified and flee before the wrath of an impotent dry leaf. And such rustling of the leaf makes the world too small and becomes our wrathful God, whom we otherwise pooh-pooh and defy in heaven and on earth." Martin Luther, WA 19:126,16ff.; Forde's translation from "Christian Life," p. 418.

59. An assumption strongly visible, for example, in Philipp Melanchthon's work.

60. See, for example, the material content of Immanuel Kant, *Metaphysics of Morals*, trans. and ed. Mary Gregor with an introduction by Roger J. Sullivan (Cambridge/New York: Cambridge University Press, 1996).

61. Luther can say extremely positive things about the power of human reason, used in its proper limits. We might think especially of the positive role of reason in Luther's *Disputatio de homine* (1536), theses 4-6. Yet Luther does not assume that humans are able to act freely and well simply on the grounds of the insights of reason itself (see *Disp. de hom.* 18; 25-27. For a more detailed discussion of this topic, see Gerhard Ebeling, *Lutherstudien*, vol. 2, *Disputatio de homine*, pt. 2 [Tübingen: Mohr, 1982], pp. 263-77). The most telling evidence of Luther's basic assumption of reason wounded by our sinful desires, habits, and practices is found, of all places, in a manual for the Christian prince, his *Commentary on Psalm 101* (1534): "This is not to condemn or reject law, sound reason, or Holy Scripture but rather the miserable admixture of the filth of our arrogance — the fact that we do not begin such a plan and proceeding with the fear of God and with a humble, earnest prayer, just as if it were enough to have a right and proper proposal and the intention to convert this plan into action speedily according to one's own ability. To do this is to despise God and to seek glory for yourself as the man who can do it. It is contrary to the First Commandment. Therefore such an admixture changes the best law into the greatest injustice, the finest reason into the greatest folly, and the Holy Scripture into the greatest error. For if the First Commandment is missing and does not give light, then none of the others will give proper light, and the understanding will be entirely faulty." Martin Luther, *Commentary on Psalm 101* (1534), LW 13:152-53.

62. In his *Commentary on Psalm 101* (1534), Luther also addresses the question of the natural law. For Luther, the natural law is not an abstract a priori "inherent in all heads that resemble human heads" (LW 13:161). Rather, it is attained through contingent insights gained by particular people in particular historical circumstances. These depend, first, on natural gifts granted contingently by God's providence and, second, on virtues and skills acquired through particular education and practices. Persons in whom these gifts, virtues, and skills coincide in an extraordinary way that results in significant historical deeds and achievements Luther calls "heroes." Now and then God sends a hero, someone who just

"knows how" to get human society in some respect or other to work as it should. Yet this designation is primarily a way for Luther to account for exceptional moral character and political genius. According to Luther, most of our access to the natural law comes by way of the inevitable messiness of the life of the human community. "The world is indeed a sick thing; it is the kind of fur on which neither hide nor hair is any good. The healthy heroes are rare, and God provides them at a dear price. Still the world must be ruled, if men are not to become wild beasts. So things in the world in general remain mere patchwork and beggary. . . . So here one must patch and darn and help oneself with the laws, sayings, and examples of the heroes as they are recorded in books. . . . Yet we never do it as well as it is written there; we crawl after it and cling to it as to a bench or to a cane. In addition, we also follow the advice of the best people who live in our midst" (LW 13:164). Now, while Luther's main concern is obviously the practical matter of governing lawfully under predemocratic conditions, his basic insight into the moral phenomenon of the "hero" still makes sense, as long as it is not misunderstood as an *Übermensch* who stands above God's law.

63. Stanley Hauerwas, "The Truth about God: The Decalogue as Condition for Truthful Speech," in *Sanctify Them in the Truth: Holiness Exemplified* (Nashville: Abingdon, 1998), p. 45.

64. Luther, WA 50:659-60; cf. Oswald Bayer, *Theologie* (Gütersloh: Gütersloher Verlagshaus, 1994), pp. 61ff.

Notes to Chapter 9

1. Martin Luther, *The Large Catechism*, in *The Book of Concord: The Confessions of the Evangelical Lutheran Church*, ed. Robert Kolb and Timothy J. Wengert (Minneapolis: Fortress, 2000), p. 425; *Die Bekenntnisschriften der evangelisch-lutherischen Kirche* [*BSLK*], Hrsg. im Gedenkjahr der Augsburgischen Konfession 1930, 8th ed. (Göttingen: Vandenhoeck & Ruprecht, 1979), p. 633.

2. There is probably no theologian who has probed the theological nature of human speech and its trinitarian root in the relationship between the Father and the Logos more profoundly and more rigorously than St. Augustine in his two treatises on lying. For what is debatably the best treatment of St. Augustine and simultaneously the most rigorously argued work, philosophically and theologically, on lying, see Paul Griffiths, *Lying: An Augustinian Theology of Duplicity* (Grand Rapids: Brazos, 2004).

3. See Thomas Aquinas, *Summa theologiae* II-II.110.1.

4. John Calvin, *John Calvin's Sermons on the Ten Commandments*, trans. Benjamin Farley (Grand Rapids: Baker, 1980), p. 216.

5. For the best recent treatment of this discussion in the middle of a clear and concise discussion of the whole spectrum of lying, see Sissela Bok, *Lying: Moral Choice in Public and Private Life* (New York: Vintage, 1989), pp. 32-56.

6. Scripture quotations are from the New Revised Standard Version (NRSV).

7. Aquinas, *Summa theologiae* II-II.110.1 corp.

8. See René Girard, *The Scapegoat*, trans. Yvonne Freccero (Baltimore: Johns

Hopkins University Press, 1986) and Girard, *The Girard Reader,* ed. James G. Williams (New York: Crossroad, 1996).

9. Friedrich Nietzsche, "On Truth and Lies in a Nonmoral Sense," in Nietzsche, *Philosophy and Truth: Selections from Nietzsche's Notebooks of the Early 1870's,* trans. and ed. Daniel Breazeale (Atlantic Highlands, N.J.: Humanities, 1979), p. 84.

10. Friedrich Nietzsche, *The Will to Power,* trans. Walter Kaufmann and R. J. Hollingdale (New York: Vintage, 1968), aphorism 495.

11. As did William H. Lazareth and Wilfried Joest. See William H. Lazareth, *Christians in Society: Luther, the Bible, and Social Ethics* (Minneapolis: Fortress, 2001), p. 206 and ch. 8, pp. 199-234; Wilfried Joest, *Gesetz und Freiheit: Das Problem des Tertius Usus Legis bei Luther und die neutestamentliche Parainese,* 2nd ed. (Göttingen: Vandenhoeck & Ruprecht, 1956), pp. 45-55.

12. I am drawing, via the title of Stanley Hauerwas's Gifford Lectures, *With the Grain of the Universe,* on an expression of John Howard Yoder. However, unlike Yoder and Hauerwas, with this phrase I refer specifically to the way the Decalogue's first voice functions as the revealed divine reminder, *post lapsum,* of the natural law, which is the rational creature's participation in the eternal law.

13. Aristotle, *Nicomachean Ethics* 4, cap. 3 (referred to by Aquinas, *Summa theologiae* II-II.110.3 corp.) and Sallust, *Bellum Catilinae* 10.6-7 (referred to by Augustine, *Enchiridion* 18).

14. For a notable Czech example of the eighth commandment's first voice, see Václav Havel, *Living in Truth,* ed. Jan Vladislav (London/Boston: Faber & Faber, 1987).

15. Luther, *Large Catechism, Book of Concord,* p. 424; *BSLK,* p. 632.

16. Luther, *Large Catechism, Book of Concord,* p. 425; *BSLK,* p. 633.

17. Paul Griffiths, "The Gift and the Lie: Augustine on Lying," *Communio: International Catholic Review* 26 (1999): 3-30; 30.

18. Stanley M. Hauerwas and William H. Willimon, *The Truth about God: The Ten Commandments in Christian Life* (Nashville: Abingdon, 1999), p. 128.

Notes to Chapter 10

1. The widespread opposition to the *Joint Declaration on the Doctrine of Justification* by many Protestant university professors in Germany is indicative of deep concern about a pervasive loss of identity — heightened, no doubt, by insinuations of a "return-to-Rome ecumenism" operative behind this particular ecumenical effort. For the text of the declaration, see Lutheran World Federation and the Roman Catholic Church, *Joint Declaration on the Doctrine of Justification* (Grand Rapids: Eerdmans, 2000). For an excellent theological discussion of this document, see in *Pro Ecclesia* 7 (1998) the Lutheran and Roman Catholic statements by Robert W. Jenson, David S. Yeago, J. A. DiNoia, OP, and Susan K. Wood, pp. 401-26, and the full-length essays by R. R. Reno ("The Joint Declaration on the Doctrine of Justification: An Outsider's View," pp. 427-48) and David S. Yeago ("Lutheran–Roman Catholic Consensus on Justification: The Theological Achievement of the Joint Declaration," pp. 449-70). Most recently, see the important volume edited by William G. Rusch,

Justification and the Future of the Ecumenical Movement: The Joint Declaration on the Doctrine of Justification (Collegeville, Minn.: Liturgical Press, 2003).

2. At the same time, this encyclical may be understood as the culmination, after thirty years of bilateral dialogues, of the Vatican II decree on ecumenism, *Unitatis Redintegratio*.

3. For the first significant reaction to this theme, see the Catholic and Protestant contributions in *Catholica* 2 (1996), which was published as a monograph under the title *Das Papstamt: Anspruch und Widerspruch: Zum Stand des ökumenischen Dialogs über das Papstamt*, ed. Johann-Adam-Möhler-Institut (Münster: Aschendorff, 1996).

4. John Paul II, *Ut Unum Sint/That They May Be One* [*UUS*] 1. Quoted from the English edition *The Encyclical Letter Ut Unum Sint of the Holy Father John Paul II on Commitment to Ecumenism*, Publication No. 5-050 (Vatican City: Libreria Editrice Vaticana; Washington, D.C.: United States Catholic Conference, 1995).

5. "To believe in Christ means to desire unity; to desire unity means to desire the Church; to desire the Church means to desire the communion of grace which corresponds to the Father's plan from all eternity. Such is the meaning of Christ's prayer: 'Ut unum sint' [That they may be one]" (*UUS* 9).

6. The encyclical quotes here *Lumen Gentium* 8, which contains the famous "subsistit" that replaces the "est" (the Catholic church "is" Jesus Christ's Church) from Pius XII's encyclical *Mystici Corporis Christi* (1943): "Haec ecclesia, in hoc mundo ut societas constituta et ordinata, subsistit in ecclesia catholica, a successore Petri et episcopis in eius communione gubernata, licet extra eius compaginem elementa plura sanctificationis et veritatis inveniantur, quae ut dona ecclesiae Christi propria, ad unitatem catholicam impellunt" ["This church, set up and organised in this world as a society, subsists in the catholic church, governed by the successor of Peter and the bishops in communion with him, although outside its structure many elements of sanctification and of truth are to be found which, as proper gifts to the church of Christ, impel toward catholic unity"]. Norman P. Tanner, SJ, ed., *Decrees of the Ecumenical Councils*, vol. 2 (Washington, D.C.: Georgetown University Press, 1990), p. 854. This "subsistit," expressing a subtle self-relativization, was undoubtedly the most decisive ecumenical breakthrough of Vatican II. Unsurprisingly, the intra-Catholic struggles after Vatican II included persistent conflicts as to how exactly to interpret the "subsistit," that is, in a maximalist sense, as virtually a synonym for "est," or in a minimalist sense, as simply "exists," leaving completely open the question of where else Christ's church also subsists.

7. Here the encyclical quotes from Vatican II's Decree on Ecumenism, *Unitatis Redintegratio* 3. Cf. *Decrees of the Ecumenical Councils*, ed. Tanner, vol. 2, pp. 909ff.

8. Here the mutual official recognition of baptism is mentioned, as well as the World Council of Churches, the liturgical reform on both Catholic and Protestant sides, the ecumenical Bible translations, and, finally, the growing kinship in practical and social witness.

9. Cf. the significance that is rightly attributed to these dialogues with regard to the discussion of the papal office by Burkhard Neumann, "Das Papstamt in den offiziellen ökumenischen Dialogen," *Catholica* 2 (1996): 87-120; 87-97.

10. "This whole lesson of the Gospel must be constantly read anew, so that the exer-

cise of the Petrine ministry may lose nothing of its authenticity and transparency" (*UUS* 93).

11. Interesting and worthy of mention is that St. Cyprian represents an important reference point for Melanchthon and Luther in their controversy with the papacy of their time. Melanchthon uses a quote from Cyprian as proof of the ancient church's collegial practice of the ordination of a bishop without explicit or implicit direction of the Roman bishop. Philipp Melanchthon, *Treatise on the Power and Primacy of the Pope* (1537), in *The Book of Concord: The Confessions of the Evangelical Lutheran Church,* ed. Robert Kolb and Timothy J. Wengert (Minneapolis: Fortress, 2000), p. 332, §§14-15. Luther, in the *Smalcald Articles* (1537), also refers briefly to St. Cyprian and his understanding of the collegial and brotherly relationship of all bishops one to another, in contrast to the papal monarchism of his time, which he condemned. *Book of Concord,* p. 307, §2.

12. See on this point the observation of the Catholic theologian Wolfgang Klausnitzer, "Der Papst . . . ist zweifelsohne das größte Hindernis auf dem Weg der Ökumene (Paul VI). Ist-Stand der theologischen Diskussion und Perspektiven einer Lösung in ökumenischer Absicht," *Catholica* 2 (1996): 193-209; 196: "While the other churches are on the *search* for a model of unity, the Catholic church claims to *possess* this unity — and indeed by authority of and under the form of a divine imperative. This claim, even when it is made moderately, actually becomes an impediment in each ecumenical dialogue in which the Catholic church is a partner, because it negates the fundamental premise of these dialogues: namely, that the partners negotiate 'par cum pari' (*Unitatis Redintegratio,* 9)."

13. Quoted from Pope Paul VI in his 1967 address to the annual assembly of moderators, members, and consultants to the secretariat for Christian Unity; *Acta Apostolicae Sedis* LIX (1967), p. 498.

14. Cf. the Roman Catholic theologian Wolfgang Klausnitzer: "The actual content of the primacy of jurisdiction remains the main problem for the ecumenical dialogues even today. The demands of the non-Catholic dialogue partners — for a renewed papacy under the Gospel, for the practice of the papacy in accordance with the Gospel, for an exercise of the primacy that respects the freedom of faith and the traditions of other Christians — signal the deep malaise and fears of an unlimited primacy of jurisdiction. A solution appears to me to be possible only if 'Rome,' in a legally binding fashion, limits itself in the legal shape of the primacy, that is, if 'Rome' renounces power. That would be profoundly in keeping with the New Testament." Klausnitzer, "Der Papst," p. 202.

15. See *Dei Verbum* 10, the expressed subordination of the magisterium to the word of God — albeit not to Scripture alone: "The task of authentically interpreting the word of God, whether in its written form or in that of tradition, has been entrusted only to those charged with the church's ongoing teaching function, whose authority is exercised in the name of Jesus Christ. This teaching function is not above the word of God but stands at its service, teaching nothing but what is handed down, according as it devotedly listens, reverently preserves and faithfully transmits the word of God, by divine command and with the help of the Holy Spirit." *Decrees of the Ecumenical Councils,* ed. Tanner, vol. 2, p. 975.

16. See Ulrich Kühn, "Papsttum und Petrusdienst — Evangelische Kritik und Möglichkeiten aus der Sicht reformatorischer Theologie," *Catholica* 2 (1996): 181-92; 183-84.

17. See Robert W. Jenson, *Unbaptized God: The Basic Flaw in Ecumenical Theology* (Minneapolis: Fortress, 1992), pp. 6ff.

18. See, for example, the two Catholic theologians Heinrich Fries and Karl Rahner, who in 1983, in the framework of the "Rahner-Fries Plan," drafted a model according to which the pope should reduce his legal powers through particular legal stipulations "iure humano" and so eliminate the basis of the non-Catholic fears of an absolute jurisdictional primacy in the case of a reunification. Heinrich Fries and Karl Rahner, eds., *Unity of the Churches — an Actual Possibility*, trans. Ruth C. L. Gritsch and Eric W. Gritsch (Philadelphia: Fortress; New York: Paulist, 1985), pp. 83-91.

19. See Ulrich Kühn, "Papsttum und Petrusdienst," pp. 190-91: "As a rule, the bearer of personal responsibility for all on a regional level is primarily the bishop. . . . A corresponding ministry on a universal level would then be conceivable. In this sense, it is possible to speak of an evangelical understanding of the sensibility, indeed the necessity, of a ministry of Peter for the whole church. It would be his task to see to it that the universal church remains in the apostolic truth, as well as full communion of the churches worldwide, and just so, to encourage the local and regional churches in contemporary faith, proclamation, and service (cf. Luke 22:32). In this sense, he would have a pastoral responsibility with respect to all churches and would at the same time be their representative and 'spokesman' both inwardly and outwardly." See also Wolfhart Pannenberg, *Systematic Theology*, trans. Geoffrey W. Bromiley, vol. 3 (Grand Rapids: Eerdmans, 1998), pp. 420-31.

20. The complete postscript reads: "I, Philip Melanthon [*sic*], regard the above articles as true and Christian. However, concerning the pope I maintain that if he would allow the gospel, we, too, may (for the sake of peace and general unity among those Christians who are now under him and might be in the future) grant to him his superiority over the bishops which he has 'by human right.'" *Book of Concord*, p. 326.

21. It seems important at this point to recall the voices in the ecumenical dialogue that indicate that the distinction between *ius divinum* and *ius humanum* is, to be sure, of central theological significance but that at the same time remind us that the *ius humanum* within the church must itself be considered theologically, that is, as related to the *ius divinum*. For a brief treatment, see Gunther Wenz, "Papsttum und kirchlicher Einheitsdienst nach Maßgabe evangelisch-lutherischer Bekenntnistradition," *Catholica* 2 (1996): 144-63, 155-62; 158-59: "Namely, insofar as the function of the ministry of unity which is perceptible in the organizational structure of the ordained ministry is inherent to the office of the church by divine right, then the multidimensional external arrangement of this function of the ministry of unity is no mere ecclesiological externality and in this sense, no mere human striving, but a divinely commanded human work. It follows from that context that the *ius humanum* is not exclusively extrinsic to the *ius divinum*, but rather is to be considered as that which, relatively speaking, belongs to it, so that the relationship between divine law and human law corresponds to the relationship between the justifying act of God, as faith perceives it, and that good human work which proceeds from faith." See also Avery Dulles and George Lindbeck, "Bishops and the Ministry of the Gospel," in *Confessing One Faith: A Joint Commentary on the Augsburg Confession by Lutheran and Catholic Theologians*, ed. George Wolfgang Forell and James McCue (Minneapolis: Augsburg, 1982), pp. 147-72; 166: "[A]lthough the differentiation of the ministry into presbyterial and episcopal offices is an historical structure arising from 'human authority' (according to Apol.

14,2), yet the guidance of God's Spirit can be seen in its development. Thus, the historic episcopate is, on the one hand, a human order, but it is also at the same time more than that." See also the report of the joint Roman Catholic–Evangelical Lutheran Commission "Das geistliche Amt in der Kirche" (Geneva, 1981) 65: "Over against all historical self-developments, it remains that the Lutheran Reformation, presuming the right preaching of the Gospel, affirms and intends to maintain the historical continuity of church order as expression of the unity of the apostolic church through the peoples and ages. For the sake of faith in the permanence of the church, this intention must be steadfastly adhered to, in view of antithetical historical developments. This is expressly emphasized in the basic declarations of the Augsburg Confession as well as in the Confession's frequent use of the Church Fathers of all eras."

22. This concerns the question of the status of the "ministry of Peter" in a collegially/synodically constituted church administration. See Wenz, "Papsttum und kirchlicher Einheitsdienst," pp. 155-62.

23. See as an introduction to this topic Pannenberg, *Systematic Theology*, vol. 3, pp. 115-28.

24. See on this theme Oscar Cullmann, *Unity through Diversity: Its Foundation, and a Contribution to the Discussion concerning the Possibilities of Its Actualization*, trans. M. Eugene Boring (Philadelphia: Fortress, 1988) and, especially, Wolfgang Klausnitzer's remarks regarding how the model of the ancient church as a pentarchy could be implemented with a plurality of regional churches (previously separated church bodies): "The common denominator of this model of church unity and the model of pentarchy is this: that the former church bodies remained autocephalic, each with its own patriarchal structure, whereby each 'patriarch' had precisely the task of preserving and safeguarding the Christian traditions and the specific peculiarities of the former church bodies. The difference lay in that precisely because of this diversity among the former confessional churches, the newly established autocephalic partner churches were not similar in many other elements. This dissimilarity or variation in unity could extend to the patriarchal vertex, which for example could be conceived synodically or collegially in certain partner churches." Klausnitzer, "Der Papst," p. 207.

25. As Martin Luther says in the *Smalcald Articles* (1537) II.4,1: "The pope is not the head of all Christendom by divine right or according to God's Word, for this position belongs only to one, namely, to Jesus Christ. The pope is only the bishop and pastor of the churches in Rome. . . ." See also Wolfhart Pannenberg's justified critique: "We should not call the holder of such an office the head (*caput*, DS, 3055, 3059, etc.) of the church or the foundation of its unity (LG 18), for the NT uses such terms specifically and exclusively for Jesus Christ (1 Cor. 11:3-4; Eph. 1:22; 4:15; cf. 5:23; Col. 1:18; 2:10). Their use for the Roman bishop has always been an occasion for justifiable offense. It would be fully sufficient if his office were truly a sign of the unity of all Christianity, not a cause and sign of its divisions." Pannenberg, *Systematic Theology*, vol. 3, p. 430 n. 1014.

26. In spite of the extremely polemical character of his theses *Propositiones adversus totam synagogam Sathanae et universas portas inferorum* (1530), Martin Luther establishes in thesis 15: "ecclesia vera est numerus seu collectio baptizatorum et credentium sub uno pastore, sive sit unius civitatis sive totius provinciae, sive totius orbis." Martin Luther, *D. Martin Luthers Werke: Kritische Gesamtausgabe*, ed. J. F. K. Knaake et al. (Weimar:

Hermann Böhlaus Nachfolger, 1883ff.), 30/2:421,19-21, hereafter cited as WA. This thesis confirms the verdict of Gerhard Müller that Luther "well into his later years [remained] of the opinion that the church should be episcopally constituted." Gerhard Müller, *Causa Reformationis: Beiträge zur Reformationsgeschichte und zur Theologie Luthers* (Gütersloh: Gütersloher Verlagshaus, 1989), p. 415. Moreover, the definition of the church in Luther's thesis implies a pastoral ministry of Peter on a universal level as the extension of the one ordained office. There proceeds from this thesis, however, a critical light upon the following assertion of Gunther Wenz: "To be sure, the ministry of unity, which constitutes the primary obligation of all church leadership, belongs inseparably to the essence of the church because it is founded upon her task of Gospel proclamation itself. Although the shape of this ministry, which extends beyond the association of the ordained ministry with the concrete worshipping congregation, is a task of inalienable historical necessity, it is precisely for that reason bound to no 'timeless' or invariable form." Wenz, "Papsttum und kirchlicher Einheitsdienst," pp. 160-61. In contrast to Wenz's interpretation, it seems to me that Luther's thesis has a stronger normative implication, particularly regarding the personal character of the universal ministry of unity.

27. The report of the joint Evangelical Lutheran–Roman Catholic Study Commission, "Das Evangelium und die Kirche," 1972 ("Malta Report") 66, the U.S. dialogue *Papal Primacy and the Universal Church*, ed. Paul C. Empie and T. Austin Murphy, Lutherans and Catholics in Dialogue 5 (Minneapolis: Augsburg, 1974), pp. 21ff., and the report of the joint Roman Catholic–Evangelical Lutheran Commission "Das geistliche Amt in der Kirche" (Geneva, 1981) 73 already point in this direction: "To be sure, the controversies handed down have not yet been fully cleared up; however, it can be said that if the question concerns the ministry of unity on a universal level, the view today, even for Lutheran theology, is directed not only to a future council or to the responsibility of theology, but also a particular office of Peter. Theologically, there is still much that is open, above all, how this universal task can be perceived to be in service to truth and unity: by means of an ecumenical council, by means of a ministerium, by means of one single bishop respected throughout all of Christendom. In various dialogues, however, there is sketched out the possibility that the office of Peter held by the Bishop of Rome as a visible sign of the unity of the whole church does not need to be excluded by Lutherans, 'insofar as, through theological reinterpretation and practical restructuring, it is subordinated to the primacy of the Gospel.'"

28. Martin Luther, WA 40/1:181; *Luther's Works*, ed. Jaroslav Pelikan and Helmut T. Lehmann, American edition, 55 vols. (St. Louis: Concordia; Philadelphia: Fortress, 1955-86), 26:99. On Luther's complex position on the papacy of his time and the office of pope as such, see the instructive essay by Gerhard Müller, "Martin Luther und das Papsttum," in Müller, *Causa Reformationis*, pp. 388-416. Müller summarizes a possible recognition of the office of the pope from Luther's perspective in the following way: "One would have to circumscribe the possible recognition of a papal primacy from Luther's side with the term 'primacy of servanthood ministry' instead of 'primacy of dominion'" (p. 414).

Notes to Chapter 11

1. Because of particular issues in the official German and English translations of *Fides et Ratio* [*FR*], I will draw primarily upon the official Latin text and refer to the German and English versions only at those points where they either clarify or obscure a particular thrust of the Latin text. Quotations in German are from Papst Johannes Paul II, *Enzyklika Glaube und Vernuft, Fides et Ratio (amtliche vatikanische Fassung)* (Stein am Rhein: Christiana-Verlag, 1998). Quotations in English are from John Paul II, *On the Relationship between Faith and Reason: Fides et Ratio*, Publication No. 5-302 (Washington, D.C.: United States Catholic Conference, 1998). On the quality of the English translation, see the telling comments by Fergus Kerr, OP, in *New Blackfriars* 81 (2000): 358. The official Latin text is to be found at www.vatican.va/holy_father/j...enc_15101998_fides-et-ratio_lt.html.

2. See "A Symposium on Pope John Paul II's *Fides et Ratio*," *Communio* 26 (1999): 455-661.

3. See Martin Bieler, "The Future of the Philosophy of Being," *Communio* 26 (1999): 455-85, and Gregor Maria Hoff, "Die Grenzen des Denkbaren: Überlegungen zum Glaubenszugang im Anschluss an 'Fides et ratio,'" *Internationale katholische Zeitschrift Communio* 29 (2000): 451-61.

4. See Cyril O'Regan, "Ambiguity and Undecidability in *Fides et Ratio*," *International Journal of Systematic Theology* 2 (2000): 319-29, and John Webster, "'*Fides et Ratio*,' Articles 64-79," *New Blackfriars* 81 (2000): 68-76, Thomas Weinandy, "*Fides et Ratio*: A Response to John Webster," pp. 225-35, and Webster, "Reply to Tom Weinandy," pp. 236-37.

5. Exploring the relationship between freedom and truth raises the question of how the two most conceptually invested encyclicals of John Paul II, *Veritatis Splendor* and *Fides et Ratio*, interrelate. While this question is important for understanding *Fides et Ratio*, I will not pursue it here. On this specific matter, see Livio Melina, "The 'Truth about the Good': Practical Reason, Philosophical Ethics, and Moral Theology," *Communio* 26 (1999): 640-61, and on the relationship between freedom and truth, see Hans Urs von Balthasar, *Theo-Logic: Theological Logical Theory*, vol. 1, *Truth of the World*, trans. Adrian J. Walker (San Francisco: Ignatius, 2000), pp. 79-130.

6. See Karl Barth, *Anselm: Fides Quaerens Intellectum: Anselm's Proof of the Existence of God in the Context of His Theological Scheme*, trans. Ian W. Robertson (London: SCM, 1960).

7. See on this dynamic the pathbreaking work by Michael Polanyi, *Personal Knowledge: Towards a Post-Critical Philosophy* (Chicago: University of Chicago Press, 1958). Polanyi offers a condensed and accessible account in his "Faith and Reason," *Communio* 28 (2001): 860-74.

8. To quote the felicitous title of the new translation of the encyclical edited by Laurence Paul Hemming and Susan Frank Parsons, *Restoring Faith in Reason: A New Translation of the Encyclical Letter Faith and Reason of Pope John Paul II Together with a Commentary and Discussion* (London: SCM, 2002).

9. The Holy Spirit is the creator of the new life that is given to believers. Hence, as Wolfhart Pannenberg rightly puts it: "Without losing their distinction from God, creatures receive through him a share in the life of God himself." Wolfhart Pannenberg, *Systematic Theology*, vol. 3 (Grand Rapids/Edinburgh: Eerdmans, 1998), p. 554.

10. My reading of the "coniunctio" in *FR* 48.

11. "Dicitur, in primis, fidem esse oboedientiae responsionem Deo" (*FR* 13).

12. "Id poscit ut Ille sua agnoscatur in divinitate, sua in transcendentia supremaque libertate" (*FR* 13). *Agnosco* carries the double connotation of "coming to know something as true" and "acknowledging something or someone in what we have come to know of it or him/her."

13. As did, e.g., Martin Luther in his *De servo arbitrio* (1525), understanding *libertas* as strictly a divine attribute — and *libertas Christiana* as participatory reality in the divine *libertas* — while using *libentia* for the freedom of choice that we exercise in quotidian matters. See Martin Luther, *De servo arbitrio*, in *D. Martin Luthers Werke: Kritische Gesamtausgabe*, ed. J. F. K. Knaake et al. (Weimar: Hermann Böhlaus Nachfolger, 1883ff.), 18:600-787, esp. 634,7-22 and 635,14-17. Cf. Robert W. Jenson, *Systematic Theology*, vol. 2, *The Works of God* (New York/Oxford: Oxford University Press, 1999), pp. 105-8, and also his "An Ontology of Freedom in the *De Servo Arbitrio* of Luther," *Modern Theology* 10 (1994): 247-52.

14. "Revelationis christianae veritas, quae cum Iesu Nazareno congreditur, quemlibet hominem percipere sinit propriae vitae 'mysterium.'"

15. "Dum perinde ac suprema ipsa veritas observat illa autonomiam creaturae libertatemque eius illam etiam obstringit ut ad transcendentiam sese aperiat. Haec coniunctio libertatis ac veritatis maxima evadit planeque Domini intellegitur sermo: 'Cognoscetis veritatem, et veritas liberabit vos' (*Io* 8,32)."

16. See *FR* 85-91.

17. "FIDES ET RATIO binae quasi pennae videntur quibus veritatis ad contemplationem hominis attollitur animus. Deus autem ipse est qui veritatis cognoscendae studium hominum mentibus insevit, suique tandem etiam cognoscendi ut, cognoscentes Eum diligentesque, ad plenam pariter de se ipsis pertingere possint veritatem (cfr *Ex* 33,18; *Ps* 27 [26], 8-9; 63 [62],2-3, *Io* 14,8; *1 Io* 3,2)." ["Faith and reason are like two wings on which the human spirit rises to the contemplation of truth; and God has placed in the human heart a desire to know the truth — in a word, to know himself — so that, by knowing and loving God, men and women may also come to the fullness of truth about themselves (cf. *Ex* 33:18; *Ps* 27:8-9; 63:2-3; *Jn* 14:8; *1 Jn* 3:2)."]

18. On exegetical grounds, this is a highly questionable claim.

19. "Philosophicis vocibus dici licet in pergravi loco illo Paulino potestatem hominis metaphysicam adfirmari." Yet is this really the case? Would we need to think of original humanity *in statu integritatis* as a school of premier metaphysicians? Should we interpret the naming of the creatures as the beginning of metaphysics? Or does metaphysical inquiry imply a distance from God and creation? To decide this question is to take a stance on the very nature of metaphysics itself.

20. While the term "autonomia" is not used in the Latin, it appears in both the English ("autonomous") and the German ("unabhängig") translations, as a second attribute next to "sovereign"/"souverän," rendering "supremos." This is regrettable, since in other contexts "autonomia" stands for the genuine autonomy of reason in its proper and genuine domain of discourse and inquiry — that is, philosophy.

21. Yet what, indeed, can "philosophy on its own" do *post lapsum*? Martin Luther captures the tension inherent in this question in three of the theses of his *Disputatio de*

homine (1536). On the one hand, he can praise reason in the highest terms, not unlike *Fides et Ratio*. Thesis 4: "Et sane verum est, quod ratio omnium rerum res et caput et prae ceteris rebus huius vitae optimum et divinum quiddam sit" ["And it is certainly true that reason is the most important and the highest in rank among all things and, in comparison with other things of this life, the best and something divine"]. Thesis 8: "Hoc est, ut [reason] sit sol et numen quoddam ad has res administrandas in hac vita positum" ["That is, that it is a sun and a kind of god appointed to administer these things in this life"]. Yet nevertheless, reason is not free *sub conditione peccati*. Rather, Thesis 24: "Quibus stantibus pulcherrima illa et excellentissima res rerum, quanta est ratio post peccatum relicta, sub potestate diaboli tamen esse concluditur" ["Since these things stand firm and that most beautiful and most excellent of all creatures, which reason is even after sin, remains under the power of the devil, it must still be concluded"]. In Gerhard Ebeling, *Lutherstudien*, vol. 2, *Disputatio de homine*, pt. 1 (Tübingen: Mohr Siebeck, 1977), pp. 16, 20; *Luther's Works*, ed. Jaroslav Pelikan and Helmut T. Lehmann, American edition, 55 vols. (St. Louis: Concordia; Philadelphia: Fortress, 1955-86), 34:137, 138-39.

22. "The Relationship between Faith and Reason," "The Interventions of the Magisterium in Philosophical Matters," "The Interaction between Theology and Philosophy," "Current Requirements and Tasks."

23. "Iterum Apostolus aperit quantopere cogitationes hominum, propter peccatum, 'vanae' factae sint ipsaeque eorum ratiocinationes detortae ad falsumque ordinatae (cfr. *Rom* 1,21-22). *Mentis oculi iam non poterant perspicue videre: paulatim facta est ratio humana sui ipsius captiva*" ["It is again the Apostle who reveals just how far human thinking, because of sin, became 'empty,' and human reasoning became distorted and inclined to falsehood (cf. *Rom* 1: 21-22). *The eyes of the mind were no longer able to see clearly: reason became more and more a prisoner to itself*"] (*FR* 22; my emphasis).

24. On this highly complex and fascinating history, see *Christliche Philosophie im katholischen Denken des 19. Und 20. Jahrhunderts*, vol. 2, *Rückgriff auf scholastisches Erbe*, ed. Emerich Coreth, SJ, Walter M. Neidl, Georg Pfligersdorffer (Graz/Wien/Köln: Styria, 1988).

25. See Robert W. Jenson, *Systematic Theology*, vol. 1, *The Triune God* (New York/Oxford: Oxford University Press, 1997), pp. 9-10, drawing upon Martin P. Nilsson, *A History of Greek Religion* (Oxford: Clarendon, 1925).

26. The exception is recent postmodern problematizing that rejects these assumptions. Yet it is clear that in the absence of an explicit constructive alternative, these critical deconstructions remain parasitically dependent on the object of their deconstruction and its commitments to antecedent transcendence.

27. A wonderful intimation of *pathos* is the shift from the grammatical active voice to the passive in John Paul II's homily on the occasion of Edith Stein's canonization: "For a long time Edith Stein was a seeker. Her mind never tired of searching and her heart always yearned for hope. She traveled the arduous path of philosophy with passionate enthusiasm. Eventually she was rewarded: she seized the truth. Or better: she was seized by it. Then she discovered that truth had a name: Jesus Christ. From that moment on, the incarnate Word was her One and All. Looking back as a Carmelite on this period of her life, she wrote to a Benedictine nun: 'Whoever seeks the truth is seeking God, whether consciously or unconsciously.'" In *L'Osservatore Romano English Edition*, 14 October 1998, p. 1; my em-

phasis. While the relationship between freedom and truth as described in St. Teresia Benedicta's journey of conversion captures the core of *Fides et Ratio*'s vision of faith and reason, the shift in voice from active to passive perhaps captures best the problem to which I am pointing. What does it mean to be conquered by the truth? Do we actually receive genuine freedom in this very event, a freedom that allows us to see the *autonomia* and *libertas* of our reason in its searching moves, in all its limitation and contingency? In what way is the will transformed or restored in this event of being conquered by the truth so that it relates differently to reason?

28. Cf. Bieler in note 3 and John F. X. Knasas, "*Fides et Ratio* and the Twentieth Century Thomistic Revival," *New Blackfriars* 81 (2000): 400-408.

Notes to Chapter 12

1. Pontifical Biblical Commission, *Le peuple juif et ses Saintes Écritures dans la Bible chrétienne* (Città del Vaticano: Libreria Editrice Vaticana, 2001).

2. Available at http://www.vatican.va/roman_curia/congregations/cfaith/pcb_documents/rc_con_cfaith_doc_20020212_popolo-ebraico_en.html.

3. Luke Timothy Johnson, "Christians and Jews: Starting Over — Why the Real Dialogue Has Just Begun," *Commonweal* 130 (31 January 2003): 17.

4. Especially relevant are articles 11 and 12 of *Dei Verbum*.

5. See article 4, on the church's roots in Israel and on her relationship to Judaism: "Since . . . the spiritual heritage common to Christians and Jews is so great, this synod wishes to promote and recommend that mutual knowledge and esteem which is acquired especially from biblical and theological studies and from friendly dialogue." Norman P. Tanner, SJ, ed., *Decrees of the Ecumenical Councils*, vol. 2 (Washington, D.C.: Georgetown University Press, 1990), p. 970.

6. See Carl E. Braaten, "A Chalcedonian Hermeneutic," *Pro Ecclesia* 3 (1994): 18-20.

7. The quote is taken from Adolf von Harnack, *Marcion* (1920; reprint, Darmstadt: Wissenschaftliche Buchgesellschaft, 1985), pp. xii, 217.

8. See especially Eberhard Busch, *Unter dem Bogen des einen Bundes: Karl Barth und die Juden 1933-1945* (Neukirchen-Vluyn: Neukirchener Verlag, 1996) and Katherine Sonderegger, *That Jesus Christ Was Born a Jew: Karl Barth's "Doctrine of Israel"* (University Park, Pa.: Pennsylvania State University Press, 1992).

9. Representative of a whole movement is Rosemary Radford Ruether, *Faith and Fratricide: The Theological Roots of Anti-Semitism* (New York: Seabury, 1974).

10. Kendall Soulen, *The God of Israel and Christian Theology* (Minneapolis: Fortress, 1996), pp. 49-52.

11. Johnson, "Christians and Jews," p. 15.

12. For two noteworthy initiatives to make this tradition of exegesis again available to a broader public and to inform the way modern Christians read the Bible, see *The Ancient Christian Commentary on Scripture* (InterVarsity), a multivolume commentary edited by Thomas C. Oden, and The Church's Bible series (Eerdmans), edited by Robert Wilken.

13. Robert W. Jenson, *Systematic Theology,* vol. 1, *The Triune God* (New York: Oxford University Press, 1997), p. 63.

14. The central notion at stake here, indeed highly contested between Jews and Christians, is "fulfillment": "The notion of fulfilment is an extremely complex one, one that could easily be distorted if there is a unilateral insistence either on continuity or discontinuity. Christian faith recognises the fulfilment, in Christ, of the Scriptures and the hopes of Israel, but it does not understand this fulfilment as a literal one. Such a conception would be reductionist. In reality, in the mystery of Christ crucified and risen, fulfilment is brought about in a manner unforeseen. It includes transcendence. Jesus is not confined to playing an already fixed role — that of Messiah — but he confers, on the notions of Messiah and salvation, a fullness which could not have been imagined in advance; he fills them with a new reality; one can even speak in this connection of a 'new creation'" (*JPSSCB* 21).

15. Now, to be fair, this tension apparent in *JPSSCB* must be read and appreciated in light of the adamant antimodernist condemnations of any form of historical-critical study of the Bible during the first decades of the twentieth century by the selfsame Pontifical Biblical Commission. (The relevant passages can be found in Heinrich Denzinger, *Enchiridion symbolorum definitionum et declarationum de rebus fidei et morum,* ed. and trans. Peter Hünermann and Helmut Hoping, 39th ed. [Freiburg: Herder, 2001], ##3372, 3373, 3394-3400, 3503-28, 3561-93, 3628-30.) The break with this antimodernist front in biblical exegesis occurred in 1943, in Pius XII's encyclical *Divino afflante Spiritu*. In a famous section of the encyclical, Pius XII allows and even calls for the use of the historical-critical method — insofar as this method defends the truth of the Bible as source of revelation, the latter understood in a quite traditional sense. With Vatican II's Dogmatic Constitution on Divine Revelation, *Dei Verbum* (especially article 12), the historical-critical method finally became a fully recognized and legitimate way of interpreting the Christian canon for Roman Catholic biblical scholars. Hence, it is no surprise that there is much greater reluctance among Roman Catholic exegetes to leave these methods behind for the sake of postcritical ways of reading the canon — precisely because their license to use the historical-critical method was experienced as a hard-won hermeneutical freedom from dogmatic strictures and magisterial tutelage. For an account of these matters as fascinating as it is informative — albeit not "neutral" — see Otto Hermann Pesch, *Das Zweite Vatikanische Konzil, 1962-1965: Vorgeschichte, Verlauf, Ergebnisse, Nachgeschichte,* 5th ed. (Würzburg: Echter, 2001), esp. pp. 271-90.

16. "The Christian interpretation of the Old Testament is then a differentiated one, depending on the different genres of texts. It does not blur the difference between Law and Gospel, but distinguishes carefully the successive phases of revelation and salvation history. It is a theological interpretation, but at the same time historically grounded. Far from excluding historical-critical exegesis, it demands it" (*JPSSCB* 21).

17. Instead of putting the matter into normative terms, *JPSSCB* prefers to intimate its leanings via a telling historical sketch: "Starting from the Middle Ages, the literal sense has been restored to a place of honour and has not ceased to prove its value. The critical study of the Old Testament has progressed steadily in that direction culminating in the supremacy of the historical-critical method. And so an inverse process was set in motion: the relation between the Old Testament and Christian realities was now restricted to a limited

number of Old Testament texts. Today, there is the danger of going to the opposite extreme of denying outright, together with the excesses of the allegorical method, all Patristic exegesis and the very idea of a Christian and Christological reading of Old Testament texts. This gave rise in contemporary theology, without as yet any consensus, to different ways of re-establishing a Christian interpretation of the Old Testament that would avoid arbitrariness and respect the original meaning" (*JPSSCB* 20).

18. This unresolved question in *JPSSCB* exactly reflects the tension between articles 11 and 12 of Vatican II's Dogmatic Constitution on Divine Revelation, *Dei Verbum*.

19. For one setting in which an ecumenical group of exegetes and historical as well as systematic theologians came to a remarkably promising consensus about the proper approach to and goal of reading Scripture, see Ellen F. Davis and Richard B. Hays, eds., *The Art of Reading Scripture* (Grand Rapids: Eerdmans, 2003).

20. This society was founded in 1995. Its board currently includes Kurt Richardson, Basit Koshul, David Ford, Daniel Hardy, Elliot Wolfson, Peter Ochs, Kris Lindbeck, Steven Kepnes, Shaul Magid, James Fodor, William Elkins, and William Young. Related to its efforts at retrieving and restoring the scriptural discourses of the Abrahamic traditions is the series Radical Traditions: Theology in a Postcritical Key, edited by Stanley Hauerwas and Peter Ochs. See also the Christian reflections by George Lindbeck, David Ford, and Daniel Hardy in *Textual Reasonings: Jewish Philosophy and Text Study at the End of the Twentieth Century*, ed. Peter Ochs and Nancy Levene, Radical Traditions (Grand Rapids: Eerdmans, 2002), pp. 252-76.

21. At this point, however, it is appropriate to remember what Vatican II has to say in its Declaration on the Church's Relationship to Non-Christian Religions, *Nostra Aetate*, article 3, about Islam: "The church looks upon Muslims with respect. They worship the one God living and subsistent, merciful and almighty, creator of heaven and earth, who has spoken to humanity and to whose decrees, even the hidden ones, they seek to submit themselves whole-heartedly, just as Abraham, to whom the Islamic faith readily relates itself, submitted to God. They venerate Jesus as a prophet, even though they do not acknowledge him as God, and they honour his virgin mother Mary and even sometimes devoutly call upon her. Furthermore, they await the day of judgment when God will requite all people brought back to life. Hence they have regard for the moral life and worship God especially in prayer, almsgiving and fasting. Although considerable dissensions and enmities between Christians and Muslims may have arisen in the course of the centuries, this synod urges all parties that, forgetting past things, they train themselves towards sincere mutual understanding and together maintain and promote social justice and moral values as well as peace and freedom for all people." *Decrees of the Ecumenical Councils*, ed. Tanner, vol. 2, pp. 969-70.

22. For this long- and unjustly neglected aspect of Yoder's work, see John Howard Yoder, *The Jewish-Christian Schism Revisited*, ed. Michael Cartwright and Peter Ochs, Radical Traditions (London: SCM, 2003).

23. See especially his essays "Confession and Community: An Israel-like View of the Church," "Martin Luther and the Rabbinic Mind," "The Church," and "The Gospel's Uniqueness: Election and Untranslatability," in George Lindbeck, *The Church in a Postliberal Age*, ed. James J. Buckley, Radical Traditions (Grand Rapids: Eerdmans, 2002), pp. 1-9, 21-37, 145-68, and 223-52. See also Bruce D. Marshall, "Christ and the Cultures: The

Jewish People and Christian Theology," in *The Cambridge Companion to Christian Doctrine*, ed. Colin Gunton (Cambridge: Cambridge University Press, 1997), pp. 81-100, and Marshall, "Do Christians Worship the God of Israel?" in *Knowing the Triune God: The Work of the Spirit in the Practices of the Church*, ed. James J. Buckley and David S. Yeago (Grand Rapids: Eerdmans, 2001), pp. 231-64.

24. Lindbeck, *The Church in a Postliberal Age*, p. 9. For a challenging argument that envisions what a relationship to Israel should mean for an emerging post-Christendom church, see Scott Bader-Saye, *Church and Israel after Christendom: The Politics of Election*, Radical Traditions (Boulder, Colo.: Westview, 1999).

Credits

The author and publisher gratefully acknowledge permission to make use of material previously published in the following sources.

The Church as Public
Pro Ecclesia 3 (1994): 334-61.

The Knowledge of the Triune God
Knowing the Triune God: The Work of the Spirit in the Practices of the Church, ed. James J. Buckley and David S. Yeago (Grand Rapids: Eerdmans, 2001), pp. 23-47.

Hospitality and Truth
Practicing Theology: Beliefs and Practices in Christian Life, ed. Miroslav Volf and Dorothy Bass (Grand Rapids: Eerdmans, 2002), pp. 206-27.

Karl Barth's "Dialectical Catholicity"
Modern Theology 16 (2000): 137-57.

Beyond Dialectics: *Est* and *Esse*
Théologie négative, ed. Marco M. Olivetti, Biblioteca dell' 'Archivio di Filosofia' 59 (Padua: CEDAM, 2002), pp. 325-40.

(Re-)Forming Freedom
Modern Theology 17 (2001): 117-61.

Freedom and Commandment
The Promise of Lutheran Ethics, ed. Karen Bloomquist and John Stumme (Minneapolis: Fortress, 1998), pp. 31-54.

The Fallen Tongue and the Freedom of Praise
The Ten Commandments, ed. Carl E. Braaten and Christopher Seitz (Grand Rapids: Eerdmans, forthcoming).

Christian Unity and the Papal Office
Pro Ecclesia 7 (1998): 182-94.

Freedom, Truth, and the Will
Neue Zeitschrift für Systematische Theologie und Religionsphilosophie 44 (2002): 268-83.

"In"
Pro Ecclesia 13 (2004): 13-24.

Index of Persons

Abraham, William, 221n.40, 232n.71
Achtemeier, Mark, 221n.40, 232n.71
Ackermann, Judge Laurie, 271n.139
Adorno, Theodor, 256n.21, 260n.59
Allison, Henry E., 257n.33
Althaus, Paul, 269n.125, 272n.5, 273n.9
Altmann, Walter, 276n.23
Ambrose, Saint, 128, 173
Andia, Ysabel de, 252n.39
Apel, Karl-Otto, 275n.17
Aquinas, Saint Thomas, 6, 52, 115, 119, 126-27, 132, 135, 143, 152, 162, 168-70, 173, 199, 219n.6, 233n.11, 261nn.69-70, 262n.72, 263n.84, 281n.54, 283nn.3, 7
Arendt, Hannah, 30-31, 226nn.26-27
Aristotle, 30, 119, 152, 173, 228n.48, 284n.13
Asendorf, Ulrich, 267n.108, 269n.125
Asmussen, Hans, 249n.53
Assel, Heinrich, 258n.40
Augustine, Saint, 6, 11, 52, 75, 128, 130, 160, 173, 179, 204, 215, 221nn.28-29, 239n.19, 261n.67, 263n.76, 280n.48

Bader-Saye, Scott C., 248n.44, 296n.24
Balakrishnan, Gopal, 271n.140
Balthasar, Hans Urs von, 6, 86, 240n.22, 246n.35, 247n.41, 251nn.17, 29, 256n.22, 290n.5
Barth, Karl, 4, 6, 21, 24-29, 32-34, 39, 46-49, 52, 54, 75, 78-94, 98, 101, 152, 209, 223n.12, 224nn.16, 18, 225nn.19-20, 234nn.14-15, 18-19, 235nn.21-22, 25, 241n.34, 242nn.1, 3-7, 244n.12, 245nn.14-17, 19-23, 246nn.24-25, 32-33, 247nn.37-38, 40, 42, 248nn.43, 46, 249nn.51, 54, 250n.15, 251nn.16-17, 254n.9, 274n.14, 275nn.19-20, 276n.26, 290n.6
Basil the Great of Caesarea, Saint, 52
Bass, Dorothy C., 237n.1
Bauer, Karl-Adolf, 225n.22
Bayer, Oswald, 220n.21, 235n.27, 251n.27, 266n.100, 267n.108, 277n.27, 283n.64
Bell, Daniel M., 280n.47
Berlin, Isaiah, 254n.4, 6-7, 256n.24, 271n.140
Berman, Marshall, 222n.3
Bethge, Eberhard, 29
Bieler, Martin, 219n.6, 255n.12, 290n.3, 293n.28
Blankenhorn, David, 219n.9
Bloom, Allan, 257n.25
Bloom, Harold, 222n.6
Blumenberg, Hans, 256n.21
Bockmuehl, Markus, 271n.137
Böhme, Gernot, 257n.35
Böhme, Hartmut, 257n.35
Bok, Sissela, 283n.5
Bonhoeffer, Dietrich, 29, 32, 100, 152, 225n.25, 238n.13, 246n.26, 275n.20, 276n.26, 278n.42, 280n.53

299

Index of Persons

Braaten, Carl E., 229n.50, 232n.71, 236n.35, 293n.6
Brecht, Martin, 267n.110
Browning, Don S., 275n.17
Brunner, Emil, 245n.20
Brunner, Peter, 235n.24, 236n.39, 240n.28
Buckley, James J., 222n.41, 236n.38
Buckley, Michael, 233n.2
Bulgakov, Sergius, 6
Bullinger, Heinrich, 250n.11
Bultmann, Rudolf, 25, 272n.6
Burrell, David B., 238n.10
Busch, Eberhard, 242n.2, 243nn.8-9, 11, 245n.13, 293n.8

Calvin, John, 50, 52, 81, 82, 115, 140, 141, 143, 151, 169, 179, 252n.33, 283n.4
Caputo, John D., 249n.3
Cavanaugh, William T., 232n.72
Charry, Ellen, 236n.37
Coats, Dan, 219n.9
Coward, Harold, 249n.3
Crüsemann, Frank, 142, 226n.29, 269n.127
Cullmann, Oscar, 288n.24
Cunningham, David S., 227n.41
Cyprian, Saint, 189

Daley, Brian, 221n.40, 232n.71
Darwin, Charles, 123
Davies, Oliver, 249n.1, 253n.40
Davis, Ellen F., 295n.19
Day, Dorothy, 239n.19
Deleuze, Gilles, 260n.56
Dennet, Daniel C., 254n.5
Denys the Areopagite, Saint, 103, 105
Derrida, Jacques, 100, 105, 251n.24
Descartes, René, 118
Dewey, John, 256n.25
Diem, Hermann, 231n.62
Dieter, Theodor, 220n.19
Dondorp, Wybo J., 276n.21
Dorr, Donal, 274n.12
Duchrow, Ulrich, 277n.29
Duff, Nancy, 276n.26
Dulles, Cardinal Avery, 132, 264n.86, 265n.91, 287n.21
Dupré, Louis, 256n.21

Dussel, Enrique, 276n.23

Ebeling, Gerhard, 282n.61, 292n.21
Edwards, Jonathan, 6
Elert, Werner, 272n.6
Elshtain, Jean Bethke, 219n.9, 228n.48, 276n.24, 280n.48
Erickson, John H., 221n.40, 232n.71

Feuerbach, Ludwig, 122
Fichte, Johann Gottlieb, 47, 105, 117, 119-22, 123, 132, 253n.42, 258nn.37, 43-45, 259nn.46, 48
Fiorenza, Francis Schüssler, 275n.17
Fletcher, Joseph, 274n.10
Foley, Grover, 242n.2
Ford, David, 295n.20
Forde, Gerhard, 252n.35, 272nn.4, 6, 274n.15, 282nn.56-58
Forstman, Jack, 258n.40
Forte, Bruno, 253n.40
Foshay, Toby, 249n.3
Foucault, Michel, 12-13, 221nn.30-34
Fowl, Stephen E., 279n.42
Fox, Matthew, 32
Frei, Hans W., 220n.22, 239n.17
Freud, Sigmund, 123, 151
Fries, Heinrich, 287n.18
Fukuyama, Francis, 219n.9
Fulkerson, Mary McClintock, 276n.24

Galston, William A., 219n.9
Gamwell, Franklin I., 275n.18
Gillespie, Michael Allen, 121, 219n.11, 233n.2, 234n.17, 256nn.20-22, 257n.28, 258nn.38-41, 259nn.49, 52
Girard, René, 171, 283n.8
Glendon, Mary Ann, 219n.9
Goethe, Johann Wolfgang von, 7, 117, 256n.22
Gogarten, Friedrich, 25
Gregory Nazianzen, Saint, 52
Gregory of Nyssa, Saint, 6, 52
Griffiths, Paul J., 179, 221n.30, 239n.14, 283n.2, 284n.17
Gulyga, Arsenij, 233n.3, 234n.16
Guroian, Vigen, 221n.40, 232n.71, 276n.26

Index of Persons

Haar, Michael, 259n.55
Habermas, Jürgen, 33, 223n.9, 256n.21, 257n.27, 260n.59, 275n.17
Hägglund, Bengt, 236n.33, 251n.26
Hahn, Ferdinand, 240n.23
Hall, Pamela, 261n.68, 262n.70, 281n.54
Hardy, Daniel, 295n.20
Harnack, Adolf von, 20-24, 27, 41, 209, 222n.5, 223n.12, 293n.7
Hauerwas, Stanley, 84, 132-33, 158, 166, 181, 238nn.10, 12, 246n.29, 263n.81, 265n.96, 271n.138, 275n.21, 276n.26, 278n.39, 280n.45, 283n.63, 284nn.12, 18
Hauschild, Wolf-Dieter, 243n.10
Havel, Václav, 275n.18, 284n.14
Hays, Richard B., 295n.19
Healy, Nicholas M., 90-91, 93, 248nn.45, 47, 249nn.52, 55
Hegel, Georg Wilhelm Friedrich, 46, 116, 121, 122, 204, 234n.13, 254n.8, 256n.19, 266n.98
Heidegger, Martin, 100, 251nn.18, 23, 254n.11
Henrich, Dieter, 120, 255n.13, 258n.40
Hermann, Rudolf, 266n.107
Hertz, Karl H., 277n.29
Hewlett, Sylvia Ann, 219n.9
Hirsch, Emmanuel, 258n.40
Hittinger, Russell, 281n.54
Hof, Otto, 267n.108
Hoff, Gregor Maria, 290n.3
Höffe, Otfried, 233n.3
Hollerich, Michael, 222nn.5-6, 223nn.10-11, 225n.25
Horkheimer, Max, 256n.21, 260n.59
Hornblower, Simon, 256n.23
Hösle, Vittorio, 259n.50
Hunsinger, George, 234n.20
Hütter, Reinhard, 218n.4, 220n.19, 231n.59, 235n.28, 236nn.31, 34, 240n.25, 241n.29, 246nn.30, 34, 36, 247n.39, 250n.10, 251n.27, 255n.18, 260n.60, 266nn.103, 105-6, 271n.2, 276n.26
Huxley, Aldous, 9, 176, 220n.18

Jaeschke, Walter, 253n.42
Janke, Wolfgang, 253n.42
Jefferson, Thomas, 6
Jenson, Robert W., 84, 221n.29, 225n.21, 229n.50, 230n.56, 232n.71, 235nn.23-24, 236n.35, 240n.21, 246n.28, 251n.17, 254nn.9-10, 266n.101, 267n.115, 269n.126, 273n.8, 287n.17, 291n.13, 292n.25, 294n.13
Joest, Wilfried, 267nn.110, 116, 270n.133, 273n.9, 284n.11
John of the Cross, Saint, 6
John Paul II, 9, 14, 76, 80, 111, 185, 188-89, 190, 210, 238n.11, 256n.24, 260n.62, 271n.140, 285n.4, 290nn.1-2, 292n.27
Johnson, Luke Timothy, 211, 293nn.3, 11
Jonas, Hans, 279n.44
Jones, L. Gregory, 230n.56, 238nn.8, 10, 279n.42
Jüngel, Eberhard, 14, 84, 221n.37, 224n.15, 244n.11, 249n.4, 252n.40, 272n.3

Kant, Immanuel, 6, 38, 43-45, 47, 100, 114, 117, 118-20, 123, 125, 132, 138, 146, 147, 150-52, 233nn.3-5, 239nn.14, 19, 251n.22, 257nn.30-31, 33-34, 37, 261n.65, 270n.134, 274nn.13, 16, 282n.60
Käsemann, Ernst, 240n.24
Kasper, Cardinal Walter, 2, 14, 40-41, 218n.2, 222n.42, 231n.64, 232n.70
Kaufman, Gordon, 32
Kenneson, Philip D., 223n.9, 233n.8
Kerr, Fergus, OP, 290n.1
Kierkegaard, Søren, 6, 48, 75, 122, 234n.13, 252n.32
Kjeldgaard-Petersen, Steffen, 255n.16
Klappert, Berthold, 247n.38
Klausnitzer, Wolfgang, 286nn.12, 14, 288n.24
Kloczowski, Jan Andrzej, 253n.41
Knasas, John F. X., 293n.28
Korsch, Dietrich, 246n.30
Kraybill, Donald B., 34
Kroeger, A. E., 259n.46
Kroner, Richard, 258n.37
Kühn, Ulrich, 126, 221n.39, 262n.71, 286n.16, 287n.19

Lamb, Matthew, 275n.17

301

Index of Persons

Lazareth, William H., 220n.23, 269n.125, 273n.9, 284n.11
Lehmann, Cardinal Karl, 231n.63
Lehmann, Paul, 276n.26
Leibniz, Gottfried Wilhelm, 100
Leo XIII, 233n.11
Levinas, Emmanuel, 249n.2
Lewis, C. S., 7-8, 56-63, 219n.14, 237nn.3-4, 238nn.5-7
Lieberman, Joseph, 219n.9
Lindbeck, George, 84, 217, 221n.40, 232n.71, 246n.27, 249n.53, 266n.102, 270n.132, 273n.7, 278n.37, 287n.21, 295nn.20, 23, 296n.24
Lochman, Jan Milič, 269n.127
Locke, John, 276n.22
Loewenich, Walter von, 252n.34, 271n.3, 272n.5
Lohfink, Gerhard, 231n.61
Lohse, Bernhard, 269n.125
Lossky, Vladimir, 96, 103, 105, 250n.7, 253n.43
Louth, Andrew, 250n.6, 252n.39
Löwith, Karl, 219n.16, 256n.21, 259n.56
Lukacs, Georg, 256n.21
Luther, Martin, 6, 7, 9-12, 35-36, 49-50, 52, 55, 75, 82, 90, 91-92, 115-16, 127, 133, 134-42, 143, 146-47, 150-51, 153-59, 162, 166, 167, 168, 173, 177, 179, 180, 193, 200, 220nn.23-24, 26-27, 229nn.50-54, 230nn.55-57, 232n.1, 235n.30, 236nn.36, 40, 240n.26, 248n.49, 249n.56, 252n.34, 254n.9, 262n.73, 263n.83, 264n.84, 265n.97, 266nn.104, 107, 267nn.109, 111-14, 268nn.118, 120-22, 269n.124, 270nn.130, 132, 272n.5, 273n.7, 277nn.28, 31, 33, 278nn.34, 36, 40, 282nn.58, 61-62, 283nn.64, 1, 284nn.15-16, 286n.11, 288nn.25-26, 289n.28, 291nn.13, 21
Lyotard, Jean-François, 33

McCormack, Bruce, 221n.40, 232n.71, 234n.14, 235n.20, 243n.11, 250n.15
McCormick, Richard, 264n.88
McDaniel, Jay B., 276n.25
MacIntyre, Alasdair, 130, 219n.10, 255n.14, 256n.21, 262n.75, 263n.82, 264nn.89-90, 265nn.92-93, 95, 274n.11
McKeon, Richard, 261n.67
Mackinnon, James, 267n.110
McSorley, Harry J., 254n.9
Mahoney, John, 264n.88, 274n.12
Malcolm, Lois, 221n.40, 232n.71, 260n.61
Mangina, Joseph L., 92, 218nn.1, 5, 248n.47
Mannermaa, Tuomo, 236n.35, 249n.53, 272n.5
Marion, Jean-Luc, 233n.12, 239n.15, 250n.5, 253n.45
Maron, Gottfried, 14
Marshall, Bruce D., 218n.1, 226n.34, 231n.66, 232n.69, 237n.2, 239nn.18, 20, 295n.23
Martikainen, Eeva, 236n.34
Marx, Karl, 122, 123, 151, 259n.51
Maurer, Ernstpeter, 235n.26
Maurer, Wilhelm, 249n.53
Maximus the Confessor, Saint, 96, 103, 250n.6, 253n.44
May, Gerhard, 251n.20
Meilaender, Gilbert, 275n.21
Melanchthon, Philipp, 50, 52, 76, 140, 141, 143, 192, 269n.125, 272n.4, 282n.59, 286n.11, 287n.20
Melina, Livio, 129, 263nn.79, 81, 83-84, 290n.5
Michalson, Gordon E., Jr., 257n.32, 36
Milbank, John, 5, 33, 35, 223n.8, 227n.38, 228n.47, 253n.46, 256n.21
Mildenberger, Friedrich, 121, 251n.25, 258n.45, 259n.47
Miles, Margaret, 280nn.48-49
Mill, John Stuart, 254n.4
Moltmann, Jürgen, 223n.12, 276n.25, 279n.44
Morse, Christopher, 241n.32
Mortensen, Viggo, 276n.25
Mouffe, Chantal, 271n.140
Müller, Gerhard, 289nn.26, 28
Musil, Robert, 256n.20

Nancy, Jean-Luc, 111, 254n.2, 255n.11, 260n.57

Index of Persons

Neumann, Burkhard, 285n.9
Neuser, Wilhelm, 243n.11
Newman, Cardinal John Henry, 111-12, 254n.3
Nicholas of Cusa, 105, 252n.31
Nichtweiss, Barbara, 222n.4, 224n.14, 243n.7, 250n.13
Nicol, Martin, 277n.32
Nietzsche, Friedrich, 7, 8, 100, 117, 122-23, 151, 165, 171-72, 219n.13, 259nn.53-54, 274n.16, 284nn.9-10
Nilsson, Martin P., 292n.25
Nissiotis, Nikos A., 235n.29

O'Regan, Cyril, 290n.4
Orwell, George, 176
Ouspensky, Leonid, 253nn.44-45

Pannenberg, Wolfhart, 84, 231nn.63, 65, 232n.72, 235n.24, 287n.19, 288nn.23, 25, 290n.9
Paul, Jean, 7, 219n.12
Paul VI, 79-80, 190, 286n.13
Pesch, Otto Hermann, 221n.39, 294n.15
Peters, Albrecht, 249n.53
Peterson, Erik, 20, 21, 22-29, 32-34, 41, 98, 222nn.4-5, 223nn.12-13, 224n.16, 225n.20, 227nn.39, 45, 232n.68, 235nn.25, 27, 246n.31, 250n.13
Peukert, Helmut, 275n.17
Picht, Georg, 257n.29
Pickstock, Catherine, 253n.46
Pinches, Charles, 263n.81, 276n.25
Pinckaers, Servais, 254n.1, 255n.15, 261n.69, 264n.88, 274n.12
Pius XII, 285n.6, 294n.15
Plato, 30
Pohl, Christine D., 238n.9
Polanyi, Michael, 290n.7
Pool, Jeff B., 218n.5
Porter, Jean, 264n.88
Purvis, Sally, 277n.26

Radner, Ephraim, 2-3, 5, 218n.1, 236n.38, 249n.57
Rahner, Karl, 287n.18
Ramsey, Paul, 275n.21

Rasmussen, Larry L., 275n.20, 276nn.25-26
Rasmusson, Arne, 276n.26
Ratzinger, Cardinal Joseph, 76, 208-9
Raunio, Antti, 220n.25, 268n.123
Rawls, John, 239n.19
Reardon, Bernard M. G., 233nn.4-5
Reno, R. R., 5, 219n.7, 221n.40, 232n.71, 284n.1
Rhonheimer, Martin, 133, 264n.88
Rieth, Ricardo, 280n.50
Rifkin, Jeremy, 220n.18
Ringleben, Joachim, 252n.32
Ritschl, Dietrich, 82
Rogers, Eugene F., Jr., 226n.34
Roloff, Jürgen, 226n.32
Root, Michael, 221n.40, 232n.71
Rorty, Richard, 33
Rosenzweig, Franz, 249n.2, 253n.45
Rousseau, Jean-Jacques, 254n.7
Ruether, Rosemary Radford, 293n.9
Rusch, William G., 221n.40, 232n.71, 284n.1
Russell, Letty, 228n.49

Saarinen, Risto, 272n.6
Sallust, 173
Sartre, Jean-Paul, 8, 219n.15
Sauter, Gerhard, 240n.28, 241n.31
Schelling, Friedrich Wilhelm Joseph, 121, 259n.50, 260n.57
Schleiermacher, Friedrich, 44, 82, 233nn.6-7, 10
Schlier, Heinrich, 21-22, 28-30, 221nn.30, 34, 224n.18, 225nn.23-24, 226nn.28, 33, 250n.12
Schmid, Dirk, 259n.50
Schmitt, Carl, 227n.39, 271n.140
Schneewind, J. B., 219n.8, 233n.2, 256n.21, 267n.117, 270n.135
Schönborn, Christoph, 253n.44
Schopenhauer, Arthur, 122
Schrag, Calvin O., 265n.94
Schubeck, Thomas L., 264n.85
Schulz, Michael, 251n.19, 256n.21
Schweiker, William, 280n.44
Sedgwick, Timothy F., 276n.26

303

Index of Persons

Senn, Frank, 240n.23
Sereny, Gitta, 238n.10
Siewerth, Gustav, 251nn.19, 21
Silber, John R., 257n.33
Simpson, Gary M., 275n.17
Sobrino, Jon, 230n.57
Sölle, Dorothee, 32
Sonderegger, Katherine, 247n.38, 293n.8
Soulen, R. Kendall, 247n.38, 255n.17, 270n.131, 293n.10
Spaemann, Robert, 220n.17, 255n.14
Spawforth, Anthony, 256n.23
Stählin, Wilhelm, 221n.35
Staniloae, Dimitru, 235n.29
Stein, Edith, 6, 292n.27
Stolina, Ralf, 253n.40
Stout, Jeffrey, 233n.2, 256n.21
Street, James L., 233n.8
Stroup, John, 227n.39, 258n.40
Suarez, Francisco, 100
Szostek, Andrzej, 260n.58

Tanner, Kathryn, 241nn.30, 33
Tanner, Norman P., 233n.11, 285n.6
Taylor, Charles, 255n.14, 256n.21, 276n.22
Teresa of Avila, Saint, 6, 75
Te Velde, Rudi A., 252n.30, 253n.46
Thomas, George F., 275n.21
Thunberg, Lars, 252n.38
Thurneysen, Eduard, 243n.11
Tillich, Paul, 272n.6
Tinder, Glen, 275n.18
Toulmin, Stephen, 256n.21
Tracy, David, 227n.43
Turner, Denys, 103, 249nn.1, 4, 252nn.36-37, 253n.41

Ulrich, Ferdinand, 219n.6, 251n.19
Ulrich, Hans G., 270n.128, 277n.27

Vattimo, Gianni, 250n.14
Vilmar, A. C. F., 255n.17
Volf, Miroslav, 14, 221n.38, 241n.30

Voltaire, François Marie Arouet, 135
Vries, Hent de, 253n.42

Wadell, Paul J., 241n.36
Wainwright, Geoffrey, 221n.40, 222n.41, 232n.71, 236n.39, 240n.28
Walsh, David, 275n.18
Walton, Martin, 276n.26
Wannenwetsch, Bernd, 264n.88, 265n.96, 277n.30, 279n.44
Watson, Gary, 254n.5
Webster, John, 275n.20, 290n.4
Weinandy, Thomas, 290n.4
Welker, Michael, 232n.67, 247n.41
Welsch, Wolfgang, 222n.1
Wengst, Klaus, 226n.35
Wenz, Gunther, 287n.21, 288n.22, 289n.26
West, Cornel, 219n.9
Wiercinski, Andrzej, 251n.19
Williams, A. N., 230n.56
Willimon, William H., 181, 263n.81, 271n.138, 284n.18
Wilson, James Q., 219n.9
Wöhle, Andreas, 269n.124, 278n.34
Wolff, Christian, 100, 233n.11
Wood, Allen W., 219n.8
Wood, Susan K., 221n.40, 229n.51, 232n.71, 236n.39
Work, Telford, 221n.40, 232n.71
Wright, J. Robert, 221n.40, 232n.71
Wright, N. T., 226n.36

Yankelovich, Daniel, 219n.9
Yeago, David S., 92, 140, 156, 221n.40, 222n.41, 229n.54, 232n.71, 236n.32, 241n.29, 248nn.48, 50, 249n.53, 266n.99, 267n.108, 268n.119, 272n.5-7, 277n.32, 278nn.35-36, 284n.1
Yoder, John Howard, 217, 229n.50, 240n.27, 276n.26, 284n.12, 295n.22

Žižek, Slavoj, 260n.57
Zizioulas, John D., 235n.29

Index of Subjects

affirmative theology, 95-106
   and danger of univocity, 99-101
   and negating the propositional vs. negative propositions, 103-4
analogia entis. *See* analogy of being
analogy of being, 4, 101, 106-7
antinomianism, 115, 133, 134-42, 143-44, 146-50, 177-78
apologetics, 73
apophasis. *See* negative theology
autonomy, 114-15, 119, 125, 129, 147-48, 152
   as derivative, 114
   and rejection of law, 114-15
autopoiesis, 114, 120-22
   as infinite approximation, 121

baptism, 36, 50, 70, 143
Bible. *See* Scripture
biblical canon. *See* Scripture
biblicism, conceptual, 99
bilateral dialogues, 188
body, the
   and eternal return, 122-23
   as "I," 121
   as "other," 118-19

cataphasis. *See* affirmative theology
catechesis, 36, 50, 73, 143, 213
cheap grace, 75
Christianity. *See* church

Christian unity. *See* ecumenism
Christology. *See* Jesus Christ
church, 1-5, 12-15, 126, 208-17
   as christological, 31, 34, 35, 39
   as community of witness, 86-90, 93
   as community "on the way," 213
   as constituted by core practices, 36
   and conversion, 37, 41-42
   and doctrine, 22-30, 31-34, 37-38, 51-53, 70-71, 73-76
   and ecclesial hermeneutics, 158-59
   as ecumenical, 2-3, 5, 12-15, 37-42, 187-88, 192-93
   as end of the subject, 44
   and eschatological fulfillment, 5, 15, 41-42
   as eschatological polis, 22, 31, 34, 41-42
   and freedom, 1-3, 5, 11-12, 127-31, 144
   as identity and difference, 87-90, 93-94
   "in" Israel, 211, 212-13, 216
   and Israel, 31, 87-88, 90-91
   and natural law, 163-65
   as *oikos*, 34-35
   as particular universality, 161
   as pneumatological, 31, 34, 37-42, 49-50, 91-94
   as problem for Protestantism, 20-22, 28-30, 85-94, 209
   as public, 20-22, 30-41
   as recipient of God's work, 43

Index of Subjects

and relative authority, 26-27
and remembrance, 38, 158-59
and world (as context), 161, 164-65
commandment. *See* law
community
and freedom, 143-44
concept, 96, 98-100, 107
as icon, 105-7
as idol, 96, 99-101
concrete catholicity, 90-94
Confessing Church
and problem of ecclesiology, 28-29
conjunction of freedom and truth, 199-200
conscience, 121, 132, 141, 162
as theological, 11, 162
creatio ex nihilo, 99
creation
as ordered toward divine communion, 9-10
creature, the condition of *(sub conditione creaturae)*, 99-100, 101-2, 104

Decalogue. *See* law
Dei Verbum, 209, 286n.15, 293n.4, 294n.15, 295n.18
desire, 160-61
determination, 113, 118
dialectical catholicity, 4, 78, 80-85, 87-94
as critical principle, 83-84, 86-90
and lack of concretion, 85, 86
and liberalism, 83-84
and particularity, 92
and Roman Catholicism, 80-82
dialectical theology, 4, 24-28, 46-48, 98, 101
and authority, 25-28
as critique of modern subjectivity, 46-47
and decentering of moral subject, 152
and pneumatological deficiency, 47-48
and pneumatology, 25, 26-27
and problem of ecclesiology, 27-28
dialogue of conversion, 188-89, 191-92
discernment, 203-6
divine participation, 199, 206
divine veiling (and unveiling), 98, 101

doctrina. *See* doctrine
doctrina definita. *See* doctrine
doctrina evangelii. *See* gospel
doctrine, 3, 21-22, 29-30, 31-34, 35, 37-40, 45, 49-55, 98, 100, 104
and distinction from a particular theological consensus (dogmatics) or teacher, 52-53
as normative specification of gospel, 50-53
as pneumatological, 22, 49
and telos of church, 31-34, 35, 38
as truth of divine hospitality, 56, 70-71, 73-74
and worship, 74-76
dogma, 21, 25-27, 49, 52, 70-71, 98, 100-101, 105, 107
dogmatics. *See* theology

ecclesial ethics, 153, 161
ecclesiology. *See* church
economy of salvation, 35-40, 96-97, 103-5, 153
and antecedence to theology, 53-55, 72-76, 96-97
and core practices, 35-40
and doctrine, 35, 37-40, 49-53, 70-71
and the new law, 125-28
ecumenism, 5, 12-15, 40-42, 185-93
and compromise, 185-86
and conversion, 40-42, 191-92
as divine gift, 189
as living concord, 192-93
and martyrdom, 186-87, 189
as reunification, 186-89
as spiritual reality, 40-42, 187
and theology of the cross, 186-87
ekklēsia. *See* church
election, 86-87, 88
eleutheria. *See* freedom
ens commune, 99
eschatology
and continuity of history, 213
as exegetical horizon, 214
esse, divine, 99, 102, 104, 106-7
est, 97-107
and affirmative theology, 97-99

Index of Subjects

and doctrine/dogma, 98
  as gift, 105
  as giving and withdrawal, 99
  as negation of negative theology, 104-5
  as scandal of kerygma, 97
eternal law, 125, 129
eternal return, 8, 123
Eucharist, 5, 36, 50, 69-70, 91, 97, 106, 143
  and ecumenism, 193
  and *est*, 97
evangelical catholicity. *See* dialectical catholicity

faith, 194-207
  as certainty, 199-200
  as form of law of Christ, 156
  as fulfillment of law, 127
  as fullness of freedom, 11, 197-99, 201
  as gift, 129
  as gnosis, 148-49
  as the good conscience, 162
  as obedience *(oboeditio fidei)*, 197
  and reason, 194-97, 202-7
  as reasoning of faith *(fidei ratio)*, 195, 197, 205
  as receptive, 143, 194, 197-98, 199, 206
  as union with Christ, 147, 148, 155-56
fides. See faith
forgiveness, 60-62, 68
freedom, 5-12, 14, 15, 111-43, 145-50, 152, 154-56, 197-99, 202, 205, 206-7
  and ancient polis, 30-31
  and autonomy, 6, 113, 114-15, 118-19, 147-48, 201
  and autopoiesis, 119-22
  and church, 1-2, 3, 5, 127-28, 129-31, 157-61, 179-80
  and communal practices, 144
  as created, 9-10, 113-14
  as crisis, 7-9
  and desire, 160-61
  and dialectic with law, 147-50
  as embodiment of commandments, 127-30, 140-41, 156-59, 161, 177-80
  as faith, 197-99, 200-201, 206-7
  as false security, 137

and gift, 9-11, 113-14, 124, 128, 129, 139, 142-43
and law, 112-13, 114-16, 124-44, 157-67, 177-81
as life with God, 5, 6-7, 9-12, 47, 127-28, 142, 157, 161, 177-78, 206
and Molinism, 199
as negative, 3, 11, 112-13, 144, 146, 147-50, 177
and obedience, 154-55
in original state of integrity, 10, 140-41, 156
as participatory, 124-33, 139, 161, 206
as political, 6, 113, 144
as polyvalent, 111-12
as positive, 3, 113, 142, 144, 177
as *potestas absoluta* (sovereign), 199
as predicate of God, 7, 115, 134, 139
and problem of definition, 111-12
as received, 11, 202, 205, 206-7
as "receiving," 113-14
of religion, 22
as self-giving love, 130-31
as spiritual discipline, 159
as theological, 6-7, 9-12, 113-14
and truth, 177-78, 179, 197-99
from will's incurvature, 154-56, 177-78, 206
and will to power, 122-23

gift, 4, 59-62, 68, 83
  of faith, 129, 195
  and freedom, 113-14, 124, 128, 129, 139, 143-44
  as God's self-revelation, 197-99
  as messianic gift of reception, 142
globalization, 164, 185
God
  and autonomous subjectivity, 150-51
  as creator, 9-10, 99-100, 161, 204
  as eschatological-temporal horizon, 151
  as faithful throughout history, 213
  and gift of communion, 157
  as giver of commandment, 10, 124-25, 140-41, 142, 152, 170, 172-79
  as ground of freedom, 9-12, 113, 142-44, 161, 178-80

307

Index of Subjects

as ground of hospitality and truth, 56, 62, 64-67, 69-70, 77
as ground of intersubjectivity, 180
as human telos, 206
and humility, 155
as judge, 87
as mystery, 98
as necessary working hypothesis, 43-44
and nonabandonment of sinners, 172
as revealer, 197
as self-giving, 47, 155
as telos of desire, 160-61, 166
as (Kantian) transcendental idea, 43-45, 47, 147-48, 151
God, knowledge of
as church practice, 44-45, 49-50
as dialectical sublation, 47
as doctrine, 51-53, 70-71
as eschatological, 55
and feeling of absolute dependence, 44
as God's self-giving, 46-48
as human impossibility, 45-46
and moral postulate, 43-44
as *pathos*, 49, 51-53, 54-55
and rational metaphysics, 43
as theology, 53-55, 73-76
as univocal, 46
and worship, 69-70, 74-76
God-talk, 100
good works, 148, 153, 161, 166, 177-79
gospel, 1, 5, 21, 26, 37, 44, 49-55, 62, 64-68, 71, 83, 86, 95, 112, 116, 130, 137, 139-43
as criterion for core practices, 49-50
as criterion for doctrine, 51-53
and *est*, 97
as forensic message, 147-48
as ground of moral subject, 149
and negative relation to law, 147
as presence of Christ, 51
and unity with law, 10, 140-41, 155-57
and utilitarianism, 149
grace, 87, 197-98, 199-200
and freedom, 197-98
and judgment, 87
and the will, 199-201

heaven, 59-62

heteronomy, moral, 10, 119, 127, 145-50
heuristic use of law. *See* law, political use of the
historicism. *See* Scripture, and historical-critical exegesis
Holy Spirit
and concrete mediating forms, 38-39, 49-50
and ecumenical spiritual space, 3, 40-41, 188-89
as giver of faith, 195
as ground of church, 37-39, 49, 92-94
as ground of doctrine, 37-40, 49, 51-53
as ground of ecclesial multiplicity, 193
as inner-trinitarian relationship between Father and Son, 47-48
and new law, 125-27
and *pathos*, 49-53
as subject and agent of church's core practices, 37-40, 45, 48, 49-50, 54-55
as subject and agent of theology, 22, 25, 26-28, 53-55
and transformation of desire, 177
hospitality, 3
and entertainment, 62-63, 75
and functionalization, 63
as God's practice, 62
as participation in God's hospitality, 56, 62-64, 66, 77
and truthfulness, 56-77
human agent. *See* subjectivity

iconic theology, 4, 102, 105-7
individualism. *See* subjectivism
In One Body through the Cross: The Princeton Proposal for Christian Unity, 14, 41, 232n.71
interiorization
and law, 163
intrinsically evil acts, 115, 131-33, 164
intrinsically good acts, 161, 166
Islam, 216
Israel, 4, 22, 31-32, 34, 62, 68, 87, 90-91, 97, 99, 126, 127, 142, 143, 210-13, 215-17
and church, 87-88, 90-91
"in" the church, 211-13, 216-17
iudicium. *See* discernment

Index of Subjects

Jesus Christ
    as basis of *est*, 97-98, 105-6
    as center of salvific economy, 213, 217
    and conscience, 162
    as divine exegete, 65-66, 131
    as elected by God, 86-87, 89
    as example (or paradigm), 128-29, 130-31, 135, 155
    and Eucharist, 62, 66, 67, 69-70
    as form of faith, 51, 148, 155-56
    and form of freedom, 148-49
    as fulfillment of the law, 128-29, 136, 142-43
    as gift, 135, 142-43
    as God's goodness, 115
    as God's hospitality, 64-67, 68-70
    as grounding confidence for truthful speaking, 13
    as ground of Christian unity, 193
    as ground of freedom, 10-11, 128-30, 141-43, 156, 177
    as ground of icon, 106-7
    as human telos, 115
    and humility, 155
    as immediate authority, 26
    and the inseparability of church and Israel, 212-13
    as law of love, 11, 141
    as liberator of reason, 206
    as Messiah, 214
    as moral paradigm, 43-44
    and negative theology, 101-7
    as paradigm of human religiosity, 44
    and *pathos*, 51
    and recognition, 65-66
    as restoration of divine communion, 11, 141
    as self-revelation of God, 177, 197
    and truth, 64-67, 177
    as wisdom incarnate, 201
Joint Declaration on the Doctrine of Justification, 14, 284n.1
Judaism. *See* Israel
justification by grace through faith alone, 146-49, 156
    as formal principle, 146-47
    and its misuse, 147-50

kerygma, 31, 97, 102, 104
koinōnia, 129

law, 113, 114-16, 124-44, 145-50, 153, 155-67
    and concrete community, 158-59
    as delight, 11-12, 141, 177
    and desire, 160-61
    as embodiment of freedom, 10, 12, 146, 156, 161
    as external code, 127, 141, 156, 166
    as form/gestalt of Christian life, 10, 12, 124-31, 135-44, 154-61, 165-67, 177-78
    and freedom from facticity, 159
    as gift of God, 126
    as the good, 124, 127
    and gospel, 116, 165-67
    as limit, 124
    as love, 11, 113, 137, 141
    and moral imagination, 166
    as moral law, 118, 125, 132
    and proper perception, 159
    as received, 125, 140-41, 142-44
    as summary of natural law, 163-64
    as transmoral, 161, 162
law, first use of the. *See* law, political use of the
law, pedagogical use of the. *See* law, spiritual use of the
law, political use of the *(usus politicus legis)*, 141, 172-75
    in classical wisdom, 173
    and modern autonomy, 147-50
    and unreliability of natural law, 173-74
    as witness to fallen world, 174-75
law, second use of the. *See* law, theological use of the
law, spiritual use of the, 10, 141, 156-58, 161, 173, 177-79
    and delight in law, 11, 141, 177
    as embodied form of life with God, 127-28, 177-79
    and freedom, 140-41, 156-61, 177-80
law, theological use of the *(usus theologicus legis)*, 141, 172-73, 175-77
    and conviction of sin, 162, 175-76
    excessive focus on, 147
    and inability to transform desire, 177

Index of Subjects

and restlessness of heart, 175-76
static dialectic of, 139
law, third use of the. *See* law, spiritual use of the
liberation ethics, 152-53, 165
libertas. *See* freedom
liberum arbitrium. *See* will
license, moral, 8-9, 114-15, 131-32, 136-37
Lord's Supper. *See* Eucharist
love
   as ethically formal, 148-49
   and freedom, 11, 154-55
   and law, 141, 159, 160
   as restoration of the will, 11
   as self-giving, 130-31
lying, 168-76, 180
   as destructive of human existence, 174-75
   and homicide, 170-71
   and origin of civilization, 171
   as parasitic on truth, 173-75
   and self-preservation, 171
   as successful deception, 170
   and its theological context, 169-72

Marcionism, 209, 217
Mariology, 80, 206
marks of the church, 36, 50, 91-92
martyrdom, 130-31
Messiah, 213-14
metaphysics, 100, 118, 151
modernity
   and freedom, 116-18, 146-52
   as hubris, 7-8
   and postmodernity, 8-9, 117-18
moral euphemisms, 176-77
moral law. *See* law
mysticism, 95
   as replacement for being church, 23, 32

narrative
   and answer-question framework, 205-6
   and myth, 66-67
   as superior to reflection, 57
natural law, 132
   and Decalogue, 163-64
   and discernment, 165

and eternal law, 129
and heroism, 165
as incomplete, 125-26
as particular discourse tradition, 163
and pluralism, 164-65
as practical reason, 164-65
as theological, 165
negative philosophy, 95-97, 100, 103-5
negative theology, 4-5, 95, 99-107
   and antecedence of affirmative theology, 95-96, 104
   as negating the propositional, 103
   as negation of imagery, 103
   as theologically necessary moment, 95-96, 101-5
neighbor
   as merely formal in ethics, 149
neo-Protestantism. *See* Protestantism
new law
   as gospel, 125-26
   and Holy Spirit, 126-27
noumenal, 118, 120

objectivism, 21, 24, 27, 30
oikonomia. *See* economy of salvation
oikos, 31, 34-35
   as "other" of ancient polis, 34-35
ontological difference, 99
onto-theology, 100

papacy
   as ecumenical barrier, 190
   as ground of ecumenism, 187-88, 189
   and post-confessional ecumenism, 190-91, 192-93
   as post-confessional sign of Christian unity, 193
parenetic prophecy, 178
parenetic use of the gospel. *See* law, spiritual use of the
parrhēsia. *See* truthful speech
participation, analogy of. *See* analogy of being
pathos, 48-55, 206
philosophy, 194, 195-96, 201, 202-4
   as metaphysics, 195-96, 201, 202, 203

Index of Subjects

and *philosophia naturae vere metaphysicae*, 196, 201
  as philosophy of being, 207
  and its pluralism of truths, 205
poiesis, 31, 37
polis, 30-31, 34-35
political theology, 31-32
postmetaphysical thinking, 100
postmodernity
  as despair, 8-9, 122-24
  as intensification of subjectivity, 44
practical reason, 43, 118-19, 125, 132
practices, core, 31, 36-40, 49-50, 69-70, 91-92
  and church's *telos*, 31, 35-37, 38
  as mediation of kerygma, 97
praxis, 31
Protestantism, 2, 5
  as critical principle, 83-90, 93
  and inadequate ecclesiology, 19-21, 22-24, 82, 83, 85
  and legalism, 148, 150
  and modernity, 19-20, 37, 43-48, 85, 134, 146-52
  and post-confessional ecumenism, 191-93
  and a post-confessional papacy, 192-93
  and Roman Catholicism, 78-85, 91, 92, 93-94
  and Scripture, 209-10
  and works-righteousness, 148, 150
public, 20-21, 30-36, 38-40, 41
  as mark of the church, 20, 31-34
pure reason, 118

ratio. See reason
rationalism, 23, 32
realist actualism. *See* dialectical theology
realized eschatology, 180
reason, 194-97, 200-207
  boldness of, 196-97
  and faith, 194-97, 202-7
  and harmonious wisdom, 206-7
  as overlapping with faith, 194-95
  as participatory, 125, 129
  as *poiesis*, 120
  as *rationis fides*, 195-97

receptivity, 113-14, 124-25, 142-44
redintegratio, 190
Reformation, church of the. *See* Protestantism
regula fidei. See rule of faith
relativism. *See* subjectivism
ressentiment, 172
Roman Catholicism, 2-3, 5, 14-15, 124-33, 189-217
  as challenge to Protestantism, 23-24, 133, 191-92, 208-10
  and commitment to ecumenism, 187-88, 189-91
  and Protestantism, 78-86, 92, 93
  and Scripture, 208-10, 214-15
rule of faith, 31, 51, 100, 209

Sabbath, 159
saeculum, 31-32, 33
Scripture, 31, 51, 100-101, 127, 208-17
  and christological exegesis. *See* Scripture, and patristic (premodern) exegesis
  and community, 215
  and historical-critical exegesis, 209, 214-16
  and the inseparability of church and Israel, 216-17
  and interreligious exegesis, 215-16
  and literal sense, 214
  and patristic (premodern) exegesis, 212, 214-16
second use of the gospel. *See* law, spiritual use of the
self-creation. *See* autopoiesis
Shoah, 209-10, 213, 217
sin, the condition of *(sub conditione peccati)*, 62, 125-26, 138-39, 181
  and conscience, 137, 162
  as estrangement from the Creator, 10, 102, 170-72, 175-77
  and ethics, 148-50, 152
  as incurvature, 102, 129-30
  and noetic effects, 46-47, 156, 158, 202-7
sola fide. See justification by grace through faith alone

311

Index of Subjects

sola gratia. See justification by grace through faith alone
sovereignty, moral, 7-9, 66-67, 114-15, 152, 178
subjectivism, 20-21, 22-24, 29, 30, 41
subjectivity, 84
  as anthropodicy, 8
  as end of the church, 43-44
  and historicism, 151
  and moral sentimentality, 71
  and nihilism, 7-8
  and Protestantism, 147-49
  as rejection of theological horizon, 6-7, 150-51
  and utopianism, 151

teleology
  of freedom and law, 124-25
telos, 30-31
  and a public, 53-55
theodicy, 8
theology
  as ad hoc apologetics, 73
  and arrogance, 74-75
  as catechesis, 73
  and Christology, 34
  and concrete mediating forms, 25-28, 29
  as contextualization of doctrine, 73
  and discernment, 74
  as discourse practice of church, 33-34, 45, 53-55, 72-76
  and divine hospitality, 76
  and doctrine, 73-76
  and forgiveness, 75-76
  and forms of discipline, 32-35
  and indifference, 75
  as informed by core practices, 49-50
  as interface of doctrine and core practices, 53-55
  and joy, 74
  and persuasion, 33
  and pneumatology, 25, 26-28, 34
  as reappropriation of doctrine, 52, 73-74
  and repentance, 76
  as *theologia*, 96-97, 102-5
  and worship, 74-76
theology of the cross, 55, 102
theology of the Word of God. *See* dialectical theology
thing-in-itself. *See* noumenal
tongue, the
  and eighth commandment, 168-69
  as fallen, 170-72
  as intersubjective, 168-69
  and praise as *telos*, 179-80
  as restored, 178-80
Torah, torah, 126, 179
  as *telos* of public of Israel, 31
traditionalism. *See* objectivism
traditionalism, conceptual, 99
transcendence, 194, 196, 197, 200, 205
translation, problems of, 198-200
truth, 197-201, 205-7
  and created existence, 113-14
  and freedom, 197-99
  as Jesus Christ, 64-67
  as "other," 66
  and revelation, 197, 200, 205-7
  and will, 199-201
truthfulness. *See* truthful speech
truthful speech, 1, 3, 12-15, 168-69, 173-75, 176, 177, 179-81
  as core of positive freedom, 177
  and ecumenism, 14-15
  and free speech, 12-13
  and hospitality, 56-77
  as necessary for human existence, 174-75
  with one's own communion, 14
  as ontologically primary, 173-75
  and praise, 179-80
  as reclamation of public church, 14
  and self-deception, 63, 68
  with separated communions, 14
  as test case for genuine freedom, 12

unity. *See* ecumenism
unity of truth, 194-95, 204
  and God as Creator and Redeemer, 204
  and instrumental rationality, 197

usus politicus legis. See law, political use of the
usus practicus evangelii. See law, spiritual use of the
usus theologicus legis. See law, theological use of the
utopianism, 120, 122

veritas. See truth
Veritatis Splendor/The Splendor of Truth, 111, 112, 114-16, 124-35, 138, 140, 144, 260nn.62, 64, 261n.69, 262n.74, 263nn.77-78, 83
virtue ethics, 152
voluntas. See will

will, 194-204, 205-7
and faith and reason, 194-202, 205-7
as freedom received, 206
incurvature of, 200-206
as mediator of faith and reason, 194-95
and unity of truth, 195-96
and voluntarism, 206-7
and wisdom, 201, 206-7
will to power, 8-9, 114-15, 122-23, 171-72
as endless becoming, 122-23
wisdom, 201-2, 206-7
as Christ, 202
as harmony of faith and reason, 201
as *philosophari in Maria*, 206-7
and will's incurvature, 202-3, 206
as wisdom of the cross, 202-3
worship
as antecedent dependence, 70
and core practices, 69-70
as hospitality of divine truth, 56, 69-70
as sign of true freedom, 11-12, 179-80
and theology, 74-76